Tour Operators and Operations

Development, Management and Responsibility

FSC
www.fsc.org
MIX
Paper from
responsible sources
FSC® C013604

Tour Operators and Operations

Development, Management and Responsibility

Jacqueline Holland

*Newcastle Business School
Northumbria University*

and

David Leslie

Freelance Tourism Researcher and Consultant

CABI is a trading name of CAB International

CABI
Nosworthy Way
Wallingford
Oxfordshire OX10 8DE
UK

Tel: +44 (0)1491 832111
Fax: +44 (0)1491 833508
E-mail: info@cabi.org
Website: www.cabi.org

CABI
745 Atlantic Avenue
8th Floor
Boston, MA 02111
USA

Tel: +1 (617)682 9015
E-mail: cabi-nao@cabi.org

Library of Congress Cataloging-in-Publication Data

Names: Holland, Jakki, author. | Leslie, David, 1951- author.
Title: Tour operators and operations : development, management and responsibility / by Jakki Holland and David Leslie.
Description: Wallingford, Oxfordshire ; Boston, MA : CABI, 2017. | Includes bibliographical references and index.
Identifiers: LCCN 2017022450 (print) | LCCN 2017037506 (ebook) | ISBN 9781780648248 (pdf) | ISBN 9781780648255 (ePub) | ISBN 9781780648231 (pbk. : alk. paper) | ISBN 9781780648248 (eBook)
Subjects: LCSH: Tourism--Management. | Package tours.
Classification: LCC G155.A1 (ebook) | LCC G155.A1 H646 2017 (print) | DDC 910.68--dc23
LC record available at https://lccn.loc.gov/2017022450

ISBN-13: 978 1 78064 823 1 (pbk)
        978 1 78064 824 8 (PDF)
        978 1 78064 825 5 (ePub)

Commissioning editor: Claire Parfitt
Associate editor: Alexandra Lainsbury
Production editor: Tim Kapp

Typeset by SPi, Pondicherry, India
Printed and bound in the UK by CPI Group (UK) Ltd, Croydon, CR0 4YY

Contents

Acknowledgements   vii

Selected Supporting Websites   ix

1   Introduction   1

2   The Package Holiday and the Rise of the Tour Operator   11

3   The Operating Environment   38

4   Product Development   59

5   Small and Medium-sized Tour Operators   86

6   Customer Service   108

7   Financial Planning: Pricing the Package   130

8   Tour Operators and Key Travel Regulations (with David Grant)   146

9   Distribution (Place)   166

10   Marketing   187

11   Human Resources and Managing the Workforce   219

12   Crisis Management   246

13   Challenges and Issues: A Look Ahead   264

Index   271

Acknowledgements

No textbook can ever reach fruition without the support of many people and this text is no different. First, we would like thank CABI for its support in commissioning the book, and the reviewers of the initial proposal for their invaluable comments. Furthermore, we would like to acknowledge the support and indeed patience of Alex Lainsbury, Alison Foskett and Claire Parfitt throughout the development and production of the book.

In developing this text we have been able to draw on the expertise and advice of many people and we would especially like to acknowledge David Grant for his invaluable and major contribution on the law and travel regulations. We also express our thanks to Anne Helsby, Danielle Muir, Jo Doran, Kate Russell, Kim Jobson, Patrick 'Paddy' Boyle, for their support, and finally Susan Leslie for her ready willingness to review and comment on innumerable draft scripts.

Selected Supporting Websites

The following websites of organizations and companies provide supplementary links to themes covered in the chapters and additional support for the discussion questions and case studies.

abta.com
www.adventuretravel.biz
www.aito.com
www.amadeus.com
www.asta.org
www.chinatourism.ch
earthlingtravels.com
ec.europa.eu/growth/sectors/tourism_en
www.expedia.com
www.greenglobe21.com
www.gstcouncil.org
www.historyofpackagetours.co.uk
www.pata.org
www.responsibletravel.com
www.sabre.com
sustainabletravel.org
www.thetravelfoundation.org.uk
www.toinitiative.org
www.travelmarketreport.com
www.travelocity.com
www.unep.org
www.UNWTO.org
www.wanderlust.co.uk
www.worldtravelawards.com
www.wttc.org
www.wttc.org/tourism-for-tomorrow-awards

1 Introduction

This book aims to present a substantive foundation for the study and understanding of tour operators and their practice. These organizations operate within the wider sphere of tourism and thus it is pertinent to provide a brief overview on the development of tourism to establish the broader context within which these organizations primarily operate, which gives rise to the emergence and development of tour operations and their related opportunities and challenges.

There is no doubt that historically within any society there have been some people who have travelled for one reason or another, such as trade or out of curiosity. In earlier civilizations, such as the Roman Empire, affluent members of society travelled for recreation and education, while other members of society travelled for the purposes of trade or spiritual fulfilment (see O'Gorman, 2010). In general, little changed for more than a millennium, until the development of mechanization and what is generally termed the Industrial Revolution circa 1780–1880, leading to industrial, economic and social transformations. The overall impact on society was substantial and laid the foundations and conditions for the working life patterns of today's industrial/post-industrial societies. It was during that period that the fundamental conditions for the development of tourism, as we know it today, were laid. This is nowhere more apparent than in the UK, which has long been considered the cradle of industrialization. Therefore, the following overview of the early development of tourism and tour operators is by default predominantly UK based and to a lesser extent Eurocentric. This historical perspective of early developments in travel is remarkably similar to what has subsequently happened in other countries, albeit more quickly, as tourism demand grew. However, first we should clarify two key terms central to this book.

Two Key Terms

First, what do we mean by tourism? While there are many interpretations, one that is particularly appropriate is that presented by Przeclawski, who stated that tourism 'in its broad sense, is the sum of the phenomena pertaining to spatial mobility, connected with a voluntary, temporary change of place, the rhythm of life and its environment, and involving personal contact with the visited environment (natural, cultural or social)' (1993, p. 10). A key reason to adopt this definition is that this conveys that the tourist has a sense of involvement with the destination, which is not just limited to the physical attractiveness of the locale. The second term we must clarify is that of a 'tourist'. Within these pages, we are concerned primarily with those people, i.e. tourists, seeking a temporary change of place for leisure, rather than tourists whose trip's purpose is business, and the role of tour operators in facilitating such demand. This temporary change must involve a minimum of 24 hours away from home and in the case of international tourists include at least one destination in a country other than their own country of residence. Thus, the trip taken may be for a few days or an extended holiday.

Fundamental Conditions

As noted previously, it was during the 19th century that the fundamental conditions for tourism demand were founded. First, employment that does not tie a person to the land for their livelihood. Second, the income/salary needs to be sufficient to allow for disposable income, which is discretionary spending once all the basic needs have been met. The third condition is that of leisure time, i.e. time free from work (or other time-based commitment), which must be of a sufficiently long period to enable absence from the home environment for a minimum of 24 hours. These factors are all constraints on demand and as these ease then demand for tourism in general increases. But the easing of these constraints of time – increased leisure time – and disposable income together with transportation all take time.

In effect, as the economy of a country develops, invariably through industrialization generating employment and in due process the establishment of holiday pay and rising disposable income, so more people in society can participate. As such, what was once generally restricted to the privileged members of society and those whose business required travel becomes over time increasingly accessible to all members of society, the democratization of tourism.

However, for demand to increase and tourism to develop to any substantial degree, there is a requirement for some form of efficient mass transportation. This came into being with the development of the railways, which for decades were the primary provision for that most essential of components for tours and subsequently the development of package holidays. Surprising as it may seem, given its significance, transportation in tourism gained remarkably little attention in tourism studies for many years (see Lumsden and Page, 2004). In the absence of transport, tourism would not have developed temporally and spatially in the ways that it has, enabling today's millions of international leisure tourists to undertake a holiday at a time and to a place that is both suitable and convenient for them.

Transportation

The railways were the earliest mass transportation method and enabled the emergence of travel agents to facilitate groups of people travelling in relative ease and safety to tourist destinations. These were predominantly seaside locations, which in comparison with their home environments were perceived to be unspoilt, attractive and safe and, depending on the prevailing climatic conditions at the time of the visit, to enjoy good weather. Thus, we can identify, albeit predominantly in the UK, the rise of pleasure-seeking holidays to the rapidly developing seaside resorts of the 19th century for the masses, and for the leisured classes trips to spas on continental Europe, the Rivieras of Italy and France, and by the late 19th century, ski trips. It was also during this period and well into the 20th century that ships started to play an important role as a major means of transportation, often integrated with the railways, for international tourists. They could also be combined to create a 'package holiday' as exemplified by the emergence of cruise ships, which were popular among the affluent classes in the 19th century. Transportation has the potential to be an integral element of the trip itself, for example rail travel involving long scenic journeys and/or the grandeur of renowned trains such as the Orient Express.

Essentially, as demand gradually increased then so too tourism developed and with it the emergence of tour operators, whose products initially often took the form of guided tours to historical and cultural destinations. The oft-cited exemplar during those early years is Thomas Cook (UK), which is credited as being the first tour operator to create an international package tour, involving a trip to Paris from the UK. In effect, the leisured classes tended to set the travel trends and, as opportunity developed, the professional and middle classes then imitated the leisured classes, followed by the working classes as their disposable income increased and comparative costs declined.

Other modes of transportation were also developing after the 1920s. Travel by coach provided opportunities for tour operators to create package trips for organized groups predominantly to seaside resorts but also other parts of a country. These trips were often based around visiting cultural attractions, e.g. Bath and York, but also viewing the countryside, e.g. the Highlands and Islands of Scotland or the Lake District of England. By the late 1930s, a clear pattern of tourist travel had emerged, mainly to well-established resorts served by the railways and via a developing network of coach operators to access destinations not served by the train, such as trips to the countryside as well as more urban, cultural destinations. After the 1940s, coach tour operations expanded and experienced their most popular period during the late 1960s/1970s, although coach tours are still very much part of the tour operating sector in many countries. Over the same period, car ownership began to grow, providing opportunities for more independent travel and in due course becoming the predominant mode of transport for domestic tourism.

This pattern of tourism development is largely manifest in most countries as their economy grows and develops.

Rise of Air Travel

The next substantive development in tourist travel was the availability of air travel, from the 1940s, which was greatly facilitated by the expansion of commercial airlines and scheduled flights. This was a significant factor in the development of hitherto popular, low-key destinations such as Cuba and the Caribbean primarily for the American market, and the southern coasts of Spain and France in the case of the European market. As demand grew from the early 1950s, subsequently burgeoning in the 1960s as the previously identified key constraints eased in the major economies of the world, then so too tour operators developed and increased in number in this rapidly growing, competitive marketplace. This enabled the larger tour operators to operate on a volume basis, based on high customer numbers and lower prices. Also, the major players could negotiate block bookings of accommodation and seats with scheduled airlines. But airlines retained control of availability, choice of destination and significantly the subsequent pricing of the tour package – factors that catalysed the introduction of charter flights by tour operators, enabling operators to have greater flexibility of destinations and, more importantly, control of costs. These charter flights also served to help tour operators get around bilateral agreements between the governing agencies of different countries over agreed routes and thus air travel prices on those routes.

In time, major operators sought to develop partnerships with carriers and ultimately incorporate such operations under their own management. In combination, these factors generated a mass tourist market by the 1980s based on comparatively low cost, popular destinations, well developed for tourists and predominantly comprising 'sun, sand and sea' (3S) based package holidays. Such holidays were basically passive and invariably based on one destination.

A significant underpinning to the successful development of this mass market, and tourist travel arrangements more generally, is that of ease of access to the destination.

Ease of Access

A key point to note is that of the speed of transportation and thus ease of access in the creation and development of destinations. In general, tourists do not want to be spending significant proportions of their holiday time or short break accessing their destination. Thus, development and expansion of rail and air transportation have increasingly enabled tourists to be able to travel further, faster, more cheaply and with relative ease. It may well have taken a couple of hours to reach a seaside resort in the 1950s by train or car, but by the 1970s a similar time could be involved in air travel to the southern coast of Spain – whether from the UK or northern/eastern areas of Europe. This was in itself a significant factor contributing to growing demand for package holidays on the north Mediterranean coast. It is also the most influential factor in accounting for the growth in demand for travel to long-haul destinations, for example, UK to Australia or Beijing to Vancouver.

Since the 1950s, government attention to tourism, based on its perceived economic benefits, led to the establishment of national tourist organizations (NTOs). The main objective of these NTOs was, and is, to maximize demand for their country and region respectively, especially so in times of recession; witness the EU's ongoing policy on promoting tourism (Leslie, 2011). Destinations are in competition – more so in today's increasingly competitive marketplace, which catalysed the emergence of destination marketing and the creation of destination marketing organizations (DMOs): exemplars of this are 'The Big Apple' and 'I love New York' slogans of the 1970s. As Kotler *et al.* expressed so well 25 years ago, and which is equally applicable now, if destinations want tourists, then 'Places must learn how to think more like businesses, development of products, markets and customers' (1993, p. 346). This is perhaps nowhere more evident today than in the bidding processes involved in a destination seeking to host one of the seemingly ever-expanding array of international sporting events, e.g. the Olympic Games, World Cup Football Tournament, Commonwealth Games, Asia Games, and cultural events such as the Eurovision Song Contest. These developments all present additional opportunities for tour operators. Thus, although the popularity of the 3S package tour may be in decline, alternative opportunities are increasing and, in part at least, are facilitated by the increasing ease of access to the destinations involved.

Developments and Expansion

As the speed of air travel increased and access to airports improved, thereby reducing travel time, then demand for destinations further afield grew. This enabled the expansion of tourism to new destinations. The key point here is that as new tourist destinations emerge, often initially promoted by small tour operators operating in niche markets, they become more fashionable and demand increases, so such destinations become attractive potential markets for further development by the more mainstream operators. For example, Antarctica, which was once a destination for explorers and scientists, is now a fashionable tourist destination receiving thousands of visitors a year, largely fuelled by its increasing popularity as a cruise destination (Lück *et al.*, 2010). It is not surprising therefore that over the past half century we have seen dynamic expansion of tourism around the globe. Indeed, the number of airline passengers has virtually doubled every 15 years since 1971, a process that has been greatly furthered by airline deregulation (first in the USA and then Europe) and cheaper air fares and low-cost airlines (Calder and Lynas, 2005). The dramatic reworking of the traditional airline business model by these low-cost airlines brought new opportunities to consumers, with their low prices and convenient regional departure points, along with a frequency of service never seen before. They have enabled consumers to enjoy experiences that they previously could or would not have done; for instance, UK residents jetting off to European cities for 'hen' and 'stag' parties. Indeed, statistical evidence indicates that the increasing numbers of air passengers shows no sign of slowing down but rather substantial and continued growth; for example, it has been forecast that there will be 7 billion passengers by 2034 (IATA, 2016). Overall, greater free time, access to credit, the internet and low-cost airlines have all combined to produce today's 'wherever – whenever' consumer societies.

International Tourist Flows

The ever-expanding distances travelled by tourists can be compared with the ripples caused by a stone dropped into a still pond. The strongest ripples are close to the epicentre and may be considered to represent domestic tourism demand, while as those ripples expand and weaken they represent the generation of international demand. Thus the general pattern over time for tourists is to visit destinations within their locale, within the country and then to other nearby countries, expanding further afield as primarily transportation systems have enabled ever further travel in comparatively shorter times. In many ways the pattern of destinations visited reflects advances in technology that have made destinations further afield more attainable – for example, in aeroplanes that can accommodate more passengers, fly faster and further thereby reaching destinations that much quicker and without stopovers, or cruise ships designed to be less susceptible to bad weather or able to withstand polar conditions, or the ambient conditions created in hotels for the general comfort of their guests.

One of the truisms in tourist demand is that where the few went yesterday, the majority will follow, evidenced in the seaside resorts of the 19th century, the north Mediterranean coast of the 1970s, Florida, the Caribbean or Africa, and Thailand and Malaysia thereafter. For example, Kenya, Belize and the Maldives all doubled their tourist numbers between 1981 and 1989 (Cater, 1993). This international travel was dominated then, and largely still is, by the major generators of international tourists, namely Europe and North America. But such dominance proportionally has declined over the last 25 years as other countries have developed, e.g. Taiwan generated 1.6 million international travellers in 1988 but by 1995 that figure had risen to 5.32 million (Swarbrooke and Horner, 1999), while Asia, Eastern Europe, Russia and Africa have all demonstrated strong and growing markets (IOTP, 2011). The pattern of economic development and growth leading to increasing propensity to generate tourist activity is further demonstrated by major emergent economies such as India, Brazil and China over the last 30 years. Not surprisingly, such increasing affluence has fuelled tourism demand in those countries; initially, this is largely evident in the growth of domestic tourism, but also in a substantial increase in demand for international travel.

Since 1990, China has developed remarkably rapidly to become the second largest economy in the world, generating 1186 million international trips in 2015, with a total estimated spend of US$1260 billion (UNWTO, 2016). The majority of those trips were to nearby places, such as Hong Kong, Japan and Thailand, with long-haul trips to Europe accounting for 10% and Russia notably demonstrating growing demand.

Worldwide tourism activity continues its inexorable growth as evidenced by the doubling of international tourist arrivals between 1990 and 2010 to a projected 1.4 billion by 2020 (UNWTO, 2016). This dynamic growth in international demand has catalysed diversification of the tourism offering, away from the renowned traditional 'Sun, Sand and Sea' packages of the latter quarter of the 20th century towards offerings that are increasingly differentiated, specialized and located in ever more remote locations (see Chapter 2, this volume). This is a substantial shift that evidences changing patterns in the consumption of tourism as tourists seek out new activities and experiences.

Overall, there is no doubt that today international tourism is a global system. Its expansion both reflects and follows national/international development furthered through internationalization and **globalization** (see Friedman, 2005). As Schivelbusch stated some 30 years ago, and is all the more germane today: 'For the twentieth century tourist, the world has become one large department store of countrysides and cities' (1986; cited in Urry, 2001, p. 237). Of further note on globalization is that it also leads to homogenization of markets and places, while

continuing to fuel tourism demand and facilitating access to, and the development of, destinations, which may then expand at an ever more rapid rate to ever more remote areas of the planet.

Tourist Resorts Come Under Scrutiny

As the popular resorts of the 1970s and 1980s around the Mediterranean Sea expanded and new resorts developed further afield, largely through the influence of tour operators, they came under scrutiny (see Chapter 2, this volume). First in terms of the impact on the destination's physical environment, which to some extent was recognized in the early 1960s, for example, by the International Union of Overseas Tour Operators (now the World Tourism Organization of the United Nations) (Leslie, 2012). However, it might be more accurate to argue that it was the possible negative effect arising from degradation of the physical environment on potential tourism demand for a locality/destination that was the cause of concern rather than any degradation of the environment itself. Such criticism of tourism was (and continues to be) largely based on the negative impacts arising from the development of tourist resorts, predominantly the traditional package holiday market destinations, which became known as mass tourism destinations. The implication was that it is mass tourism which is largely to blame for any degradation of the environment and for other negative impacts such as economic leakages of tourism revenues from destinations because of the involvement of overseas companies, notably tour operators.

However, the increased attention focusing on reducing the negative impacts of mass tourism stimulated companies, in particular entrepreneurs (see Chapter 5, this volume), to create and promote alternatives to the mass tourism product. This led to the emergence of new forms of tourism differentiated from mass tourism (Mowforth and Munt, 2009). These new forms of tourism, with their plethora of terminology and definitions (Frey and George, 2010), may also be seen as a means of target marketing for tour operators to lure new custom from 'environmentally and socially conscious' tourists who are seeking an alternative to 'mass' tourism (Warnken *et al.*, 2005).

A Lack of Attention to Tour Operators

Although tour operators are key role players in facilitating tourist demand and in tourism destination development, they have rarely been the focus of research (Holland, 2015); not surprising perhaps, given that tourism enterprises themselves have received comparatively little attention in the body of tourism research (Leslie, 2015). Indeed, one of the most remarkable outcomes of any comprehensive analysis of the myriad books published in the field of tourism over the last 30 years is the evident absence of a book that is directly focused on tour operators (although to be precise there is one exception, namely Yale's 1995 book *The Business of Tour Operations*). This is further reinforced through examination of an extensive array of tourism books that are designed for tourism courses but that on close analysis give remarkably little attention to tour operators. To some degree the reasons why they gain such limited attention is understandable because of the main focus on the more general, widely applicable discourses or issue-based themes, which tend to be within the domain of academic journals. Within this context, the actual providers involved in supply invariably gain little attention (see Leslie, 2015). Even then,

the orientation is more on tourism enterprises involved in primary aspects of the delivery of services to meet the needs of tourists, i.e. hospitality operations. Yet for many of those operations the tour operator can be and often is a major source of custom.

How this paucity of attention to tour operators has come to pass is a matter of debate. Certainly, a contributing factor is the evident lack of attention given to the actual business enterprises and their operational management within the tourism sector on the part of those involved in the development of tourism, be that programmes, courses or more widely within the context of academia. That this has continued over the decades is all the more surprising when one stops to consider the importance of tour operators (past and present) in the development of tourism in many localities, which has been substantial and continues to be so, despite the perception in some quarters that the days of 'mass' tourism – of the package tour – are over.

In light of the above, the continuing absence of a fundamental book for students of tourism, whether at a foundation level, undergraduate or MSc programmes on tourism, is all the more inexplicable. It is in recognition of such paucity of attention to tour operators and their management and operations that this book has been designed, to redress this significant absence in the current tourism literature.

Chapter Outline

The book has been carefully arranged based on 13 chapters, which collectively are designed to provide a comprehensive study of the management and development of tour operators and their practices. Following on from the introductory chapter, Chapter 2 discusses the rise of tour operators and the development of the standardized package holiday in what is seen as a highly competitive and dynamic marketplace. This leads on to consideration of demand and global developments, which gave rise to new opportunities and encouraged diversification on the part of both tour operators and in the range of holiday packages produced. Significantly, and albeit briefly, attention is drawn to the importance of tour operators in tourism development and as key role players in the development of tourist destinations and resorts. Chapter 3 presents strategic concepts and tools that can be used to examine the operating environment within which tour operators work. The chapter then examines the structure of the sector and recent changes to distribution and opportunities for product development to achieve growth. Chapter 4 builds on this strategic overview and examines how tour packages are developed or adapted by major tour operators. The chapter offers a framework for developing new products and each stage is examined in depth by presenting both strategic and operational considerations. In recognizing the predominance of small/ medium enterprises in the sector, Chapter 5 presents an overview of how niche operators may create new products and identifies challenges for them, specifically the effects of varied itineraries and the use of local suppliers.

A key approach for successful tour operators is to differentiate themselves from competitors. In this, quality and customer service are considered major factors, as discussed in Chapter 6. The financial considerations of an operator are critical to their success and tour operators face many challenges, such as variable exchange rates and the need to price products a considerable time before they are purchased and consumed. These challenges are examined in Chapter 7. Chapter 8 addresses key regulations for tour operators based in the EU and recent changes in legislation in the Far East directly relating to tour operators. Chapter 9 provides an overview of how operators distribute their products and summarizes the role of agents and the importance of the brochure to both organizer and retailer. Marketing is further explored in Chapter 10, which addresses the problems faced in marketing tourism products, in particular packages. The chapter summarizes the need to clearly identify target markets, first examined in Chapter 5, and the application of the promotional mix to attract potential customers. The importance of employees to the success of the tour operator is addressed in Chapter 11, which summarizes the main challenges and key tasks of manpower planning. The chapter reviews the process from identifying the need for new recruits, the application and evaluation process, and concludes with managing performance.

The penultimate chapter, Chapter 12, introduces the need to plan for incidents by evaluating likelihood and severity using a risk assessment. More serious incidents are planned for using a Crisis Management Plan and the production of this plan is summarized at the end of the chapter. Finally, Chapter 13 considers the current environment for tour operators and raises the challenges and issues that they may face in the coming years. In the process, questions for further debate are raised.

Chapter Structure

Each chapter is designed to contain the essential information for students to understand the business of tour operations. While each chapter provides a stand-alone overview of the topic, the chapters are interwoven and linked to enable students to appreciate the interdisciplinary nature of the sector. In order to facilitate the understanding of the topic, chapters mainly follow a similar format, commencing with a set of learning objectives. At the end of each chapter, discussion questions are provided, which cover the main points raised and can be used to develop classroom discussion and encourage further investigation. This is developed further by including an internet exercise to encourage students to interact with the sector by analysing a specific aspect of a company. Chapters also include a mini case study, describing a company situation or example that can be used to illustrate how the content of the chapter relates to companies and practice, and a further and more comprehensive case study, complete with questions that can be used either for class discussion or for student directed learning. A glossary of key terms is also presented. The information provided is supported by selected recommended reading. Selected websites have been collated and are presented in the preliminary pages, which provide links to company web pages and also organizations that relate to chapter content.

Key Term

- **Globalization:** Primarily this describes the process whereby business operations and capital increasingly transcend national boundaries encouraged by deregulation.

Recommended Reading

For a contemporary, comprehensive and lively discourse on tourism, both the good and the bad, as a global phenomenon:

Becker, E. (2013) *Overbooked. The Exploding Business of Travel and Tourism.* Simon & Schuster, New York.

On early environmentalism:

McCormick, J. (1989) *Reclaiming Paradise.* Indiana University Press, Bloomington, Indiana.

References

Calder, S. and Lynas, M. (2005) Feel good travel: cheap flights: a force for good? Or a threat to the planet? *The Independent on Sunday* 19 June, 2.

Cater, E. (1993) Ecotourism in the third world: problems for sustainable tourism development. *Tourism Management* 14(2), 85–90.

Frey, N. and George, R. (2010) Responsible tourism management: the missing link between business owners' attitudes and behaviour in Cape Town tourism industry. *Tourism Management* 31, 621–628.

Friedman, T. (2005) *The World is Flat: A Brief History of the Globalised World in the 21st Century.* Allen Lane, London.

Holland, J. (2015) The understanding and implementation of responsible tourism for adventure tour operators. Unpublished dissertation, Northumbria University, Newcastle, UK.

IATA (2016) IATA air passenger forecast shows dip in long-term demand. Available at: http://www.iata.org/pressroom/pr/Pages/2015-11-26-01.aspx, accessed 2 May 2017.

IOTP (2011) *Travel and Tourism 2011 – Measured Analysis and Focused Response.* International Council of Tourism Partners, Hawaii.

Kotler, P., Haider, D.H. and Rein, H. (1993) *Marketing Places: Attracting Investment, Industry and Tourism to Cities, States and Nations.* Free Press, New York.

Leslie, D. (2011) The European Union, sustainable tourism policy and rural Europe. In: Macleod, D.V.L. and Gillespie, S.A. (eds) *Sustainable Tourism in Rural Europe – Approaches to Development.* Routledge, New York, pp. 43–60.

Leslie, D. (ed.) (2012) *Responsible Tourism: Concepts, Theory and Practice.* CAB International, Wallingford, UK.

Leslie, D. (2015) *Tourism Enterprise – Developments, Management and Sustainability*. CAB International, Wallingford, UK.

Lück, M., Maher, P.T. and Stewart, E.J. (2010) *Cruise Tourism in Polar Regions: Promoting Environment and Social Sustainability*. Earthscan, London.

Lumsden, L. and Page, S.J. (2004) *Tourism and Transport: Issues and Agenda for the New Millennium*. Elsevier, Amsterdam.

Mowforth, M. and Munt, I. (2009) *Tourism and Sustainability – Development and New Tourism in the Third World*. Routledge, Abingdon, UK.

O'Gorman, K.D. (2010) *The Origins of Hospitality and Tourism*. Goodfellow, Oxford, UK.

Przeclawski, K. (1993) Tourism as the subject of interdisciplinary research. In: Pearce, D. and Butler, R. (eds) *Tourism Research: Critiques and Challenges*. Routledge, London.

Swarbrooke, J. and Horner, S. (1999) *Consumer Behaviour in Tourism*, 2nd edn. Butterworth-Heinemann, Oxford, UK.

UNWTO (2016) *UNWTO Tourism Highlights*. Available at: http://www.e-unwto.org/doi/pdf/10.18111/9789284418145, accessed 9 February 2017.

Urry, J. (2001) Transports of delight. *Leisure Studies* 20, 237–245.

Warnken, J., Bradley, M. and Guilding, C. (2005) Eco-resorts vs. mainstream accommodation providers: an investigation into the viability of bench marking environmental performance. *Tourism Management* 26, 367–379.

Yale, P. (1995) *The Business of Tour Operators*. Longman, Harlow, UK.

2 The Package Holiday and the Rise of the Tour Operator

Learning Objectives

After studying this chapter, you should be able to:

- Appreciate the factors that have enabled the growth of package tourism.
- Understand the increased standardization of tourism packages.
- Appreciate the terminology used within the tour operating sector.
- Identify the different categories of tour operators.
- Explain the impacts of tour operations in the context of tourist destinations.

Introduction

The objective of this chapter is to examine the development of the package holiday and the rise of tour operators. It is without doubt that economic growth creates the conditions that lead to the demand for tourism. This provides the opportunities for the launch of entrepreneurial tour operators and their potential for growth and expansion. The chapter first focuses on the emergence of tour operations in the 19th century, which gradually expanded temporally and spatially across Europe and North America as opportunity grew and demand increased. This overview of the rise of the tour operator is therefore primarily UK-centric. However, just as tourism has expanded internationally, so too does the scope of our examination, in the process highlighting how, in contrast to most of the 20th century, tour operations have expanded comparatively quickly in emerging economies because of economic growth and development.

Discussion centres on the growth of the traditional package holiday, as we know it today, based on sand, sun and sea (3S). Attention is drawn to the development of what we may rightly describe as the standardization of the traditional 'package holiday' and the significance to its success of convenience and associated key attributes such as safety and comfort. This leads to consideration of how this expanding marketplace and shifts in demand generated opportunities for diversification in tour operations and their products, as illustrated by the classification of package tours. The correlating development of the tour operating sector and major expansion, catalysed by growing demand, leading to an increasingly competitive market, is then highlighted. In response, tour operators developed varied management strategies to increase turnover, market share and further international expansion, but in the process some operators overextended their position, leading to market failure.

Following on, the chapter highlights the potential influence of tour operators on tourist flows and destinations and the continuing opportunities both for companies and entrepreneurs, supported by sustained demand for package holidays as well as through diversification. Their importance as key players in tourist destination development is recognized, noting that such developments have not been without their critics. This situation has brought into contention the view that tour operators have a responsibility both for a resort's environment and to the indigenous population.

Early Developments

During the early development of travel and tourism in the mid-1800s, we can discern the emergence of the retail travel agent (more commonly termed travel agent) who recognized an opportunity to profit through helping to arrange the travel of customers (initially in groups) through the sale of train tickets bought in bulk at lower prices, and subsequently began also arranging accommodation. These were generally arranged and sold as separate services and not as a 'package'. The early leaders in retail travel recognized the potential of facilitating international travel, which was aided by two key factors. First, a growing knowledge and expertise of destinations overseas and second, their ability in being able to manage foreign exchange transactions, travel documents and so forth; a combination which at the time was beyond the ability of the general public. It was not long before these agents saw the potential to develop a complete package for tours. For example, Thomas Cook staged its first tour of America in 1866, Henry Lunn founded its tour operation business in 1893 and pioneered skiing holidays in Switzerland, while American Express and the renowned company Cox & Kings became synonymous with the travel business in the USA (Burkart and Medlik, 1981). The 19th century therefore saw the emergence of two key players in the holiday market – the travel agent and the tour operator, that is, the retailer and the organizer. Customers could make their own vacation plans via a travel agent who could, depending on the destination, not only arrange their travel requirements but also accommodation, providing them with the necessary tickets and accommodation vouchers for their trip. In effect, the more entrepreneurial travel agents began to see the potential for arranging a 'total package' and thus the concept of the package holiday was born and with it the practice of tour operators.

The typical package holiday generally consists of transport to and from the destination and accommodation, which are provided by companies, referred to as 'principals'. In addition, a package will include transfers (e.g. between arrival airport and accommodation), and, as appropriate or required, activities at/within the destination. Thus, the role of the tour operator is to create convenient packages to meet demand by bundling two or more of these principals into a single package, in the process making them appealing to consumers. They are thus producers and wholesalers as these packages are then distributed through the **intermediaries** of the time, namely travel agents (see Chapters 3 and 9, this volume). The holiday packages are then readily available to potential customers at an attractive price, which, in most cases, they would not have been able to obtain. However, as we generally know it today, the traditional package holiday involving international travel, accommodation and ancillary services did not really start until the 20th century. According to the archives of Thomas Cook, the first travel package to include an air flight took place in 1908, but the forerunner of what is termed the 'package holiday' did not occur until the end of the 1940s. After the Second World War, a combination of factors such as increasing prosperity, paid holiday leave and the growth of media such as radio and television encouraged the demand for international travel. The first flight-inclusive package was arranged by Vladimir Raitz, who set up Horizon Holidays and operated his first overseas package to Corsica in 1949, at a cost of £32 10s., which included a return charter flight, tented accommodation on the beach, meals and 'as much wine as you could put away' (Anon, 2010, p. 27).

Tour operators continued to develop through the early 1950s, by which time air travel was beginning to play an increasing part in international tourism, consequently creating opportunities for tour operators to expand. Thus, by the 1960s the travel sector was well positioned to take advantage of the growing demand for holidays and the ongoing expansion of tourism.

The Rise of the Package Holiday

In the 1960s, tour operators sought to exploit the growing market demand for the package holiday. The most successful operators in terms of market share developed an approach that enabled them to replicate their offering to create a degree of standardization. In effect, the aim of mainstream tour operators was/is to present a package to the consumer that is standardized, reproducible, consistent and, above all, safe. In developing this approach, operators in the major holiday markets based their operations on the product type (e.g. summer sun) rather than specific destination. As an indicator of their success, package holiday demand in the UK quadrupled between 1963 and 1971 (Burkart and Medlik, 1981) and continued to rise in the major markets of Europe and North America.

In the early 1970s, the growth of international holidays in post-industrial countries was aided by changes in major markets fuelled by determinants of demand such as improved holiday allowances and greater prosperity. While tourists with limited experience of international travel were generally buying packages to established resorts, their more experienced and more affluent counterparts were seeking destinations further afield. That is, generally away from the now increasingly popularized resorts of the 1960s/1970s to find something different and better in terms of quality and experience. Thus, we can identify the first major indications of demand for longer-haul tourist destinations seen to be more 'exotic' and also signs of a trend for independent holidays, allowing more flexibility in configuration and choice of destination(s). This development reflects that tourism products, like general consumer goods, are invariably first taken up by the elite in society and then gradually by wider society. This is well illustrated in the statistics that in 1994 over 27 million holidays were taken by UK citizens, 56% of which were package holidays (Baxter, 2013).

Tourist demand had become a mass market, one that was not difficult for the entrepreneur to enter (see Bray and Raitz, 2001). However, the competition was strong and profit margins limited, because major operators generally based their business strategy on high volume/low margin operations offering standardized packages. As Ritzer and Laska so cogently expressed: 'What people really want is vacations that are highly predictable, highly efficient, highly calculable and highly controlled' (1997, p. 99). This approach contributed to the substantial growth of tourism in Europe and North America throughout the latter part of the 20th century, in what Vladimir Raitz (founder of Horizon Holidays in the late 1940s and now part of TUI) referred to as the 'package holiday revolution' (Bray and Raitz, 2001, p. 21).

However, by the 1990s many consumers were no longer naïve and inexperienced tourists as they gained more experience of travelling to foreign destinations and of other cultures. This shift in demand, coupled with growing interest for alternative offerings, generated new opportunities and further diversification within the marketplace. New destinations emerged packaged for the 'sun, sand and sea' (3S) market as well as new products orientated to specific market segments, many of which are the forerunners of today's highly diversified products presented by a myriad of operators. This also led to the attractiveness of 'special interest' holidays. In marketing terms, such a package is described as a **'positional good'**, built on the idea of 'ego-tripping' whereby the customer seeks to gain status among his/her peers in terms of the 'wow' factor; for example, the tour operator Black Tomato specializes in what they consider to be extraordinary activities in extraordinary destinations, such as motorbike safaris in the Namib Desert.

Overall, this largely accounts for the situation where the overall market grew by almost 65% during the 1990s, although the proportion of packages sold had declined by 10% by 2000. Although in mature markets the number of package holidays purchased may have declined, they are still a dominant form of holiday taken by consumers, predominantly to short-haul destinations accounting for some 50% of the market for package holidays (Mintel, 2016). For northern Europeans, these tend towards destinations around the Mediterranean Sea or off the northeast coast of Africa, e.g. The Canaries. Similar tourists from the USA favour countries with close proximity to North America, with Mexico and the Caribbean being the most popular with over 32.5 million American tourists in 2013 (Mintel, 2014).

The Convenience of Package Holidays

Basically, the primary principle underpinning a 'package' holiday is convenience. That is convenience for the purchaser – the prospective tourist – and this encompasses a range of wants. First, that it is convenient to the customer in terms of home departure point, travel time, fitness for purpose and cost. As Hanefors and Mossberg (1999) argued, packages are perceived as being effective and less expensive in comparison with buying flights and hotels separately. Second, safety and security are fundamental influences on the customer's choice of package, as is often demonstrated by the sudden drop in demand for a destination or region after some type of crisis. Indeed, the perceived safety of package holidays in Europe has become an area of intense scrutiny over the last few years, primarily due to terrorist events that have affected destinations. Third, comfort, which is considered to include such factors as the language, type/style of food and wider culture of the destination. Hence the trend in tourist resort development in popularized destinations was to be attuned to the tastes of predominant generating markets; in effect, the creation of an 'eco-bubble', which is still very much in evidence today, for example in the all-inclusive package and the cruise market.

These factors become more influential in times of trouble, such as witnessed in major popular destinations around the eastern and southern coastal areas of the Mediterranean Sea in the 2010s, which saw a decline in visitor numbers. Conversely, alternative short-haul destinations may often benefit as a result of such negative events; for example, tourists with previous experience and a degree of familiarity may opt for such potential alternative resorts. This is well illustrated by the resurgence in demand for the Balearic Islands in the Mediterranean Sea in the summer of 2016, which was largely attributed to terrorism and political upheaval across a swathe of North African and Middle Eastern countries on the Mediterranean Sea.

In combination, these influential factors largely explain the consistent demand for the '3S' holiday package from tourists living in temperate climes, in which the attraction of warm, coastal resorts is the product type and, as such, not place-specific. However, these package holidays from their early development had a significant weakness in terms of consumer protection, primarily in terms of what happened if their tour operator's business collapsed and second, as regards redress if some aspect of their package holiday was not as it should be.

Customer Protection

In the early days of the package holiday, customers had all too little protection (see Grant and Mason, 2012) and operating practices often left much to be desired in what was then a largely unregulated sector with little representation outside of the International Union of Official Tour Operators (IUOTO), established in the 1940s. The first real signs of recognition of problems were heralded by the formation of the Association of British Travel Agents (ABTA) in 1955 as a first step towards professional representation at a national level, and the introduction of the Air Transport Licensing Board (subsequently the Civil Aviation Authority), which became responsible for the approval and issue of the Air Transport Organizers Licence (ATOL). Both of these organizations are widely recognized today (see Chapter 8, this volume). In the late 1960s, the Federation of Tour Operators (FTO) was established, which primarily represented the interests of the

UK's major tour operators and aimed to 'improve conditions for holidaymakers' (Yale, 1995, p. 248) (note: the International Federation of Tour Operators represented European operations). More representative of small tour operators was the formation of the Association of Independent Tour Operators (AITO) in the 1970s, which at the time comprised some 120 operators.

It was through ABTA, and the FTO, that the practice of 'bonding' was introduced in the early 1970s (subsequently becoming a legal requirement), whereby operators commit to contributing a percentage of their turnover to an independent fund, basically to provide for rescuing customers left stranded by the collapse of their tour operator (see Chapter 8, this volume). This initiative was supported by AITO, which also established their own bond arrangements. This development was very much influenced by the first financial crash of a major tour operator, namely Court Line in 1974 (see Yale, 1995). With a background of rising oil prices and the onset of recession in the UK, the Court Line holiday company went bankrupt, along with several other smaller operators, leaving thousands of package holidaymakers stranded overseas, while others who had already booked and paid for a forthcoming holiday with those operators faced losing their money. As a result, there was a loss of confidence in the holiday market by consumers, although the Air Travel Organizers' Licence (ATOL) system had been launched in 1972, so there was some financial protection in place and the stranded tourists were brought home. The UK Government consequently set up the Air Travel Reserve Fund, which was funded by £5 million from the Treasury, and a levy equivalent to 2% of a tour operator's turnover was introduced to reimburse the Treasury. The full value of bonding arrangements is illustrated by the collapse of the International

Leisure Group in 1991 (see Yale, 1995). It should be recognized that these bonding arrangements were the only major direct consumer protection regulations for UK tourists at the time, outside of which customers had very little protection beyond general legislation and regulations, which often failed to protect them adequately. That remained the case until the introduction of the EU's Package Travel Directive in December 1992 (see Chapter 8, this volume). A further point on bonding is that it is potentially a barrier to an entrepreneur seeking to set up as a tour operator in that s/he is required to provide for the necessary bond funds in advance of any tour.

Global Developments

In summary, historically Europe is the cradle of the international holiday package, both in terms of demand and the rise of tour operators. Thus, it is not surprising that within Europe the tourism sector is highly competitive and is characterized by the dominance of the mass market model; that is, the production and consumption of tourism 'en masse'. The mass tourism product here has been defined as 'the sum of industrial and commercial activities that produce goods and services wholly or mainly for tourist consumption' (Weaver and Lawton, 2006, p. 47). These product offerings have traditionally tended to be '3S' holidays to popular destinations. Tour operators in this market base their business on regular departures to well-known destinations and developed resorts. They achieve profit through the mass production of standardized holidays by buying components in bulk, which allows them to negotiate favourable rates and sell at low prices – an approach that could be described as a Fordist production model characterized by a lack of product differentiation

together with high standardization (Aguiló and Juaneda, 2000; Claver-Cortés et al., 2007). However, during the late 1990s, as noted above, within Western Europe this traditional high-volume, low-priced operating model came under threat as changes in demand led to a growth of more differentiated products, while alternative distribution channels created new opportunities.

Certainly, in make-up these 'new' packages may have changed from the traditional '3S' of the latter part of the 20th century familiar to many in the 'western world'. Although they have declined in terms of proportion of market share, we have seen a marked development in the diversification of the package holiday market creating opportunities and fuelling differentiation between tour operators (see Chapter 4, this volume). This shift in composition involves more bespoke packages, including the trio of eco/nature/adventure tours and myriad niche products – a composite that certainly lends itself to Urquhart's (2006) argument that the 'package' is a mere literal description, incorporating a wide variety of products and therefore experiences, which is well illustrated by the classification of package holidays (see below).

Over the last quarter century, much has been said on the death of package travel and the growth of independent, 'build it yourself' packages. Certainly, the development of low-cost airlines has made independent travel more accessible and attractive due to the low prices, but package holidays will still be important for many customers worldwide. Today, and even allowing for information communication technologies, arranging such trips independently might otherwise be time-consuming and in some cases difficult to organize if also seeking to obtain the equivalent or better overall cost. Furthermore, there is a significant risk in loss of consumer protection (see Chapter 8, this volume) as well as the value attached in terms of security through booking a holiday with a well-recognized company. It is therefore understandable why the package holiday or short break designed by tour operators was, and still is, a very attractive product.

In part, these developments, as discussed above, have balanced the decline over the last 30 years in the more traditional package-style holidays. Furthermore, those very factors that underpinned the successful development of the traditional package holiday also largely account for the rise in popularity over the last 20 years of cruising and the 'all-inclusive' resort package, and new resorts based on artificial environments such as the Disneyland theme parks around the world, Las Vegas (USA), Sun City (South Africa) or Nusa Dua (Bali). Furthermore, such new tourist resorts/attractions can now be created in a much shorter time, as seen in Dubai, particularly its underwater hotel complex, the Hydropolis (see www.dubaiunderwaterhotel.net).

New markets in the major emergent economies of the world have developed, encouraged by international operators as well as local companies and entrepreneurs, none bigger than China. Indeed, the 1978 open door policy (see Chapter 8, this volume) and changes to the approved country listing resulted in many more countries being added to the Chinese Government's list of acceptable destinations. China has become the major tourist-generating region in the world and the world's top spender since 2012 (UNWTO, 2015) as a result of a booming economy and growing middle class. This situation was recognized comparatively early by TUI, which established the China Travel Company in 2003, the first joint venture with an overseas company in tourism. This is also demonstrated in the establishment of the tour operator Biewei 55 in the UK, which employs local guides

fluent in Mandarin. Furthermore, although group travel is still the most popular tourism product purchased by Chinese residents, there is a growing market in independent travel mirroring that of the European and USA markets.

Classification of Package Holidays

Today, such is the diversity, it is difficult to categorize 'the package holiday/break' beyond rather broad general terms, which often relate to climatic conditions (e.g. tropical, arctic) and seasonal variations (such as winter skiing and summer sun). There will also be potential variations to such broad categories, according to the main determinants of demand arising in a tour operator's home market and country. Packages can also be classified based on accommodation type and by mode of transportation throughout the trip (e.g. coach, rail, bicycle). Alternatively, categorization could be based on the main activity involved, which is more complex than first appears. This is well illustrated by AITO, whose members collectively offer well over 100 different forms of packaged adventure holidays – this is a category that has developed from the camping trips and outdoor activities, targeted at young people, by PGL Travel Ltd (USA) dating from the 1950s. Today, 'adventure tourism' is a major market, which itself can first be divided into 'hard' or 'soft' and involves myriad activities, that has seen substantial growth and expansion since the early 2000s (Holland, 2015).

Thus, we begin to discern the potential complexity of classification. In an attempt to overcome this, classification is usually made on the type of operation and services provided. The nature of these packages can be divided into whether they are consumed in one destination (static) or several destinations (a tour).

Even then, within each category there are types of products that are too numerous to mention, though what follows seeks to provide a range of insights.

Static

Static holidays, or single-destination holidays, as the name suggests, take place in a single fixed location, for example a beach resort, an increasingly popular form of which is the all-inclusive holiday. There are different levels of all-inclusive, from those that include only the meals (which echo holidays of yesteryear, when hotels often offered 'full-board'), those that include meals, local drinks and snacks, to those that include all food and beverages, sporting activities and entertainment. The level of all-inclusiveness depends on the company brand and target market. They are seen by customers as being less of a risk and far more transparent as to the total cost of the holiday. All-inclusive holidays are not new, but have seen a tremendous growth in the market within Europe in the 2010s, partially due to tourists' concern about exchange rates, recession and because they enable customers to plan and budget for their holiday spending. Operators also recognized the attraction of all-inclusive packages, which not only meet such criteria as security, comfort and attractive destinations, but also well-defined prices. For example, in the mid-1990s First Choice was promoting all-inclusive tours, notably in Cancun, Mexico, and now all of their holiday packages are all-inclusive, as are those of Starwood Hotels and Resorts. As Tibbott opined, 'The all-inclusive resort and cruise has become the perfect product for the cash-rich and time-poor who, above all else, want to minimize risk' (2001, p. 15).

Also illustrating diversification within this category is the recognition of younger adults as a potential market segment. A notable example was the launch of Club Mediterranean, which established the potential of the 18–30-year-old market group, the success of which was notably copied by other tour operators, e.g. Intasun's Club 18–30, but which by the 1990s became more of an 18–21-year-old group, renowned for excessive partying in destinations such as Faliraki.

Multicentre

A multicentre holiday combines two or more destinations into one trip; for example, a city break followed by a beach escape. This type of holiday product allows tourists to see more than one place. Mass market operators offer twin-centre holidays that may involve several days spent visiting cultural sites and other days relaxing on a beach.

Tours

Tours in general can be considered in two categories:

- An escorted tour: a prearranged travel programme escorted by a tour manager or a tour leader who commonly provides a wide variety of services and information throughout the tour. Coach tours, adventure and activity packages often use a tour manager. These types of tours may include additional guides with particular expertise on the localities/region involved. More recently, the term tour is being replaced by 'guided vacations' as some operators believe that the term tour has negative connotations (Baran, 2012).
- Guided tour hosted packages. These offer travellers the opportunity to travel independently but also receive

guidance and assistance from a host based in the tourist destination(s). The host is a representative of the tour company, or a ground handling agent, who provides meet and greet services and assists tour participants with the planning and organization of their activities, including arranging transfers and entry tickets. They may also serve as an information specialist facilitating other needs, such as arranging guides.

Independent

An independent tour is a package designed for independent tourists. These participants travel independently without a group, for example on 'fly-drive' tours or self-guided walking or rail holidays where tourists visit multiple destinations but follow a predefined route. These holidays are designed by selecting specific destinations, type of accommodation, transport and may include other services such as sports, cultural events or excursions. The tour includes air tickets, hotel bookings, transfers and additional services (if requested by the customer).

Tailor-made packages

Tailor-made itineraries involve deciding all aspects of a holiday to meet the customer's needs on an individual basis rather than selling ready-assembled holidays. This category may also include custom tours or independent tours. These packages are termed tailor-made because they are designed to fit the requirements of the customer and as a result may be expensive compared with pre-packaged itineraries. Many tour operators offer this form of package and have specialist staff designing the itineraries, for example Audley Travel and Travelbag.

Cruising

Cruise holiday packages have shown a remarkable increase in popularity over the last decade, albeit based on the repackaging of long-standing products. Cruise ships, as noted earlier, have long been popular, but were very much associated with the more affluent in society and seen in some quarters as old fashioned as well as expensive. In the 1970s, Carnival Cruise Lines of the USA sought to make cruising more attractive to a wider market, creating a livelier approach. However, it was not until the 1990s that cruising gained substantial popularity, and was noted as the most rapidly growing type of tourism in the Caribbean (Duval, 2004). Today it is arguably the most globalized of all forms of tourism.

A Competitive Operating Environment

The rapidly growing market of the 1960s/1970s not only enabled established operators to expand but also became an attractive opportunity for entrepreneurs to set up their own tour operations, leading to an increasingly highly competitive market. As Yale (1995) demonstrates, this was a period of not only the rise of tour operators but also one of flux in the sector, with takeovers and market failures. Some operators, in order to compete, cut costs and adopted poor practices and/or overstretched their capacity, leading to business failings and often to the cost of their customers. This is not surprising, given that

> For many tour operators during the 1960s and 1970s, a major share of their profits was attributable to how they managed their cash flows, currency fluctuations and additional 'offers' rather than from the actual price of the tour itself. However, by the 1980s such

opportunities were becoming limited which led to a shift in emphasis on making the tour package in itself more profitable. (Goodman, 1984, p. 7)

Small profit margins also meant that companies might lack the necessary resources to cope with extraneous factors; for example, a decline in demand such as witnessed in the early 1970s due to a hike in the price of oil, a rise in interest rates or price increases as a result of an unfavourable major shift in currency exchange rates (see Chapters 3 and 12, this volume).

In the face of increased competition from entrepreneurs, as well as other tour operators, established market leaders realized that, although they may have had considerable buying power enabling block bookings of airline seats, accommodation and services, at the destination they were still paying their principals for those services. Thus, they adopted various strategies to increase their market share and/or improve their financial performance (see Chapter 3, this volume). In particular, and as Coles identified, 'Strategies of horizontal, vertical and even diagonal **integration** among major, transnational TOs allied to the rationalisation of operations have been pursued as a means of developing market share, enhancing price and competitiveness and responding to global market imperatives' (2004, p. 238). An established tour operator could adopt the strategy of vertical integration involving merging with or taking over a travel agency and/or purchasing or developing a chain of hotels in their most popular resorts. A comparatively recent example is that of TUI Travel, which owns approximately 150 aeroplanes, over 3500 retail shops and hotel chains like Grecotel, Iberotel and Rui-hotels (Mosselaer *et al.*, 2012, pp. 74–75). The operator therefore has not only guaranteed air flight seats and accommodation, more control over the costs of provision and

retention of profits, but also greater control over the quality of the various service offerings. It is largely because of successful adoption of such strategies that even today many major transnational operators are based in North America or Europe and are extensively vertically integrated; as such, they draw on their own resources and chains of supply in the destinations they operate. This situation has implications for the development of tourism in many places, not least due to the economic leakages that arise through using their own companies rather than destination-based independent suppliers (see Chapters 5 and 10, this volume).

Further, the more directly a tour operator is involved in the delivery of the various components of the package, the more susceptible it is to sudden changes in demand. This is well highlighted by major conflicts arising in destination regions, as in the case of the Gulf War of 1991, which is considered a major factor in the collapse of the tour operator Leisure International. Also terrorism, the bane of tourism in the 21st century, can cause major shifts in demand for destinations. Thomas Cook announced a warning to investors that profits would be down in the summer of 2016 due to loss of bookings attributed to the state of flux around the Mediterranean Sea, which led to a drop in their share price at the time of approximately 20% (a decline in the value of the company of £260 million).

In terms of the business sector more widely, major successful tour operators also became potentially attractive to external investors, as evidenced by those companies with a stock market listing. Comparatively smaller companies are also potential targets for external investors, as illustrated recently in the cases of specialist tour operators. A particularly noteworthy example in this context is that of Audley Travel, a comparatively large upmarket operator with a turnover of approximately £150 million and 350 employees. They started as Asian Journeys in the 1990s, specialising in bespoke holiday packages to destinations in India, Thailand, Botswana and Kathmandu, before expanding their operations in America in the early 2010s (Armstrong, 2015). Also, small successful operators in niche markets gaining in popularity are potential targets for takeovers. As their success grows, the market risk declines and the enterprise can then become attractive to a major tour operator as an opportunity to maintain market share and/or diversify its portfolio (or reduce competition!).

Overall, a combination of factors ensured the continued growth and development of tour operators, fuelled by sustained demand in traditional markets. Even so, it should be recognized that during the substantial expansion of tour operators and their operations since the 1960s, there have invariably been periods of difficult trading conditions often due to falls in demand. However, demand has always recovered and subsequently increased. To date, probably the most sustained difficult period of trading arose due to the wide-scale recession that began in 2008 as a result of the international banking crisis. This led many tour operators and travel agencies across Europe to fail, but by 2015 the total number of these businesses had returned to pre-2008 levels (Hayhurst, 2016). This resurgence may well have been justifiably expected because over time tour operators have demonstrated a remarkable resilience to challenging issues and changes in demand. Not all operators survive: as Cavlek so succinctly expressed, those 'who are not successful in adapting to change are wiped out of the market' (2013, p. 3).

Further fuelling the development and expansion of tour operators is the rising demand in emergent and developing economies across the world. This brings new opportunities and new destinations, leading to increasing diversification not only in terms of product offering but also within the tour operating sector itself.

Types of Tour Operator

Tour operators are traditionally divided into three major categories comprising five main types of operations, as illustrated in Fig. 2.1.

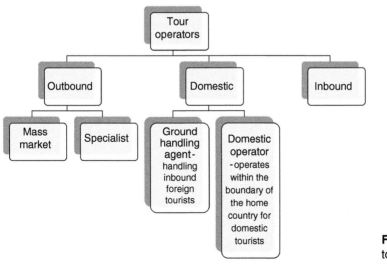

Fig. 2.1. Types of tour operator

Domestic tour operators

Domestic tour operators are those who assemble and combine components into inclusive tours/packages designed and promoted to the domestic market, i.e. residents within their own country, either as part of a package or a tailor-made itinerary. They tend to focus on very specific markets, such as the grey or youth market segments, offering city breaks, coach holidays or short breaks. It is very difficult to estimate the size of the sector because within many countries data are often not collected or collated on **domestic tourism**. Additionally, it is often difficult to differentiate between domestic tourists, international tourists and day visitors in popular localities.

In the mature markets of post-industrialized countries, domestic tour operators are a relatively small sector because it is increasingly easy for customers to package their own holidays using the Internet – a benefit that is aided by the fact that there is no issue with language. The prospective tourist can purchase air, train or coach tickets with relative ease and book directly with accommodation suppliers and often directly with attractions and other services.

By way of contrast, many developing destinations have domestic tour operators that work alongside international tour operators and facilitate their tours in the destination on behalf of the overseas tour operator. In this context, they are often referred to as ground handling agents (see Chapter 5, this volume).

Outbound tour operators

Outbound operators package together accommodation and transport and usually include transfers in the traditional inclusive tour format for destinations outside of their client's home country. These operators are traditionally subdivided into either mass market (undifferentiated, major markets) or specialist/niche/tailor-made. The main differences between these categories are summarized in Table 2.1.

Mass market operators usually offer a wide range of destinations and products and concentrate on volume of sales rather than profit. These operators focus on mainstream popular destinations. For example, within Europe these large operators focus on destinations around the Mediterranean. TUI UK Ltd, the largest operator in the UK, has an ATOL licence allowing them to sell over 5 million packages (CAA, 2017).

Specialist tour operators offer products that are generally considered not within the mainstream market. That is, from a westernized perspective, package holidays that are not based around the 3S. However, the differences between mainstream packages and the specialist tour operators are becoming ever more blurred as the mass market operators increasingly develop their portfolios and offer specialized products.

Inbound tour operators

Inbound tour operators devise and coordinate travel arrangements on behalf of international/overseas tour operators or travel organizers (see Chapter 5, this volume) and, as noted above, may also operate within their own domestic market.

Further to the above types of tour operator, we can also identify sub-categories based on the types of package they offer, characterized by:

- Mode of transport. The transport element of the package holiday may include air travel, but also may involve

Table 2.1. Summary of tour operators by market. (Adapted from Laws, 1997, p. 139, with permission from Cengage Learning (EMEA).)

Holiday element	Market sector		
	Mass market	Exclusive/tailor made	Specialist/independent
Accommodation	Large, member of a chain/operator owned or contracted	High star rating/as customers require	Small, local style
Airline	Charter	Business class/as customers require	Scheduled/occasional use of charter
Departure airport	Local airports	Regional/as customers require	Regional/major
Transfers	Group coach, multi-drop	Individual taxi/limo/as customers require	Group coach (dependent on size of group)/taxi
Journey schedule	'Market days'	Any day	Ad hoc/determined by destination and duration
Duration	Seven-day multiples	As requested	Determined by holiday and activity
Excursions	General interest by coach	Individual excursions as requested	Key element of the holiday, specific to each holiday
Cost	Low price	Premium price	Varies
Ethos	Relaxation, informal, group activities	Exclusive, personal recognition of individual clients	High degree of contact with local hosts. Focus on individual interest and involvement in activities

ships (such as ferries, cruises, chartered yacht), rail, coach, bicycle and car (such as self-drive holidays and fly drive).

- Mode of accommodation. The accommodation component of the package holiday may be based on specific serviced accommodation (e.g. hotel room, guest house, bed-and-breakfast) or non-serviced accommodation (e.g. self-catering apartments, tents and static caravans).
- Location of destination. Categorization is based on operators that offer products to specific destinations, e.g. Greece (Olympic) or China (Wendy Wu), or a region, e.g. South America (Journey Latin America).

- Demographics of target market. Some operators choose to focus on specific demographics. For example, SAGA Holidays focuses on those over 50 (also termed the grey market), whereas Solo Holidays offers packages for single travellers.
- Inclusive services. Operators may differentiate themselves by the services offered; for example, all-inclusive holidays (where meals, drinks, activities and entertainment are all included) or self-catering.
- Length of holiday. The length of holiday package offered can differentiate tour operators: from the traditional mass market operators offering 7 or 14 nights to operators offering

more flexible periods. Such packages may vary from a short break (1–3 nights; e.g. a city break), to those offering extended trips of several months (overland trips) or extended stay winter-sun holidays.

- Location of client base. The source market differentiates many companies, which can be advantageous to operators. For example, multinational companies maintain individual brands specialising in specific tourist-generating regions: TUI own and operate Marmara for Dutch tourists and Fritidsresor for the Scandinavian market.
- Distance from the originating market. The majority of package holidays take place intra-regionally and are considered to be short, that is up to 4 hours' flight time, but some operators specialize in the long-haul market with flights over 7 hours.
- Activities or specialisms. Experiential holiday products are growing in both demand and specialism. These can include holiday-specific activities, such as sport, trekking or water sports, or could be event-based (e.g. weddings and honeymoons).

Influence of Tour Operators

Tourism is a catalyst of change (see McKercher, 1993) and although it has diverse impacts on the destination and the host's environment, it has been more readily recognized for its potential economic benefits, notably at the macro-level, for foreign exchange earnings and contribution to the balance of payments. At the regional and local levels, it is generally considered to create jobs, especially in the hospitality sector and more broadly as a tool for regional development (see Leslie, 1991). Indeed, following the dramatic financial upheavals of 2008 and subsequent long-term economic effects, tourism in some quarters has been considered to hold a strategic economic benefit, such that 'It is increasingly seen as part of the solution and a key sector to help the world avoid a jobless recovery' (IOTP, 2011, p. 1). This is a view apparently widely held by international organizations such as the United Nations World Tourism Organization (UNWTO) and the Organization for Economic and Cultural Development (OECD), in addition to many professional bodies representing the interests of tourism businesses. As Lipman argued, in relation to the recession of the late 2000s, there was a need to facilitate 'building new opportunities for small entrepreneurs and community development' and to recognize 'that travel and tourism is an important driver of inclusive/shared economic growth, rapid job creation, service exports, happiness/well-being of individuals and communities, and social development and, as such, that there is a massive social good embedded in the sustainable development of the sector' (2011, p. 2). To varying degrees, this is understandable given claims that tourism is the largest global 'industry' accounting for billions of international travellers and their associated spending. In this, tour operators are a major role player. However, one of the remarkable outcomes of any study into tour operators is the lack of available statistics that could be utilized to provide insights into the significance of these enterprises in tourism. One set of data, however, is particularly useful in that it conveys the limited size of this category of tourism enterprise compared with the other main categories, while also drawing attention to the substantially greater share of gross tourism revenues attributable to tour operations (see Table 2.2).

There is no doubting that tour operators are still influential. As Mosselaer *et al.* stated, 'Although the tourism sector

Table 2.2. Gross share of tourism by category of tourism enterprise within the EU. (Derived from Leidner, 2004, p. III.)

	Share of supply (%)	Share of turnover (%)
Hotels and other accommodation	15	22
Restaurants, cafés, catering	82	49
Travel agents and tour operators	3	29

includes many actors, to date tour operators still have significant power in selecting and assembling suppliers in a holiday package, as well as in influencing consumers' choices with respect to destinations, accommodations and additional services' (2012, p. 74/5). This goes some way to explaining why, despite market developments suggesting otherwise, there is still growing tour operator activity (see Cavlek, 2013; Hayhurst, 2016). The package tour is still a key component of the tourism sector. For example, in the UK it is considered to account for some 30% of all international travel, which equated to 14.4 million package holidays in 2010 (Mintel, 2010) and is similar to the mid-1990s (KPMG, 2012). Such a level of demand has generally been maintained and indeed, contrary to underlying trends, increased in the mid-2000s by approximately 10%, partly due to rising concerns over security (Smith, 2015). These market trends were recognized in 2012 by TUI, which announced that it had strong profits after a change in business strategy, and heralded the resurgence of the package holiday.

Opportunities Continue to Increase

If we base our perceptions of the scale of tourism on gross tourist data, then it would be quite rational to perceive it as an international sector of substantial global significance. However, such a basis is potentially misleading given that a relatively small percentage of total tourist travel involves trips across national borders and many of the latter are attributable to business activities. Furthermore, tourism itself is considered by some commentators as a major force in globalization, yet such arguments are often based on the scale of tourism as indicated by the number of international arrivals. This is potentially misleading as most international arrivals are accounted for by intrastate movements, e.g. Europe, given the number of countries in close geographic proximity. Even allowing for such intrastate tourist flows, domestic tourism still accounts for the major share of tourism demand, while North America, Europe and Northeast Asia account for most travel and tourism activity (Aramberri, 2009). Thus, tourist flows from the major generators to less developed regions of the world perhaps account for less than 10% of international leisure-based tourists. Certainly, the propensity of countries in Asia, South America and the Pacific to generate international tourists will continue to increase over the coming years, with a correspondingly proportional decline in share on the part of North America and Europe, although total international arrivals will also continue to increase. This expansion has been, and to an extent still is, dominated by operators based in Europe and the USA, which clearly has implications for the host destination, not least in terms of limiting the potential economic benefits to the destination locality.

Key Role Players

Over the last 50 years, this substantial short-term annual migration of tourists to destinations near and far from their home environment has spawned a major business sector comprising a substantial array of tourism enterprises promoting diverse products and services. The major players in this market for decades have been, and continue to be, tour operators. It is their presence in the marketplace that has not only provided for and encouraged consumers in their desire for a holiday, but also largely contributed through the success of their operations to the development of past, present and emerging tourist destinations into what have become generally considered tourist resorts. These popular resorts, for example, around the Mediterranean, the Caribbean or in Thailand, are highly dependent on tour operators to sustain their supply of tourists. As Carey *et al.* (1997) noted, it is not just their influence on destinations but also their ability to influence market trends and demand for new areas, arguing that they hold more influence than the marketing efforts of a destination. For example, major tour operators in the early 1990s recognized the potential of Turkey as a major tourist destination, resulting in visitor numbers increasing from 7 million in 1995 to 40 million by 2014 (Anon, 2016). As a result, tour operators are often major stakeholders in many destinations and hold substantial influence in their development and growth to become destinations where tourism can be a dominant, transforming vector of the economy.

In many such cases, tourism developed from a low-impact, low-key activity (i.e. what would now be termed alternative tourism) and then expanded as demand grew and supply increased. As has been argued, 'Even monster resorts like Benidorm and Ibiza were once sleepy villages, frequented by a privileged few who thought they were in on a secret' (Anon, 2008, p. 13). This is well illustrated by the WTTC *et al.* (2002):

- The Balearic Islands were the poorest province in Spain in the early 1950s, but by the year 2000 they had become one of the richest.
- The Maldives by 2001 was no longer classified as a 'lesser developed country'.
- Cancun, Mexico, was once a poor area of perhaps 600 people, but by the early 2000s, primarily due to tourism, it had substantially changed with a population of over 0.5 million.
- In the case of Turkey, 30% of commodity revenues in 2000 were attributed to tourism.

In effect, the development of any destination/region is invariably incremental from small beginnings of little noticeable impact, e.g. 'alternative tourism' (Smith and Eadington, 1992), to renowned resorts. This is well illustrated by Whinney's (1996) discourse on the Alternative Travel Group's early experience in Turkey. They were very successful and as word spread so others followed. 'Tourism began to grow insidiously' (1996, p. 223), degrading their culture and leading to conflict between locals and tourist companies. More renowned destinations bear witness to similar tourist development, but on a more substantive scale; for example, the village of Kuta on Bali or Goa, India, which were very popular with backpackers in the 1960s and by 1990 had become major tourist destinations. More recently, tourism development and economic growth have expanded with the rise in popularity of East Africa and Nepal in the 1990s, along with Thailand and the development of Pattaya and Phuket as tourist destinations.

Major Players in New Destination Developments

A new destination today can develop in popularity largely due to promotion on the part of major tour operators, especially with the favourable support of the destination's national and local governments. This can also take place over a much shorter time than was the case many years ago; witness the growth and development of Dubai (www.visitdubai.com/en-uk/). However, it is not the case that tour companies operate in isolation; there are other role players and stakeholders involved, not the least of which is government. For tourism to expand to any significant extent, there needs to be government support, which, albeit rarely, might seek to constrain tourism development and consequently reduce the influence of transnational tour operators. For example, the Dominican Republic was considered to be an alternative tourism destination and was constrained in its early tourist development by government policy and a strong bias on local enterprise (Weaver, 1992). However, that was in the 1980s and much has changed since then due to a shift in government policy and constraints on external investment: now it is a major tourist destination featuring in the products of a raft of tour operators. In similar ways, the tourism policy of the Government of Bhutan seeks to limit tourism development and the involvement of external investors, as well as limiting the number of foreign visitors (especially from the 'west') allowed each year, a condition leading to low-volume, high-value tourists. Ironic as it may seem, to confine tourism development to low-key, low-scale may increase the attraction of the place and status as a positional good, meaning comparatively high prices and thus more favourable opportunities for tour operators. Such a situation to some degree illustrates how places can become **commodified** as high prices act as a barrier to access, potentially limiting demand to the affluent in society. But what is fashionable now will in time become passé, as is so often seen with tourism demand.

The Obverse Perspective

As the popular tourist resorts developed and expanded in the 1960s and beyond, so too did the impacts of tourism development on the environment become increasingly recognized. An early indication of this was flagged up by the International Union of Official Tour Operators, which in 1960 encouraged 'all IUOTO member countries to exercise increased vigilance regarding the attacks on their natural tourist resources' (Jenner and Smith, 1992; cited in Leslie, 1999, p. 181). Such a view heralded the beginnings of the debate over the following years on the negative impacts of tourist resort developments on the environment. This gathered pace through to the 1980s, subsequently gaining impetus following the **Brundtland Report** of 1987 and more so in the wake of the UN's World Congresses on Sustainable Development in Rio de Janeiro in 1992 (the 'Earth Summit'; see Hunter and Green, 1995) and in Johannesburg in 2002. Although tourism gained substantive attention over that period as regards its impact on the environment, comparatively little attention was given to tour operations, despite a general theme of much of that attention being that mass tourism was, and is, to blame for the ills of tourism development. Indeed, it was widely considered that alternative tourism was and is more in tune with sustainable development, as is made clear in recurrent themes in much of the tourism literature (see Leslie, 2009). Consequently, mass tourism is seen as less sustainable than smaller scale activities, such as those implied, for example, by eco/green/ethical tourism offerings (see Leslie, 2012). This critique is debatable, especially if one considers some of the ills arising from what are considered as alternative forms of tourism (see Leslie, 2012). For example, Seabrook argued that 'Adventure tourism scatters debris and waste in formerly inaccessible places on the earth; pristine mountain slopes, ice-floes and high plateaux receive their quota of mementos from the unquiet visitations of people avid for sensation and novelty' (2007, p. 14). Conversely, adventure tour operators may be comparatively far more attuned to the precepts of **responsible tourism** (see Holland, 2015) with notable major international players in this market such as Intrepid, (Melbourne), Southern Sea Ventures (Queensland) and World Expeditions (Sydney) all based in Australia (see Buckley, 2012). However, it is inescapable that such low-impact tourism can do harm by attracting the attention of the big operators, as Whinney well-illustrated (see above).

It is not surprising that, away from the renowned tourist resorts, other places of the world, comparatively all the more accessible today, have gained nicknames such as the 'Coca Cola Trails' of the Peruvian Andes or the 'Toilet Paper Trails' of Nepal. Latterly the Chinese Government has decried the graffiti scrawled on monuments and signs around Everest, and in 2016 vowed to publicize the names of anyone identified. Meanwhile, the oceans around popular tourist regions are the playground of cruise ships, which generate substantial air pollution and waste (Johns and Leslie, 2008), although The International Council of Cruise Lines (ICCL) promotes responsible management practices. Cruise ships also gained attention for their impact on destinations for reasons including the little economic gain (see Duval, 2004) arising from passengers' short day-visits and overcrowding, as in the case of the Cinque Terre coastal

villages of Italy (e.g. Manarola, Vernayza): during the cruise season they are inundated with passengers from cruise ships calling in to the nearby port of La Spezia. The capacity of the port has been expanded, largely due to the significance given to the economic benefits attributed to the cruise sector by regional and national government, fuelling further increases in visitor numbers and adding to congestion.

> **Box 2.1.** Venice and Cruise Ships
>
> During peak season, approximately 30,000 tourists disembark from cruise ships every day in the port of Venice, with around 22 million visiting each year. The number of tourists visiting Venice has led locals to protest about the damage to the environment and the increase in prices that affects the local community, resulting in many inhabitants moving out of the city. Venice is a UNESCO World Heritage site and it has threatened to add Venice to the list of endangered heritage sites if Italy fails to ban cruise ships from the lagoon.

As noted, the major tour operators in the holiday mass tour market are in a potentially powerful position to influence the development of resorts and, in the process, encourage wider distribution of the perceived benefits and ameliorate negative impacts associated with such development. They, more than any other tourism agent, through creating and delivering holiday packages, hold substantial potential to influence a responsible approach on the part of the other enterprises involved in their tours and thus the importance of supply chain management is stressed (see TOI, 2005). Also, due to their potential lobbying power to influence government, they can support/advocate for the protection of the environment and through their supply chains can encourage the introduction of best **environmental management** and socially responsible practices (Leslie, 2015). But they can also use their influence to counter government policies favouring positive action such as conservation-based initiatives. Witness the outcry from concerned operators when the Balearics (Spain) first mooted a tourism tax in the 2000s and more recently in September 2015, when again proposed by government, with the suggestion of 2 Euros per day per visitor, which has largely been derided by the major tour operators with operations in that area. This proposal is by no means unique in Spain; for example, Barcelona, which already had a tourist tax, sought to extend this in the spring of 2016 to include day-trippers.

International professional organizations representing major role players in tourism, including tour operators, such as the World Travel and Tourism Council and the Travel Foundation, have been promoting what is generally termed '**sustainable tourism**' or 'responsible tourism'. This has largely arisen in the wake of the Brundtland Report and the UN Earth Summits of 1992 and 2002, and the correlating promotion of the agenda for sustainable development and subsequently that of climate change (see Leslie, 2012), rather than any clear demand from tourists or indigenous populations.

Certainly, broadly speaking, tour operators, large and small, are seeking to improve their environmental performance; for example, encouraging environmental management and corporate **social responsibility** practices (see Cavlek, 2002; Mosselaer *et al.*, 2012). To some extent, this is exemplified by their establishment of the Travel Foundation. International operators such as Thomas Cook have embraced ABTA and the Dutch ANVR travel association's environmental programme, branded as Travel Life, while their airline business was the first tour operator to achieve ISO 14001 for its approach to environmental management. Similarly, TUI has introduced environmental policies both within their own tour operations and along their company-owned supply chain. But the promotion of such initiatives can be counterproductive, as Hudson and Miller argued: 'Communication of an environmental message can achieve many potential benefits including increased custom and better, more motivated employees, yet the possible cost of a raised profile is increased attention from groups seeking to ensure the message is matched by action' (2005, p. 394). Be that as it may, tour operators generally are reluctant to accept responsibility for the environments in which their operations are based, though it should be recognized that this is certainly less applicable to small enterprises and notably less in the case of adventure tour operators (see Holland, 2015). As Ioannides (2008, p. 57) argued, the overriding priority of members of the International Federation of Tour Operators (IFTO) is maintaining the appeal of their products, and thus their focus is invariably on the short term. But, and rather contrary to the foregoing, Richard Branson of Virgin Enterprises has not only argued for all his operations to be environmental leaders in their fields, but more generally that 'We need to address the environmental issues, both those created by travel and those generated at the destinations themselves, before others do it for us' (2006, p. 3).

Summary

The growth and development of tour operations has been driven by entrepreneurs and this entrepreneurial spirit is still very obvious today. This is most evident in the comparatively recently developed economies of the world, such as India and China, a situation which reflects the correlation between economic development and demand for tourism as well as in combination engendering opportunities for tour operators. These opportunities have been facilitated, and indeed furthered, through developments in transportation as well as by the expansion of the infrastructure and superstructure at and within destinations. Thus, as demand for tourism worldwide has grown, so too has the competitive environment within which tour companies operate. A combination of demand and supply has led over time to a growing diversity in the types of tour operator as well as in their product offerings aligned with the continuing success of the package holiday. The sector has expanded and new operators have entered the marketplace, which is still highly competitive. This is manifest in takeovers and mergers as well as in the collapse of some tour operators, both large and small, witnessed since the 1960s, which well illustrate the dynamic nature of the increasingly challenging market within which tour operators operate.

Indeed, the challenges continue and in general people are travelling more and are increasingly arranging their own holidays, facilitated by the availability of the internet and the ever-growing array of supporting consumer advisory websites and 'apps' (see Chapter 12, this volume). Even so, the long-term trend in mature holiday markets is shifting away from the standard package of yesterday.

Reflecting on the rise and growth of tour operators, their operations and the development of tourist resorts over the last 50 years leads to identifying the significance of their role in influencing tourist demand and the ongoing development of their favoured resorts over time, which might be termed 'tourisurbanization'. As such, and to varying degrees,

tour operators are a significant factor in a tourist destination's economic development. However, such influence has not been without criticism, initially arising over concerns on the impact of tourism on the physical environment and subsequently in relation to perceived disbenefits to the local/regional economy and peoples, criticisms which gained impetus under the umbrella of the agendas of sustainable development and climate change. Hence tour operators, be they the myriad of small companies operating in niche markets or major international companies, are being encouraged to adopt the policies and associated practices promoted under the umbrella of 'responsible tourism' by a host of international agencies and non-governmental organizations and by professional organizations within tourism. How effective they are is very much a matter of debate, a debate that may be more academic than practical given the evident lack of customer demand. But then, what little demand there is opens up potential opportunities for tour operators to develop holiday packages tailored to that specific, target market!

Overall, this discussion of the development of the package holiday and correlating rise and growth of tour operations serves as a background and foundation to the different facets of managerial practices in and issues relating to tour operators, which are discussed in the following chapters.

Discussion Questions

1. When considering the history of tourism, what are the key factors that have enabled the growth of tour operators?
2. Why did 3S tourism products become the dominant product in the marketplace?
3. When reviewing the role of travel agents and tour operators, what are their commonalities and where do they differ?

4. How have the major European tour operators remained successful, despite the growth of specialist operators?

5. What roles do national tourism organizations have when working with tour operators?

6. Why have specialist tour operators offering niche products grown in importance within the sector?

7. Are tour operators responsible for the impacts of their products on a destination?

Key Terms

- **Brundtland Report**: The United Nations Report *Our Common Future* (1987) by the World Commission on Environment and Development that was chaired by Gro Harlem Brundtland. The Report is most widely known for establishing the concept of sustainable development.

- **Commodified**: The transformation of goods, services, ideas and people into commodities, or objects of commercial use; for example, using a destination's culture to make profit or support the economy.

- **Domestic tourism**: Tourism activity that is generated by residents of a country taking trips/holidaying within their own country.

- **Environmental management**: Managing an organisation's activities 'that give rise to impacts upon the environment...and essentially therefore...the interaction between the organisation and the environment... It is the environmental aspects (as opposed to the financial or quality aspects) of an organisation's activities, products and services that are subject to management' (Sheldon and Toxon, 1999, p. 2). For example, BS7750, EMAS or ISO 14001.

- **Integration**: A combination of businesses that are at the same or different stages of the distribution channel.

- **Intermediaries**: Companies or individuals who act as brokers, or go-betweens, between the tourist and the supplier, e.g. travel agent, tour operator.

- **Positional good**: An object that is especially valued by the possessor because it is not possessed by others and so is considered a status symbol, such as a particularly high-status and desirable holiday destination.

- **Responsible tourism**: Tourism that 'emphasises the principles of conservation, creating and maintaining a balance of tourism and preservation of the local culture and environment, and balances the interests of all stakeholders, including the tourists, rather than solely reducing or limiting the numbers of tourists' (Holland, 2015).

- **Social responsibility**: The International Standards Organization defines social responsibility as: 'The responsibility of an organization for the impacts of its decisions and activities on society and the environment, through transparent and ethical behaviour that contributes to sustainable development, health and the welfare of society; takes into account the expectations of stakeholders; is in compliance with applicable law and consistent with international norms of behaviour; and is integrated throughout the organization and practiced in its relationships' (see Dodds and Kuehnel, 2010, p. 222).

- **Sustainable tourism**: Tourism 'which is economically viable but does not destroy the resources on which the future of tourism will depend, notably the physical environment and social fabric of the host community' (Swarbrooke, 1999, p. 13).

Using data from *UNWTO Tourism Highlights, 2016 Edition* (available at www.e-unwto.org/doi/pdf/10.18111/9789284418145), compare the international arrivals for Europe and Asia and the Pacific.

Questions

- Why is the average annual growth in international tourism in Asia and the Pacific almost double that of Europe?
- UNWTO suggest that by 2030 the dominance of Europe as a tourist generating region will decline. What evidence is there to support this statement?

CASE STUDY

The following two articles illustrate the differing opinions about the future of package holidays.

The first article by Lueck, is taken from 2005, and predicts a very pessimistic view of the future of the sector:

Sunset for the package holiday

In the 1950s only 1% of Brits had ever travelled abroad on holiday, but with the growth of air travel and post war prosperity millions of us were soon travelling to the sun on all-inclusive deals. Package deals revolutionized the travel industry.

By the 1970s, Spain was a favourite destination and resorts like Lloret de Mar on the Costas were full of Brits on seven or 14 night package deals. Holiday companies such as Thomson grew big as people escaped to the sun.

The 1990s heralded a big change in travel as the internet expanded and low cost carriers offered new ways to travel. Low cost carriers like Easyjet and Ryanair offered flights to the sun for less than their competitors and they allowed customers the opportunity to travel when they wanted.

Massive savings

In the last few years the growth of the internet has meant that many people have now become travel agents in their own home, doing away with the need for agents' shops on the high street. Many travellers shop around for cheap deals.

Some independent travellers think they can get a better deal on the web. Julia Gerrard from Barnsley reckons she can save £800 on a holiday by booking it herself. 'I gave up on the package because I knew they were never going to be any cheaper,' she says.

For the first time ever, more of us are choosing to book our holidays independently and fears are being expressed for the future of the big holidays firms. Household names like Thomsons are seeing their core package holiday product suffer a dramatic loss in market share. The travel industry is growing by around 12% a year. The package however is stagnating and on the Spanish Costas it's in decline.

Continued

Brits buying abroad

Another threat to the traditional Spanish package holiday is the number of British people buying property abroad. So far over half a million own a foreign property and Spain is growing in popularity. New developments are spreading and this means a very real threat to the package holiday companies. Now people will no longer need a holiday to Spain, just a cheap flight. (Lueck, 2005)

Questions

1. Why did people buy package holidays?
2. Why are tourists no longer buying package holidays?
3. What has enabled them to arrange their own holidays?
4. What type of holidays do you think people arrange for themselves?

The second article, by A. Lusher from the *Independent* newspaper (5 August 2015), presents a contrasting view about the package holiday sector.

A history of package holidays: rising numbers indicate a renaissance with an updated and classier holiday experience

It was supposed to have gone into terminal decline sometime after 2003. The great British all-inclusive flights-and-accommodation package holiday – first pioneered in the Mediterranean in 1950 – was, we were told, being killed off by the budget airline and the internet; both tempting us to find our own cheap fares and board without needing a tour operator.

A smidgen of snobbery from the independent traveller crowd, a healthy dose of revulsion at boozed-up Brits abroad, and an unmourned demise was guaranteed. Now, however, the Office for National Statistics (ONS) has revealed that the death of the package has been greatly exaggerated. Figures – released, as luck would have it, on the 65th anniversary of the first Mediterranean package holiday – have shown that the number of Britons taking package holidays abroad is rising again, from 15.3 million in 2013 to 15.9 million last year. And additional research by the travel association ABTA suggests that more than half of UK holidaymakers (51 per cent) going abroad last year booked a package.

Compare that with 2008 (when the proportion of us choosing the option had slumped to just 37 per cent) and it seems that, as it celebrates its 65th birthday, the British package holiday is looking not so much at retirement as renaissance. True, ABTA's Sean Tipton thinks that the cause may lie in post-2008 austerity – after all, with operators' economies of scale, they can be cheaper and easier than web-based DIY – but taking another look at packages has allowed us to discover an updated, classier, more flexible holiday experience.

'The package holiday has become a different animal since the decline,' says Tipton. 'Customers now understand it offers huge variety, including complicated itineraries, but with all the old positives like convenience.' Banish any thought of the bucket-spade-and-sun-lounger fortnight in a hotel, then, and forget the rep: 'You can go on your own tailor-made safari, just you and the guide. You can have a yachting holiday in the Med.

Continued

CASE STUDY. Continued.

So long as it's sold at an all-inclusive price, with transport and another service (which will be accommodation 99.9 per cent of the time) then it's a package.' As for the old fixed-period formula: 'It used to be, that's what you get. Seven nights or 14, and such inflexibility used to be a real weakness. Now you can go for as long or short as you like.' (Lusher, 2015)

Questions

1. Why are we seeing an increase in the purchase of package holidays?
2. What advantages do package holidays have over independent travel?
3. What has changed from the traditional packages of the 1970s/80s to those in the 2010s?
4. What has happened in the interval between the first article (2005) and that of the second article (2015) that may account for the apparently very different opinions?

Recommended Reading

For an overview of the growth of the package holiday that is both informative and entertaining:

Richardson, D. (2016) *Let's Go: A History of Package Holidays and Escorted Tours.* Amberley, Stroud, UK.

For a global picture on tourism developments:

Boniface, B., Cooper, R. and Cooper, C. (2016) *Worldwide Destinations: The Geography of Travel and Tourism.* Routledge, London.

For a discussion on the rise of tourism in China, described as the 'new giant' in tourism, and also an interesting discussion on cruising:

Becker, E. (2013) *Overbooked: The Exploding Business of Travel and Tourism.* Simon & Schuster, New York.

For an applied economics text book explaining many economic theories and applying them to a range of tourism activities, which will further your understanding of the economic dimensions of travel and tourism:

Tribe, J. (2011) *The Economics of Recreation, Leisure and Tourism.* Routledge, London.

On the subject of responsibility and tour operators:

Harmon, L. (2007) *The Final Call – In Search of the True Cost of Our Holidays.* Transworld, London.

Leslie, D. (2015) Sustainable supply chain management. In: *Tourism Enterprise: Developments, Management and Sustainability.* CABI, Wallingford, UK, Chapter 2.

References

Aguiló, E. and Juaneda, C. (2000) Tourist expenditure for mass tourism markets. *Annals of Tourism Research* 27, 624–637.

Anon (2008) Trains planes and automobiles. *Ethical Consumer*, May/June, 8–13.

Anon (2010) Vladimir Raitz. Obituaries. *The Daily Telegraph* 3 September, 27.

Anon (2016) Travel news. *The Daily Telegraph*, 11 June, 9.

Aramberri, J. (2009) The future of tourism and globalisation: some critical remarks. *Futures* 41, 367–376.

Armstrong, A. (2015) Tour operator Audley Travel sets off on £200m sales journey. *The Sunday Telegraph*, 2 August, 7.

Baran, M. (2012) Tour giants Trafalgar and Globus take different marketing paths. Available at: http://www.travelweekly.com/Travel-News/Tour-Operators/Tour-giants-Trafalgar-and-Globus-take-different-marketing-paths, accessed 11 February 2017.

Baxter, S. (2013) A brief history of the package holiday. Available at: https://www.theguardian.com/travel/2013/jun/14/brief-history-package-holidays, accessed 12 October 2016.

Branson, R. (2006) The environment. *The Tourism Society Journal* IV, 3.

Bray, R. and Raitz, V. (2001) *Flight to the Sun: The Story of the Holiday Revolution.* Continuum, London.

Buckley, R. (2012) Environmental performance. In: Leslie, D. (ed.) *Responsible Tourism: Concepts, Theory and Practice.* CAB International, Wallingford, UK, pp. 82–89.

Burkart, A.J. and Medlik, S. (1981) *Tourism: Past, Present and Future.* Heinemann, Oxford, UK.

CAA (2017) 250 largest ATOLs for sales to the public. Available at: http://publicapps.caa.co.uk/modalapplication.aspx?catid=1&pagetype=65&appid=4&mode=results&top=250&type=publicsales&pageIndex=1), accessed 10 February 2017.

Carey, S., Gountas, Y. and Gilbert, D. (1997) Tour operators and destination sustainability. *Tourism Management* 18, 425–431.

Cavlek, N. (2002) Tour operators and sustainable development – a contribution to the environment. *Journal of Transnational Management Development* 7, 45–54.

Cavlek, N. (2013) Tour operator marketing strategies: from 'made by tour operators' to 'made by tourism'. *Tourism Tribune* 28, 2–15.

Claver-Cortés, E., Molina-Azorín, J.F. and Pereira-Moliner, J. (2007) Competitiveness in mass tourism. *Annals of Tourism Research* 34, 727–745.

Coles, S. (2004) What makes a resort complex? Reflections on the production of tourism space in a Caribbean resort complex. In: Duval, D. (ed.) *Tourism in the Caribbean: Trends, Development and Prospects.* Routledge, London, pp. 235–256.

Dodds, R. and Kuehnel, J. (2010) CSR among Canadian mass tour operators: good awareness but little action. *International Journal of Contemporary Hospitality Management* 22, 221–244.

Duval, T. (2004) *Tourism in the Caribbean: Trends, Development and Prospects.* Routledge, London.

Goodman, H. (1984) Leisure. *Financial Times*, 8 December, 7.

Grant, D.J. and Mason, S. (2012) *Holiday Law: The Law Relating to Travel and Tourism*, 5th edn. Sweet & Maxwell, London.

Hanefors, M. and Mossberg, L. (1999) The travel and tourism consumer. In: Hogg, H. and Gabbott, M. (eds) *Consumers and Services.* John Wiley, Chichester, UK, pp. 141–162.

Hayhurst, L. (2016) Number of agents and tour operators return to pre-recession levels. *Travel Weekly*, 26 February, 2.

Holland, J. (2015) The understanding and implementation of responsible tourism for adventure tour operators. Unpublished PhD, Northumbria University, Newcastle, UK.

Hudson, S. and Miller, G. (2005) Ethical orientation and awareness of tourism students. *Journal of Business Ethics* 62, 383–396.

Hunter, C. and Green, H. (1995) *Tourism and the Environment: A Sustainable Relationship?* Routledge, London.

Ioannides, D. (2008) Sustainable development and the shifting attitudes of tourism stakeholders: toward a dynamic framework. In: McCool, S.F. and Moisey, R.N. (eds) *Tourism, Recreation and Sustainability – Linking Culture and the Environment.* CAB International, Wallingford, UK, pp. 55–76.

IOTP (2011) *Travel and Tourism 2011 – A Measured Analysis and Focused Response.* International Council of Tourism Partners, Haleiwa, Hawaii.

Jenner, P. and Smith, C. (1992) *The Tourism Industry and the Environment.* Special Report No. 2453. The Economic Intelligence Unit, London.

Johns, C. and Leslie, D. (2008) Leisure consumers of air miles – the unlikelihood of change in leisure consumerism and sustainable development 'mission impossible'. *Leisure Studies Association Newsletter* 80, 35–38.

KPMG (2012) *Leisure Perspectives*. KPMG, London.

Laws, E. (1997) *Managing Packaged Tourism*. International Thomson Business Press, London.

Leidner, R. (2004) *The European Tourism Industry – A Multi-sector with Dynamic Markets. Structures, Developments and Importance for Europe's Economy*. EC, Enterprise DG (unit D.3) Publications, Brussels.

Leslie, D. (1991) Tourism in Northern Ireland: 1969–1989. Troubled times. Unpublished MPhil Thesis, University of Ulster, Jordanstown, Northern Ireland.

Leslie, D. (1999) 'Sustainable tourism' – or more a matter of sustainable societies? In: Foley, M., McGillivray, D. and McPherson, G. (eds) *Leisure, Tourism and Environment: Sustainability and Environmental Policies*. University of Brighton, Leisure Studies Association, Brighton, UK, pp. 173–193.

Leslie, D. (ed.) (2009) *Tourism Enterprises and Sustainable Development: International Perspectives on Responses to the Sustainability Agenda*. Routledge, New York.

Leslie, D. (ed.) (2012) *Responsible Tourism: Concepts Theory and Practice*. CAB International, Wallingford, UK.

Leslie, D. (2015) *Tourism Enterprise – Developments, Management and Sustainability*. CAB International, Wallingford, UK.

Lipman, G. (2011) Travel and tourism 2011 – a measured analysis and focused response. International Council of Tourism Partners. Available at: http://www.forimmediaterelease.net/pm/4317.html, accessed 7 November 2016.

Lueck, M. (2005) Sunset for the package holiday. BBC News. Available at: http://news.bbc.co.uk/1/hi/business/4417793.stm, accessed 5 August 2015.

Lusher, A. (2015) A history of package holidays: rising numbers indicate a renaissance with an updated and classier holiday experience. *Independent*. Available at: http://www.independent.co.uk/travel/news-and-advice/a-history-of-package-holidays-rising-numbers-indicate-a-renaissance-with-an-updated-and-classier-10306101.html, accessed 7 November 2016.

McKercher, B. (1993) The unrecognised threat to tourism: can tourism survive 'sustainability'? *Tourism Management* 14, 131–136.

Mintel (2010) Package holidays UK. Available at: http://academic.mintel.com/display/479781/, accessed 24 November 2014.

Mintel (2014) US outbound. Available at: http://academic.mintel.com/display/702130/?highlight#hit1, accessed 16 January 2016.

Mintel (2016) Package vs independent holidays. Available at: http://academic.mintel.com/display/748212/, accessed 16 January 2016.

Mosselaer, F., Duim, R. and Wijk, J. (2012) Corporate social responsibility in the tour operating industry: the case of Dutch outbound tour operators. In: Leslie, D. (ed.) *Tourism Enterprises and the Sustainability Agenda across Europe*. Ashgate, Farnham, UK, pp. 71–92.

Ritzer, G. and Laska, A. (1997) McDisneyization and post-tourism. In: Rojek, C.C. and Urry, J. (eds) *Touring Cultures: Transformation of Travel and History*. Routledge, New York, pp. 96–109.

Seabrook, J. (2007) Tourism, predatory or omnivorous? *Third World Resurgence* 207–208, 13–14.

Sheldon, C. and Toxon, M. (1999) *Installing Environmental Management Systems – a Step-by-Step Guide*. Earthscan, London.

Smith, O. (2015) More Britons book package holidays. *The Daily Telegraph*, 27 April, 5.

Smith, V. and Eadington, W. (1992) *Tourism Alternatives: Potentials and Problems in the Development of Tourism*. John Wiley, Chichester, UK.

Swarbrooke, J. (1999) *Sustainable Tourism Management*. CAB International, Wallingford, UK.

Tibbott, R. (2001) New lives, new leisure. *Locum Destination Review* 5, 3–4.

TOI (2005) *Integrating Sustainability into Business: A Management Guide for Responsible Tour Operations, United Nations Environment Programme*. Tour Operators Initiative, Paris.

UNWTO (2015) *Tourism Highlights*. United Nations World Tourism Organization, Madrid.

Urquhart, C. (2006) From jet set to carbon offset. *The Times*, 26 October, 19.

Weaver, D.B. (1992) Tourism and the functional transformation of the Antiguan landscape. In: Conny, A.M. (ed.) *Spatial Implications of*

Tourism. Geographical Perspectives, Groningen, The Netherlands, pp. 161–175.

Weaver, D. and Lawton, A. (2006) *Tourism Management*, 3rd edn. John Wiley, Chichester, UK.

Whinney, C. (1996) Good intentions in a competitive market: training the people and tourism in fragile environments. In: Price, M.F. (ed.) *People in Tourism in Fragile Environments*. John Wiley, Chichester, UK, pp. 221–230.

WTTC, IFTO, IH&RA and ICCL (2002) *Industry as a Partner for Sustainable Development*. World Travel and Tourism Council, International Federation of Tour Operators, International Hotel and Restaurant Association, International Council of Cruise Lines, London.

Yale, P. (1995) *The Business of Tour Operations*, 5th edn. Pearson Education, Harlow, UK.

3 The Operating Environment

Learning Objectives

After studying this chapter, you should be able to:

- Understand the structure and distribution of tour operator products.
- Explain the importance of integration.
- Appreciate the impacts on tour operators of the macro environment.
- Describe and use the PESTEL framework relevant for tour operators.
- Appreciate the micro environment.

Introduction

As with any business, tour operators must work within their environment and respond, as necessary and appropriately, to changes in that environment. However, in this their situation is different from general business. This is because their activities are not only subject to or influenced by the prevailing forces and events in the country within which they are based, but also of those destinations with which they are involved; for example, differing regulations or significant events (see Chapters 8 and 12, this volume). To develop and prosper they need to be both attuned to market demand within their home country and the market in other countries as well as potential opportunities in new destinations. A primary consideration is how to reach the actual and potential markets and thus we need to examine the distribution process and the intermediaries between the tour operator and their potential customers.

In total, this is effectively a tour operator's channel of distribution. Here we consider the general chain of distribution and the possibilities for a tour operator to become more directly involved, for example taking over a travel agency, thereby reducing the role of other companies in their chain of distribution. Although not discussed here, it should be recognized that the channels of distribution for tour operators have changed substantially since the 1990s (see Chapter 9, this volume).

No company can afford to stand still in today's changing times and the tour operator needs to be aware of external influences on its operating environment and the opportunities for and threats to its business operations that may arise as a result. This is considered below in the broad context of the external operating environment. Being well prepared is good for the company and its future, but this also requires the development of a management strategy to guide the company forward while recognizing the competition and potential opportunities for growth. Therefore, our attention turns to appropriate frameworks that can be applied by tour operators in developing their management strategy.

External Operating Environment

For any organization to be successful or to maintain success, it is important that the organization understands the current operating environment and is aware of developing and potential future trends in the wider, i.e. macro, environment (sometimes referred to as the broader or external environment). Further it must be able to react to changes that may influence the operations of the company. The operating environment can be analysed at two different levels – the macro environment and the micro environment.

Macro environment

The assessment of the environment outside an organization's control is termed macro environment analysis. Although the macro environment is beyond a company's influence, it can have a significant impact on a company's operations and thus overall performance. As the tour operating sector operates in an 'extremely volatile and dynamic external environment' (Dale, 2000, p. 361), it is susceptible to changes in both consumer demand and the environment. Therefore, the ability not only to recognize but also to appreciate the potential significance of such changes enables operators to adapt their activities. The most frequently used model to analyse the macro environment is the framework known by the acronym PESTEL.

PESTEL

PESTEL, generally considered to be the simplest tool, is a useful framework that enables an organization to appreciate the macro environment, identify potential issues that may have an implication for the organization and consider such issues in terms of whether they present opportunities or threats to the organization. In the context of tour operators, the application of macro analysis needs to consider issues that arise according to the different countries within which they operate as

well as the potential markets in their home country. Further adding complication is the need to take into consideration different levels of government and regulation, i.e. international, intraregional (such as the EU), national and local levels of government.

POLITICAL The political environment is that which is under direct control or influence by government. This may include legislation and regulation (e.g. airport regulations and tourism policies), economic policy (e.g. exchange rate stabilization, control of inflation, taxation, trade tariffs) and governmental international policy. Political acts such as war and terrorism can have devastating impacts on destinations and their tourism sector. Terrorist attacks, such as those in Paris, Bali, Nairobi, Madrid, London and New York, have immediate impacts on the destinations involved through a reduction of tourist numbers. However, it should be recognized that such acts tend to switch demand to other localities. Political risk must also be considered and therefore companies must assess the political situations of and within countries, particularly those in less stable areas such as sub-Saharan Africa, parts of the Middle East and South America.

ECONOMIC Economic analysis can include the price of oil, fuel costs, exchange rates, interest rates, minimum working wages and inflation – all factors that indirectly may impact negatively on disposable income and thus demand for tourism and/or on the expenditure of tourists as well as the costs of tour operators. An overview is required of how these may affect patterns of consumption, potential market growth and/or construction of the market. For example, the global recession after 2007 saw a decrease in the number of UK residents taking international package holidays, while domestic holidays increased

(Davidson, 2015). Changes in exchange rates can affect an operator's profit margins considerably and many tour operators forward buy currency to try and minimize the impact of exchange rate fluctuations (see Chapter 7, this volume). A destination may introduce a higher value added tax rate for food/accommodation or introduce an airport tax on departing passengers, which will not only affect demand for a destination but will also impact on the operator's pricing strategy. For example, in 2016 the Balearic Islands introduced a Sustainable Tourism Tax with the aim of improving and maintaining the quality of tourism on the islands, which could add up to £80 to the price of a two-week holiday for a family of four.

SOCIOCULTURAL Sociocultural influences include demographics, e.g. population statistics and profiles, lifestyle, education, holiday entitlement and workforce changes. A demographic trend in post-industrial countries is marrying later in life and having fewer children and, of particular significance, when compared with earlier generations in such societies, people are living longer and are fitter and more affluent. This is a growing market segment, often referred to as the 'grey market' or 'silver panthers'. They are also more experienced travellers and more likely to seek alternative experiences. Consideration also needs to be given to the composition of families, which leads to market opportunities such as family adventure holidays or grandparent/grandchildren holidays.

TECHNOLOGICAL The travel sector has always been at the forefront of new technologies; for example, computer reservation systems/global distribution systems (**CRS/ GDS**). Technological changes, such as innovations in reservation systems and **yield management** (see Chapter 7, this volume), the internet and web 2.0 capabilities, have all influenced change in the way businesses operate. The emergence of online travel agents (OTAs) has proved to be a fundamental change to how holidays are bought and sold. Trends such as dynamic packaging (the ability of agents to build a customer's own choice of flights, accommodation and car rental instead of purchasing a pre-defined package) have enabled travel agents to react to consumer demands in a more effective way, using a range of communication tools such as a computer, tablets and phone applications.

ENVIRONMENTAL Environmental issues can involve **climate change**, the reduction of natural resources and pollution and potentially therefore the response of national and international government agencies, which may directly or indirectly affect tour operations.

Environmental factors can be considered to comprise two distinct categories. First, disasters caused by natural events, e.g. hurricanes, floods, earthquakes. The tsunami in 2004 affected a large number of countries, including Thailand, Sri Lanka, Indonesia and notably the tourism-dependent Maldives. Certainly, such disasters are unpredictable. However, this does not mean an operator should not have plans in place addressing how they would cope in such an eventuality (see Chapter 12, this volume). The second category encompasses diverse issues such as initiatives arising from the promotion of sustainable development – 'sustainability' – by international and national agencies; similarly, reactions to climate change. The responses to such issues are diverse and more policy based. Promotion of best practices may herald subsequent and significant legislation, as in the introduction of a carbon or sulphur tax which indirectly affects operators through its effects on fuel costs.

LEGAL This includes the legislation and regulation of companies, which is usually under the control of the government. Legislation covering employment, consumer protection, contracts and taxation will be set by the government. For example, the Monopolies and Mergers Commission in the UK allows the government to intervene on mergers, markets and regulation to ensure fair competition for the benefit of companies, customers and the economy. Tour operators must be attentive to developments in this field in all the countries within which they operate, e.g. the USA has legislation on fair trade practices and employment that potentially impinge on operational practices.

Table 3.1 presents an outline of a PESTEL analysis by category and associated implications.

PESTEL's simplified framework can be used to identify and sort the pertinent information drawn from what in practice is termed 'environmental scanning'. This involves searching and reviewing the wider environment for indicators of change that may hold implications for the ongoing operations of the company, which can then be further considered in terms of opportunities or threats. When conducting such a scan, it is important that the analysis is focused on that information which is highly relevant to the organization's circumstances. Indeed, such analysis could result in contradictory information and, due to the dynamic nature of the sector, the information identified could become out of date relatively quickly. Therefore, managers should be aware of the limitations of such a scan and constantly update it, particularly when new sources of information are found. As such, it needs to be recognized that environmental scanning is very much an ongoing process.

While PESTEL provides a very useful tool to aid recognition of the importance of attention to, and a better understanding of, the macro environment, that is only half the picture. To complement this, organizations need to have a thorough understanding of their competition and the marketplace. This brings into focus the competitive environment.

Micro environment

An analysis of the micro environment involves an assessment of the environment within which the business operates and

Table 3.1. Illustration of PESTEL analysis.

Factors	Example	Implication
Political	Increase in minimum wages	Increasing costs
	Increasing air passenger duty	Impact on cost of packages
Economic	Increase in interest rates	Less disposable income
	Changes in exchange rates	May affect cost of holiday and profit
Social	Demand for experiential holidays	May need to introduce a new range of products
Technological	Growth of internet distribution	Reduction in 'bricks and mortar' travel agents
Environmental	Drought	Less water available for the maintenance of golf courses
Legal	Changes to the EU Package Directive	Unknown until implemented
	Introduction of the Disability Discrimination Act	Need for accessible facilities e.g. transport access, accommodation provision

interacts, e.g. suppliers, customers and competitors. The simplest tool is a SWOT (Strengths, Weaknesses, Opportunities and Threats) analysis, which can be used to audit the organization and its environment. Strengths and weaknesses are internal factors, whereas opportunities and threats are external factors. Ideally, a company would look to improve weaknesses and turn them into strengths, and to turn threats into opportunities. For example, an operator may consider one of their strengths to be an innovative and specialist product, but they may consider their lack of marketing skills to be a weakness. Opportunities may include improving their website or attracting new markets, whereas threats could be the introduction of a new competitor with a similar product or a competitor that has access to superior distribution channels.

There are several key elements within a business environment that affect the level of competition for any organization. Therefore, it is important that organizations not only recognize this but are also aware of and react appropriately, ideally swiftly, to changes in this competitive environment. According to Porter (1980), there are five major forces within a competitive environment that represent strong threats to a company's success. Collectively, these forces can provide valuable insights into most organizations, destinations or attractions (Evans, 2015).

Porter's Five Forces

Porter's Five Forces framework is a popular technique that provides an easy-to-use model that can be used to analyse the tour operating sector and help explain the need for horizontal and vertical integration. It is widely viewed as an approach that is complementary to a SWOT analysis, i.e. the opportunities and threats, informed by an understanding of the competitive environment and developed from analysis of the macro environment as identified through the PESTEL framework. It is important to remember that Porter's Five Forces framework is designed to facilitate analysis of the industry within which the company operates. If the organization has a diverse portfolio of products and services, then separate models should be created for each of them. To be effective, it must be borne in mind that the outcomes of utilizing this framework provide only a snapshot of the market at that moment in time. Therefore, without regularly reviewing the operating environment, knowledge gained from using Porter's Five Forces may become out of date quite quickly. These forces, as illustrated in Fig. 3.1 and discussed below, are:

- Industry rivalry.
- Suppliers' bargaining power.
- Buyers' bargaining power.
- Threat of new entrants.
- Threat of substitutes.

INDUSTRY RIVALRY One of the key factors for success in any business is the ability to understand the competitors, in particular their marketing strategies and product. A competitor analysis will enable operators to understand the extent and nature of the products on offer and specifically the differentiation of such products. Evans (2015) suggests that competition can either take place on a price or a non-price basis; that is, price competition involves undercutting competitors, whereas non-price competition is based on a range of activities, such as branding, advertising, promotion, product innovation and customer service. In highly competitive markets, price changes may be necessary to match a significant competitor in order to maintain sales. Within the overall market, factors that need to be considered include the degree of concentration of competitors,

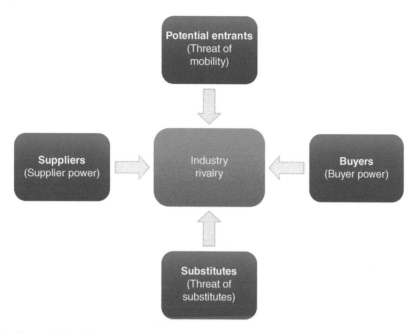

Fig. 3.1. Porter's Five Forces.

including the number and relative size. Furthermore, it is imperative to assess the growth potential of the market.

If the market is dominated by one or two organizations, new entrants are likely to encounter difficulties in sustaining their operations because larger organizations may be able to stop or limit the growth of smaller competitors. For example, the mass market product of beach holidays in Europe is dominated by two major vertically integrated tour operators and because of their marketing power and pricing strategies it is difficult for new entrants to compete against them. In sectors where there are high fixed costs, such as cruising due to the investment in purchasing cruise ships, the ability of new entrants to compete is often limited. In addition, high cost entry barriers (sunk costs) mean potentially significant problems later if a company encounters financial difficulties; for example, once a company has invested in cruise ships, they cannot use them for other purposes. Witness the collapse of the UK's All Leisure Group at the start of 2017, which operated cruise lines Swan Hellenic and Voyages of Discovery.

An appreciation of supply in relation to demand and the characteristics of that demand means that in markets that are mature, the competition is likely to be more intense than in those markets that are developing. In a mature market, companies will only be able to gain market share by taking customers from existing competitors. Therefore, such factors as customer service and customer loyalty become all the more significant. Clearly, it is more difficult to attract customers away from competitors with high levels of repeat custom. However, traditionally the tour operating sector has low levels of loyalty (Richard and Zhang, 2012) due to low switching costs and numerous alternatives available, although independent specialist operators tend to have high levels of repeat custom (see Holland, 2012). In contrast, developing markets present new opportunities where sales can be increased without taking customers from existing operators.

In sectors where differentiation is greater, there is less likely to be high levels of rivalry; for example, operators working in specific destinations or with specific activities usually encounter less competition, such as Wendy Wu, which is the UK's leading China holiday specialist, or Intrepid, an Australian company specializing in small group adventure holidays.

In summary, the intensity of competitor rivalry increases with:

- large number of firms in the market;
- number and relative size of competitors within the industry;
- slow market growth;
- high fixed costs;
- low switching costs;
- low levels of **product differentiation**; and
- high exit barriers.

SUPPLIERS' BARGAINING POWER The bargaining power of suppliers relates to the supply side of the sector. Operators often rely on third-party suppliers and therefore the uniqueness and scarcity of potential suppliers will dictate the level of bargaining power of the tour operator. The company that is offering differentiated products with reliance on a small number of suppliers means suppliers hold significant power over the operator regarding provision of supply and costs. Conversely, if the destination can be easily substituted for an alternative one, then suppliers have less power. For example, a tour operator such as Intrepid offering specific tour itineraries that include Everest base camp is reliant on the suppliers to provide mountain guides and tented accommodation. If that supplier were to be offered better rates by a different tour operator, then they may readily switch their allegiance to that operator. In some cases, switching between suppliers may be costly for operators, therefore,

where appropriate, it is important to build relationships over time that should encourage the loyalty of their suppliers.

BUYERS' BARGAINING POWER The bargaining power of buyers translates in the case of tour operators to the demand for their products by tourists. Clearly, this has an impact on the price that can be charged by operators. Generally speaking, the more power buyers have, the lower the price of the product. That said, the power is dependent on the number of customers and the volume of their purchases. In effect, customers can have significant bargaining power when it is easy and cheap for them to substitute their chosen product for a very similar alternative, as is the case with the typical 3S package. In economic terms, this is referred to as **price elasticity**. In this case, the traditional 3S package holiday is generally seen to be price elastic, whereas a specific tour involving a particularly special destination would be considered as price inelastic.

Operators are generally reliant on retailers to promote and sell their products, thus retailers can exercise a level of power over tour operators due to their potentially large customer base. Therefore, when there are many tour operators trying to place their products in travel agencies, agencies may limit the number of operators with whom they work. In the case of vertically integrated tour operators, through their own retailers they have a secure distribution channel and can guarantee that those retailers will sell their product. Conversely, non-integrated operators are reliant on encouraging retailers to promote their products through the practice of offering commission and other incentives.

In addition, tour operators and retailers can be viewed as buyers and have substantial influence on their suppliers. Large operators purchase elements of the package from selected principals, e.g. accommodation, and when purchasing in large numbers they can achieve very competitive rates from those suppliers, which may not be in the suppliers' best interest. For example, destination accommodation suppliers are reliant on tour operators to use their accommodation and thus may accept a reduced price for a guarantee that the rooms will be sold (see Buhalis, 2000).

THREAT OF NEW ENTRANTS The threat of potential new entrants to the market varies according to the ease or difficulty involved on the part of new operators seeking to enter the market. If the market has little brand awareness and loyalty and is one where distribution channels are easy to access, then there is greater likelihood that new rivals may enter the market. In general, the tour operator sector has traditionally been relatively easy to enter as there are very few barriers to entry. There is easy access to principals, related services and retailers and relatively little in the way of start-up costs.

As a result of the ease of entrance to the market, tour operating companies often need to grow or specialize to maintain their market share. Horizontal integration (by the purchasing of other operators) or vertical integration (establishing a retail distribution centre) provide quick ways to achieve this – for example, the purchasing of many independent adventure tour operators by First Choice (prior to the merger with TUI) enabled the company to introduce specialist products to a focused market.

Companies that achieve significant **economies of scale**, or have substantial experience and can achieve lower operating costs, will have an advantage over new entrants. Furthermore, a high level of brand awareness and customer loyalty could hamper any new entrants to the market. However, given the general low levels of customer loyalty, which is certainly a weakness factor for many operators, the

potential opportunity for new entrants increases.

THREAT OF SUBSTITUTES The tour operator sector is very susceptible to substitute products due to the large number of operators' products in existence that are readily available to potential customers, whether through retailers or the internet. In this instance, a substitute product is a package that basically meets the same customer needs as other packages. As a result, this can limit the opportunity for companies to raise prices.

Substitute products could include:

- replacing one destination/country for another;
- independent travel instead of a package;
- all-inclusive instead of self-catering;
- adventure holidays instead of beach holidays;
- short breaks instead of longer holidays; and
- one company's product for another.

The extent to which alternatives may form a threat depends on two factors: the closeness of the substitute in terms of price and performance and/or the willingness of buyers to switch. Within tour operations, many products can be easily replaced/substituted for others because many companies offer similar products, while consumers are increasingly looking towards new experiences. Horizontal integration has allowed many operators to diversify and introduce 'substitute' products, thereby offering new experiences to help retain their customers. For example, TUI operates an adventure section, Peak Travel, to meet the recognized demand for adventure holidays.

Overall, the threat of substitutes is high when consumer switching costs are low and the substitute product may be cheaper and/or better quality than the original. Conversely, the threat of substitutes is slow when switching costs are high and/ or the product is more expensive and/or considered as inferior in quality and service.

It is important to note that there has been substantial research that either supports, revises or complements Porter's basic model (see Andriotis, 2004). In particular, it is noted that the model does not acknowledge some of the monumental changes that have affected the sector over the last 30 years. For example, change is more rapid and the model does not consider nonmarket forces such as technology and the impact of government regulation. There is no doubt that information technology offers new opportunities to improve communication with customers, and technology provides information systems that change the way operators work and the way customers can purchase the holiday (see Chapter 9, this volume). Government involvement in tourism is wide in scale, from activities encouraging tourism development to the control and regulation of airlines, and therefore must also be considered as an additional force (Andriotis, 2004).

Porter's Generic Strategies

Once operators understand their competitor analysis, this information can be used to determine the strategic direction the company may take. Porter suggests that the way to build sustainable competitive advantage and market dominance over rivals is to develop a strategy that best fits the organization's competitive environment (Porter, 1985). Porter's Generic Strategies (see Fig. 3.2) suggests three possible competitive stances:

- differentiation;
- cost leadership; and
- focus.

Each of these generic strategies has a different approach to achieving competitive advantage, based on the characteristics of the product mix and the company's ability to create and distribute the product.

DIFFERENTIATION A differentiation strategy, while it can be applied in different ways, is often based on creating and informing consumers that their product is superior or different from that of their competitors. This focus on premium product features, which are specifically targeted to the needs of customers or to create customer perception that the product is substantially better than that of the competition, may be achieved through advertising and promotional campaigns. This strategy invariably involves offering a

Target scope	Advantage	
	Low cost	Product uniqueness
Broad (Industry wide)	**Cost leadership strategy**	**Differentiation strategy**
Narrow (Market segment)	**Focus strategy** (low cost)	**Focus strategy** (differentiation)

Fig. 3.2. Porter's Generic Strategies.

superior (exceptional) level of service and the use of selective distribution channels with the aim of developing a strong brand name and image coupled with loyalty programmes and a distinctive product. This approach achieves a competitive advantage because operators will be able to command premium prices, and customers will be willing to pay the additional fee, resulting in higher profit margins.

Differentiation strategies rely on innovation, research and development, and can create customer loyalty, which is generally considered rare within the tour operating sector.

COST LEADERSHIP Cost leadership is a strategy based on reducing costs, thus enabling lower selling prices to achieve increased demand. Cost leadership does not focus on creating a new product but rather replicating an existing product while utilizing less-expensive resources. Economies of scale are achieved by high-volume purchasing from principals and locating the holidays in destinations where costs are comparatively low to reduce the overall price. The key to this strategy is standardization.

Basically, this strategy aims to achieve the lowest production costs or service within the sector. This can allow companies to achieve high profits if they can produce their products more cheaply than their competitors, leading to lower prices and increased sales and market share. Adopting this approach for the introduction of new products can mean that operators offer these new products at lower prices than their competitors, gaining market share and sales. Such tactics can produce barriers to entry (see Porter's Five Forces) and is appropriate in a market where customers are price sensitive. An example in the European mass market are the holiday companies Thomas Cook and Thomson (part of TUI), in which there is high capacity utilization of the aircraft, high bargaining power over suppliers and subsequent economies of scale, combined with low operating costs through standardization and high-volume sales.

However, the cost leadership model appears to be losing its attraction within mature markets because tourists are increasingly able and confident enough to organize their own holidays and are demanding more experiential and personalized holidays.

FOCUS A focus strategy, either using differentiation or cost leadership, is aimed at a specific segment of the market, a niche, that may be identified on the base of demographics, location or interests and/or specializing in a particular geographic destination (see Chapter 10, this volume). A focus strategy is most likely to be adopted by small or medium-sized enterprises (SME) as a way of competing in the sector by concentrating on specific target group(s) and providing a product designed to meet their needs (see Chapter 5, this volume). For example, The Aurora Zone specializes in holidays to see the Northern Lights, while the Family Adventure Company creates family activity-based holidays.

While SMEs adopt this strategy to survive in a complex marketplace, some of the larger tour operators within Europe have purchased small operators to provide niche products. For example, TUI own and operate a number of activity-based companies that target specific segments of the market, such as Marco Polo, which specializes in long-haul tailor-made holidays. Thus they operate two different strategies for the different brands within the company. Within a focus strategy, in this instance the company charges a premium price for a particularly special holiday package and also offers the lowest priced package in the mass market sector (one reason for retaining the brand of a company taken over).

Porter suggests that organizations that fail to clarify their strategic stance are in danger of being 'stuck in the middle'. Essentially, such companies are a little of both – a differentiator and a cost leader – and as a result rather 'sit in the middle of the road' with a lack of focus. Thus they are unlikely to achieve substantial market growth and are liable to be subject in terms of success to the influence and actions of their competitors, achieving little in moving forward beyond what may well be perceived by potential customers as rather standard fare. To sustain the business, organizations must decide whether to gain competitive advantage by:

- differentiating the products and services and achieving higher prices (or differentially charging average price to gain market share) or
- producing its products and services at lower costs than its competitors.

In addition, organizations must decide whether to target a large section of the market or a specific narrow section (segment) of the market. As such, the tour operator logically either operates in a niche market or the general market. This largely explains why a major player in the marketplace would seek to buy a small tour operator specializing in a niche market and retain that operator's name; e.g. TUI owns and has retained the names of Marco Polo, Crystal Ski holidays and Exodus.

It should be noted that Porter's Generic Strategies model is not without criticism (Garau, 2007), with suggestions that cost leadership does not in itself sell products and differentiation strategies can be used to increase sales rather than price. Despite such limitations, this model provides a useful framework enabling managers to focus on assessing where their advantage lies. Indeed, Porter's original model has been adapted by Bowman and Faulkner (1997) to include eight different strategies that can be evaluated at varying levels of price and perceived value (see Evans, 2015).

A complementary approach to the preceding frameworks of PESTEL and Porter, which we can draw from the successful manager's toolbox, is that of Ansoff's Matrix (1987) to aid decision making as regards opportunities for growth.

Opportunities for growth

One of the most commonly applied models for assessing the possible growth of an organization is Ansoff's Matrix. This is a basic framework to guide examination of products and markets to identify opportunities for growth. The framework comprises four main types of strategy that organizations can implement: market penetration; product development; market development and diversification (see Fig. 3.3).

MARKET PENETRATION Market penetration covers an operator's products currently in the marketplace. If the market evidences growth potential for a specific product offering, e.g. due to the collapse of a major competitor, there are opportunities for the organization to take advantage of their experience and reputation in the marketplace to grow their customer base. This means that the product does not need to be changed, but can be exploited further through the use of promotions such as pricing and advertising and/or finding new ways to distribute the product, thereby reaching potential new customers. Market penetration usually involves the least risk, because there is an established base of customers and the opportunity to attract customers from operators who have ceased trading. However, if the reason that an operator has withdrawn from the market is because it is declining, then the company should rethink and perhaps focus on growing other products and alternative markets.

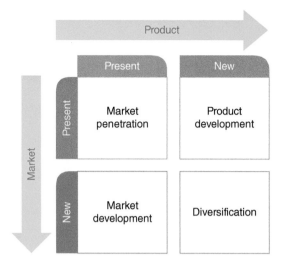

Fig. 3.3. Ansoff's Matrix.

PRODUCT DEVELOPMENT In the product development growth strategy, new products are introduced to existing markets or existing products are modified in some appropriate way. The aim is to increase the level of purchase by existing customers and thereby increase market share, rather than primarily to attract new customers. In terms of product development, tour operators may develop their product offerings by identifying additional destinations, e.g. 'City Break' packages now include new destinations such as Bilbao in Spain or Chang Mai in Thailand, rather than the expected capital cities. This may be due to customers' preferences changing or the emergence of new opportunities, such as creating packages to destinations that have only just become easily accessible to the source market, perhaps as an outcome of the development of a new airport, or have become more stable politically (e.g. Myanmar). This is well illustrated in the case of the German division of Thomas Cook, which added an additional 21 flights to Bulgaria for the summer of 2016 as demand for holidays near the Black Sea increased. Additional capacity on flights was acquired through obtaining seats on charter flights provided by Germania, Sun Express and Air Via, and increasing the number of departure airports in Germany. Product development may also be a reactionary strategy if the competition has already launched new products. It should be noted, however, that product development has a higher risk than market penetration because the modified products may fail to take off.

MARKET DEVELOPMENT Market development focuses on the entry to a new market, which is also sometimes referred to as market extension. By adopting this strategy, a tour operator sells its existing products to new markets, which could be a potentially new target market segment or targeting a new geographical source of potential customers or adopting new methods of distribution. For instance, a company that has traditionally sold their products domestically may look to find distributors overseas; e.g. Explore Worldwide have a range of distributors in the USA and Canada. Market development works on the assumption that the current market has been fully exploited, hence the need to move into new markets. This strategy has more risk than market penetration because the new market may not respond to the product as well as anticipated.

DIVERSIFICATION The final strategy is that of diversification. This requires the operator to identify new products and new markets concurrently and is recognized as the riskiest of these strategic options because it involves two unknowns. Therefore, this strategy should only be adopted if the tour operator is confident that they understand the new market and that they have created a product that specifically meets the needs of that target market. Operators can diversify in two ways, either into products that are unrelated to the market they work in or, and the more likely, they diversify within the same market (**diagonal diversification**). While diversification clearly has commonality with vertical and horizontal integration, integration usually involves a takeover or merger with a competitor, whereby the latter is integrated into the existing organization, whereas diversification involves developing internally or integrating a competitor through joint developments.

There are some instances where organizations may implement a strategy of withdrawal from the product or market. This strategy may be a result of a number of factors, such as a decline in the size of the market, more effective and successful competition, poor performance, utilizing resources for different products or a decision that the product is no longer beneficial to the company's strategic direction. This strategy of consolidation may be chosen and can be implemented in a number of ways, such as a reduction in the range of products offered or the number of market segments targeted, which may be a result of the strategic decision for the business to maintain market share but not increase it. For example, in 2015 Kuoni Group sold its European tour operating business to DER Touristik so that it could concentrate on its core businesses, Global Travel Distribution, Global Travel Services and VFS Global.

The analysis so far allows us to have a picture of the macro (external) and micro (competitive) environment. Porter's Generic Strategies and Ansoff's Matrix also provide ways of thinking about strategic direction. The next section will build on these ideas and concentrate on some of the actual activities organizations in the tourism sector might have to undertake in order to become and/or remain competitive. To do this we will utilize the concept of the chain of distribution.

Chain of distribution

Tourism products primarily consist of transport, accommodation and ancillary services, which are traditionally referred to as principals in the tourism chain of distribution. These include transport providers, such as airlines, railways, cruise ships; accommodation suppliers, such as hotels, guesthouses; and finally, ancillary services, which may be visitor attractions, conference venues or entertainment. Often the principals promote their own products/services directly to potential customers. However, in the case of the holiday package created by a tour operator, the chain of distribution, sometimes called channel of distribution, is used to illustrate how products and services are created and distributed. This illustrates how different segments of the travel and tourism sector work together to create and distribute package holidays. The tourism package therefore comprises a number of services provided by principals that are bundled together and presented to customers as a single product. The traditional chain of distribution shows that products are distributed through a number of intermediaries, who are considered either wholesalers or retailers (see Fig. 3.4).

Wholesalers are companies that buy large quantities of products and services from suppliers, package them together and then sell them on an individual basis to consumers: as such, tour operators can be seen as wholesalers. Although tour operators may be seen as wholesalers, they

Fig. 3.4. Chain of distribution.

are also producers of new products in that they create a single product from an amalgamation of components. For example, a package of accommodation and transport in a beach resort is a different product from accommodation and transport combined as part of a tour visiting many cities.

Tour operators are not the only wholesalers; there are also **brokers** and **consolidators** who can also be considered as wholesalers.

- Brokers usually operate in the airline industry, but may also offer accommodation or other services. They purchase in bulk and sell on to tour operators or travel agents, either individually or in larger amounts. As brokers purchase large numbers of airline seats or hotel rooms, they are able to acquire these at low prices and make a profit, while allowing the agent or tour operator to add their own price mark-up.
- Consolidators are specific brokers working in the airline industry who purchase tickets directly from airlines, enabling them to resell to travel agents or consumers at discounted rates. There are specialist consolidators

who work with charter aircraft operators, enabling airlines to sell unsold stock.

Retailers are customer facing and the final link in the chain, selling either packages created by the wholesalers or products on behalf of the principals.

There are generally considered to be two different levels to distribution:

- Level one distribution, also called direct distribution, is the simplest form of distribution because there is no intermediary and tour operators sell direct to the customers. This is predominantly through a sales team based in the company or through websites. Benefits of selling directly to customers include the ability to control the quality of the information being given to potential customers and the opportunity to sell additional products or upgrades. As there are no intermediaries involved, no commission is given to agents acting on behalf of the company, which reduces costs and potentially means greater profit for the supplier.
- Level two distribution involves an intermediary such as a travel agent

selling products on behalf of the tour operator for which a commission is paid to the agent.

The structure of the tour operating sector is very dynamic. Major changes within the distribution chain, such as the internet, and difficulties with the economy, such as a recession, have led many companies within the chain of distribution to consolidate and forge alliances or mergers to control costs of production and distribution. In addition, this can be a way of growing the business as well as surviving in an increasingly competitive sector. There are many benefits to working closely or merging with other organizations, and this process is known as integration, which Cooper describes as 'an economic concept to describe formal linking arrangements between one organization and another' (2012, p. 206). The tourism sector in northern Europe is reaching maturity, with tourism organizations integrating, concentrating, forming alliances and investing in mass distribution techniques; as yet, this is not replicated in developing markets such as Korea and India, where distribution is more fragmented and suppliers remain independent (Sharda and Pearce, 2006).

Horizontal integration

This occurs when companies buy or merge with other companies at the same level in the chain of distribution. The most usual form of integration is between companies offering similar products, for example, a travel agency chain purchases another travel agency chain, or a tour operator purchasing or merging with another tour operator. The benefit of horizontal integration for tour operators is that by increasing their demand from suppliers, e.g. accommodation, they gain further economies of scale through bulk purchasing as well as integrated marketing and awareness campaigns. An obvious benefit is that of increased market share, either through expansion or diversification of the products available. Furthermore, the takeover of or merger with another tour operator reduces competition. The 1980s were notable for companies across Europe undertaking horizontal integration (Yale, 1995). More recent examples of horizontal integration include Carnival (USA), the leading operator in the cruise business, which bought Cunard Cruises and P&O Cruise operations while maintaining their brand (Buhalis and Ujma, 2006); the merger of First Choice with TUI in 2007; and The Co-operative Travel's merger with Thomas Cook in 2011. An example of integration at principal level is EasyJet's purchase of the airline Go from British Airways.

In many instances, tour operators may decide to retain the brand name of the purchased company and so consumers may not be aware that it is part of a bigger company. TUI, for example, own specialist holiday companies such as Crystal Ski and Headwater Holidays that maintain their own brand. Alternatively, integration may occur between companies offering complementary products at the same level on the chain of distribution, such as a coach company purchasing a small hotel group, e.g. Shearings and the Coach Holiday Group merged and now own over 200 coaches and 52 hotels. Such mergers or acquisitions are less frequent today, though the purchase of Starwood by Marriott International in 2016 is a notable example. Integration at principal level tends to take place in the form of alliances between airlines, such as the merger of British Airways with Iberia to create the International Airlines Group.

Vertical integration

This occurs when a company develops its own operations or takes over or merges with another component at a different level within the chain of distribution. An example would be a travel agent introducing their own tours (e.g. Thomas Cook in its early days) or purchasing a tour operator, or a tour operator purchasing a charter airline or accommodation. As demonstrated by Thomas Cook, whose portfolio includes accommodation operations, travel agents, tour operators; each of these deal in a different part of the distribution chain. The reverse scenario of a tour operator buying out a travel agent is equally applicable. For example, Airtours developed from the purchase of two small travel agencies in the early 1970s to become one of the leading UK-based tour operators by the mid-1980s and through a dynamic approach to both vertical and horizontal integration, including the takeover of other leading operators in other European countries, developed into MyTravel plc in 2002 – one of the largest operators in Europe at the time.

Vertical integration provides a competitive advantage for a company by ensuring that they have control over supply and standardization of service quality through alignment of service values and competencies (Theuvsen, 2004). This approach can enable global or regional expansion; for example, a small travel agent may position themselves in a niche market by partnering with hotels that have golf courses or spas. As such, these expansions may create barriers for new entrants to the market by gaining significant market base and a reduction in costs and potential financial gains from economies of scale.

There are two types of vertical integration – forward or backward:

- Forward vertical integration

Forward (downstream) vertical integration is when a tour operator is involved in the later stages of production, such as the distribution of the products. For example, Thomas Cook is a large UK tour operator and has a collection of travel agents branded as Thomas Cook. It also entered into a joint venture with The Co-operative Travel in 2011, which enables it to promote its own products and maximize revenue streams.

Forward vertical integration enables tour operators to secure a direct source of customers, for example those loyal to the travel agency, and gain better control over the distribution of their own packages. Also, the aim is to promote their own products in preference to those of competitors by virtue of owning that retailing operation. This is termed 'directional selling' and can account for up to 80% of an agency's bookings. It may also reduce the cost of sales through reduced marketing effort, which may ultimately have an impact on pricing.

- Backward vertical integration

Backward (upstream) vertical integration occurs when the original company merges or acquires another company earlier in the distribution chain. For example, a travel agency merging with a tour operator or a tour operator purchasing an airline, which is unusual as they are more likely to set up their own charter airline. This is advantageous because they are not then dependent on scheduled providers or chartering flights for the provision of seats. In addition, operators can maintain airport slots, which is particularly important at congested, high-demand airports.

Backward integration secures the supply of a product/service, such as hotel rooms and transport, at a lower cost and ensures guaranteed access to that component of the package. For example, in 2013 Canada-based travel company Sunwing Travel announced a US$250 million investment to develop a 1250-room resort in Mexico, while the Spain-based travel company Grupo Piñero also announced a US$250 million investment in 2012 for seven resorts under its Bahía Príncip brand in the Dominican Republic and Mexico. These hotel groups also planned further expansion initiatives in new destinations in the Caribbean, Central America and Latin America.

Both backward and forward vertical integration ensure control over supply and pricing and enable operators to ensure a consistent level of customer service. This is particularly significant to tour operators based within the EU abiding by the Package Travel Regulations (see Chapter 8, this volume) for whom it is very important to be able to control the quality of the package and services provided therein. Owning the chain of distribution enables operators to control service delivery at every stage, from initial contact at a travel agency (or online) to their clients' return at the end of a holiday. A further benefit is that the quality management of the service experience can lead to an enhanced image and increased brand loyalty.

Vertical integration, both forward and backward, provides tour operators with the opportunities to reduce transaction costs and gain economies of scale because the buying power of integrated companies means they can achieve advantageous rates from principals with which they are not integrated. This approach also helps minimize the costs of distribution and ensure increased awareness of the product through merchandising and advertising. Integration may also enable a continuous supply of both transport and accommodation. In combination, this leads to gaining competitive advantage over non-integrated competitors (Theuvsen, 2004). In addition, vertically integrated companies may achieve overall profitability even if one component of the chain is operating at marginal or sub-marginal profit.

Diagonal integration

Diagonal integration occurs when a travel business enters into a related service. Saga, the UK's largest tour operator targeting the over 50s market, offers travel insurance and vehicle insurance which can be purchased at the same time as the holiday package; TUI owns a car rental company in Mallorca. This form of integration is also known as 'related diversification', whereas 'unrelated diversification' (see Ansoff, 1987) is when the travel business enters a new market that is unrelated to the core business, as illustrated by Virgin plc, which is highly diversified and whose brand extends across a range of businesses, including media, banking and credit cards. There are many risks involved in pursuing strategies such as this, not only in terms of success but also the impact on the brand image.

Although integration appears to offer substantial benefits, there are disadvantages.

Disadvantages of integration

There have been numerous reports (Lafferty and Van Fossen, 2001; Theuvsen, 2004) considering the impact of integration, primarily raising concerns that it may restrict consumer choice, and that many consumers are unaware of the ownership of the brands. For example, seemingly independent brands such as Exodus and Crystal Ski Holidays are part of TUI. Vertical integration has had a serious effect on independent travel agents because operators can control the amount of commission that agents receive from them, potentially reducing their income streams. A further factor is the element of choice limitation on the part of travel agents owned by tour operators, because the agent's staff direct customers to own-brand products. In addition, operators and airlines selling their products directly to customers, in particular through the internet, are reducing income streams for agents (see Chapter 11, this volume).

Also of consideration for those tour operators extensively integrated and operating on a basis of high-volume, low-price and thus low profit margins per sale is that they are more exposed to risk. They are potentially less able to cope in the event of sudden decline in market demand – witness the collapses of Clarkston (the UK's largest tour operator at the time) in 1974 and the International Leisure Group in 1991.

Summary

This chapter provides an overview of the structure of the tour operating sector, in particular the integration of the chain of distribution, which is clearly evident among many of the large tour operators. As such, the chapter provides a fundamental basis to the business management of the tour operator that will contribute to a more comprehensive understanding of the operations of, and decisions made by, tour operators discussed in subsequent chapters.

Irrespective of the size of a tour operator, they all need to develop a comprehensive understanding of the marketplace, the customer and the competition. Such knowledge is so important in guiding the successful development of the operation and should be maintained through ongoing environmental scanning to keep abreast of consumer trends and developments, particularly in relation to what is happening elsewhere that may impinge on the operation, be that in other destinations or among competitors.

As discussed, this knowledge can be used to full effect in tandem with management tools developed to aid assessment of the macro environment, in particular the utilization of a SWOT analysis drawing on PESTEL and Porter's Five Forces, which facilitates identifying threats and opportunities within their portfolio. Such an approach lays a foundation for the application of Porter's Generic Strategies, which helps the operator to identify the core competencies, and Ansoff's Matrix, which helps identify opportunities for growth. Through such methods, the tour operator is then better placed to address their chain of supply, to consider integration or indeed disintegration. All of this will be subject to the scale of the tour operator and the prevailing (and forecast) financial position.

Discussion Questions

1. Select a travel operator and conduct a macro environmental scan. What factors impact on the operations of the business?
2. Using a tour operator as an example, apply Porter's Five Forces to analyse the competitive environment.
3. Conduct a PESTEL analysis for TUI.
4. Develop a SWOT matrix for an organization of your choice.
5. What are travel and tourism intermediaries? What role and function do they perform and are they likely to be placed under increased pressure because of the internet?
6. Using examples, explain what is meant by integration in the context of mass market European tour operators? Suggest implications for suppliers, consumers and small and medium-sized enterprises.
7. Examine why a significant number of tour operators, both large and small, have collapsed. What might be done to reduce the risks of business failure on the part of those experiencing difficult times?
8. Discuss the circumstances under which disintermediation occurs in the tourism chain of distribution. Explain why this may be perceived as both an opportunity and a threat by tour operators.
9. Is there a future for tour operators?
10. With reference to a country of your choice, examine the structure, organization and operation of travel and tourism intermediaries. What are the main problems that these businesses face?

11. Do you consider that tour operators face a significant threat as a result of global agreements on climate change that aim to reduce air pollution?

Key Terms

- **3S:** Standardized pre-packaged holiday to a beach destination, termed 'sun, sand and sea' destination.
- **Brokers:** An individual or company that bulk-buys tourist products and sells them in smaller quantities. Online intermediaries such as ebookers and Opodo are examples of modern brokers.
- **Consolidators:** A form of broker that specializes in airline capacity, by buying unsold charter aircraft seats and selling them through intermediaries, enabling the airline to offload surplus capacity.
- **CRS/GDS:** A computer reservation system/global distribution system, which operates worldwide and offers information, reservations, ticketing for airlines, hotels, car rental companies and other services.

- **Diagonal diversification:** Diversification of the company into offering products and services that are related to their core offerings, usually by targeting their existing customers. Diagonal diversification may be related or unrelated.
- **Directional selling:** This is when a travel agent promotes the products of the operator that owns them and then promotes services by a 'preferred supplier'.
- **Economies of scale:** Usually refers to the reduction in cost associated with increasing the scale of the operations for the production of a single product.
- **Price elasticity:** The measurement of consumer demand for a product and how such demand responds to changes in price; if the demand is affected by price, then demand is elastic.
- **Product differentiation:** Making a product, in this case a package, that is different from other competitors.
- **Yield management:** Control and allocation of the services of a tourism provider by offering these to travellers at different price levels to maximize income.

INTERNET EXERCISES

Access Travelmole.com and adjust the settings to your local region (Asian/Pacific, United Kingdom, USA). By looking at the news, in particular tour operator news, reflect on the number of different operators that are being merged, bought or sold.

Questions

- Why is the tour operating sector so changeable?
- What are the trends in integration?

The Specialist Holiday Group (SHG) is a wholly-owned subsidiary of TUI. SHG is a collection of niche holiday brands operating in 23 different markets. Each of the businesses are run independently. (www.specialistholidays.com/about-us/)

Question

- Why do TUI not unite these products under a single brand, e.g. TUI?

MAJOR CASE STUDY

The Aurora Zone

The Aurora Zone is an independent tour operator company based in the north-east of England, which specializes in holidays to see the Aurora Borealis, also known as the Northern Lights. The Northern Lights are a spectacular natural light show created by the interaction of electrically charged particles in the atmosphere.

The Aurora is most frequently visible in northern Scandinavia within a certain latitude, which may increase depending on geomagnetic activity, but usually localized to an area just above the Arctic Circle. In order to have the best chance of seeing it, viewers need to be as far removed as possible from any significant light pollution, such as cities, and there has to be limited cloud cover. The best time of year to visit is during the winter months due to the long dark nights, but also because heavy snowfall provides lots of opportunity for sledding during the day.

Seeing the Northern Lights has become a 'bucket list' trip, i.e. one of the ultimate travel holidays to do in a lifetime along with activities such as whale watching, swimming with dolphins and seeing the Grand Canyon. The problems of offering trips of a lifetime is that once a passenger has been on the trip, then there is no reason for them to repeat book. Furthermore, such trips are often expensive and the Aurora Zone is no exception due to the remoteness of the destination, the activities involved and the equipment necessary.

Questions

- Using the Aurora Zone (or a similar product), how can the company expand to take advantage of their current market and create a product that would encourage repeat bookings?
- What information would you need to review to aid the decision?

Recommended Reading

For comprehensive coverage of the fundamental strategic management principles in tourism, hospitality and events:

Evans, N. (2015) *Strategic Management for Tourism, Hospitality and Events*, 2nd edn. Routledge, Abingdon, UK.

For an analysis of the growth and structure of the UK tour operating industry which draws on several of the strategic management tools mentioned:

Dale, C. (2000) The UK tour operating industry: a competitive analysis. *Journal of Vacation Marketing* 6, 357–367.

To consider Porter's Five Forces model in further depth, in this case applied in an examination of the travel and tourism sector specifically in Greece:

Andriotis, K. (2004) Revising Porter's five forces model for application in the travel and tourism industry. *Tourism Today* 4, 131–145.

References

Andriotis, K. (2004) Revising Porter's five forces model for application in the travel and tourism industry. *Tourism Today* 4, 131–145.

Ansoff, I. (1987) *Corporate Strategy*. Penguin, London.

Bowman, C. and Faulkner, D. (1997) *Competitive and Corporate Strategy*. Irwin, London.

Buhalis, D. (2000) Relationships in the distribution channel of tourism. Conflicts between hoteliers and tour operators in the Mediterranean region. *International Journal of Hospitality and Tourism Administration* 1, 113–139.

Buhalis, D. and Ujma, D. (2006) Intermediaries: travel agencies and tour operators. In: Buhalis, D. and Costa, C. (eds) *Tourism Business Frontiers: Consumers, Products and Industry*. Elsevier Butterworth-Heinemann, Oxford, UK, pp. 171–180.

Cooper, C. (2012) *Essentials of Tourism*. Pearson Education, Harlow, UK.

Dale, C. (2000) The UK tour operating industry: a competitive analysis. *Journal of Vacation Marketing* 6, 357–367.

Davidson, L. (2015) The rise of the staycation: more Brits holidaying at home. *The Telegraph*. Available at: http://www.telegraph.co.uk/finance/newsbysector/retailandconsumer/leisure/11396195/The-rise-of-the-staycation-more-Brits-holidaying-at-home.html, accessed 12 February 2017.

Evans, N. (2015) *Strategic Management for Tourism, Hospitality and Events*, 2nd edn. Routledge, Abingdon, UK.

Garau, C. (2007) Porter's generic strategies: a re-interpretation from a relationship marketing perspective. *The Marketing Review* 7, 369–383.

Holland, J. (2012) Adventure tours: responsible tourism in practice. In: Leslie, D. (ed.) *Responsible Tourism: Concepts, Theory and Practice*. CAB International, Wallingford, UK, pp. 119–129.

Lafferty, G. and Van Fossen, A. (2001) Integrating the tourism industry: problems and strategies. *Tourism Management* 22, 11–19.

Porter, M. (1980) *Competitive Strategy: Techniques for Analysing Industries and Competitors*. The Free Press, New York.

Porter, M. (1985) *Competitive Advantage: Creating and Sustaining Superior Performance*. The Free Press, New York.

Richard, J.E. and Zhang, A. (2012) Corporate image, loyalty, and the commitment in the consumer travel industry. *Journal of Marketing Management* 28, 568–593.

Sharda, S. and Pearce, D.G. (2006) Distribution in emerging tourism markets: the case of Indian travel to New Zealand. *Asia-Pacific Journal of Tourism Research* 11, 339–353.

Theuvsen, L. (2004) Vertical integration in the European package tour business. *Annals of Tourism Research* 31, 475–478.

Yale, P. (1995) *The Business of Tour Operations*. Addison Wesley Longman, Harlow, UK.

4 Product Development

Learning Objectives

After studying this chapter, you should be able to:

- Explain the need for itinerary planning.
- Appreciate the complexities of designing itineraries.
- Understand the basic stages involved in creating a package.
- Explain the different contracts available for accommodation, flight components and ancillary services.

Introduction

Tour operators are pivotal in their role of acting as wholesalers and packaging together transport to the destination, transfers, accommodation and ancillary services. However, a successful tour operator has to ensure that the selected destinations are attractive and the products offered can be sold at prices that are acceptable to customers. Furthermore, given the highly competitive marketplace within which they operate, all tour operators need to invigorate their portfolio to remain competitive. Despite their wide variety in terms of size and scope, they largely follow a similar process in the planning and development of a package.

This chapter therefore aims to provide an overview of how a tour operator creates a static **itinerary**, i.e. a holiday package to a single destination as part of a charter package, which could be, for example, a holiday in Cancun, Mexico or a week's skiing in Whistler, Canada. The key considerations involved in this process are discussed, although it should be recognized that each company will follow their own procedures for product development or review and amendments to their current products, as 'each season the entire product range is repriced, repackaged and relaunched' (Riley, 1983). The development of other types of tour package, such as adventure tours, is discussed in the context of small and medium-sized enterprises in Chapter 5 (this volume).

Itinerary Development (or Review)

Planning a new itinerary is a complex procedure and is obviously critical to the success of the company because an operator needs to provide maximum satisfaction for customers at a price that appeals to the market while remaining profitable. When planning an itinerary, the operator must not only ascertain the principal components of the package, i.e. accommodation and transport, but must also consider the logistics at the destination, transport between destinations, activities, excursions and suppliers.

Tour operators design new packages but also review current offerings and make changes to their itineraries. Such changes to packages may be small, such as changing hotels, levels of service or the introduction of new excursions, or more substantive, including the introduction of new destinations or products to attract a different market. Changes may be the result of customer feedback or the need to diversify to maintain a competitive advantage after reviewing sales and forecast planning or to address seasonality. For instance, mass market operators achieve most of their revenues during the high season (usually summer), which may result in cash flow problems during the off-season, thus a 'summer sun' operator may look to introduce a winter programme as another source of income during low season. For the purpose of this chapter, we will illustrate the process by way of using a flight inclusive, single destination (i.e. resort) pre-packaged holiday, for example, a 3S beach holiday.

Planning a Packaged Holiday

The production of a tour package will take on average 18 months to develop, from product conception to marketing the product, and then a period of lead time before the holiday operates. The time frame may vary between 12 months to three years for a standardized 3S packaged tour, considering the need to market and promote the tour, as illustrated in Table 4.1.

In contrast, a small, specialist tour operator may be able to create an itinerary in a much shorter development time. However, the construction of all packages needs to follow a similar process as regards the planning stages involved, irrespective of the time factor and type of tour operator. This product development process does not happen in isolation, and should be all-encompassing, drawing on staff expertise throughout the company, e.g. product, marketing, operations, human resources and finance departments.

Stages in Product Development

Essentially, there are nine stages in product development when planning an inclusive tour programme, commencing with review, research and planning. These stages are presented in Table 4.2 and discussed below.

1. Review, research and planning

Review company strategy and objectives, profitability and performance

The planning and development of a package originates from the strategic direction of the company and their business objectives (see Chapters 3 and 10, this volume). Therefore, the creation of new packages should meet the needs of the longer term business objectives as laid out in the company's strategy, such as increased market share. The objectives and strategy of the company are frequently presented in terms of a Mission Statement and Company Values, i.e. the aim of the company and how they plan to achieve it. The principal short-term objective of most companies is to stay in business and make a profit for the owners (or shareholders). However, how companies plan to achieve this depends on their size and scale. For example, small tour operators may focus on specialist operations distributing a niche product, whereas larger tour operators may focus on increasing their market share at the expense of their competitors.

Prior to any product being developed, it is essential that the tour operator conducts research to determine the destinations, prices, **capacity** and type of holiday to be offered. Research should not only include a review of the company's performance within the context of the company's objectives, but also identifying changes/trends in demand (the macro

Table 4.1. Typical timeframe for planning a package holiday. (From Holloway and Humphreys, 2012, p. 583, with permission from Pearson Education Limited. © Pearson Education Limited 2012.)

Stage	Time	Period	Activities
		September/December	Second stage of research
			In-depth comparison of alternative destinations
	Year 2	January	Determine destinations, hotels and capacity, duration of tours, departure dates
			Make policy decisions on size and design of brochure, numbers of brochures to print, date for completion of print
Negotiation		February/March	Tenders put out for the design, production and printing of brochures
			Negotiate the charter flights with the airlines
			Negotiate with hotels, transfer services, optional excursion operators
		April/May	Typesetting and printing space booked with printer, copies of the text commissioned
			Illustrations commissioned or borrowed
			Early artwork and text under development at design studio, layout suggestions
			Contracts completed with hotels and airlines, transfer services, etc.
		June	Production of brochures starts
Administration		July	Determine exchange rate
			Estimate selling price based on inflation, etc.
			Galley proofs to printer, corrections made
			Any necessary reservation staff recruited and trained
		August	Final tour priced
			Brochures printed and reservation systems established
Marketing		September/October	Brochure on market, distribution to agents
			Initial agency sales promotion, including launch
			First public media advertising, and trade publicity through press, etc.
	Year 3	January/March	Peak advertising and promotion to trade and public
		February/April	Recruitment and training of resort representatives, etc.
		May	First tour departs

environment), sales data and customer feedback (see Chapter 3, this volume).

A review of the market trends and opportunities for growth should be analysed and changes in consumer demand and global tourist flows should be reviewed.

Customer preferences vary and as such, holiday destinations may be attractive to different market **segments** over time (see Chapter 10, this volume). Identification of trends specific to a tour operator's specialism is key to developing new products

Table 4.2. Stages in planning an inclusive tour.

Stage	Activity
Review, research and planning	• Evaluation of company performance • Market research, including changes in demand and identification of trends • Competitor analysis
Second stage of research	• Evaluation of alternatives, including basic feasibility and capacity predictions • Identification of new product possibilities
Product planning	• Itinerary planning, including destinations, grade of holiday, capacity and departures • Initial costing which may result in reviewing itineraries • Marketing materials production
Contracting	• Negotiate with airlines and accommodation suppliers • Negotiate contracts with ancillary services e.g. transfers, excursions
Brochure production and website design	• Commission designers and printers • Finalize contracts
Finalize sales and marketing plan	• Design and implement marketing strategy • Preparation of administrative support • Sales training agents and staff development
Operations and administration training Recruit specialist staff	• Recruit staff – this may be for overseas, such as resort reps, tour managers, drivers etc.
Product launch and subsequent evaluation of sales	• Review sales and introduce recovery tactics if sales are poor
Product review and post tour management	• Review product and plan changes necessary • Quality review and implement changes

or amending current offerings. As Callaghan *et al.* (1994) proposed, there are five areas of trends that should be considered:

• **Destination** While many traditional European destinations remain popular, such as Spain, France and Greece, other popular destinations, such as Turkey and Tunisia have suffered a decline in numbers due to political instability. In Asia, destinations that are considered good value for money remain popular. A destination's popularity is constantly affected by external influences (see the section on PESTEL, Chapter 3, this volume).

• **Transport** The accessibility of the destination will impact on the type of holiday that can be offered. For example, destinations with international airports and good road infrastructure encourage the growth of mass market products, whereas destinations that are more remote and may involve substantial transfer distances will attract a different type of market and thus product offering.

• **Accommodation** The type of accommodation, such as star rating (or grading standard) and hospitality packages, varies in attractiveness to different markets. The growth of all-inclusive packages is testament to this.

- **Duration** The traditional 7- or 14-day package holiday offered in Europe is today less popular given the opportunities for alternative time periods. That said, packages such as cruises, adventure holidays and tours all must be planned with a specific duration.
- **Holiday type** The traditional European beach holiday, although still popular, is being challenged by destinations that were once considered inaccessible. Due to technological changes, such as improved aircraft, destinations further afield are more readily accessible, as can be witnessed by the growth of package holidays from Europe to South Africa, Goa (India) and the Maldives.

An analysis of the company's existing product(s) and competitive position is essential to evaluate its current product offerings and gaps in the market (see Chapter 10, this volume), a process that involves drawing on the following key sources of information:

- **Internal sales data** An examination and detailed analysis of previous years' sales performance will ascertain consumer trends for the company's products. Also, comparing predicted sales with actual sales from the previous year will identify destinations and products that are exceeding expectation and those products that fail to meet targets (see Product Life Cycle and BMG Matrix below).
- **External sales data and competitor analysis** By examining the performance of competitors, tour operators can identify trends in the provision for similar market segments.
- **Market research reports and media** Articles about upcoming destinations are frequently included in the travel sections of national newspapers and consumer magazines. In conjunction with media reports, such as TV travel programmes and social media commentators (e.g. bloggers), potential new destinations may be identified and/or destinations declining in popularity.
- **Customer satisfaction and feedback** Most tour operators conduct customer satisfaction audits using questionnaires, which often include questions about future destinations, repeat visitation and areas for improvements. Questionnaires can be extremely useful in providing substantive data extremely quickly, which can identify potential new products or destinations.

The product strategy is derived from analysis of the research. Although research identifies the needs of clients based on products currently on offer, if used alone it can be retrospective rather than identifying new opportunities. Thus part of the strategy is to assess the existing products and identify if there are opportunities for improvement, either in terms of component provision and/or customer service.

Review current portfolio

In the case of major tour operators, it is likely that they offer a range of products aimed at different markets and this is termed their portfolio. Established tour operators will have most of their offerings fixed and will be confident that the destinations they already market will be successful, although there may be changes made to the products such as introducing new hotels or new resorts in established destinations. A company with a broad portfolio means that they offer many products to different market groups, whereas a narrow portfolio implies that the tour operator focuses on few, even one, market segment. Broad portfolios spread the risk of a downturn in one destination's attractiveness or demand, but also may be perceived as the company lacking in focus. Tour operators offering a narrow portfolio of products run the risk of being susceptible if there is a change in the market; for example, following terrorist attacks in the summer of 2016, Anatolian Sky Holidays, which specializes in holidays to Turkey, ceased trading due to subsequent low demand for holidays. Major operators are also not immune; for example, TUI witnessed a drop in demand of 40% for their tours in Turkey as demand from Russia declined because of Moscow imposing sanctions and cancelling flights (Rodionova, 2016).

Evidently, a company needs to manage its portfolio effectively. To aid this process there are differing management tools that can be used to assess and analyse current portfolio offerings, for example the Boston Consulting Group Matrix and the Product Life Cycle.

BOSTON CONSULTING GROUP MATRIX (BCG MATRIX)
The BCG Matrix is a useful, albeit simplistic, tool in examining the portfolio of products on offer and compares market share and market growth (see Fig. 4.1). This helps companies focus and allocate their resources more effectively and in the process identify new opportunities or products that should be culled. Market share is the measurement relative to competitors and market growth relates to the growing markets where there is an expectation that these will continue to grow.

- Cash cow: products with high market share, but low market growth; usually mature products needing little amendment or investment. These are normally profitable and generate high sales numbers benefiting from economies of scale, although they do not have an indefinite lifespan. These profitable products can finance growth of other products. Examples of cash cows include 18–30 age group products, summer sun packages and city breaks.
- Dogs: products with low market share and little opportunity for growth, e.g. packages that were once popular but are no longer achieving the quantity of sales previously achieved. These packages may require major rethinking

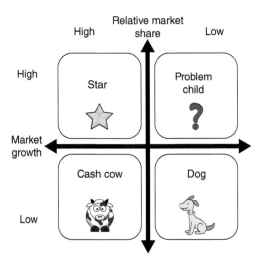

Fig. 4.1. The Boston Consulting Group Matrix.

and rejuvenating or may be best deleted from the portfolio. For example, the decline in UK coaching holidays may suggest that these are dogs, but some itineraries may be more successful than others. Therefore, each coach operator could apply this matrix to each of their different products and thereby identify overall which may be cash cows and which one(s) may benefit from investment or differentiation.

- Stars: products with high market share in a rapidly growing market. It is probable that these products, although selling well, require substantial investment to continue, for example continuing or increasing spend on advertising and promotion. The long-term desire is for these stars to become cash cows, although there is a risk that if the market share is lost they will become a dog. The larger tour operators' stars may be new products, such as spa breaks and other niche products, introduced in direct competition with other smaller companies' offerings.
- Question marks: products of uncertain future. The matrix demonstrates that they have high market growth but low market share; for example, a new product that has seen good sales but is not dominant in the market and if not managed correctly could become a dog. Tour operators may consider trying to increase the market share of these packages through investment or advertising, although this is a high-risk strategy because it means investment in a product that may not recoup the spend.

PRODUCT LIFE CYCLE   Another tool that operators can use to review their current product offerings is that of the Product Life Cycle (PLC) Model. This is perhaps one of the most famous theoretical models in marketing and strategic planning. The PLC curve describes the growth trajectory

for products from their introduction to their decline (see Fig. 4.2). The PLC is based on the premise that products, in this case holiday packages, have a limited life and that product sales pass through distinct stages, each of which hold implications for marketing in that products at different stages of the life cycle require different strategies. As a result, profits from products at different stages in the life cycle will vary.

The BCG and PLC can be important for the marketing plan (see Chapter 10, this volume) by enabling the operator to make decisions as to which product to promote to increase market share or sales, those that they need to maintain market share or to exploit for immediate cash returns and those that they need to withdraw from the market.

Essentially the tour operator needs to decide if the product is practical and viable and if there is sufficient market demand. Other considerations include whether the operator has specialist knowledge of the type of product and has the resources to support any new offerings; for instance, if the operator is looking to diversify and develop packages in new destinations or incorporate specialist activities. In such cases, the operator needs to evaluate whether they have the skills in-house or whether they will need to recruit specialist staff to develop further the initial product plan.

2. Second stage of research

Once a shortlist of destinations and products has been identified, the company will evaluate the available options. Identification as to whether a destination is suitable requires a feasibility study to assess the facilities available in the destination, whether the superstructure is available to support tourism (such as accommodation suppliers) and the accessibility of the

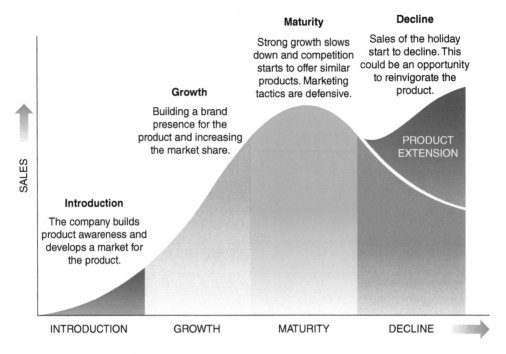

Maturity

Strong growth slows down and competition starts to offer similar products. Marketing tactics are defensive.

Decline

Sales of the holiday start to decline. This could be an opportunity to reinvigorate the product.

Growth

Building a brand presence for the product and increasing the market share.

PRODUCT EXTENSION

SALES

Introduction

The company builds product awareness and develops a market for the product.

INTRODUCTION GROWTH MATURITY DECLINE

Fig. 4.2. The product life cycle.

destination (infrastructure such as relative locality of airport). For example, a specific destination may be identified, but if there is insufficient accommodation it is unlikely that an operator will continue to investigate that destination. Alternatively, if the destination is proving popular with other tour operators, then there may be a shortage of accommodation and the operator must decide whether they wish to pay more for the accommodation, which will in turn put the package price up, or reconsider the destination. A review of exchange rates is also necessary to assess the stability of the currency because this may affect the costing of the package. This also applies to contracting, i.e. whether the payments to suppliers are made in the tour operator's home currency or the currency of the destination (or, as applicable, in US$). An appraisal of the airport may be necessary to ensure that the facilities can handle the number of proposed passengers, the runway is sufficient for the

size of plane proposed and the fees and charges made by the airport.

Mass market operators are looking for destinations that are sustainable, i.e. they will be attractive on a long-term basis and will look to grow the destination. Small operators will invest less in the destination and may be able to switch destinations if the product fails to sell or they encounter operational difficulties. Once the tour operator has identified a suitable destination, then analysis of the product development opportunities can begin. Further research may be necessary to ensure the attractiveness and viability of the proposed product.

3. Product planning

Once the final decision about new products is established, specific decisions need to be made about the itineraries, including accommodation, capacity and departure dates.

Itinerary planning

When planning a new tourism product or itinerary, it is useful to consider Kotler's (2000) analysis of products, comprising the following three elements.

- The core: this is what is being offered: for example, a beach holiday or a city break.
- The tangible product: the physical elements, such as core elements of a package tour, the flight and accommodation.
- The augmented product: extra features the supplier of the product adds to be competitive, such as guides, free transfers.

In terms of planning, the tangible elements, such as the identification of suitable accommodation, are key. For example, operators need to assess the accommodation available in terms of location, health and safety provision, quality and service. Essentially this applies to all elements of the tour package:

- Transport from the generating area to the destination – for example, flights. Operators need to ensure that flights are available to the destination, potentially introducing flights from regional airports, and that the holiday locality is accessible within a reasonable time of landing.
- Accommodation at the destination. Is there sufficient accommodation available at the destination and is this of the appropriate quality/grading? Accommodation may be hotel or apartment (self-catering), and graded by quality rating, type and board basis. Local accommodation, such as pension, auberge, chalet, may be offered. Decisions about board basis need to be made; for example, bed-and-breakfast, half-board or all-inclusive, and availability of single rooms and whether there are penalties for single occupancy.
- Transfer from the airport to the accommodation and return. Transfers from airport to hotel are usually completed by coach with potentially each coach offloading passengers at several hotels, which means some passengers may experience lengthy transfers. This is often the cause of many complaints. Ski tour operators, due to the location of ski resorts, will operate longer transfers, but this is accepted by the clients because of the nature of the activity.
- Ancillary services, such as the need for a representative or manager, availability of car hire, equipment hire, excursions and local attractions.

Additional components include gratuities, baggage handling, service charges, taxes, ski lift passes, etc. Some packages may also include promotional gifts or complimentary drinks at a welcome event or reception.

Costing

An initial cost base analysis will be completed to identify the approximate price of the package, which as Table 4.3 illustrates through three similar tour packages, is complex. It is at this stage that operators may review the proposed package and compare it with competitors offering similar packages and identify whether the price will be attractive to the market. Tour operators may try to keep their prices low by negotiating low prices from suppliers, reducing profit margins or attempting to cut their cost structures, for example using their own charter flights.

As noted previously, an inclusive package will include transport, accommodation and ancillary services (which may

Table 4.3. Cost base analysis for a tour package: illustrative examples. (Source: T. Barnett, 2017, unpublished data; T. Barnett, Hemel Hempstead, 2017, personal communication.)

Stage 1 – Inputs for cost base analysis. May include:

		May Sat 7 night Half Term Family Hotel	August 14 night Family Holiday	September 7 night Adult Differentiated	Comments
a	Flight costs (Sterling)	300	370	280	Vertically integrated tour operator cost flexed to reflect seasonality; Operator using external airline, rate flexed to reflect anticipated market rate
b	Hotel costs (Euros)	350	800	400	Rates will vary based on board basis, seasonality, terms of contract, level of differentiation (e.g. kids clubs), cost structure (e.g. child reductions, price per room or price per person)
c	Commission	8%	8%	8%	Commissions may vary based on holiday type, e.g. cruise, package, flight seat
d	Foreign exchange rate assumptions and hedging position	70% @ 1.2 Euros to Pound	70% @ 1.2 Euros to Pound	70% @ 1.2 Euros to Pound	May be supported by sensitivity analysis to validate level of risk
e	Fuel assumptions and hedging	80%	80%	80%	May be supported by sensitivity analysis to validate level of risk

Stage 2 – Assumptions for cost base analysis. May include:

		May Sat 7 night Half Term Family Hotel	August 14 night Family Holiday	September 7 night Adult Differentiated	Comments
a	Volume assumptions by duration	80% of holidays sold for 7 nights	55% of holidays sold for 14 nights	70% of holidays sold for 7 nights	Hotel costs dependent on assumptions
b	Volume assumptions by hotel	30 passengers	40 passengers	20 passengers	Assumptions used to review analysis at an aggregated level
c	Volume assumptions by room type	60% basic, 40% superior	60% basic, 40% superior	60% basic, 40% superior	Hotel costs dependent on assumptions

d	Volume assumptions by departure date	24 passengers	22 passengers	14 passengers	Assumptions used to review analysis at an aggregated level
e	Party size assumptions	2.8	2.9	2.1	Hotel and flight costs dependent on assumptions

Stage 3 – Pricing policies/strategy. May include:

a	Tactical offers, e.g. free child places, 8 nights for 7, group discounts, single parent offers		Free child place		May be 'part funded' by supplier (e.g. terms in hotel contract), may be implemented as a tactical pricing lever. Where deployed, must be accounted for when evaluating estimated margins
b	Board upgrade pricing	40% All Inclusive supplement for adults, 20% for children			May be 'part funded' by supplier (e.g. terms in hotel contract), may be implemented as a tactical pricing lever. Where deployed, must be accounted for when evaluating estimated margins
c	Child pricing				May be 'part funded' by supplier (e.g. terms in hotel contract), may be implemented as a tactical pricing lever. Where deployed, must be accounted for when evaluating estimated margins
d	3rd adult reductions			3rd adult reduction	May be 'part funded' by supplier (e.g. terms in hotel contract), may be implemented as a tactical pricing lever. Where deployed, must be accounted for when evaluating estimated margins
e	Flight supplements	£80 – 7 night Saturday flights vs £40 for 14 night Saturday flights			Priced to reflect fluctuations in cost between different UK airports, variations in seasonality (e.g. supplements for Scottish flights may be higher at beginning of July to reflect school holiday periods)

Continued

Table 4.3. Continued.

	May Sat 7 night Half Term Family Hotel	August 14 night Family Holiday	September 7 night Adult Differentiated	Comments
Stage 4 – Target margins and seasonality: Based on above costs, what margin (+ve or –ve) want to achieve based on:				
a Different resorts	Popular family destinations with shorter flight times may be able to command a higher price than less family-friendly resorts		Destinations like Greece and Italy that are popular with couples may be able to command a higher margin than a more family-focused destination, e.g. Menorca	
b Different product types				
c Different durations		Longer durations will be able to command a higher margin in August than they would in June		

| d | Different departure dates | £100 | £180 | £120 | Taking all of above into account, sample margins that holidays could be priced to achieve |

Stage 5 – Validation of prices, whereby any of stages 1–4 may be reviewed

Historical performance and trends may support this analysis, prices sense checked for anomalies/errors, exceptions reviewed (holidays with highest estimated margins/lowest estimated margins), margins reviewed vs initial targets, year-on-year variances assessed

Stage 6 – Programme goes on sale. Prices are then optimized up until departure date using yield management technology and processes

Sales trends are monitored compared to previous year performance and sales plans. Costs may fluctuate (e.g. hotelier may provide a reduced rate), and prices will be regularly increased/decreased based on such circumstances include a resort representative, car hire etc.), which all need to be considered alongside fixed costs (company office expenses), distribution costs, marketing costs and additional expenses (see Chapter 7, this volume). Reviewing the pricing strategy of the company provides information about how customers will perceive the products. If products are frequently discounted to fill late availability, then there is a disparity between the perception of the product by the management and perception of the product by the customer. This tactical late price discounting to fill unused stock has a detrimental effect on the company brand.

Capacity

Planning the capacity refers to the number of holidays the tour operator can supply in the marketplace, which is frequently decided 12–18 months ahead of the holiday season, and target capacity figures are confirmed 12 months prior to departure date. Although it is complex trying to predict demand for the purchase of holidays, it is a critical part of the planning process because poorly planned capacity predictions can lead to overcapacity or under capacity.

Overcapacity occurs when a tour operator contracts to provide more packages than there is demand for. Essentially, over supply will result in either the cancellation of departures, consolidation of flights or discounting. While discounting is an effective method of encouraging sales and attractive to customers, for tour operators it can be costly, because any reduction in price will affect the profit margins. Due to overcapacity and subsequent cancellation of departures, tour operators may still need to pay for components such as accommodation that will not be used, thus effectively making a loss on that departure, again affecting profit margins.

Under capacity is when a tour operator has fewer holidays to supply than market demand, which means that customers will have been unable to buy the product they want and may look for alternatives such as different operators and so the operator loses the sale and possibly future repeat bookings. Adding capacity can be problematic, particularly if destinations or hotels are proving popular and there is no additional bed space. Smaller operators may be able to negotiate additional last-minute beds and flights, but these will not necessarily be at the same discounted price and additional costs have to be passed on to the customer.

Marketing materials

A provisional plan for marketing materials will be costed. This may be as straightforward as additional pages in a brochure and on the web, or it may involve a specialist marketing campaign. For example, the launch of a new product may involve a national TV campaign in conjunction with website updates, promotional material made available to travel agents, advertisements on social media and websites, direct mail and brochure production. At this stage, initial tenders for design, production and printing of brochures will be obtained from suppliers, and copy text and illustrations commissioned.

4. Contracting

An important element of designing an inclusive holiday package is negotiating with principals and subsequently contracting the components. This is generally carried out by senior members of staff because it requires an in-depth knowledge of the company's background, financial standing, long-term goals and objectives. If the contracts manager fails to supply sufficient capacity in terms of transport, accommodation and ancillary services with the appropriate quality of provision, then the company is unlikely to achieve the market share expected and maintaining customer loyalty may be problematic.

Key decisions need to be made about suppliers providing components of the holiday product and therefore contracting suppliers requires good communication and negotiating skills. Large tour operators have specialist departments dealing with contracting because this involves specialist knowledge of both the operator's home country and overseas legislation. Larger tour operators may have contracting departments based overseas that will work with all the accommodation suppliers in the region. For example, a tour operator based in the UK but operating throughout Europe may have regional offices that liaise directly with the hotels. Small tour operators do not usually have a specific department and contracting will often be part of the operations team's role.

Contracting for existing products can often be done relatively quickly by using previous suppliers if they have maintained their quality and minimal price increase. Difficulties always arise in acquiring new components, for example flight seats to new destinations, new accommodation suppliers in existing destinations or new suppliers in new destinations, which may involve competing with rival companies for limited supply, because this can enable suppliers to increase rates and tariffs.

Accommodation

The fundamental decision that needs to be made by an operator is the number of rooms that they plan to offer, or need to achieve the planned capacity, to ensure there is sufficient supply. Potential accommodation suppliers are identified through site visits, promotional events such as the **World Travel Market** or staff working in the destination. Initially, contracting accommodation is usually conducted in the destination and will be negotiated directly with the owners/managers involved, although tour operators may utilize the experience and knowledge of a local agent to operate on their behalf. Established operators working in the same destinations will renew contracts with accommodation suppliers based on capacity predictions. Operators need to contract sufficient beds to match the number of flight seats available on their flights. Large tour operators can secure the cheapest rates from accommodation suppliers, given their buying power and predicted sales. Smaller tour operators do not have the leverage to gain substantial discounts and therefore will not be able to secure the cheapest price. As contracting is often carried out 12 months in advance, there are risks associated with exchange rate fluctuations (see Chapter 7, this volume).

It should be noted that popular destinations are not usually generating region specific, meaning there is very little destination loyalty and therefore operators will be in competition with other operators from different countries. Thus, if a hotel is in such a competitive situation their tariffs may increase, which will affect consumers and the price they pay. For an operator, it is beneficial to secure exclusive contracts for a hotel, which means it can control the client group and avoid conflict between different market segments, for example the youth market versus the family market, although this may not be practical for many large hotels (e.g. 100 rooms or more). Conversely, hoteliers may prefer to spread their rooms across competing companies to reduce the risk of being reliant on one company.

TYPES OF CONTRACT Beds are usually contracted in three different ways, based on the level of risk and predicted sales.

Commitment. A commitment contract is when a tour operator agrees to buy a predefined number of beds for the season, regardless of the number it sells, for example 200 bed nights for a season lasting six months. The operator will pay for these beds whether they are used or not and the higher number of committed beds, the lower the price from the hotelier, and the contract may stipulate that the hotelier may not be able to offer the beds to another operator. For the tour operator, this can be very profitable if all beds are sold, although there is a level of risk if there are changes in market demand and the destination proves unpopular or suffers from negative publicity (e.g. health scare; terrorist threat) and beds remain unsold.

At the beginning of the season, the operator will pay a non-refundable deposit, and if the destination proves unpopular there will be a substantial cancellation charge imposed by the hotelier if the operator decides to withdraw the holidays. The rates charged by accommodation suppliers can vary throughout the seasons with low-season prices approximately 20% lower than high-season prices, so even a commitment contract may have variable pricing. Large tour operators may negotiate to contract the whole hotel or facility, such as a chalet for skiing holidays, which enables the operator to control the market for which the accommodation will be used. Long-term contracts may be used in destinations that are already popular; for example, five-year contracts are not unusual, but frequently involve renegotiation mid-term due to fluctuations in exchange rates.

This type of contracting offers very little flexibility and is usually used by operators in well-established destinations in a mass market. Over supply of accommodation enables mass market operators to sell packages such as 'allocation on arrival' to use up additional contracted beds, although it should be noted that unsold beds are less expensive than unsold flight seats. It is also important that full utilization of beds is planned in advance to avoid the conflict between markets, such as elderly couples being placed in a hotel full of young adults.

Allocation (also called allotment). A second option of contracting is that of allocation. This is also seen as a 'sale or return' option. The tour operator will agree with the hotel a defined number of rooms, which they will use. Allocation contracts can be used for a specific period, such as the whole season or specific dates. Allocation is often used by small and medium-sized tour operators, because they may be less certain that itineraries are going to run or maximum numbers achieved, and by larger operators wishing to top up their commitment accommodation. These blocks of rooms will be available to the tour operator until a predefined release date, when the rooms revert to the hotelier if they are unsold. Although release dates are usually 4–6 weeks in advance of the holiday date, companies with stronger buying power may be able to negotiate later dates. This method of contracting reduces the financial risk for operators, but is usually considerably more expensive than a commitment contract. For example, an activity-based tour operator with a multi-destination itinerary may confirm the dates of the tour for the hotel as being for the season, but confirm the actual number of rooms needed 2–3 weeks before they are required. This is more labour-intensive for the tour operator because they must contact hotels in advance and confirm numbers.

For hoteliers, this is riskier than commitment contracting because they run the risk of beds being unsold and returned to the hotelier for sale. Thus, beds contracted using this approach will be more expensive than those contracted through a commitment. Hoteliers may be tempted to double-book rooms if they are unsure of the numbers, although tour operators may introduce a penalty clause in the contract to prevent such actions. However, if a hotel is double booked, the immediate pressure is to find accommodation for those customers.

Ad hoc. Ad hoc contracting is the costliest method of buying rooms. However, there is no risk to the tour operator. Ad hoc arrangements involve buying rooms when needed and for this reason this contracting method is used by organizers offering tailor-made itineraries and specialist operators. As rooms are only paid for when they are used, there is no risk involved for the tour operator. Operators may also have to use this method of contracting rooms when there is overbooking. The use of online bed retailers such as hotelbeds.com means that travel agents and operators can compare accommodation prices quickly and buy easily to incorporate into a package.

Large tour operators may use a mix of contracts, using allocation to top up their bed supply contracted through commitment, whereby most accommodation is booked on commitment throughout the season, but additional beds contracted on allocation during shoulder periods when the operator may be uncertain of the level of demand.

The contract needs to specify the exact requirements of the operator, including the number of rooms, the beds (single, twins, triple/family rooms), balconies, sea views and facilities. The contract will also need to stipulate the board basis (room only, bed-and-breakfast, half- or full-board and all-inclusive) and how additional services will be paid for by the guest. Further additions to the contracts may be included, such as porterage fees, provision of inclusive meals (e.g. expected vegetarian dishes, local food, halal), fire safety provision and access to communal areas for resort representative briefing sessions. Operators

may also be able to request free accommodation for the resort representative.

Transport

The contracting of transport is crucial to the success and profitability of any tour. In this example, the package includes flights.

FLIGHTS   As flights usually account for approximately 40% of the overall package holiday price, unsold seats may result in significant loss to the company. Aircraft seats can be contracted in different ways. As noted in earlier chapters, companies that are vertically integrated and have their own aircraft need to focus on the maximization of the aircraft. The aim is to keep the aeroplanes in the air as much as possible. If operators fail to fill their own chartered airlines, then they may offer to sell blocks of seats to other operators.

Charter aircraft are usually single-class layout with low seat pitch (the distance between each row of seats) to maximize the number of customers who can be fitted into the cabin. As an example, scheduled operators offer seat pitches between 30 and 32 inches, whereas charter craft offer 28 inches, although pre-booking or upgrading can enable bigger pitches. To maximize capacity, charter airlines tend to reduce the number of toilets, storage and galley space (in-flight catering tends to be basic). Charter airlines work on a load factor of 85% or more, compared with short-haul scheduled airlines that work on 50–75%. The cost savings include the utilization of regional airports, where fees are cheaper, and off-peak flying, which reduces airport costs. That said, some of the larger tour operators such as TUI and Thomsonfly have reconfigured their aircraft to increase the seat pitch to 33 inches in economy for long-haul destinations because customer expectations have changed. The traditional tiny aisle screens have been replaced by seatback televisions, and pre-ordering food and beverages enables operators to maximize revenue and reduce waste.

However, the majority of tour operators do not own their own aircraft and therefore they need to reserve seats either on scheduled airlines or on charter craft operated by other companies. Packages involving scheduled aircraft are usually more expensive and therefore tend to be utilized by specialist tour operators or agents offering tailor-made itineraries, or on long-haul packages. Seats on charter aircraft are comparatively cheaper and therefore tour operators have various options:

Whole season chartering
- Part (or split) chartering – booking a block of seats on specific flights (usually with other tour operators).
- Ad hoc chartering – an arrangement for single return-trip (rotation).
- Time series chartering – a contract for a regular sequence of flights and the exclusive use of an aircraft throughout the season.

For operators considering chartering their own aircraft from suppliers, the prices may vary according to the reputation of the tour operator and their experience in using chartered aircraft, with those operators who have used the charter supplier previously receiving preferential pricing.

Whole season/time series chartering.
Time series charter is where a tour operator charters a whole aircraft for a specific period, which may be for one day, occasional weeks or for the whole season (or longer) and is a usual method of working in Europe and North America. Charter flights do not operate according to published schedules but are planned in such a way that their air time is maximized. As the tour operator is responsible for the full utilization of the aircraft, it is essential that they maximize the craft in the charter period. For example, a tour operator will plan flights between differing departure and arrival airports, often described as a W flight pattern (see Fig. 4.3).

Such intensive flight patterns can be problematic. If a flight is delayed at one of the destinations or there are technical problems, the delay will affect all other subsequent flights using that plane.

Chartering an aircraft is an expensive and potentially high-risk strategy because the tour operator is responsible for selling all the seats. Some operators may offer 'seat-only' sales on charter flights to ensure

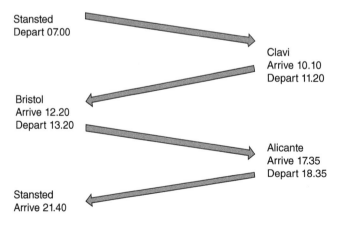

Stansted
Depart 07.00

Clavi
Arrive 10.10
Depart 11.20

Bristol
Arrive 12.20
Depart 13.20

Alicante
Arrive 17.35
Depart 18.35

Stansted
Arrive 21.40

Fig. 4.3. Series charter.

that they fill all the seats on the flight when they do not have capacity in tour sales to fill the aircraft. According to Doganis (2009), this trend was led by the German charter airlines in order to obtain lower seat/kilometre costs – approximately 20% of total capacity would be seat only.

Although it is a high-risk strategy, the chartering of air services provides for a low cost per seat and operators have a degree of flexibility in terms of destinations and departure points. If an operator has chartered an aircraft, then they have the option of subcontracting the plane to other operators, either on a daily basis or even a return flight on a specified day. For example, the operator that charters the plane may not wish to offer night flights but can subcontract the plane out to another operator who is happy to have night-time departures or arrivals.

When a company owns or charters its own plane, it has greater control over the service provided by the airline, although it also bears the risk if seats or holiday packages have not been sold.

Part charter. Some operators will not want to contract the whole aircraft as they predict that they have insufficient sales and may opt for a part charter instead. The contract will determine whether the operator part charters for specific days but ultimately the operator is responsible for selling those seats. As mentioned above, if a company charters aircraft and they have excess capacity they may part charter their seats directly to other tour operators or use an airline broker to dispose of the additional seats, often selling them on to small operators. Part chartering reduces the financial risk, although they still are responsible for the flight plan and the initial seat cost.

Low-cost carriers. Low-cost carriers (LCC) in Europe have impacted on the inclusive holiday market by launching scheduled services to traditional holiday destinations around the Mediterranean, lake resorts in Eastern Europe and some Alpine destinations. By targeting these established destinations, low-cost airlines are challenging the role of charter airlines, as they are both budget alternatives to scheduled airlines. LCC are more flexible than charter airlines because they have greater levels of differential pricing, which can be applied to the air component of a package holiday, but also allow passengers to book flight components independently of the destination operations. As the choice of airline route and availability has expanded, enabling customers to build their own travel experiences, it has also facilitated the growth in dynamic packaging for tour operators and travel agents.

The traditional view of LCC was that they provided a poor experience, but their popularity increased due to their price. Some LCC have started to differentiate their products, offering what is termed a hybrid model attracting both business and leisure and the ability to upgrade, such as buying additional luggage allowance, pre-book meals, purchase extra legroom or priority seating and priority boarding. LCC are not necessarily about the traditional costing models (prices increase as departure date gets closer), but use demand-driven pricing using sophisticated yield management systems (see Chapter 7, this volume) and aggressive marketing strategies.

LCC such as Germanwings are making available block sales to tour operators, thus allowing operators to purchase the airline component of a package cheaper than an incumbent airline. Further developments such as the increased number of low-cost airlines available globally will increase the number of destinations; for example, the Ministry of Transport in Russia has recently adapted legislation to encourage the development of LCC. A greater number of LCC are moving into the medium- and long-haul markets, which will provide greater opportunities for operators to provide competitively priced offerings in more remote locations.

Scheduled flights. Scheduled air services tend to be used by long-haul operators and specialist/tailor-made organizers, because they provide fixed itineraries or 'scheduled departures' and operate regardless of the number of passengers on board. Their use of scheduled flights in holiday packages allows greater flexibility because tickets can be booked to arrive in one destination and depart from another, known as '**open jaw**' tickets. However, mass market package operators to mainstream destinations are more likely to use charter aircraft because of the price. The increase in long-haul destinations and availability of numerous carriers flying to destinations has made the utilization of scheduled aircraft more accessible. For example, it may be more cost effective for a UK-based operator to contract seats on a scheduled airline to Sri Lanka rather than attempt to charter a craft for a package holiday to Sri Lanka.

In general, the operator would normally contract a specific number of seats on dates that would be sold at a Special Inclusive Tour by Excursion (ITX) fare or a Special Group Inclusive Tour (SGTI) fare. The fare would not be shown on the ticket, as with other scheduled services. Seats that are not sold would be released back to the airline by an agreed date (usually one month before the departure).

This sale-or-return system is particularly attractive to operators introducing new untested destinations because it reduces the risk. They are particularly useful for one-off, tailor-made or specialist packages, but are generally too expensive for mass market operations.

Land-based transport. Although contracting beds and flight seats is important,

an operator will need to contract additional services such as transfers from the airport to the accommodation, excursion transport and, where necessary, public transport such as trains and taxis.

Transfers. Many companies use coaches for the transfer of passengers between airport and accommodation and for optional excursions. Vertically integrated companies such as TUI have their own coaches, which are scheduled to move passengers efficiently from the airport as quickly as possible. Smaller companies, those that are not vertically integrated, will need to negotiate with local transport companies to provide such transfers, either on an allocation or ad hoc basis.

Car hire. If the holiday packages involve car hire, such as fly-drive holidays, which are popular for tourists in the USA, then they need to contract vehicle hire through a car hire company such as Europcar or Hertz, although making arrangements with local companies invariably will be cheaper. In the case of fly-drive holidays, the expectation is that the car will be available at the airport on arrival.

Ancillary products and services

These products and services include tickets to events, guides, and the availability of private transfer services. Operators may work with local companies to provide excursions and guides, and these will have to be contracted for the season, or on an allocation basis allowing the operator to cancel if the itinerary does not operate.

5. Brochure production

Brochure production and e-brochure production are key elements of the promotional materials and take time to prepare and produce because of the need to check and recheck information. This, and a company's website, are discussed in detail under the umbrella of marketing (see Chapter 10, this volume).

6. Finalize sales and marketing plan

Finalizing the sales and marketing plan involves finalizing and implementing the marketing strategy (see Chapter 10, this volume). But, and significantly, it also requires ensuring staff involved in sales are as well prepared as possible. Thus, comprehensive staff training is a requisite if the company is to be efficient and effective.

Sales staff training

Sales training may be conducted for both in-house sales staff and also for travel agencies retailing the products. Training for in-house sales staff is easier to manage logistically because the staff may be in the headquarters or within a specialist telesales department. Operators recognize the importance of product knowledge when selling tours and packages, and training sessions are arranged so that staff who have visited the destination can share their experiences with the sales team. Larger operators may send out sales staff to the resort so that they can experience the destination. Promotional tactics to encourage sales, in addition to commission, can include cash bonuses, competitions and incentives.

Working with travel agents may be more problematic if they are not part of the same company. To promote new destinations, representatives (or trained agents) may visit travel agents to promote brochures and advise on details of the new products on offer.

More recent innovations include online training programs for travel agents that provide information about the company, the products and information about destinations, activities and other holiday-specific information. For example, Saga Travel launched an online training program in December 2015 to create Saga Experts, and some companies, such as the cruise company MSC Cruises North America, hold major conferences for travel agents. Agents that are knowledgeable about specific products and companies are more likely to recommend those products to customers because thorough product knowledge is a powerful sales tool. Information that will aid sales includes:

- Departure airports and the opportunity to use regional-based airports.
- Information about alternative methods of transport; for example, train or coach.
- Transfer times to hotels or resorts.
- Product-specific information such as variety of accommodation, their facilities and their appropriateness for different market segments.

Recently the use of '**webinars**' for training has become very popular as a way of training sales staff over large geographic regions. Webinars may be recorded and watched later, but in order to encourage interactivity between the travel agents and the operator, operators encourage live attendees by offering exclusive offers or competitions. Lists of webinars can be found on travel industry magazine websites such as *Travel Weekly* and can be filtered by destination, activity and market segment.

Other methods of encouraging sales include the familiarization trip (fam trip), sometimes termed educational, which historically was always seen as a perk of being a travel agent. These fam trips may be sponsored by the tour operator, equally they may be sponsored by national or regional tourism organizations, cruise lines or several companies working together, such as a National Tourist Office, airline and hotels. A typical fam trip will be for 10–30 travel agents and a representative of the sponsor organization. A fam itinerary will usually include visiting many hotels and resorts as well as briefings about the destination, activities and excursions available. These trips may be free or heavily subsidized and are frequently used to encourage travel agency loyalty and/or for high-performing agencies.

7. Operations and administrative staff training

Operations staff training

Briefings will be held to ensure that all operational staff are aware of the new product, the staff involved and any anticipated issues. Reservation systems and procedures are confirmed and finalized. Confirmation is made with suppliers to ensure all components are ready, which will also include confirmation about payment dates to suppliers.

Administrative staff training

All major operators utilize computerized systems, so the inclusion of a new package is unlikely to require much staff training. The company may require additional staff to cope with anticipated demand and thus training will take place as part of the recruitment and induction process (see Chapter 11, this volume).

Recruit specialist staff

The traditional mass market product relies on carrying many passengers to established destinations and in many cases these operators still provide resort representatives (reps) (a comprehensive discussion of the role and responsibilities of representatives can be found in Chapter 11, this volume). For operators providing reps, the immediate decision is whether to employ representatives from the generating region or to use home-based staff. Clearly, the benefit of using representatives from the generating region is that they understand the culture and language of the customers. Conversely, a local representative will have a better insight into the destination and have contacts that will enable problems to be resolved quickly. There is also a cost implication for the tour operators in that recruiting staff from within the destination may be less expensive.

8. Product launch and subsequent evaluation of sales

Once the product is in operation, the company will need to deal with any issues arising at the destination. This is usually handled through the resort reps. Most problems will occur at the start of the season and it is usual to put an experienced member of staff in the destination to handle any incidents. Immediate review of customer feedback is essential because customers may identify areas for improvement, some of which may be able to be implemented immediately. In this era of hyper-communication, it is essential that operators include a review of user-generated content sites such as Trip Advisor or Trust Pilot, where customers give feedback on their experiences.

Although each product is different, it is important to review sales against targets. Therefore, a well-organized tracking system, usually computer-based, will enable operators to review bookings instantaneously.

As the season commences, operators may face a number of challenges, such as lack of sales. In this instance, operators must make decisions about how to increase sales to achieve forecasted figures. One of the most frequent methods of disposing of surplus offering is the use of 'allocation on arrival'. Allocation on arrival is frequently used by operators to increase sales of low-selling products; for example, the customer will buy the package with a known departure date and duration, but the hotel, and even the resort, will be allocated on arrival. For the customer, there is a higher degree of risk, but the discounted price compensates for the lack of certainty and increased risk of the transaction.

Tour operators may also look to relaunch their brochures, which enables operators to consolidate flights from airports, react to the pricing strategies of competitors and, if sales are particularly bad, to delist the hotel or even the resorts that are failing to sell. Other opportunities include introducing cheaper hotels at popular resorts or, if sales are good and there is capacity in the destination, operators may look to increase the number of holiday products available.

9. Product review and post tour management, including quality review

Towards the end of the season, it is essential to review the performance of the company's products. This will involve comparing predicted sales with achieved sales and reflecting on any discounting or additional promotion that was necessary, enabling operators to make decisions about capacity for the next season.

Where possible, sales data should also include market share, enabling managers to assess how the holiday package is performing in relation to those offered by competitors. Informed decisions may be made about advertising spend and investment in promoting the product, including potential price reductions if sales were low, or potentially price increases if demand exceeded supply. It may be necessary to amend the product if there have been repetitive difficulties and to relaunch the holiday in the next brochure.

Summary

This chapter has provided a general overview of the processes tour operators employ when creating or adapting a package holiday. Although the key procedures are identified, it should be noted that operators will have their own practices, depending on the generating and receiving regions, target market and size of company.

However, a common factor for all tour operators is that the success of a package holiday primarily depends on the attractiveness of the destination and the provision of services to ensure the smooth transit of the customer from the home locality to the accommodation in the destination. On superficial consideration, this may appear to present little difficulty. As the foregoing stages in the planning and development of a package holiday demonstrate, this is not the case. Indeed, managing current products effectively and efficiently in the first place is not such an easy task, nor is the ongoing need to review those products to ensure they continue to meet target market expectations and identify potential new opportunities. Furthermore, to achieve such objectives within a highly competitive environment on a scale sufficient to achieve profit margins becomes more complex, requiring careful and detailed planning, which itself is time consuming and to an extent largely dependent on the skills and knowledge, not to mention ability to negotiate, of the personnel involved. To varying degrees, this is equally applicable to all tour operators, whether they are micro/small enterprises (see Chapter 5, this volume) or multi-national businesses with a stock market listing. The key difference is the scale of the operation(s) involved thus a tour operator may develop from a small office of three or four people to a leading player in the market, with a substantial workforce (see Chapter 13, this volume). As the enterprise develops, so too does the scope of marketing research, product review and the potential options available in each of these nine stages in the product development, and therefore the degree of complexity involved.

Discussion Questions

1. What are the risks involved in developing a product that diversifies from the tour operator's core market?
2. What are the risks in withdrawing products from the market due to unexpected incidents?
3. Should operators continue to promote products in medium- or high-risk destinations?
4. Identify a selection of countries or regions that are rarely included in mass tour operators' brochures. Discuss the reasons why they fail to be promoted.
5. Why are mass tour operators less loyal to destinations?
6. How relevant is the product life cycle to a tour operator's products?
7. What are the risks in using the allocation method to contract accommodation?
8. In terms of responsibility, should tour operators be required to meet the guidelines for best practice in sustainable supply chain management when developing their product(s)?

Key Terms

- **Capacity:** This refers to the maximum number of passengers.
- **Itinerary:** This is the travel arrangements made including all the activities that will take place e.g. changing hotels, transfers etc.
- **Open jaw:** This is an airline return ticket where the destination and/or the origin are not the same in both directions.
- **Segments:** Submarkets of consumers who have been chosen as the target groups and are marketed to specifically.
- **Webinars:** Short for web-based seminar. Can include presentations, lectures or workshops transferred over the web using video conferencing software.
- **World Travel Market:** Global event for the travel industry which enables operators to network with industry suppliers, and for suppliers to promote their offerings.

INTERNET EXERCISE

All-inclusive packages are growing in popularity because of the fixed costs that enable customers to plan their budgets. In the UK, First Choice markets all their products as all-inclusive.

Review the Tourism Concern website: www.tourismconcern.org.uk/all-inclusives/ and read their research report: http://www.iuf.org/w/sites/default/files/WorkingConditions inHotels.pdf

Continued

Questions

- What are the benefits for tour operators of offering all-inclusive?
- What are the benefits for customers?
- Are all-inclusive packages fair for the host communities?
- What can tour operators do to try to ensure that destination-based organizations can benefit from tourism in their locality?

MINI CASE STUDY

Much has been made of the impacts of climate change and their effects on the tourism sector, none more so than that of snow-based tour operators. Examine what tour operators are doing to improve the sustainability of their product.

Questions

- How are tour operators adapting their products?
- What is the future of ski tourism?

MAJOR CASE STUDY

Product development

In the days of the boom in Mediterranean beach holidays during the 1980s, tour operators were constantly looking to develop and grow their market share by product differentiation. One major tour operator from the UK, Thomson Holidays, attempted to do this by conducting intensive research drawing on their family customer base in order to determine the elements of their package holiday considered most important by the market.

The results of the survey revealed the following aspects of the holiday were high on customers' list of priorities:

- Entertainment – both daytime and evening.
- Food – customers didn't want lack-lustre buffets with no variety and overcooked vegetables.
- Accommodation – customers wanted 'home from home' comforts, not electrical sockets positioned away from mirrors, coarse lavatory paper or rough bathroom towels.

Consequently, the Product Development Department compiled a 300-point specification, which was the focus of changes. To make these changes, it was important to gain the suppliers' commitment to implement the proposed changes, especially the hoteliers. Hotels in family resorts such as Santa Eulalia (Ibiza) and Sa Coma (Majorca) and on Rhodes and Cyprus were singled out for the newly designed products.

Continued

The hoteliers bought into the concept and the new product was underway. In agreeing to make the changes, the hoteliers were guaranteed beds would be filled, staff training, increased bar takings (as a result of a professional entertainments programme) and improved quality ratings (as a result of improved customer satisfaction).

Refurbishment began in the hotels and the catering staff attended an intensive five-day programme. The programme offered breakfast suggestions, lunch and dinner menus – all especially selected to appeal to the tastes of British holidaymakers. The chefs were shown how to cook vegetables 'al dente' and were given the opportunity to practise their newfound skills. Patisserie and dessert making sessions were included. The training was well received by all.

Recruitment of entertainment representatives was advertised via *The Stage* magazine (a UK-based magazine for the arts and entertainment industry) and applicants were invited to attend auditions as opposed to interviews. A professional team of consultants was enlisted for the selection and training process. The training lasted three weeks pre-season, during which time new recruits were put through their paces. Microphone and compering skills were emphasized. Specialists were brought in to teach them how to run daytime activities such as aquafit. The finale consisted of an all-singing, all-dancing show, which had been professionally scripted and choreographed.

On-going training and monthly quality reports ensured that all staff were fully informed of their progress and that any initial teething problems could be ironed out.

The new programme was hugely popular with staff, suppliers and the customers. Hoteliers were recognized by the Gold Award system and today you can see their awards displayed in reception (just like a pop star would display their gold discs).

Questions

- Why was it necessary to professionalize the provision in the destination by improving quality and provision?
- How difficult is it to manage the suppliers, e.g. hoteliers, and ensure that they provide the quality expected?
- How have customer expectations changed since the case study?

Recommended Reading

A substantial range of cases on, or relating to, product development:

Horner, S. and Swarbrooke, J. (2004) *International Cases in Tourism Management*. Elsevier, Oxford, UK.

A suitable text to further the study of product development in the broader context of marketing:

Kotler, P., Bowen, J. and Makens, J. (2014) *Marketing for Hospitality and Tourism*. Pearson Education Limited, Harlow, UK.

References

Callaghan, P., Long, P. and Robinson, M. (1994) *Travel and Tourism*, 2nd edn. Business Education Publishers, Sunderland, UK.

Doganis, R. (2009) *Flying Off Course: The Economics of International Airlines*, 4th edn. Routledge, London.

Holloway, C. and Humphreys, C. (2012) *The Business of Tourism*, 9th edn. Pearson Education Limited, Harlow, UK.

Kotler, P. (2000) *Marketing Management*. Prentice Hall, Englewood Cliffs, New Jersey.

Riley, C. (1983) New product development in Thomson Holidays UK. *Tourism Management* 4, 23–25.

Rodionova, Z. (2016) Turkey holiday bookings dropped 40% over terrorism fears, TUI says. Available at: http://www.independent.co.uk/news/business/news/turkey-holiday-bookings-drop-40-over-terrorism-fears-tui-says-a6862961.html, accessed 9 September 2016.

5 Small and Medium-sized Tour Operators

Learning Objectives

After studying this chapter, you should be able to:

- Demonstrate an appreciation of the significance of small and medium-sized tour operators.
- Explain the terminology used for suppliers based in the destination country.
- Analyse the role ground handling agents play in the creation of tourism packages.
- Understand how to cost a tour package.

Introduction

The general holiday tour market, i.e. the 3S type of international package in many post-industrial countries, is largely dominated by a small number of major, vertically integrated international companies. This can be considered an **oligopolistic** business market. Despite such domination, most tour operators are small and medium-sized enterprises (**SMEs**) offering specialist products, 'enterprises which employ fewer than 250 persons and which have an annual turnover not exceeding €50 million and/or an annual balance sheet total not exceeding €43 million' (Enterprise and Industry Publications, 2005, p. 3). On this basis, the majority of these SMEs are in the small category, employing fewer than 50 people. It is this category that has seen a continuous growth in the number of businesses since the 1990s, which has been facilitated by the rapid development of information technology and changes in consumer preferences. This is well illustrated in the UK, where in 2015 there were 1920 tour operators (an increase of approximately 12% on 2004; Keynote, 2015), in total employing 22,215 people and with a combined turnover of £13.3 million (Hayhurst, 2016).

Today there are many small tour operators that offer specialist products that do not compete directly with the mass market products of the major players. In effect, there has been an increase in the provision of more segmented, specialized and sophisticated products that may be loosely considered under the umbrella of special-interest tourism (Nylander and Hall, 2005). It should be noted that this does not mean that the larger companies do not offer these products, because many of the vertically integrated tour operators own sub-brands that specialize in those markets. Even so, their *modus operandi* will differ, not least due to the size and scope of their business operations.

This chapter examines the role of small and medium-sized tour operators and explores the use of destination-based suppliers who are particularly significant to the operations of the smaller tour companies in that they play a key role in the creation/delivery of the tourism product. These suppliers handle activities and operations in the destination country on behalf of an international tour operator (in effect a form of partnership), for example arranging boat trips, tours and accommodation. They have many different names, such as ground operators, inbound agents, local service providers or more generally ground handling agents (GHAs). It is this latter term that we will use here. They can be considered representatives of the international tour operator at destination level and are engaged in a range of different activities generally known as trade services, the extent of them depending on the contract with the tour operator.

Many of these GHAs are very small companies, often owner-operated, and they may further subcontract some activities to other agencies or suppliers, such as self-employed guides and drivers. According to Buhalis (2001), GHAs are the least well-known element of the tour operators' supply chain and because of their involvement bring varying degrees of complexity to their operations. Thus, our first consideration is to establish the general role and function of GHAs and in the process to illustrate the potential complexities arising from their role(s) in the supply chain. To further our consideration of small and medium-sized tour operators and their operational strategies, we will focus on three different categories of tour drawn from within the **niche** tourism sector, specifically adventure tourism, tailor-made and all-inclusive.

Ground Handling Agents

The first step is to differentiate the role of GHAs from inbound operators as they may, on the surface, appear to offer similar services in that they not only retail products on behalf of principals but also provide tour packages at the destination level.

To clarify, an inbound travel agency or tour operator provides services for tourists coming from outside the country or region and are generally referred to as inbound operators. These inbound tour operators create and retail products and services directly to overseas customers by packaging and providing itineraries for independent travellers, for example organizing a tour in India based around New Delhi and visiting cities such as Agra and Jaipur, having liaised directly with the customer. In addition, they also may run their own tours and market them directly to potential customers. In contrast, a GHA provides travel services and destination-based activities on behalf of a tour operator based in another country which that operator then includes in their packages. In this context, the GHA may be considered a domestic tour operator, albeit offering domestic tours for international passengers, and usually does not sell these products directly to overseas customers. Basically, a GHA undertakes 'all commissionable jobs at a destination, [including] identification, negotiation, contract and reservation of appropriate tourism products [and] acting as legal representatives' (Buhalis, 2001, p. 27).

The GHA will act as the tour operator's representative in the destination and potentially be involved in diverse activities in supplying specific components of a package trip, from basics such as contracting accommodation and transportation to identifying possible new itineraries, purchasing admission tickets for visitor attractions, arranging tickets for public transport, and where necessary organizing any equipment requirements for tours such as boats, jeeps, porters. Further, and as required, they will liaise with local service providers for specific activities such as guided tours, sightseeing bus trips, diving trips, or contract transport such as required for desert safari expeditions. The potential extent of their involvement and the scope of expertise required leads to some GHAs developing a range of strategic partnerships with international operators from different countries to maximize revenue streams and spread the risk, i.e. they are not reliant on one source market. Contracts for agreed services vary between the operators but generally are based on an annual, seasonal or *ad hoc* basis. The contracts may include payments for handling fees, which is a per passenger fee paid for each departure.

Externally based tour operators may operate with different supply chain structures in different locations depending on the number and type of tours, the experience of the company operating in that destination and local legislation, which may involve fully subcontracting packages to a GHA. In this case, the GHA could arrange the accommodation, transport and activities on behalf of the tour operator. As such, the company is essentially buying places on the local operator's itinerary, whereby the groups comprise passengers that have purchased their product through a variety of international tour operators or direct sales by the GHA. At the other end of the scale, the operator may independently contract directly with accommodation suppliers, transport agencies and activity providers on an individual basis. Thus the external operator generally has three options:

- Purchase places on a package offered by a GHA; the customers are therefore part of a bigger group not aligned to a single operator.
- Purchase a package offered by a GHA but that is supplied only for the passengers of that international tour operator.
- Work with a GHA to produce a package designed by, or in conjunction with, the international tour operator.

As noted, small tour operators generally target their products to segments of the market based on specific interests and/or activities. Therefore, to illustrate both the role of these operators and the complexities involved in their operations, we can examine them in the context of special interest tourism through three specific categories, as discussed below.

Niche Tourism

Niche tourism, also known as special interest tourism, is seen as an alternative to mainstream, general market offerings and provides more specialized and unique products. According to Robinson and Novelli (2005), niche tourism has the following characteristics:

- It is the counterpart to undifferentiated mass tourism.
- It refers to specific tourism products focused to meet the needs of particular market segments.
- Niche products may be considered on a continuum from macro niches operating in large markets, e.g. city breaks, to micro niches, e.g. battlefield tours.

Basically, niche tourism is a comparatively small specialized sector of tourism that meets the needs of a correspondingly specialized market segment. These distinct products allow tour operators to differentiate themselves from other operators and provide a unique experience. Needless to say, there is a potentially endless list of such niche products, as is conveyed in the main and sub-categories presented in Fig. 5.1.

Within Fig. 5.1 there are several broad categories that might be considered as macro niche sectors, given the overall demand for the type of product offering that could be included within that category, e.g. Urban (see Robinson and Novelli, 2005). Conversely, micro niche tourism products provide a more focused, highly individualized experience, driven

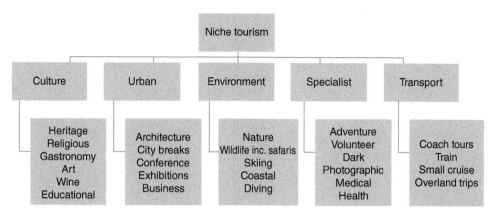

Fig. 5.1. Major categories of niche tourism. (Derived from Robinson and Novelli, 2005, p. 9.)

by the growing demand for tailored experiences creating further opportunities for SMEs to play a key role in providing products and services to meet the specific interests of their customers (Holland, 2012). Many niche tourism companies' products can be placed in the initial stage of the product life cycle (see Chapter 3, this volume) and as their product life cycle evolves and reaches maturity, successful companies need to reinvent their offerings to reinvigorate the market. This results in a constantly changing portfolio of products on offer to consumers, essentially leading to more refined and increasingly specialized products.

Adventure Tourism Products

Adventure tourism is one of the fastest growing types of tourism. According to one tour operator, the offerings are appealing to 'more families, older travellers, more women. We are now on the cusp of adventure travel becoming more mainstream' (Mintel, 2010, p. 3). The types of adventure products available are wide ranging, vary in destination and the activities involved, the market segments and level of experience of customers. The most accepted typology of adventure tourism is based on classifying the activity in terms

of 'hard' or 'soft' adventure, which commonly relates to the level of risk involved in the activity. Not surprisingly, soft adventure tours, i.e. low difficulty products for unskilled clients (Buckley, 2006) that carry little risk for the clients, represent most offerings in this sector and have received relatively little attention to date, specifically research relating to operational aspects. As with so many 'new' contemporary tourism product offerings, the adventure sector is not a new market but stems from the 1960s 'hippy trails', with overland journeys from Europe to Asia via places such as Kathmandu, Goa and often on to the Far East. It is from these roots that many of the UK adventure operators developed, often with ex-tour leaders and in some cases customers setting up their own companies (Holland, 2015).

Operations

The complex supply chain that SMEs in the adventure tour market need to negotiate is well illustrated by Fig. 5.2, which is based on a small UK company, and each of the suppliers indicated will need to be contracted for the tour. The linkages between these destination-based suppliers and the UK-based tour operator will vary according to the itinerary

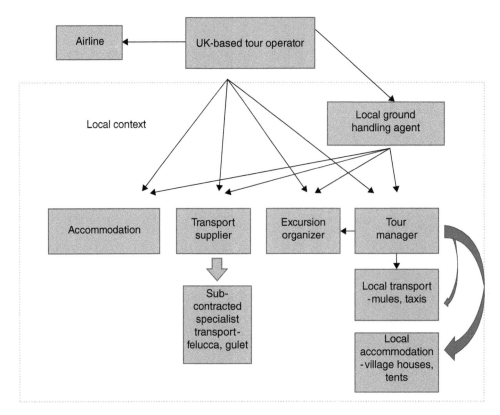

Fig. 5.2. Illustration of UK adventure tour supply chain.

and destination. Further complicating matters is that operators may use differing sub-contractual agreements in different locations. Also, the extent of involvement of GHAs in any tour will depend on several variables, for example, the legal regulations within some countries may enforce the use of an agent, such as in Morocco, whereas in countries such as China the inclusion of a local guide is compulsory.

Operators design a series of tours that will run back-to-back. Well-established itineraries and popular destinations may be offered year-round, and it is not unusual for a season of tours to last eight months. Where possible, this will be managed by the same member of staff, thus reducing the costs (e.g. air flights) involved as a result of changing the staff.

Accommodation

Specialist adventure tour operators such as The Family Adventure Company (UK) and Intrepid (Australia) identify the use of locally owned accommodation as a key component of their product because their chosen destinations are often remote and the availability of major hotels is unlikely. Accommodation can include standard hotels, guesthouses, village houses and lodges. Where little or no accommodation is available, home stays or camping (wild, bush or basic) will be used. Ideally, the accommodation is chosen to reflect the style of the tour, for example sleeping on a felucca on the Nile or in village houses in the Atlas Mountains, which all need to be arranged by the tour company directly or by GHAs.

Transport

One of the key operational aspects of adventure tours is that they are multi-destination and, as such, rely heavily on transport between destinations. As these tour companies promote the use of small groups, the transport tends to take the form of minibuses, jeeps and, in some instances, local public transport. This may involve such diverse transport as overnight or high speed trains, local taxis or, on occasion, auto or cycle rickshaws, even camels. For example, one tour offered by a leading adventure operator includes 14 different types of transportation, from the usual bus, jeep and train to the more unusual services of mules, camels and water taxis. For trips that cover extensive distances, flights are often used; for example, trips visiting several destinations in China may make use of several internal flights to maximize the time spent at destinations rather than on transfers. Other specialist operators may use the method of transport as the focus of the package, e.g. trains such as the Trans-Siberian Express and Orient Express or boats such as caique cruises in Greece and Turkey or houseboats in Kerala.

Adventure tour managers and guides

Pre-packaged adventure itineraries are usually accompanied by tour guides or tour leaders/managers, who play a crucial role in adventure tour operations. The importance and value placed on the quality of the tour leader is often demonstrated by inclusion of leader profiles within the brochure and on their web pages. The general practice is for leaders to be from the home region combined with destination-based staff, though the trend is towards engaging local leaders and thereby providing local employment opportunities. Also, local leaders with a passion for and knowledge of their culture and heritage enhance the tourist experience (Holland, 2012). However, this is limited by the availability of suitably qualified staff such as mountaineers or dive masters.

Itinerary

Designing an itinerary for an adventure package is complex and requires a good knowledge of the customer segment and creativity. Due to the number of destinations visited, itinerary planning requires an excellent understanding of the practical implications of such a tour and timings – for example, distances travelled during the day, departure times for flights, length of time necessary in each destination and places to visit on the way. Many of the decisions involved in establishing the itinerary require further consideration than just place and time, as illustrated in Table 5.1.

While these considerations are important in themselves, they also need to follow the philosophy of the company and their marketing strategy and recognize the potential cost implications of what may or may not be included, particularly for accommodation and land-based transportation. These considerations are pertinent not only to adventure tour operators but also to all operators offering multi-destination tours (see the following sections on coach tours and tailor-made packages).

To further our analysis of itinerary planning, let us consider a nine-day tour starting in Cairo, Egypt, which involves six nights of hotel accommodation in different towns, an overnight on a train and a felucca, entrance to architectural sites, and finishing in a beach resort on the Red Sea. The accommodation is comfortable but not luxury. Tours such as these are available flight-inclusive (in this instance, the departure point is the UK), but are available as land-only for people arranging

Table 5.1. Illustration of factors to consider in designing an adventure tour. (Adapted from Mancini, 2012.)

Demand	Issues	Considerations	Examples
Market segment	What are the customers' needs, expectations and interests?	Specific activities such as birdwatching, heritage, trekking Consideration of energy levels	Some trekking destinations may be inaccessible for parts of the year How active do the tourists need to be? Does the tour require previous experience, e.g. mountaineering?
Theme of the trip	Good titles make tours attractive to potential customers	Intriguing and effective titles and images generate more sales Tours incorporating specific events should include the event name in the title	'A trip round Japan' is less attractive than 'A visit to the land of the Rising Sun' or 'Trail of the Shogun' Specific itineraries could include 'Sapporo Snow Festival' or 'Toubkal Ascent'
Time of year	Is the destination or attraction seasonal? Is the market targeted only likely to travel during holiday periods?	Birdwatching tours will only be available during the appropriate season Snow-based itineraries will be dictated by snow availability Weather conditions Flight availability	Viewing migratory birds depends on when they arrive in and leave the destination and this will dictate the best time to operate these tours
Departure day	Midweek or weekend flights	Midweek flights are usually less attractive because customers have to take more time off work	Certain calendar dates, like Christmas Eve or Christmas Day, New Year's Eve and New Year's Day, are less attractive
Length of trip	Seven or nine days 14 days or longer	A trip leaving on a Friday evening and returning on a Sunday evening means customers only have to take five days of annual leave	This means that tours may overlap, i.e. all departures on Friday for a nine-day trip
Type of itinerary	Circle itinerary	Circle itineraries start in the same city and depart from the same city	Return flights to and from the same destination are often cheaper and essential for charter flights This may be a hub airport that is used for many tours, with each group then embarking on their own itinerary
	One-way itinerary	Tourists arrive at one airport and depart from another	The so-called 'open-jaw' itineraries

Suppliers	Availability and quality of suppliers	The quality and availability of accommodation, local transport, attractions and guides may dictate the ability to operate	Lack of suitable accommodation able to cope with the maximum number of passengers on a tour may limit potential destinations. In Greece some ferry services stop during the winter months
Flights	Availability of flights	Some scheduled flights and charter itineraries may not be available all year round	If flights are not available throughout the year, this will dictate when the itinerary can operate. Seasonal flight itineraries may result in an inability to secure seats on these planes, e.g. flights to Lapland over the Christmas season due to the number of operators offering Santa Claus trips
	Flight schedule	Using early morning flights means passengers may have connections requiring overnight accommodation or risk connection failure	If there are no direct flights and the trip involves connecting flights, if the initial flight is delayed this may result in missing the connection, problems with luggage, etc.
Arrival and departure city	Suitability of gateway airport destination	Passengers often enjoy free time towards the end of the holiday to relax, so the departure airport destination needs to provide suitable attractions and opportunities for relaxation	A tourist's arrival and departure can strongly influence their perceptions of their holiday. Including welcome meetings and interesting attractions can improve tourist satisfaction
Schedule	The number of destinations and attractions visited	Passengers may dislike packing and unpacking every day, so it is always worth considering spending two or three nights in the same destination. It is often best to avoid one-night stays during the trip	Logical planning of the tour to enable tourists to see each destination and incorporating free time. Unless the tour is promoted as one that moves on, for example trekking or camping trips. It is often easier to plan trips where tourists stay in one city and take day trips to other destinations (hub-and-spoke itineraries)
Split itineraries	The option of dividing the group in two	This may involve some passengers taking part in certain activities while alternative activity options are provided for the other members of the group	In golfing holidays, some partners may not play golf and may wish to take part in other activities such as shopping or sightseeing

Continued

Table 5.1. Continued.

Demand	Issues	Considerations	Examples
Activities	The number of sites and activities available	While providing many activities there also should be optional activities available for those who wish to do more Too many activities may limit the opportunities for passengers to explore the destination themselves	A trip to Aswan, Egypt is very interesting but some passengers may wish to take additional excursions to Abu Simbel Incorporating free time in destinations will allow passengers to have a later wake up or free time to shop and relax
Distances covered	The distance travelled between each destination	Tourists do not want to spend a long time on transfer transport, so it is important to balance the time in transfer with time at the destination	Planning transfers between destinations is important. Considerations include how long the transfer will take and whether there are any interesting sights to be seen along the way. What provision is available for food and toilet breaks?

their own flights or non-UK passengers. An overview of the itinerary is mapped out in Table 5.2.

This itinerary involves the following contract main suppliers:

- Four different hotels.
- Full day on a boat.
- Overnight on a felucca.

Many of the overnight stays in hotels also include dinner. While this reduces the additional expenses for passengers, it limits the opportunities to try local restaurants. There are many reasons why this may be included, but often it is a demand made by the accommodation supplier to guarantee the accommodation reservation, as they are therefore guaranteed additional income. The suppliers may be contracted directly with the tour operator or by the GHA, which will:

- Confirm accommodation bookings and numbers.
- Arrange half-day sightseeing trip in Cairo.
- Book tickets for train and sleeping berth.
- Arrange transfers when using coaches.
- Liaise with felucca operators.
- Reserve boat and transfers to port.
- Arrange optional excursions, such as Treasures and Tut, flights to Abu Simbel.

Optional excursions are provided but are not included in the price because this ensures that the brochure price remains low. Optional excursions are usually paid locally.

The tour leader will play a fundamental role in the operations of the tour, being required to:

- Arrange and pay taxis.
- Pay entrance fees and local guide (e.g. Valley of the Kings, Museum, Sphinx/Pyramids).

- Arrange and pay horse-drawn carriage.
- Arrange and pay donkey excursion.

Adventure operators often note that itineraries may change following feedback from past travellers and seasonal changes of transport. For example, the felucca trip is on board a sailing boat with no engine and therefore is reliant on currents and winds; flight timings can also change.

Costing

Costing tours is complex in comparison with single-destination mass market holidays because there are many individual components to be included, as evidenced above and illustrated in Table 5.3. The use of GHAs means that rather than contracting each component individually, these are subcontracted to the GHAs, who in turn coordinate and contract with the individual suppliers. These individual suppliers (service providers) may be micro-enterprises, such as individual guides or small groups, such as in this instance the owners of feluccas. The complexity of costing means that the use of tour operations costing software is very popular because it enables costing to be managed more efficiently and effectively.

The profitability of tours varies according to the number of people taking part in the trip and the costs incurred. Usually, one of the most expensive costs on tours are the charges for ground transport such as a coach. In the case of adventure tours, these involve the use of minibuses with a seating capacity of eight persons. Therefore the tour will be at its most profitable when they have eight or 16 passengers (two minibuses). If the tour has ten passengers, then two minibuses will be needed but they will not be full, so the cost of the minibuses is split between

Table 5.2. Itinerary overview of adventure tour.

Day	Overnight accommodation	Transport	Included excursions (paid)	Optional excursions (additional cost)[a]	Included meals
1	Arrival in Cairo	Flight to Cairo (if UK departure) Transfer to hotel (if UK departure)			
2	Overnight train (two-bed berth)	Coach (tour) Coach/taxi to train station	Half day sightseeing trip – Giza (pyramids/sphinx) and Cairo Museum	Sound and light show at pyramids (EGP 100) Treasures and Tut (GBP 46)	Breakfast (hotel) Dinner (train)
3	Aswan	Taxi to hotel (on arrival)		Camel ride Visit to obelisk Philae Temple (EGP 60) Abu Simbel (short flight)	Breakfast (train)
4	Nile felucca	Walk to felucca departure point (luggage transferred by taxi)			Breakfast (hotel) Lunch (felucca) Dinner (felucca)
5	Luxor	Taxi to Luxor hotel on arrival	Kom Ombo		Breakfast (felucca)
6	Luxor	Taxi to Valley of the Kings donkey ride	Valley of the Kings Hatshepsut Tomb, Karnak Temple	Sound and light show Hot air balloon ride Tutankhamun tomb (EGP 100)	Breakfast (hotel)
7	Red Sea (Hurghada)	Horse-drawn carriage Bus to Red Sea	Karnak		Breakfast (hotel)
8	Red Sea (Hurghada)	Bus to port (return)	Boat trip		Breakfast (hotel) Lunch (boat)
9	Departure	Bus to airport Flight (if UK departure)			Breakfast (hotel)

[a]GBP: UK Pounds; EGP: Egyptian Pounds. Costs noted in EGP are paid in local currency.

Table 5.3. Overview of basic costing for an adventure tour.

Service suppliers	Currency[a]	Ex-rate	Cost per person	Pax	Mark-up (%)	Total net cost Forex	Total net cost (GBP)	Total gross sell (GBP)	Gross profit subtotal (GBP)
GHA1	USD	1.3	1,345	4	40	5,380	4,138	5,794	1,655
GHA2	THB	55	5,450	4	35	21,800	396	555	159
SS3	USD	1.3	765	4	50	3,060	2,354	3,295	942
Domestic flight in destination	GBP	1	325	4	20	1,300	1,300	1,820	520
Airlines ex UK	GBP	1	280	4	15	1,120	1,120	1,568	448
	GBP	1		4	0	0	0	0	0
UK departure tax	GBP	1	20	4	15	80	80	112	32
Other flight taxes	GBP	1	6	4	15	24	24	34	10
Visa fees	GBP	1	50	4	35	200	200	280	80

Financial analysis

Total revenue	£13,458
Total gross profit	£3,845
Travel agent commission	£1,346

[a]GBP: UK Pounds; USD: US Dollar; THB: Thai Bhat.

the ten passengers, meaning the cost per head is higher. It is for reasons like this that operators push sales for departures that are not at capacity or have yet to achieve maximum profitability and may close sales of tours if they will not achieve the best possible numbers. Thus, unlike mass market operators that seek to achieve 3–5% profit per sale, adventure operators may achieve between 10% and 35% profit, varying according to the number of passengers and the cost of the variable components.

It is often easy to make many mistakes when costing a tour. For example, Lubbe (2000) cites common failings are forgetting room costs will be divided by two to achieve a per person rate and wrongly counting the number of nights' accommodation required, e.g. a seven-day tour will spend only six nights in a hotel; also if porterage fees are included then the fee involved will be double because baggage transfer involves both into and out of the accommodation.

Tailor-Made Itineraries

Demand for tailor-made itineraries has increased globally and this type of product delivers high levels of repeat business (Mintel, 2015) but relies heavily on the knowledge and experiences of the organizer (Buckley and Mossaz, 2016). A tailor-made programme is a bespoke itinerary created for the customer(s) and therefore may vary in timing, length and contents and often be flexible and modifiable. Tailor-made itineraries are designed specifically for the client and can vary according to:

- Group size.
- Departure date.
- Guide or tour manager.
- Accommodation.
- Included activities.

The potential passenger can stipulate style of accommodation, type of transportation, the destinations and any excursions. Itineraries such as these can be time-consuming to create, involving substantial negotiations with the client. These products can be designed by travel agents, adopting a tour operator role, or provided by specialist tour operators who liaise directly with the client, e.g. the UK tour operator Audley Travel or the international operator Tucan Travel.

Organizers of these tours need to have excellent in-depth knowledge of the destination so that they can make recommendations about the best time of year to travel and advise on attractions and accommodations based on the client's interest and budget. Tailor-made itineraries can also be offered for small private groups, school groups or groups with a specific interest such as photography.

Operators that specialize in these products will often have example itineraries on offer that can then be customized in conjunction with the client. Usually these tailor-made itineraries are not accompanied by a tour manager, but local guides can be arranged in advance and costed into the itinerary.

Operations

These types of tours rely heavily on GHAs because they are designed individually and accommodation and services are booked on an *ad hoc* basis. Due to the lack of forward planning, accommodation suppliers cannot be contracted using the usual allocation or commitment contracting and thus will be more expensive (see Chapter 4, this volume). That said, operators have access to discounted prices, which are not available to the general consumer or may have a contract with the accommodation provider to receive special rates.

Costing

It is obviously critical that every component included in the tour is costed. Each component of the package is priced based on contracts with suppliers and prices accessible to operators. Once each component is agreed, then a mark-up is added. This mark-up covers company costs and overheads such as marketing, premises and wages. A simplified overview of how a costing can be produced manually is presented in Table 5.4. However, it is unusual to do this manually because there are many computer programs designed specifically for SME operators that enable the construction of a package and costing.

Coach Tours

Coaches are predominantly used as part of the touring package, whereby holidays include visiting a variety of destinations as part of one itinerary, e.g. tours throughout China, USA or Turkey. The line between coaching and other types of escorted tour holiday is becoming increasingly blurred as coach tour operators may offer other types of holiday, e.g. rail or escorted cruise tours. Some companies position themselves specifically as escorted tour companies rather than coach operators (Mintel, 2014), because in some countries the term 'coach tour' appears to have negative associations largely dating back to the mid/late 20th century. However, there has been a noticeable transition from the large-scale mainstream coach holiday to smaller group sizes and upmarket accommodation specifically targeting the luxury end of the market. Also there has been a growth in all-inclusive coaching holidays that provide passengers with the reassurance that all the costs are included. Although coaches may be seen as restrictive due to the lack of flexibility in itineraries

and the close proximity of the passengers, companies are amending itineraries to give more free time in destinations, optional excursions, and focusing on travelling with like-minded people rather than strangers. Indeed, coach tours have long been held as an attractive option for older, single people, providing opportunities to meet others with similar interests. However, since the 1990s cruise trips have become increasingly attractive to such a market, especially given the general quality of the accommodation, the excursion options and the fact that there are no changes in overnight accommodation during the trip, which partly accounts for the decline in UK demand for coach tours. Even so, scheduled coach travel throughout Europe is increasing; for example, in Germany coach travel is very popular when accessing Alpine resorts due to the lack of alternative transport.

Coach tours offer a number of attractions to passengers:

- Low prices.
- Convenience of door-to-door travel.
- No baggage or transfer problems.
- Assistance from tour manager, which makes travelling to and throughout an unknown destination easier, particularly if there are language barriers.
- No problems of language and handling documentation, e.g. visas.
- Companionship.
- Security of feeling part of the group.

Traditionally, within Europe it is generally considered as a product for third age customers with domestic or trans-European itineraries, a market that may well increase as the number of fit, over 75-year-olds doubles in the next 20 years (Mintel, 2014). Further stimulating contemporary demand are developments in the coaches themselves. Coach operators are continually adapting their products to meet changing consumer needs and expectations, such as coaches with air

Table 5.4. Basic tailor-made tour costing model.

Reference:	1234	CB	Visa fees in the UK included?
Version:	A	SR	Taxes included for UK originating flights?
Number of Pax:	4	CB	Are the ex-rates correct and up to date?
Travel Agents Comm:	12.0%	SR	Are your quotes based on per person rates or totals for the couple/group?
Specialist Comm & Bonding:	3.0%	CB	Correct markups used/is it an agency sale?

Service Suppliers	Currency	Ex-Rate	Cost PP	Pax	Markup	Total Net Cost Forex	Total Net Cost £££s	Total Gross Sell £££s	Gross Profit Subtotal £££s
Fastour	USD	1.51	1345	4	40%	5380	£3,563	£4,988	£677
Journey Planner	THB	59	5450	4	35%	21800	£369	£499	£55
Exotissimo	USD	1.51	765	4	50%	3060	£2,026	£3,040	£557
Thai Intl UK	GBP	1	325	4	20%	1300	£1,300	£1,560	£26
Malaysia Airlines UK	GBP	1	280	4	15%	1120	£1,120	£1,288	–£25
		1		4	0%	0	£0	£0	£0
UK Departure tax	GBP	1	20	4	15%	80	£80	£92	–£2
Other flight taxes	GBP	1	6	4	15%	24	£24	£28	–£1
Visa fees	GBP	1	50	4	35%	200	£200	£270	£30
							£8,683	£11,764	£1,317

Financial Analysis
Total Revenue £11.764
Total Gross Profit £1,317
Travel Agents Commission £1,418
Sales Person £355
Comm & Bond
%age Gross Profit 11.2%

Notes:
Exotissimo quote includes Vietnam visa auth charges
Journey Planner quote based on Baan Boran as cheaper Dusit fully booked

conditioning, toilets and Wi-Fi access coupled with more comfortable seating, better external visibility and entertainment systems such that the latest models begin to copy airline travel. Many operators have reconfigured the large coaches of 53–57 seats to accommodate fewer seats (40). This reduction in maximum passenger numbers means that each passenger has additional window space and more room for luggage and high-deck motor coaches have become the expectation.

Many adventure and specialist operators utilize coaches (for example, historical tours, budget travellers and those seeking a multi-destination package), but these operators usually work on smaller group sizes. We can also identify a number of relatively new developments, for example, the rise of international fly–coach products, which reduces the need to access the destination by coach, such as on offer to Canada, China or Italy – as mapped out in Table 5.5.

While coach tours appear synonymous with older clients because of their ease of access, there are several brands (e.g. Contiki) that target the youth market, offering more adventurous trips such as high-energy tours (focusing on nightlife), camping (for longer low-cost trips) and other non-coach-related itineraries.

Table 5.5. All-inclusive coach luxury tour.

Day	Overnight accommodation	Transport	Included excursions/ activities	Meals included
1	Arrival in Rome	Coach transfer	Welcome dinner and wine	
2	Rome	Coach	VIP entrance to Vatican Museum including local guide, Sistine Chapel, St Peter's Basilica, Forum and Coliseum	Breakfast Dinner in local restaurant
3	Island of Capri	Coach, hydrofoil, taxi	Guided tour of Pompeii	
4	Capri	Cruise ship (small)	Guided tour by boat	Breakfast Dinner – choice of local restaurants
5	Perugia	Hydrofoil, coach	Guided tour of Perugia	Breakfast Dinner
6	Mugello Valley (near Florence)	Coach	Wine tasting in Chianti hills, artisan ice cream parlour	Breakfast Dinner
7	Mugello Valley (near Florence)	Coach	Museum with guide	Breakfast Dinner in local restaurant
8	Rapallo	Coach	Guide at Pisa and Lucca	Breakfast Dinner
9	Rapallo	Coach, train	Excursion by train to Portofino	Breakfast Dinner
10	Venice	Coach		Breakfast
11	Venice	Cruise ship (small)	Guided tour, evening cruise to Burano	Breakfast Dinner
12	Transfers to airport	Coach transfer		Breakfast

Another growth area in the coaching market is the polar opposite of the luxury market, the budget coach tour aimed at young adults with a limited budget (e.g. 'hop on–hop off' coach travel throughout Europe) giving passengers the flexibility to design their own itinerary. Specialist coach tours are also growing in both provision and customer numbers. For example, there are specialist tours visiting destinations made famous in films and television programmes, historical sites from the First and Second World Wars and culinary-themed trips.

Many well-known coach tour companies are operated by The Travel Corporation, which has 24 travel brands, operates in over 60 countries with 35 offices worldwide and has annual sales involving over 2 million customers. The brands are independently managed and target specific markets, and include well-known brands such as Evan Evans tours, Haggis Adventures, Insight Vacations, Trafalgar Tours, and Creative Holidays. It also operates boutique hotels under the Red Carnation brand and cruises through its Uniworld brand.

Operations

Best practice today for many coach operators is to offer door-to-door itineraries, which means passengers are collected from their home or local collection depot and taken on feeder buses to interchanges where passengers join their coach tour. For example, Shearings (UK) have over 650 joining points nationwide and operate from a number of interchanges (Shearings, 2016). This hub-and-spoke system is similar to many scheduled airlines.

Escorted coach tours include the services of a tour manager (also called tour director) in addition to the driver(s). Tour managers play a key role in ensuring that the tours run smoothly. For example, they ensure fast and efficient group check in at hotels, luggage transfer from coach to the rooms (and reverse) without customer involvement, provide information about the destination, deal with customer complaints and queries and liaise with local suppliers such as guides. Tour managers are usually contracted for a tour, but some companies may offer seasonal contracts whereby a tour manager will be expected to run back-to-back tours in the same or different locations. Within Europe, drivers are constrained by the number of hours that they can drive. They may not drive for more than nine hours in one day (extended to ten hours twice a week) or drive for more than 56 hours in a week (90 in any two consecutive weeks), and they must have a break of 45 hours after six consecutive days of work. These regulations limit the distances the drivers can cover and so on many longer trips there may be two drivers working, or on occasional days local drivers will be used.

Costing

Costing a coach tour is comparable with generic tour market products in that they also work on a load factor; for instance, a 70% load factor means that ideally at least 28 seats of a 40-seater coach need to be sold, although the per person costs will increase, as rooms, baggage and entrance fees (e.g. for attractions) would multiply if all seats are sold. An illustration of a tour costing is presented in Table 5.6, which shows the major costings that need to be included. Obviously, any additional activities included will need to be added as necessary.

One of the biggest expenses that coach operators need to give particularly careful attention to is that of fuel because fluctuations in fuel prices, for example, due to a rise in oil price or currency exchange rates, will have a substantial impact on profitability.

Table 5.6. Costing for a 9-day coach tour (ex London).

Destination		Cost	Currency		GBP total cost
Hotels					
Brussels hotel	Bed-and-breakfast (double occ)	40	GBP	280.00	280.00
Berlin hotel	Three nights: evening meal, bed-and-breakfast (double occ)	45	GBP	315.00	315.00
Dresden hotel	Two nights: evening meal, bed-and-breakfast (double occ)	40	GBP	280.00	280.00
Kassel Hotel	One night: evening meal, bed and breakfast (double occ)	40	GBP	280.00	280.00
Brussels hotel	One night: evening meal, bed and breakfast (double occ)	45	GBP	315.00	315.00
Excursions	Berlin bus tour (invoiced direct to HQ)		GBP	100.00	100.00
1 EUR = GBP 0.86	Berlin guide (direct payment)	135	Euro	135.00	114.75
	City guide (direct payment)	150	Euro	150.00	127.50
	Leipzig guide	105	Euro	105.00	89.25
	Dresden guide (direct payment)	95	Euro	95.00	80.75
	Erfurt guide (direct payment)	70	Euro	70.00	59.50
Entrance fees	Leipzig Church entrance (p/p)	1.2	Euro	16.80	14.28
	Colditz entrance (p/p)	7.5	Euro	105.00	89.25
Welcome drink	Day 2 Berlin hotel (p/p) (paid direct by tour manager)	3	GBP	42.00	42.00
	Day 5 Dresden hotel (p/p) (paid direct by tour manager)	3	GBP	42.00	42.00
Baggage handling	Five hotels × 2 = 10	2	GBP	28.00	28.00
Ferry costs					850.00
Fuel				3000.00	3000.00
Drivers costs	Wages		GBP	450.00	450.00
	Accommodation (often gratis)				
Tour manager costs	Wages 9 × £60/day		GBP	540.00	540.00
	Accommodation (often gratis)				
Total costs					7097.28
Mark-up (30%)					2129.18
VAT on mark-up (20%)					425.83
TOTAL					9652.29
Cost per person					690.00[a]
SELLING PRICE					745.00[b]

[a]Rounded figure; [b]including 8% commission.

Summary

In general, all tour operators start out as a micro-enterprise (less than ten employees). From such a base, the successful operator will grow and develop into a sustainable enterprise and potentially into a major international company with a stock market listing. However, in numerical terms the latter are relatively few among the myriad of tour operators. Obviously, there are many steps in between as well as different growth strategies (see Chapter 3, this volume). But, as success of operators has been evident and demand sustained, then so too have the opportunities for entrepreneurs to enter the marketplace, often through identifying a niche market or presenting an offering that differentiates that operator's package from similar packages available. Hence it is not surprising that, in the developed economies of the world, we can identify the presence of a remarkable number and range of small and medium-sized tour operators.

A significant factor about these small operators is that they are neither vertically nor horizontally integrated (though there are exceptions) and therefore they require the support of ground handling agents and often other similar-sized principals in their package destinations to provide the key services, e.g. transfers, accommodation, activities. As such, they are arguably contributing more directly to a destination's locality and economy. This is not only because of their size and therefore capacity to operate tours, but also due to operating predominantly in the niche tourism market, away from the macro-niche end of the spectrum in localities more attuned to their tours, e.g. adventure, nature. This adds to the complexity of their tours and thereby means costing a package is often more complex, more detailed and fraught with potential errors.

However, these SMEs are not only evident in the broad markets of adventure and nature, but also, as Fig. 5.1 exemplifies, in a host of other areas, which even then can be further subdivided. But each in their own way still require the support of service providers on the ground. The extent of their reliance on such suppliers clearly varies with the operator, as illustrated by coach tours. This market could be considered to have had its day between the 1930s and 1970s, subsequently surpassed by international air travel packages and car ownership. Today it is a macro-niche market evidently providing further opportunities for small/medium-sized operators tuned into new itineraries, new style coaches with more attention to customer comfort and interests, albeit their major source markets have and continue to be attracted to cruising. An alternative strategy for an SME in the tour operating marketplace is to build 'in-house' expertise to create packages for customers seeking their own experience but who do not have the time and/ or expertise to organize such a trip themselves. Hence the appearance in the sector of tailor-made packages, developed according to customer requirements by agents with the requisite knowledge and skills to create their customized trip.

Overall, it is the SMEs that comprise the bedrock of the sector. Obviously, some will fail while others will grow and prosper, developing into a major business potentially to be taken over by a larger operator seeking to expand and/or diversify its own product portfolio. However, some of these specialist operators, especially in the adventure/nature sector, will continue to operate as a SME presenting quality products, attuned to their customers' interests and requirements.

Discussion Questions

1. What are the typical problems faced by small to medium-sized tour operators? Illustrate your answer with specific examples.

2. Tourism and entrepreneurship are intrinsically linked – without entrepreneurial skills any tourism business will fail. Examine the validity of this contention with specific reference to small-sized tour operators.

3. Examine the problems faced in establishing a tour operator business and the extent to which they need to develop niche products.

4. With reference to two notable tourism entrepreneurs, examine the problems they faced establishing the business, the extent to which they developed niche products and the impact of larger tourism organizations on the ventures.

5. Are small tour operators offering low-key, small group tours more in keeping with the concept of responsible tourism and sustainability than international operators offering 3S-style package holidays?

Key Terms

- **Niche:** A niche means a segment is very small and specialized.
- **Oligopoly (oligopolistic):** An oligopoly is a market structure that is dominated by a few firms and is said to be highly concentrated.
- **SME:** Small and medium-sized enterprises. (Medium = less than 250 employees; small = less than 50 employees; micro = less than ten employees.)

INTERNET EXERCISE

UNWTO have produced a Global Report on Adventure Tourism: cf.cdn.unwto.org/sites/all/files/pdf/final_1global_report_on_adventure_tourism.pdf

Questions

- Discuss the benefits of adventure tourism to local economies.
- What problems do these companies face in commodifying adventure?

MINI CASE STUDY

Read 'Capturing the Asian millennial traveller', available from www.yoursingapore.com/content/dam/MICE/Global/bulletin-board/travel-rave-reports/Capturing-the-Asian-Millennial-Traveller.pdf

Questions

- What are the issues in trying to attract these customers?
- What type of products could you design to encourage potential customers to book package holidays rather than create their own?

Overland tours

Overland tours are long road trips using self-reliant vehicles usually for a maximum number of 22 passengers (see Intrepid, Oasis Overland, Dragoman), often termed expedition tours. The principal goal of these tours is to cover large distances using road routes rather than flights, often visiting places where the infrastructure is poor and locations are remote. For example, an 84-day trip from Kathmandu to Singapore via New Delhi, Bhutan, Myanmar, Vietnam, Cambodia and Malaysia, or a central Asia overland trip starting in Tehran, Iran and finishing in Kazakhstan taking 40 days.

The majority of these tours use tented camping or local hostels and guesthouses for accommodation. The quality of the accommodation will vary due to the remoteness of the stopping point. Food is cooked on equipment carried on board. Packages usually include breakfast and an evening meal, with lunch being bought along the way.

Specialist expedition vehicles are used because of the types of roads encountered. These trucks are basic but comfortable and are equipped for mechanical breakdown (e.g. toolkits and spares) or getting stuck (e.g. sand mats, ropes, shovels and pickaxes). In addition, they carry substantial amounts of water and are equipped with cooking facilities, solar showers and toilet tents for bush camping.

The tours are usually operated by two expedition leaders/drivers who need to be trained as garage mechanics as well as cooks. These leaders are not guides but will be knowledgeable about the route and attractions. Passengers are expected to work together as part of a team, including daily shopping, cooking, cleaning and disposing of rubbish. Other jobs such as collecting water and firewood, managing the food stores and loading luggage are allocated on a rota basis to team members.

Questions

- What are the difficulties in organizing and operating overland trips?
- What type of passenger would purchase such expeditions?

Recommended Reading

An excellent overview of the breadth of adventure holidays on offer is presented in:

Buckley, R. (2006) *Adventure Tourism*. CAB International, Wallingford, UK.

Interesting coverage of a niche product with growing support can be found in:

Dickinson, J. and Lumsden, L. (2010) *Slow Travel and Tourism*. Routledge, London.

As many small operators are reliant on third-party suppliers, integrating sustainability into their supply chains is important. See:

Font, X., Tapper, R., Schwartz, K. and Kornilaki, M. (2008) Sustainable supply chain management in tourism. *Business Strategy and the Environment* 17, 260–271.

References

Buckley, R. (2006) *Adventure Tourism*. CAB International, Wallingford, UK.

Buckley, R. and Mossaz, A.C. (2016) Decision-making by specialist luxury travel agents. *Tourism Management* 55, 133–138.

Buhalis, D. (2001) Tourism distribution channels: practices and processes. In: Buhalis, D.

and Laws, E. (eds) *Tourism Distribution Channels*. Continuum, London, pp. 7–32.

Enterprise and Industry Publications (2005) *The New SME Definition: User Guide Model Declaration 2005*. Publications Office, European Commission, Luxembourg.

Hayhurst, L. (2016) Number of agents and tour operators return to pre-recession levels. *Travel Weekly* 26 February, 2.

Holland, J. (2012) Adventure tours: responsible tourism in practice. In: Leslie, D. (ed.) *Responsible Tourism: Concepts, Theory and Practice*. CAB International, Wallingford, UK, pp. 119–129.

Holland, J. (2015) The understanding and implementation of responsible tourism for adventure tour operators. Doctorate of Business Administration, Northumbria University, Newcastle, UK.

Keynote (2015) *Tour Operator Activities*. Available at: https://www.keynote.co.uk/market-digest/travel-leisure/tour-operator-activities-0, accessed 5 January 2016.

Lubbe, B. (2000) *Tourism Distribution: Managing the Travel Intermediary*. Juta & Co. Ltd, Kenwyn, South Africa.

Mancini, M. (2012) *Conducting Tours: A Practical Guide*. Thomson Learning, New York.

Mintel (2010) Activity Holidays – UK. Available at: http://academic.mintel.com/display/508054, accessed 2 August 2016.

Mintel (2014) Coach Holidays UK. Available at: http://academic.mintel.com/display/679817/, accessed 24 July 2016.

Mintel (2015) Luxury Travel – UK November. Available at: http://academic.mintel.com/display/756040/, accessed 10 July 2016.

Nylander, M. and Hall, D. (2005) Rural tourism policy: European perspectives. In: Hall, D., Kirkpatrick, I. and Mitchell, M. (eds) *Rural Tourism and Sustainable Business*. Channel View, Bristol, UK, pp. 17–40.

Robinson, M. and Novelli, M. (2005) Niche tourism: an introduction. In: Novelli, M.M. (ed.) *Niche Tourism: Contemporary Issues, Trends and Cases*. Routledge, Oxford, UK, pp. 1–14.

Shearings (2016) Interchanges. Shearings Holidays. Available at: http://www.shearings.com/about-us/our-interchanges, accessed 26 July 2016.

6 Customer Service

Learning Objectives

After studying this chapter, you should be able to:

- Understand the importance of customer service.
- Appreciate the importance of service quality.
- Understand methods of measuring service quality.
- Understand the importance of managing service encounters efficiently and effectively.
- Understand the role of customer satisfaction.
- Examine customer loyalty.
- Examine the impacts of service failure and recovery.

Introduction

Tour operators' products encompass many individual components and while some may be owned by the tour operator, many components of the holiday experienced by a tourist are not under their direct control. For example, the airline the passengers travel with, the hotel they stay in and the hospitality enterprises or attractions they visit may be operated by other companies. This is particularly pertinent in the tour operating sector, which has unique characteristics (see Chapter 10, this volume), and wherein the interactions between customers and staff play a fundamental role in the holiday experience. This is because it is a service-based sector that relies on staff to co-create the tourist experience with the customer. Positive interactions with staff can add value and delight to the consumer experience and are frequently the focus of training. Therefore, it is important that operators recognize it is not only the management of their own components of a tour that will contribute to success. It is also about managing service, managing the experience and managing customer expectations if such success is to be sustained. Thus, the overall importance of customer service and service quality cannot be overstated. Furthermore, service quality has been identified as providing opportunities for long-term competitive advantage.

The focus of this chapter is therefore on customer service and how tour operators can improve service quality, which is not just a matter of managing the customer/provider interface but also how service quality may be assessed. This leads on to addressing **customer satisfaction** and loyalty and ways in which the tour operator can seek to improve their own performance. The key matter of managing **service recovery** in the event of adverse incidents concludes the chapter.

Customer Service and Satisfaction

In an age of hyper-competition, simply meeting the requirements of the customer by providing quality products is no longer sufficient to maintain market share and market position. As service capabilities increase and tourist expectations are more demanding, **value-added** services and customer-focused strategies are necessary for survival. Not surprisingly, therefore, customer service has been promoted as being a method of achieving sustainable competitive advantage (see Chapter 3, this volume) by adding value to the tourist experience. This is well encapsulated by Lucas, in what is arguably the most comprehensive definition of customer service: 'the ability of knowledgeable, capable, and enthusiastic employees to deliver products and services to their internal and external customers in a manner that satisfies identified and unidentified needs and ultimately results in positive word-of-mouth publicity and return business' (2014, p. 7). This definition clearly reinforces the importance of the role of staff in delivering quality service. It is unequivocal that positive experiences lead to customer satisfaction, which in turn engenders loyalty and potential repurchase (Brunner *et al.*, 2008), and also '**word-of-mouth**' (WOM) and '**e word-of-mouth**' (eWOM) recommendations that can differentiate the tour operator from competitors.

Customer satisfaction, in effect, is a feeling of pleasure that results from comparing a product or service's perceived performance or outcome with expectations (Kotler *et al.*, 2009). As Pearce (2005) observes, satisfaction is a post-experience attitude based on evaluating the experience once it is complete, which will then inform future purchases. Satisfaction is linked to the customer's expectation (level of fulfilment) and can be considered a long-term evaluation, whereas quality is linked to consumption and is evaluated invariably within the context of a single event interaction (see below). The relationship between satisfaction and service quality is key to understanding customer satisfaction. Matzler and Sauerwein (2002) suggest that the factors affecting customer satisfaction can be considered in three categories:

- Basic factors: These are the minimum requirements that are expected of a product – the basic attributes of the service – to prevent the customer from being dissatisfied. They do not necessarily cause satisfaction, but lead to dissatisfaction if absent.
- Performance factors: These are the factors, such as reliability and friendliness, that lead to satisfaction if fulfilled or dissatisfaction if not fulfilled.
- Excitement factors: These are factors that increase customer satisfaction if fulfilled, but do not cause dissatisfaction if not fulfilled.

In other words, tour operators need to ensure that the basics of their package are in place to meet the essential elements of the holiday and that these are delivered throughout the holiday at an acceptable standard at the very minimum. However, given the level of competition, this in itself may be considered unsatisfactory and tour operators should be aiming to achieve outstanding customer service. Thus the whole process of delivery needs to be set in a context of striving to achieve service excellence. As Cronin and Taylor (1992) argued, outstanding customer service has been seen to be one of the most effective and least expensive ways to promote a business. Companies that recognize the importance of this may also be particularly attractive in terms of being a good employer. As McCarthy stated, 'whenever you find a company whose customers report an exceptionally high level of satisfaction, almost invariably that company also has high levels of employee satisfaction' (1997, p. 4).

Service quality

One of the main elements determining customer satisfaction is the customer's perception of service quality. In general, a customer's perceptions of service quality arise from comparison of their expectations before they receive a service with their actual experience of that service. However, tourists judge the satisfaction of tourism products based on the quality of their experience, and interactions within the complex tourist system, in comparison with their expectations. Thus tourists have initial expectations (formed through advertisements, brochures, mass media and internet searches, information from friends and relatives) about the type and quality of products and services offered by the tour operator and at the tourist destination. To meet and exceed those expectations it is important to understand what expectations tourists have and how tour operators can seek to ensure satisfaction, which is an important antecedent of loyalty. Outstanding service (or service excellence) is therefore about managing customer perceptions and expectations such that the customer feels that their experience has fulfilled their expectations. Ideally, the aim of the tour operator is therefore not only to satisfy the tourist's expectations as a minimum but to exceed them.

Significantly, the provision of a high-quality experience ultimately falls on the front-line staff and therefore tour operators must promote a customer-focused approach, ensuring that not only do their products meet the expectations of their customers but also that the service delivery is of the highest standard. Indeed, a quality experience can only exist to the extent that the operator's product and service meets the needs and expectations of the customer. In effect, that the customers receive the service they envisaged and ideally it surpasses their expectations. Thus as Berry and Parasuraman suggest, 'the proof of service [quality] is in flawless performance' (1991, p. 15), which has its roots in 'zero defects' of **total quality management**, a tool used in the manufacturing industry. As Berry *et al.* (1988) argued, service quality has become a significant differentiator and the most powerful competitive weapon which is manifest in leading service organizations and is set as the key operational goal in many organizations (Foster, 2014).

In summary, excellent service quality delivers the outcomes that tour operators look to achieve, that is customer satisfaction, repeat purchases, customer loyalty and positive promotion of the company, which can lead to lower marketing costs, opportunities for premium pricing and ultimately increased profitability.

Managing the Service Encounter

The service encounter can be defined as the interaction between the tourist and a representative of the tour operator, essentially front-line staff or subcontracted employees. The outcomes of the service depend on the knowledge, personality, behaviour and performance of these employees and when implemented successfully will lead to positive outcomes: satisfaction, loyalty and positive reviews. Thus, it is important that tour operators understand how to manage these interactions. Furthermore, as service quality is a nebulous concept, with each customer assessing the product or service from his/her own perspective, it is essential to try to understand what customers are looking for and what they consider to be quality services. As such, tour operators must manage service quality based on the expectations of the tourist, that is they should make the customer/the tourist the focal point, in what is termed a 'customer centric' rather than a 'product centric approach' (Kandampully, 2006).

In the case of tour operators, the potential customer may have dealings with different organizations before they have any interaction with the holiday operator. Further, once on holiday, they will have service encounters with other suppliers, thus the experience is gauged not by the separate elements but the totality of experiences. This is made even more complex because of the length of duration of the holiday, the numerous service providers and geographical locations where the service takes place. However, throughout this delivery process the tour operator should recognize that there are many extraneous factors that can affect tourist satisfaction, in particular stress. Stress caused by any aspect of the trip can lead to dissatisfaction with the holiday product, as Swarbrooke and Horner (2016) illustrate in the following examples:

- Difficulties over money.
- Transport delays.
- Unfamiliar customs and food.
- Performance of service staff.
- Failure of accommodation services.
- Relationships with other tourists.
- Personal safety and health.
- Unforeseen incidents.
- Problems with foreign languages.

For escorted packages and those that include the services of a tour manager and/or a resort representative, the performance of the staff is critical to achieving customer satisfaction. The staff are the ones who sell the next package because their performance affects not only the satisfaction of the tourist, but also the company image and reputation. Therefore, the interaction between tour operators' representatives (tour manager or resort rep) is critical to the success of both the package and the operator.

Managing the tourist–employee encounter is perhaps one of the most difficult aspects for tour operator managers and critically important because many of the employees involved in service encounters will not be in the employment of the tour operator, e.g. airline and hospitality staff. Customer service, in particular the role of the resort representative, is the most frequently complained about facet of a package holiday. It is ironic therefore that the majority of front-line staff who deal with customers are often the youngest employees and that despite the gradual move to technology, e.g. self-check in, off-line sales, they still provide the key feature of the package holiday, yet they are more than likely to be the least trained staff and frequently receive low pay.

Moments of Truth

Service encounters are the interactions between customer and service delivery, which may be a brief encounter or form a key component of the holiday and will vary according to the employee's role. Jan Carlzon, the former CEO of Scandinavian Air Systems (SAS) (Carlzon, 2001) coined the concept 'Moments of Truth', referring to all the interactions that the customer, or even potential customer, will have with an organization. But, as Baum (2002) argued in the case of tourism, each Moment of Truth is not equal, as each interaction does not have the same intensity as far as the customer is concerned, yet delivering a quality experience is central to managing each such moment. These encounters may be remote (no direct contact between the customer and the service provider, e.g. automated services), by telephone, or face-to-face; for example, Disney claim up to 74 encounters per visit.

As Carlzon (2001) argued, the first '15 golden seconds' during which an organization is assessed by the guest are the most critical. In the instance of package holidays, that first 15 seconds is not necessarily under the control of the tour operator; for example, purchasing the holiday from an independent travel agent

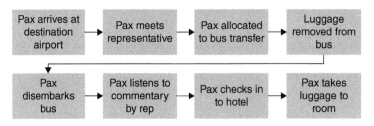

Fig. 6.1. Arrival at destination and transfer to resort; indicative interactions.

or interactions with cabin crew on a scheduled flight. The frequency and number of service encounters and therefore potential opportunities for failings can be extensive, as illustrated in the sequence of stages presented in Fig. 6.1. For many customers, a call centre or email exchange may be the first interaction with the company, and these are frequently the focus of many customer concerns.

The varying degrees in interaction intensity between the tourists and the employees all contribute to constructing an impression of the company, the destination and the holiday. High levels of interaction at the pre-travel stage will vary depending on whether the customer visits a travel agent, engages in online negotiations with a tailor-made operator or simply visits the website. Lower levels of interaction may take place between the airline and the passenger, with the customer being a passive recipient of the experience. That said, unacceptable experiences on the outbound flight may negatively impact on the customer's perception of the whole holiday. As Ryan (2002) argues, whilst tourists gauge each individual element of their holiday experience, they base their evaluation of the holiday on their overall experience.

Measuring Service Quality

Today's tourist has become more discriminating and discerning. Tourists are more likely to be well-travelled and have a greater number of experiences to compare with when evaluating whether the product has met their expectations. According to Voss *et al.*, service quality is defined from the provider's perspective in terms of 'the ability of the provider to consistently meet customers' requirements' (2004, p. 213) and therefore it becomes critical that customers' opinions are sought and service delivery is monitored.

There are many ways to collect data on customers, which largely depends on the type of information required and its purpose. In general, data collection is usually divided into two different approaches: qualitative methods, which collect data in the tourists' own words and quantitative methods, which usually generate numerical data. Table 6.1 illustrates some of the different research methods (further explored below) that can be applied to collect information that can then be used to aid analysis of service quality.

Qualitative Data Collection

- Customer interviews. Interviews can be used to obtain detailed information directly from customers. Due to the time-consuming nature of this method, in terms of time for the interview and transcribing the recording and then analysing the data, it is not a frequently used approach. This approach is usually used only when responding to comments made on customer service questionnaires.

Table 6.1. Illustration of customer-based research.

Survey method	Qualitative	Quantitative
Customers	Customer interviews Focus groups Complaint monitoring Critical incident technique Customer service questionnaires – open-ended questions	Customer service questionnaires Internet and email surveys Customer comment cards Online reviews
Travel agent	Mystery shopper	
Suppliers	Critical incident technique Incident logs	
Tour guides/ managers	Tour reports Incident logs	

- Focus groups. This is a time-consuming method of collecting data but the information generated can be particularly informative as a way of generating new ideas and comparing experiences.

- Complaint monitoring. Monitoring complaints and sources of dissatisfaction can help organizations identify trends, facilities or behaviours that are consistently causing complaint. Traditionally complaints focus on the facilities used, specifically the quality of the facilities and services, food and beverages and dissatisfaction with the description of provision in comparison with the actual provision. This will enable operators to make decisions such as changing accommodation suppliers, requesting additional provision and even working with accommodation suppliers to improve menus.

- Critical incident technique. This is a useful technique for studying service quality questions and assessing tourists' perspectives of service (Chen and Hsu, 2012). It can be used to analyse data collected in several ways, including interviews, focus groups and questionnaires, by classifying it into categories such as transportation, accommodation and experiences.

- Mystery shopper. This method of data collection is used by many organizations, e.g. airlines, hotel chains, restaurants, bars and in particular travel agents. Mystery shopper services interact in different ways, including visits in person, in writing, over the telephone and by email. *Travel Weekly*, a UK travel industry newspaper, regularly reports mystery shopper experiences. The feedback from mystery shoppers is frequently used to identify training needs and benchmark company operations against competitors. In order to increase the reliability of the results, organizations provide set standards to the mystery shopper, which they can use to assess service; e.g. did the employee acknowledge you with a smile; what were the first impressions of the shop; and was the information provided accurate?

- Incident logs. These logs record specific incidents that happen during the holiday. They may be related to health and safety or specific incidents such as loss of personal items.

- Tour reports. These reports are completed by tour managers/leaders at the end of each tour. They are used to analyse the level of service and provision by suppliers. These are not the same as accident report forms, which are additional documents. Tour managers/leaders are in the unique position where they can interact with the customer as front-line staff.

- Online reviews. These reviews are posted by customers and are available to potential customers (see Chapter 10, this volume).

Quantitative Methods of Data Collection

The most usual method for collecting quantitative data is customer service questionnaires. These are sometimes referred to as exit surveys, designed to evaluate the performance of the holiday. Open-ended questions or comment boxes allow passengers to provide extra detail about their experiences. They are usually devised by each company with the aim of obtaining qualitative and quantitative data that can be analysed easily, particularly if online data collection methods are used. A customer service questionnaire will garner details about the customer's actual holiday experience, but they do not address the expectations the customer had prior to the holiday. There has been much debate about the relevance of questionnaires, but they are still a useful tool for large tour operators to identify possible potential issues. The benefits of collecting and analysing information about service delivery are numerous, ranging from the identification of frequent causes of complaints, areas where improvements could be made, identification of provision that is not included and feedback about the accuracy of marketing materials. This is illustrated in Box 6.1.

There are several tools utilizing customer service questionnaires that have been developed to assess customer satisfaction and quality. In this text, we consider two of the most widely recognized tools. The first is **Importance Performance Analysis (IPA)** (Martilla and James, 1977). IPA shows the importance of various attributes and the performance of the company, identifying areas for service quality improvements (see Hudson and Shephard,

---

Box 6.1. Customer service questionnaires – Exodus

Exodus, a UK adventure tour operator, use customer service questionnaires, which they refer to as holiday evaluation forms (HEF), as part of their customer feedback process, which is implemented via email. After customers return from their holiday each customer is emailed a unique personal link to the HEF. Customers who did not book directly with Exodus may request the link to be sent to them.

The survey has 23 questions addressing the booking process, the trip experience, specific parts of the trip and additional information. Most questions use a Likert scale, although there are several Yes/No questions and all have comment boxes for additional feedback. In order to encourage completion, the tour leader gives passengers reminder cards and also enters them into monthly voucher competitions. Currently the overall response rate is approximately 48%. Two weeks after the trip, the returned information is consolidated into a single trip report (STR) for that departure. The information is reviewed internally and comments are sent to any ground handling agents and tour leaders involved (see Chapter 5, this volume). The STR provides an overview of the feedback, identifying where problems have occurred, using a traffic light system, green meaning no problems, amber needs reviewing and improving and red meaning immediate action needs to be taken.

1998). In effect, IPA assesses importance and performance information related to a customer's experience. It is a popular method for measuring the significance placed on various attributes and their perceived performance. IPA can be used to measure both the extent to which tourists are satisfied and also how important certain attributes are by rating on a Likert scale. The importance-performance attributes are analysed and placed in a matrix based on their perceived importance and performance to the customers (see Fig. 6.2).

The four quadrants can be summarized as follows:

- Keep up the good work. This quadrant contains attributes that tourists think are important and that perform highly. Attributes should remain in this quadrant.
- Concentrate here: This quadrant includes attributes that are important to the tourist but for which performance is low. Attributes in this quadrant require the most attention.
- Possible overkill: This quadrant contains attributes that received low importance ratings and high performance ratings, indicating that resources should be reallocated.

- Low priority: This quadrant includes attributes that receive low scores for both the importance and performance scales. The tourist views these attributes as being low in importance and therefore these attributes require little attention.

IPA identifies attributes performing at a satisfactory level and attributes that require attention. For the tour operator, it enables better identification of customer products and services that need to be improved, where high importance and low performance attributes are identified.

The second tool to consider is that of SERVQUAL (Parasuraman *et al.*, 1985). SERVQUAL is a model that aims to measure the gap between consumer expectations of the service and perceptions of the actual service received. An overall service quality score can be assessed based on five dimensions: tangibles, reliability, responsiveness, assurance and empathy (see Table 6.2). Expectations and performance can be measured using pairs of questions, for example questions to measure expectations could be presented as 'organization X should be dependable', whereas questions to measure performance could be presented as 'organization X is dependable.'

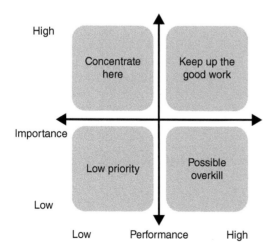

Fig. 6.2. Importance performance analysis matrix. (From Chen *et al.*, 2012, p. 49.)

Table 6.2. The dimensions used in SERVQUAL. (Derived from Hudson *et al.*, 2004; Cheyne *et al.*, 2006; Wirtz *et al.*, 2012.)

Dimension of service quality	Definition	Tour operator illustration
Tangibles	The appearance of physical facilities, equipment, personnel and communication material	Quality of the brochure, website. Attractiveness of accommodation, representative appearance
Reliability	Ability to perform the promised service dependably and accurately	Confidence in the product purchased, that the package bought is what will be received
Responsiveness	Willingness to help customers and provide prompt service	Speed at which problems are resolved
Assurance		
Credibility	Trustworthiness, believability, honesty	Honest and helpful information provided by sales teams, knowledge and experience, specialist staff. Reputation of the tour operator
Security	Freedom from risk, danger or doubt	Confident about payment security, safety of facilities, e.g. accommodation, safety of destination. Insurance policy. Provision of guide or representative to help if something goes wrong
Competence	Possession of skills and knowledge required to perform the service	Product knowledge and ability to answer questions
Courtesy	Politeness, respect, consideration and friendliness	Interpersonal skills by all staff interacted with, e.g. demeanour, politeness and consideration
Empathy		
Accessibility	Approachability and ease of contact	Approachability of staff or operator, e.g. phone number. Location of accommodation. Access to attractions
Communication	Listening to customers and keeping them informed in a language they understand	Keeping customers informed if there are issues. Providing guidance and information in a suitable language
Understanding the customer	Making the effort to know customers and their needs	Adapting products to meet customer needs, e.g. flexible itineraries, upgrades, optional excursion provision

The results for each of the five dimensions of the customer service can be analysed using data analysis packages such as IBM SPSS Statistics or Excel to identify areas where customers' expectations are not being met.

Both tools are not without criticism. Buttle (1996) summarizes several theoretical and operational criticisms, commenting that SERVQUAL is based on a disconfirmation paradigm (meaning that the customer either agrees or disagrees) rather than an attitudinal paradigm, that the five dimensions are not necessarily applicable to all service encounters and that the administration of two separate surveys (expectation questions and performance questions) for collecting data is confusing.

Improving Service Quality

Clearly the key to managing customer service and demonstrating service quality is to know what the customer wants and to develop the right products and services to support their expectations.

There are many ways in which tour operators have tried to manage service encounters, such as providing standardized information, staff training, adopting a customer-centric culture and recruiting new staff with customer service experience who appreciate the company's customer service values. Staff are particularly important because they represent the face of the company. There are many challenges that tour operators and their staff face in their multi-dimensional role; for example, not only completing their operational tasks but also problem solving, health and safety matters and 'up selling'. Therefore, as Mill (2002) argues, an emphasis on training is crucial to an organization. However, management too often see training as an expense rather than an investment and yet it is an essential tool for not only providing service quality but also enhancing employee motivation. Although many benefits of training are hard to measure due to their intangible nature, there is a raft of evidence to support the theory that comprehensive training leads to a higher level of return on investment. Training staff provides the employee with the competence to do the job, which leads to job satisfaction, which in turn can improve productivity and ultimately profitability. Furthermore, positive training to develop employees rather than addressing deficiencies is key to attracting prospective employees and thus recruitment, retention, engagement and innovation (see Chapter 11, this volume).

Customer Loyalty

Customer loyalty is important to all businesses. It is the feeling of attachment for a company, the product or service, and the commitment to re-patronize that company in the future despite alternatives being available. Developing and maintaining customer loyalty, that is creating long-term relationships with customers, is key to an operator's growth and success. Loyalty can be both behavioural, that is when a consumer repurchases the same brand without considering others, and/or emotional, that is a psychological preference and an attachment to a brand. Customer loyalty is not to be confused with customer satisfaction. The latter is an indication of how well a customer's expectations have been met, whereas customer loyalty indicates how likely customers are to repurchase. Loyalty is achieved when a customer feels that the company best meets their needs in comparison with the competition to the point that they exclude other companies from their consideration.

There are many ways through which companies can encourage loyalty. According to Wirtz et al. (2012), these include:

- Managing service encounters.
- Providing customer incentives.
- Offering enhanced services to loyal customers.
- Developing pricing strategies to encourage repeat purchase, e.g. discounts.
- Maintaining up-to-date information about customer purchase history and preferences.
- Communicating with customers individually.

While marketing generally focuses on attracting new customers, it is much more cost-effective to seek to retain customers. In the highly competitive marketplace of tour operators, it is not surprising therefore to find that the emphasis of their marketing strategies has shifted from customer acquisition to customer retention; that is, gaining and keeping loyal customers. One of the most frequently used models to demonstrate customer loyalty is the Customer Loyalty Ladder, which characterizes customers in the context of loyalty (see Fig. 6.3).

This model is a simple construct suggesting that companies should convert suspects into prospects and so forth.

- Suspect: this relates to when customers have heard about the holidays from advertising or from a brochure; they may or may not be interested in the product.
- Prospect: these are suspects who have taken some form of action such as visiting the tour operator's website, subscribing to their newsletter or giving some form of information to enable the operator to contact them. They are people who may turn into customers.
- Customer: this is someone who has bought a product and therefore should be more important to the company in comparison with a prospect who has yet to buy.
- Client: once at this stage, these customers have developed a degree of trust in the company and like the products on offer. Research suggests customers who make more than two purchases are ten times more likely to purchase another one in comparison with those who purchase just one. Logically, these types of customers particularly deserve attention.
- Advocate: this is a customer who has not only purchased an operator's product but actively engages in WOM/eWOM promotion. This may be to friends and family but also includes participation in consumer review sites such as Trip Advisor, travel blogs or comments on company websites.

Several authors (see Blanchard and Bowles, 2011; Kazanjian, 2013) have suggested that there is a further rung on the loyalty ladder, the 'Partner', sometimes referred to as 'Raving Fan', which can only be attributed to 5% of customers or less. These are the most valuable customers in that they automatically choose the same tour operator for their holidays and are likely to remain loyal if the product continues to meet their expectations.

Maintaining Loyalty

Undoubtedly customer loyalty helps achieve higher profits for companies, increased employee satisfaction and greater potential growth for the company. That said, the relationship between satisfaction and loyalty is not linear because

Fig. 6.3. Customer loyalty ladder. (From Christopher *et al.*, 1991, p. 48.)

there are many influences on loyalty. Therefore, tour operators need to understand the needs of their target market and critically what influences satisfaction and loyalty. This will vary by type of product and the targeted market. For example, for operators offering premium products, the quality of the accommodation will have a high customer priority, whereas speed and efficiency may be the critical attributes for other customers.

Loyalty schemes exist and are extremely popular for many principal components of the holiday product, such as accommodation suppliers, and for many airlines who reward passengers with onboard credit, premium upgrades, VIP airport access and waived supplements. Some tour operators, such as the Australian adventure holiday company Intrepid, have recognized the value of loyal customers and introduced loyalty schemes to encourage repeat bookings. These schemes often involve discounts on subsequent purchases, and/or a discount for referrals, e.g. introducing a friend who makes a purchase. It is surprising that more, particularly the mainstream tour operators, currently do not have such loyalty schemes.

Loyalty schemes do not only exist for tourists, but also for distributors of their holiday products (B2B – Business to Business loyalty schemes). Most leading travel companies offer exclusive schemes that recognize top-performing agencies and can include black-tie events and exclusive insider training programmes that help agents stay ahead of the competition. By offering agents discounted travel, free travel and/or a points-based shopping catalogue of merchandise, gift cards and other prizes, operators (or brands) are hoping to increase agent loyalty. There are many small and medium-sized tour operators (or sub-brands) that offer loyalty schemes to travel agents to encourage agents to promote and sell their packages.

Customer Relationship Management

Developing a relationship with existing customers invariably will lead to repeat business as well as the promotion of the company through positive WOM/eWOM. Therefore, good customer service and quality, which itself is a key part of a company's strategy, is a primary objective and should not be understated. Trust and commitment are key to developing a relationship with customers, and for customers to feel committed to an organization it is likely that they will have shared values. That is, they feel the company represents their interests and they trust the company to deliver what they expect, which is primarily achieved through marketing communications.

These important facets of customer relationships develop over time and ideally lead to a long-term relationship. The maintenance of such relationships aligned with encouraging repeat purchasing will ultimately increase the **customer lifetime value** (CLV) of the customer to the business, which brings into focus **customer relationship management** (CRM) (see Fig. 6.4). This is the 'ability to identify and establish, maintain and enhance and, when necessary, terminate relationships with customers and other stakeholders, so that the objective of all parties involved are met; and that this is done by mutual exchange and fulfilment of promises' (Grönroos, 1997, p. 407).

Fig. 6.4. Customer relationship management.

CRM is integral to the marketing strategy and often part of a promotional campaign. For example, when a tourist views a tour operator's website, they may enter their email details to receive additional information and most certainly if s/he proceeds to make a reservation. The data gained can then be used to send information, newsletters or interaction via social media, about other products that are tailored to their interests.

As customers develop a relationship with the company, they usually expect some form of recognition. The introduction of CRM software and integrating this into booking systems will enable companies to track and monitor repeat customers, which could then be used to automatically reward them. Such an approach has been adopted by TUI. Their CRM system includes a comprehensive loyalty scheme facilitating the offer of free excursions, room upgrades and possibly VIP invitations for cocktail parties, most of which will be provided by their suppliers and therefore have little cost to TUI. In addition, TUI are looking to incentivize customers to book their next holiday while still on their current holiday. Cliff Hudson, the Head of CRM at TUI UK, stated that 'effective CRM is less to do with the automation of systems and more to do with the integration of customer-focused learnings so you can target your clients with a marketing message in an appropriate manner. It's not rocket science. It brings together technology, data and common sense' (Travelmole.com, 2002).

Service Recovery

A service failure is not always the fault of the tour operator or their representatives. A scheduled flight as part of a package holiday is not controlled by the tour operator and yet any unsatisfactory experience on that flight may impact on the tourist's holiday experience and their impressions of the tour operator. In fact, many of the problems that do arise are unforeseen and/or uncontrollable. But for the customer, the problem needs to be resolved and they will turn to the staff that they see regardless of where the problem originated and therefore not necessarily the service provider.

Service recovery is critical to managing customer expectations and reducing negative WOM/eWOM commentaries. Dealing with problems swiftly can prevent a small complaint becoming a larger issue and going from 'in-house' to the public domain via social media. A brief review of posts on TripAdvisor will provide sufficient evidence to see how quickly negative posts and comments can spread and how frequently comments are more about how a complaint was handled rather than the complaint itself. Therefore, it is essential that tour operators deal with problems as quickly as possible and in the process handle complaints either face-to-face or online swiftly and effectively to a positive resolution for the customer. Furthermore, the attention of EU-based tour operators to customer complaints is encompassed within the EU's Package Travel Directive (see Chapter 8, this volume), which sets out specific processes and timelines for dealing with such matters. Many tour operators employ staff to deal specifically with customer complaints; certainly, the large operators have specific departments dealing with post-holiday customer contact to enable swift resolution.

There are several key techniques for dealing with customer complaints, including:

- Respond quickly to the customer, thanking them for their contact.
- Ensure that clear procedures and timelines are provided to the customer.
- Adopt a patient and empathetic approach in all communications without

apportioning blame and accept constructive criticism where appropriate.

- Complete the appropriate research which may involve requesting reports from resort representatives, tour managers, suppliers and other third parties.
- Maintain contact with the customer and involve them in the process by updating them on a regular basis.

Many customer complaints can be dealt with *in situ*, that is while the customer is on holiday. Companies such as Thomson and First Choice empower their resort representatives to make decisions about dealing with complaints and, if appropriate, decide on the level of compensation, working within a framework when making decisions on service recovery. It is important to find out what the customer values in the service and how the company can put it right, but any form of compensation has to be proportional and appropriate, e.g. giving a guest a bottle of wine when s/he does not drink wine is hardly appropriate. Compensation can include free activity sessions or admissions to kids clubs, which do not necessarily mean an additional cost to the company yet could be very acceptable to customers and can result in positive feedback. Also noteworthy is the Thomson Travel Buddy scheme, introduced by the tour operator Thomson, which provides an online system to deal with customer queries and complaints in resorts and enables representatives to swiftly deal with queries and issues.

The speed at which problems are resolved to satisfactory outcome is becoming necessarily faster as opportunities to post social media reviews and ratings have raised the stakes, and thus the cost of a negative experience is possibly higher. Therefore, skilled service recovery in this age of hyper-media can be used to the benefit of the company as a speedy service recovery can result in positive WOM/ eWOM promotion of the company, in spite of the fact that there was a problem in the first place.

Customer Satisfaction and Profitability

Ensuring customer satisfaction is one of the key strategic goals of many organizations. This is widely recognized as being a contributory factor to performance outcomes such as profit. Basically, retaining custom and ensuring repeat purchases is cost effective because the cost of keeping a customer is substantially less than trying to attract new customers through advertising and promotion. There are several tools tour operators can use to assess customer loyalty and profitability, although many of the strategic tools include other variables such as employee satisfaction and productivity. The tools we consider here are the Service Profit Chain and the Balanced Score Card, which are frequently used for evaluating profitability and customer loyalty.

The Service Profit Chain

The Service Profit Chain (SPC) was developed in the late 1990s and assesses the sources of profitability and growth in service organizations, i.e. those service companies in which staffing is both an important component of the total cost and capable of differentiating the company service from competitors. Essentially, the SPC establishes relationships between profitability, customer loyalty and employee satisfaction, loyalty and productivity (Heskett *et al.*, 1994). The framework establishes that profit and growth are stimulated by customer loyalty, which is a direct result of customer satisfaction and this is largely influenced by the value of services provided to the customers. The value is created by satisfied, loyal and productive employees.

Employee satisfaction, in turn, results primarily from high-quality support services and strategies that enable employees to deliver results to customers (see Fig. 6.5).

The SPC implies that the main objective is to achieve customer loyalty by providing value. There are a number of techniques that can be employed to improve performance, including:

- Feedback from customers – using instruments such as those discussed in the section above on measuring service quality.
- Input from employees – feedback from front-line staff who deal directly with customers and will therefore be aware of problems that are affecting productivity, satisfaction and loyalty.
- Implementation of interventions – collecting data and identifying issues is only part of the solution; companies need to ensure that they address the issues efficiently and effectively, e.g. employee empowerment, training,

The Balanced Score Card

The Balanced Score Card (BSC) is an effective tool that can be applied by tour operators to manage and improve their performance. In effect, it is a means of translating the operator's mission into more tangible measurable goals, actions and performance measures (Kaplan and Norton, 2001). No single performance indicator can capture the complexity of an organization's performance and so the BSC helps managers to examine the business from many different perspectives based on the company's strategic objectives (see Fig. 6.6).

Technically, it is a management system rather than a measurement system because it is used to set strategic goals and objectives for an organization by providing feedback based on internal processes and external outcomes (see Evans, 2015). Based on Cooper and Hall (2008), the application of the BSC framework provides the answers to four basic questions.

- How do customers view the company? (Customer measure)
- How do owners/shareholders view the company? (Financial measure)
- What must the company do and excel in to satisfy customers? (Internal processes measure)
- How can the company continue to improve and grow? (Knowledge, education and growth measure)

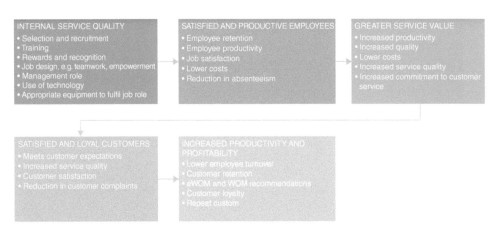

Fig. 6.5. The service profit chain. (Adapted from Heskett *et al.*, 1994.)

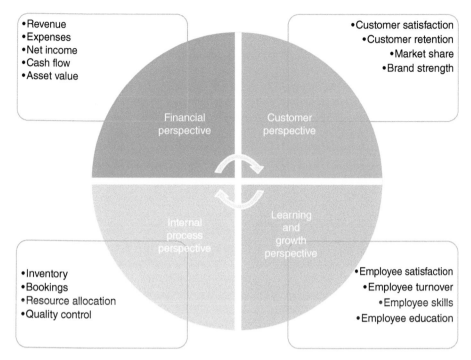

Fig. 6.6. The balanced score card.

For each of the measures, a tour operator needs to identify key objectives, stipulate how the objectives will be measured, decide on targets and identify and introduce initiatives necessary to make improvements. In addition, operators may rank the measures according to priority. For example, if the operator has identified that reducing customer complaints made to representatives in a resort is a key priority, they may look to measure results by evaluating the number, severity and sources of the complaints and introduce workforce training initiatives to reduce the complaints and empower staff to provide appropriate compensation such as free excursions or a room change. The BSC can be applied at different levels of an organization such as individual operation units, e.g. agencies, a resort, or even individuals.

Summary

There is no doubt that the quality of customer service is fundamental to the sustained success of any business. This is all the more so for tour operators whose products and related services are so often entwined with staff in the delivery process. Indeed, staff are integral to the quality of service and therefore tour operators should seek to recruit and retain staff with excellent interpersonal skills who are attentive to their personal presentation (see Chapter 11, this volume). Operators not only need to recognize these traits but also actively support and encourage them through training and personal development. Therefore, it is not surprising that the staff of those companies who realize this enjoy a comparatively high degree of employee satisfaction. But it not only affects the operator's own staff; many others may be involved in the delivery process, as illustrated in the discussion of Moments of Truth.

The quality of service clearly cannot be overstated and is fundamental to achieving customer satisfaction. This should be a keystone of the operation. How is customer satisfaction assessed? As noted, this is rather nebulous when examined in the context of package holidays in that the service provision for one group of customers, or even within the same group, potentially will vary according to previous experience and expectations of the individuals within the group. There are diverse methods to gain such feedback, most commonly through customer comment cards and questionnaires, which are increasingly being encouraged via tour operators' websites. Through such methods, the operator can assess the degree to which customers of any specific package are satisfied and in the process, identify areas for improvement and potentially opportunities for development. Customer loyalty, as discussed, is a progression of customer satisfaction and is to be encouraged because this will not only lead to positive WOM/eWOM promotion but potentially further purchases. Thus, loyalty schemes are to be encouraged. However, customer loyalty schemes, which are widely accepted as encouraging repeat business (notably so in the retail sector) are something of a conundrum within the tour operating sector. A tour operator may enjoy high levels of customer satisfaction but not gain repeat purchase because the choice of holiday was for a particular purpose or event and, as such, a 'one-off' occurrence. Even so, the importance of achieving service excellence should not be undervalued because such customers may well promote that company through WOM/eWOM. Another factor in this is that 3S-type packages invariably present choices between similar packages and prices, thus a customer may opt for a destination not served by that operator. Such factors help to account for the evident lack of customer loyalty generally in the tour operator sector. Even so, the value of loyal customers and thus potential for further purchases and positive promotion is not to be dismissed.

The attention given to customer loyalty and how to encourage this draws attention to the customer loyalty ladder and loyalty schemes designed to help maintain and develop positive, ongoing customer relationships. All of this is encouraged within the context of customer relationship management (CRM). But no matter how good a tour operator is in terms of customer service and CRM, there will be occasions when some aspect of service provision fails in some way. Tour operators therefore need to develop a service recovery strategy to ensure that such failings are dealt with efficiently and effectively without rancour, irrespective of the cause of the failing.

Overall, customer service is not just about achieving excellence in delivery and thereby very satisfied, potentially loyal customers, nor about the standing of the tour operator in comparison with competitors. It is also about sustaining the continuing success of the business, which in terms of the operator's 'bottom line' is profit.

Discussion Questions

1. Why are service encounters so important to tour operators?
2. Devise a customer service questionnaire for a tour operator of your choice. You need to identify what information is needed and the best way to measure it.
3. What is the difference between tourist satisfaction and service quality?

4. How may a tourist's nationality affect their perception of customer service and the way they may complain?

5. Undertake a mystery shopper exercise at a travel agency. What are the limitations of using a mystery shopper?

6. Is SERVQUAL a useful tool for tour operators?

7. Devise a loyalty scheme for an identified operator. What challenges do they face in trying to achieve loyalty and how may the loyalty scheme overcome such challenges?

8. How would you devise a relationship marketing strategy for an identified tour operator?

9. Is the tour operator responsible for the environmental behaviour of their customers? If an operator considers they do have some responsibility, how would you, as their tour manager, handle customers who behave in environmentally inappropriate ways?

Key Terms

- **Customer lifetime value (CLV):** A view of customer relationships that looks at the long-term cycle of customer interactions rather than single interactions.

- **Customer relationship management (CRM):** To select customers and maintain relationships with them to increase their lifetime value to the business.

- **Customer satisfaction:** The extent to which a company's business ethics matches or exceeds the expectation of the customer.

- **Importance Performance Analysis (IPA):** Technique used to measure service quality.

- **Moments of Truth:** A customer's interaction with front-line employees.

- **Service recovery:** Actions taken that result in a customer being satisfied after a service failure has occurred.

- **Total quality management:** An organization-wide process and system of ensuring that all activities carried out adhere to pre-agreed standards.

- **Value-added:** Features and benefits over and above those presented by the standard product.

- **Word-of-mouth/eword-of-mouth (WOM/eWOM):** When someone hears about a product or service from someone else/finding out about a product or service via electronic media such as email, chat lines, social media sites, bloggers.

INTERNET EXERCISE

According to the Consumers Association in the UK, the big holiday companies are not providing satisfactory service experiences for their customers. *The Telegraph* lists some of the most amusing complaints: http://www.telegraph.co.uk/travel/galleries/ridiculous-complaints-made-by-holidaymakers/

Question

- How can tour operators respond when customers make reasonable complaints?

The following scenarios are real examples of complaints received by tour operators.

Case 1

Mr and Mrs Reynolds have been on holiday to Italy, where they booked a superior room with balcony. The basic cost of the holiday was for a standard room and to get a superior room along with a balcony they had to pay a supplement. On arrival at the hotel, they were allocated a standard room without a balcony. They complained to the reception that this was the wrong room but the hotel did not have any superior rooms available for two nights. The Reynolds accepted the standard room for the first two nights as long as they were moved for the remainder of their holiday.

Once they had returned home, they contacted guest services and complained about being given the wrong room.

Questions

- What could be the guest services' response to the guests?
- How could a tour operator prepare for such eventualities?

Case 2

Dear Smartsun,

My husband and I have just been on a holiday organized by you (Smartsun) to Corfu from 1st June to 8th June. I am writing today to complain about building works going on in our hotel – the Hotel Kalimera – that meant that we were unable to relax properly whilst in our room.

You (Smartsun) had already written to us to advise of the building works as follows:

'We have been advised by the management team that the hotel will undergo some renovation works between 14th May and 2nd June on some of the hotel rooms. We have been advised that noise and visual disruption will be kept to a minimum and no facilities at the Hotel Kalimera have been affected. Hotel management have confirmed rooms will be allocated away from the work.'

As we were arriving on 1st June we felt that one day of possible disruption would be acceptable. What we found was that the workmen were conducting building works throughout our stay on the floor above our room. They [the workmen] arrived at around 7am and left at 7pm. During that time, there was drilling, banging and shouting – all of which we could hear only too well given that they were on the floor above and not away from the work at all. Whilst not consistent throughout the day, it meant that such things as relaxing or reading or even an afternoon nap would be interrupted.

The building works over-ran and continue to over-run the date you (Smartsun) gave us – we had not been advised of this before we went. We consider the nature and long hours of building works in the floor above us as unacceptable in a hotel and certainly not minimal disruption. For these reasons we expect to receive compensation for having to holiday in a hotel where the management clearly had no regard for their guests.

I look forward to hearing from you.

Continued

Case Studies. Continued.

> **Questions**
>
> - How should the tour operator respond?
> - Should the tour operator consider compensating the guests? If so, what would the compensation be based on?
> - What could the representative of the company based in the resort do to resolve the problem at the time?

Case 3

Dear Sir/Madam,

I have just returned from my holiday in India and whilst I had a great time once I got there, the flight was delayed which meant that I missed out on the first day of my holiday and my overnight hotel. It was really annoying as no-one told us what time the flight would leave, we didn't get refreshments, and when we did get to our destination, we were expected to have a quick freshen up then go on a sightseeing tour. I was too tired to enjoy this and missed out on the first proper day in India. I believe that you should be giving me back the cost of the hotel as I didn't use it.

> **Question**
>
> - What would be the response from the tour operator?

Case 4

Mr and Mrs Kumar and their two children booked a skiing trip to Austria. When they got to their hotel the rooms they were given were not adjoining. They had specifically requested rooms together as the children were quite young and adjoining rooms had been confirmed. The hotel insisted that they had not received this request from the tour operator and there were no other rooms available. They contacted their resort representative to explain the situation and their unhappiness with the situation.

The resort rep did have confirmation that the adjoining room had been requested but the hotel said they didn't have any rooms like this currently available. Although the rooms given to Mr and Mrs Kumar were close, they were not adjoining. The Kumars reluctantly accepted the rooms but said they would be contacting the tour operator once they got home as they were very disappointed.

> **Questions**
>
> - Who is responsible for the failure to provide adjoining rooms?
> - Should the tour operator provide compensation?

Recommended Reading

The following article is particularly interesting because it not only explores the measurement and importance of service quality but considers this in the context of dive tourism experiences:

O'Neill, M., Williams, P., MacCarthy, M. and Groves, R. (2000) Diving into service quality – the dive tour operator perspective.

Managing Service Quality: An International Journal 10(3), 131–140.

For an illustration of using the Balance Score Card for assessing tour guide performance:

Huang, L. and Kao, P.-H. (2011) How to tell a good tour guide under different strategic orientations. *African Journal of Business Management* 5(27).

For a study identifying five of the most important service quality factors among seniors from Taiwan and China:

Wang, K.-C., Ma, A.-P., Hsu, M.-T., Jao, P.-C. and Lin, C.-W. (2013) Seniors' perceptions of service features on outbound group package tours. *Journal of Business Research* 66, 1021–1027.

A very interesting overview of the difficulties involved in managing tour groups for a tour leader and an operator:

Bowie, D. and Chang, J.C. (2005) Tourist satisfaction: a view from a mixed international guided package tour. *Journal of Vacation Marketing* 11, 303–322.

References

Baum, T. (2002) Making or breaking the tourist experience: the role of human resource management. In: Ryan, C. (ed.) *The Tourist Experience.* Continuum, London, pp. 94–111.

Berry, L. and Parasuraman, A. (1991) *Marketing Services.* The Free Press, New York.

Berry, L., Parasuraman, A. and Zeithaml, V. (1988) The service-quality puzzle. *Business Horizons* 31, 35–43.

Blanchard, K. and Bowles, S. (2011) *Raving Fans: A Revolutionary Approach to Customer Service.* Harper, New York.

Brunner, T.A., Stocklin, M. and Opwis, K. (2008) Satisfaction, image and loyalty: new versus experienced customers. *European Journal of Marketing* 42, 1095–1105.

Buttle, F. (1996) SERVQUAL: review, critique, research agenda. *European Journal of Marketing* 30, 8–32.

Carlzon, J. (2001) *Moment of Truth.* Ballinger, Cambridge, Massachusetts.

Chen, J., Stanis, S., Barbieri, C. and Xu, S. (2012) An application of Importance-Performance analysis to recreational storm chasing. In: Fisher, C.L. and Watts, C.E. (eds.) *Proceedings of the 2010 North-Eastern Recreation Research Symposium.* US Forest Service, Newtown Square, Pennsylvania, pp. 45–51.

Chen, W.-Y. and Hsu, C.-Y. (2012) Assessing travel business partners using the critical incident technique and the analytic hierarchy process. *Tourism Economics* 18, 295–310.

Cheyne, J., Downes, M. and Legg, S. (2006) Travel agent internet: what influences travel consumer choices? *Journal of Vacation Marketing* 12, 41–57.

Christopher, M., Payne, A. and Ballantyne, D. (1991) *Relationship Marketing.* Butterworth Heinemann, Oxford, UK.

Cooper, C. and Hall, C.M. (2008) *Contemporary Tourism: An International Approach.* Butterworth Heinemann, Oxford, UK.

Cronin, J.J. and Taylor, S.A. (1992) Measuring service quality: a re-examination and extension. *Journal of Marketing* 56, 33–55.

Evans, N. (2015) *Strategic Management for Tourism, Hospitality and Events,* 2nd edn. Routledge, Abingdon, UK.

Foster, C. (2014) Customer satisfaction in tourism. The search for the holy grail. In: McCabe, S.S. (ed.) *The Routledge Handbook of Tourism Marketing.* Routledge, Abingdon, UK, pp. 165–178.

Grönroos, C. (1997) Value driven relationship marketing. *Journal of Marketing Management* 13, 407–520.

Heskett, J.L., Jones, T.O., Loveman, G.W., Sasser, W.E. Jr and Schlesinger, L.A. (1994) Putting the service-profit chain to work. *Harvard Business Review* 72, 164–174.

Hudson, S. and Shephard, G. (1998) Measuring service quality at tourist destinations: an application of importance-performance analysis to an Alpine ski resort. *Journal of Travel and Tourism Marketing* 7, 61–77.

Hudson, S., Hudson, P. and Miller, G. (2004) The measurement of service quality in the tour operating sector: a methodological comparison. *Journal of Travel Research* 42, 305–312.

Kandampully, J. (2006) The new customer-centred business model for the hospitality industry. *International Journal of Contemporary Hospitality Management* 18, 173–187.

Kaplan, R.S. and Norton, D.P. (2001) Transforming the Balanced Scorecard from performance measurement to strategic management: part I. *Accounting Horizons* 15, 87–104.

Kazanjian, K. (2013) *Driving Loyalty: Turning Every Customer and Employee into a Raving Fan for Your Brand*. Crown, New York.

Kotler, P., Keller, K., Brady, M., Goodman, M. and Hansen, T. (2009) *Marketing Management*. Pearson Education, Harlow, UK.

Lucas, R.W. (2014) *Customer Service Skills for Success*, 6th edn. McGraw-Hill Education, New York.

Martilla, J.A. and James, J.C. (1977) Importance-performance analysis. *Journal of Marketing* 41, 77–79.

Matzler, K. and Sauerwein, E. (2002) The factor structure of customer satisfaction: an empirical test of the importance grid. *International Journal of Service Industry Management* 13, 314–332.

McCarthy, D. (1997) *The Loyalty Link. How Loyal Employees Create Loyal Customers*. John Wiley & Sons, New York.

Mill, R.C. (2002) A comprehensive model of customer satisfaction in hospitality and tourism: strategic implications for management. *International Business and Economics Research Journal* 1, 7–18.

Parasuraman, A., Zeithmal, V.A. and Berry, L.L. (1985) A conceptual model of service quality and its implications for future research. *Journal of Marketing* 49, 41–50.

Pearce, P. (2005) *Tourist Behaviour: Themes and Conceptual Schemes*. Channel View, Bristol, UK.

Ryan, C. (2002) *The Tourist Experience*. Continuum, London.

Swarbrooke, J. and Horner, S. (2016) *Consumer Behaviour in Tourism*, 3rd edn. Routledge, Abingdon, UK.

Travelmole.com (2002) CRM in the Travel Industry. Available at: Travelmole.com: http://www.travelmole.com/news_feature.php?id=84833, accessed 7 December 2016.

Voss, C.A., Roth, A., Rosenzweig, E.D., Blackmon, K. and Chase, R.B. (2004) A tale of two countries' conservatism, service quality, and feedback on customer satisfaction. *Journal of Service Research* 6, 212–230.

Wirtz, J., Chew, P. and Lovelock, C. (2012) *Essentials of Services Marketing*, 2nd edn. Pearson, Singapore.

7 Financial Planning: Pricing the Package

Learning Objectives

After studying this chapter, you should be able to:

- Understand the importance and role of costing and pricing in achieving the overall objectives of the operating company.
- Appreciate the major financial issues involved in costing packages.
- Appreciate the relationship between costing and pricing.
- Understand the different pricing techniques used by organizations.

Introduction

This chapter provides an overview of financial considerations pertinent to tour operators and their impact on pricing. A good understanding of financial management and accounting is essential for tour operators; however, it is not within the remit of this chapter to go into the fundamentals of accounting practices and performance measurements. This is better dealt with through the study of accounting and finance textbooks such as Kotas (2010) or Harris and Mongiello (2012). Further, it should be noted that it is difficult to obtain accurate and current financial information about tour operators due to confidentiality in this highly competitive sector.

Fundamental to a tour operator's financial performance is that of establishing the right price for their package holidays and managing the revenues effectively in order to achieve the required profit margin and thereby sustain the business. This is not as simple as might first be considered; for example, deposits and the outstanding balance for the holiday package are paid in advance, while payment of the principals involved is often towards the end of that package holiday season. This necessitates good cash-flow management. Further, operators invariably have to deal in more than one currency and thus currency exchange rates can have a significant influence on the net profit margin. While these factors all require careful financial management, there is then a further factor to take into account, particularly in the mass market sphere of operations, that of the prices of competitors in the same market. The pricing of an inclusive holiday is therefore complex because it needs to be competitive and profitable (see Chapters 4 and 5, this volume).

For tour operators, the price that is charged for the holiday is the main source of income; indeed it is the only element of the marketing mix that generates turnover for a company and therefore needs to attract the customer as well as provide sufficient profit for the company. For customers, the purchase of a holiday package is framed by considerations such as disposable income, evaluation of alternatives, family situation and other constraints, but the price is a critical element in decision-making. As customers purchase their holidays in advance, the price of the holiday product acts as a signal of the quality and accessibility.

In addition to the price charged, the package must be attractive to the customer and must offer benefits that make it more attractive to them than the possibility of purchasing the individual components separately. To establish the price involves a complex process of planning, which needs to take into account:

- Company objectives and positioning strategies, e.g. increase market share, increase profitability (see Chapter 3, this volume).
- The fixed and variable costs of operating the company.
- Operational costs, i.e. the cost of distribution and commissions; also price variation according to season and capacity.
- Cash management and **cash flow**.
- Strategic pricing decisions.

In order to understand how operators price their products, it is essential to develop a good understanding of the costs involved in producing a package. In Chapters 4 and 5 (this volume), the illustrated packages were costed by including a **mark-up**, i.e. a percentage added to the cost of the product which will cover the costs of operating the business.

This chapter will examine those principal costs in greater detail.

Operating Costs

Before operators can determine the price for their products, they need to consider the costs of operating as a business, their expected profit margin and the costs associated with distributing their products. Chapters 4 and 5 (this volume) illustrate the complexities of costing products due to the number of components included in packages. The profit margin is then added to the actual costs of the offering. In addition to costing the individual components of a package, operators must also include contributions to the company's fixed and variable costs incurred when operating, selling and fulfilling the bookings. The actual profit made by operators is affected by the cost of running the company, termed operating costs. These costs include the following and are illustrated in Fig. 7.1:

- Fixed costs. Fixed costs do not vary; they stay the same no matter how many passengers the company carries. These include annual business costs

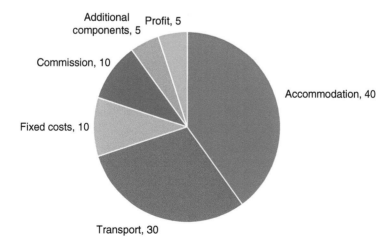

Fig. 7.1. Average tour operator cost (%) breakdown (mass market product)

such as advertising and marketing, loans and repayment, energy suppliers, equipment lease and hire, insurance, bank charges, membership of professional organizations, licences, rent or mortgage, stationery and office supplies, wages and salaries, vehicles.

- Variable costs. These are costs that vary according to how much business is achieved, e.g. sales. The variable costs of holidays include tickets on scheduled services, *ad hoc* accommodation bookings, temporary and casual staff, trade events, familiarization trips for agents. These costs vary with the number of passengers because they only have to be paid for the people who actually travel.

As Fig. 7.1 illustrates, in this example profit is minimal due to the competitive environment for mass market products. The higher the operator's costs, the more expensive the prices will need to be to cover those costs. Clearly, these percentages will change depending on the type of tour operator and package on offer, the country of origin and destination.

Operational Costs

While tour operators can price packages competitively, there are a number of additional costs that need to be included when determining the package price.

- Air Tax: many governments impose a tax on all passengers flying out of the country. In the UK, this is called Air Passenger Duty and is considered to be the highest passenger tax levied anywhere in the world (WTTC, 2017). Other taxes include departure tax, landing fees, fuel surcharges and additional accommodation taxes.
- Charges: airport departure and landing fees.

Load Factor

Operators do not assume that all seats on aeroplanes or accommodation packages will be sold. If they did not allow for a shortfall, then given the generally low profit margins involved they would make a loss. Therefore they base the price of a package on less than 100% capacity. They thus work to a load factor, which is the percentage of flight seats they expect will sell, as a charter aircraft has to be paid in full regardless of how many seats are sold. For example, a flight costing £5000 has 100 seats available; the operator assumes a load factor of 90%, i.e. that 90 seats will be sold. Therefore, the cost per seat would be 5000/90 = £55.56 per seat. If a low load factor of 80% was adopted, then the price per seat would rise to £62.50. Operators wishing to keep prices down therefore work on high load factors, i.e. high forecasted sales, but this obviously presents a risk if the target sales are not achieved and the costs may not be covered. Conversely, operators who work on low load factors have higher prices and this can be detrimental to sales because customers in some markets are price sensitive. Operators who sell more holidays than they forecast will therefore realize higher profits. Overall, profit margins need to be realistic and prices appropriate for the target market, taking into consideration the prices of competitors.

The tour operating industry is a very low net profit business for mass market operators, with suggested net profit margins of 1–2%, with net profit of 4–5% being considered exceptional for mass market products (Cavlek, 2006), margins that would be considered unacceptable in other industries (Fitch, 1987). Profit margins for specialist and niche tour operators may be considerably higher, because customers will usually pay a premium for these products.

Empty Leg

When chartering planes, either part or full charter, operators need to factor in additional costs such as 'empty legs'. For example, when operating the first package departure of the season, a plane will be loaded with passengers from the source market and fly to the destination, but as there are no passengers to collect in the destination the plane will return empty. At the end of the season, the licensed return flight will involve an empty leg flying out to the destination but will return with the last package holiday makers. This will affect the costing of the flight element of the package, as demonstrated in Box 7.1.

The smaller specialist tour operators usually cost the basic elements of the holiday and then add a mark-up of 20–35% to cover fixed costs, travel agents' commission and profit. The larger mass market tour operators are more conscious of the prices of their competitors and introduce a pricing strategy. This could mean that holidays in the low season are offered at the breakeven point where no actual profit is made, while during the peak season prices are inflated to cover fixed costs, agents' commission and profit. Selling without profit is regarded as better than not selling at all, especially if the tour operator owns the airlines and hotels involved. However, reducing prices to a bare minimum can be a risky business. Imagine a situation where the tour operator has overestimated the number of holidays they will sell in a year, and as a consequence they contract to buy more than they need. If they have costed their holiday at the cheapest possible price, there is no margin to offer holidays at a discount if they do not sell. This happened to International Leisure Group in 1992 and led to their collapse.

Box 7.1. Exemplification of costing a charter flight seat.

A tour operator contracts a flight series for a 130-seater Boeing 737 every Thursday at a cost of £15,000 per return flight.

$$29 \times £15,000 = £435,000$$

Their season covers 28 weeks, which gives a total of 29 return flights:
The first return flight to the destination will return empty (as no passengers to bring back) and the last return flight of the season will be empty on the outbound flight and will return with passengers.

So effectively there will be 28 return flights as a source of income.

The total cost of a return flight with passengers is:

$$£435,000 \div 28 = £15,536$$

The aircraft holds 130 passengers, but a load factor of 90% would assume only 90% of 130 passengers would actually fly:

$$130 \times 90 = 11,700 \div 100 = 117$$

Therefore 117 passengers are expected to cover the cost of the flight.

The cost per person will be:

$$£15,536 \div 117 = £132.78$$

If more than 117 people book, then the extra fares are clear profit for the company. If less than 117 people book, then no profit, and even a deficit situation may occur. In this case, a decision may be made to consolidate flights and ask clients to fly at another time or from another airport.

Distribution Costs

The distribution of the packages is how the products are made available to the customer (this is considered in depth in Chapter 9, this volume). The utilization of intermediaries such as travel agents is a cost because it is usual practice to provide commission. Essentially, if there is no commission at an acceptable rate, then it is unlikely that the intermediaries will distribute or promote your product.

Sales agent commission (e.g. travel agent, telesales, online travel agent)

Tour operators pay agents commission to encourage sales. Travel agents' commission can be examined from two perspectives: the 10% the travel agent receives (which is fairly standard) or the 10% the tour operator pays, which is illustrated as follows:

A travel agent usually receives 10% of the selling price:

Holiday price (£)	Commission earned (£)	Amount due to tour operator
652.00	65.20	586.80
724.00	72.40	651.60

The tour operator pays 10% commission:

Net revenue required (£)	Agent's commission (£)	Holiday price (nearest £)
139.23	15.47	154.70 (155.00)
245.17	28.24	273.41 (274.00)

If the travel agent is to receive 10% of the final selling price, this means that the tour operator must add another one ninth (or 11.1%) to the actual cost of the holiday (before fixed costs are added). This is a rather simplistic view of commissions, because commission is often paid based on sales (see Chapter 9, this volume). Some tour operators introduce a tiered commission level, whereby the commission paid to the agent increases proportionally to an increase in sales; this may be counted on an income revenue basis or as a passenger count. Agents working as part of a consortium will be able to consolidate all sales figures and achieve higher commission levels.

The payment of commission may be based on **net rate** (price minus taxes) or **gross rate** (including taxes). It is usual for cruise liners to adopt a net rate as the selling price for a package includes substantial taxes. This is referred to as non-commissionable fees. Commission may also vary according to how the booking was made with the agent, the destination (some destinations have different commission levels) and whether price matching was involved, which will result in a lower commission level. The cost of commission must be factored into the overall published price, as shown in Box 7.2.

If operators choose to distribute their product directly to the customer, many operators reward their sales staff with commissions (although this is not at the same rate as those paid to agents) to motivate and incentivize staff. In some companies commissions are not paid on the basic package that is being sold, but will be paid for '**up-selling**', for example encouraging the customer to purchase additional excursions, private transfers or a room upgrade.

Seasonality

One of the most common ways of setting price differentials is to use seasonal banding. In high season, prices may be more expensive than low season. Using the example above, the operator may:

- sell the holiday at this price of £399.00 in low season, knowing that immediate costs would be covered;

Box 7.2. Illustration of impact of commission on costing a tour [VAT excluded]

The transport cost per person for the flight	£210.00
Assume the hotel cost per person per week	£90.00
Transfers	£17.00
Cost per person	£317.00

This £317.00 is required to cover the client's actual costs and now the operator must calculate a price at which fixed costs and travel agent's commission can also be covered. If the fixed costs are generally marked up at 9%, and the travel agent's commission at 10%, then the final price is known as the break-even point.

Costs per person	£317.00
Travel agent's commission	£35.22
Mark-up for fixed costs	£31.69
Final break-even cost	£383.92

The tour operator could then round up the selling price to £399.00, which could be charged throughout the season. Large tour operators usually cover the cost of travel agent's commission and then adjust the price according to the season.

- raise the price to £499.00 in high season and £449.00 in the shoulder season.

The clients who travel in the high or shoulder seasons are in effect paying towards the fixed costs and profits for the whole year. This is a very simple example, but it should illustrate the reasoning that could go into producing a price grid which varies throughout the season. When investigating pricing per season, you will note that some of the cheapest prices are in the early weeks of the season, and the most expensive over holiday periods such as Christmas and New Year or school holidays. This is because the operator knows there will be sufficient people looking for holidays in peak times and can increase the prices without fear of losing custom.

Depending on the type of contract made with suppliers, there may be different prices paid for the components depending on the season. For example, hotels may charge more during high season and that additional cost is transferred to the price of the holiday. Alternatively, if the operator has commitment contracts, then the price of the components, e.g. a hotel room, may not fluctuate as a set agreed price has been contracted. If a tour operator chooses to increase the price during high season, it is not obvious whether their suppliers have also increased prices or whether the tour operator is taking advantage of supply and demand.

Forecasting and Capacity Management

Accurate forecasting of costs and sales is critical. The first step is to forecast the number of packages that can be supplied and ensure that there is sufficient demand. This is problematic and high risk, as evidenced by the fate of the International Leisure Group (ILG) (Box 7.3).

As this case illustrates, the forecasting of demand and subsequent pricing of holidays is critical to the success of any holiday company. These anticipated sales are determined by historic booking patterns and research in order to predict capacity. As companies frequently plan the number of holidays on offer months, if not years, in advance, it is important that they continually monitor demand to avoid being left with unsold stock. Further complicating the situation is that customers are becoming increasingly price conscious and will spend time comparing prices and products prior to purchase. Since the early 1990s, customers now anticipate the tactical discounting practices (Hoeseason and Johns, 1998), resulting in a shift in purchasing patterns. Rather than book early, often with 6–8 months lead time, customers are purchasing packages much closer to departure.

Operators have introduced several interventions to help manage cash flow and maximize revenue. The introduction of **yield management** is one of those interventions, replicating other sectors of the travel and tourism sector. Yield management can be defined as 'the optimization of revenue through differentiation of prices' (Dwyer and Forsyth, 2006, p. 169); the term 'revenue management' is often used interchangeably and is perhaps a more accurate description. Yield management involves the implementation of a variable pricing strategy that anticipates customer behaviour during different time periods and aims to increase the net yield or profit through predicting capacity and purchases to previously identified market segments at an optimum price. Essentially, a very basic yield management system has historically been used by the tour operating sector: reduced prices in off-season when demand is low and high prices in high season when demand is greater. For tour operators, yield management is more complex than accommodation and airline sales because it is multidimensional, meaning that it involves not only flights but could involve a number of hotels, each with different contracting arrangements. The adoption of yield management systems enables operators to change prices based on demand in an attempt to try to overcome late booking, unsold capacity and achieve the best price for each product; this is illustrated in the following examples.

Mass market tour operators

Mass market tour operators do not expect to sell all of their products at brochure price. The mass market tour operating sector frequently uses price fluctuations, and the market is used to such changes, particularly since the price wars and late deals offered in the early 1990s. There are three different strategies that can be adopted.

1. The price increases as the departure date comes closer. This is not a strategy that is used by most mass market operators because there is wide competition and alternatives available. Last-minute bookers would be looking for discounts, while early bookers are usually price sensitive.

2. Decrease prices closer to departure date. This tactic was used in the 1990s and creates an expectation from customers that the later they book, the cheaper the holiday will be. This will affect tour operators' cash flow and sales predictions for the destination.

3. Prices are optimized every day based on sales, available capacity and market conditions. With this option there is no expectation from the customer as to when the price will be best, and this allows flexibility in pricing. This is best obtained by using a computerized yield management system.

The first stage of implementing yield management systems is to align the price with the peaks and troughs in demand, i.e. seasonality. A more complex yield management system is a lead time differentiation, where prices are set in incremental stages and operators would allow a predefined number of holidays to be sold at each price. The stages are set through the analysis of historical bookings and review of sales lead times, in addition to the strategic objectives of the company: for example, if the operator wishes to move large numbers of bookings earlier or later in the season, price positioning, online sales and competitive pricing. Incentivizing early sales in addition to low prices may include free child places, free insurance and additional free nights.

Specialist tour operators

Specialist tour operators, particularly those where tourists spend time as a group, are less likely to use dynamic pricing and yield management because they need to ensure the passengers paid similar prices to avoid dissatisfaction of the customer. Some markets may be resistant to fluid or dynamic pricing and expect the price published in the brochure or online to be the price paid. Rather than adopting a fluid pricing structure, specialists are more likely to increase capacity with the price remaining the same. For example, using the adventure itinerary presented in Chapter 5 (this volume), the tour can be run as planned, and in addition the itinerary can be reversed. This will double capacity and not impact on the tourist experience or reduce prices.

Bonds, Insurance and Membership Fees

Within the UK, all tour operators offering a flight inclusive package need to purchase an Air Tour Operators Licence (ATOL) (see Chapter 8, this volume). As ATOL is concerned with the flight, this protection also covers flight-only bookings as well as packages. It is a financial protection scheme and each holder has a unique identifiable number, which enables customers to check that the claim of a licence is bona fide. Each operator must contribute to a protection fund called the Air Travel Trust. In 2017 the fee was £2.50 for every passenger booking an air inclusive package.

The European Package Travel Regulations (PTR) requires European tour operators to be able to provide sufficient evidence of security of monies in case of refund or the need to repatriate the customer. There are three main ways in which operators can provide financial protection to customers:

- Insurance.
- Bonding through organizations such as ABTA, CPT and ABTOT.
- Trust Account.

Operators offering coach holidays can join the Bonded Coach Holidays organization, which requires members to provide a bond from a bank or major insurance company. The bond is used to refund money to customers should the company cease trading. For operators offering cruise holidays including air transfers to the departure port, then an ATOL licence is needed. In addition, a UK tour operator that markets or sells financial products such as insurance will come under the scrutiny of the Financial Conduct Authority, although many tour operators forward details to a company licensed to sell financial services or become an appointed representative of an approved company.

Cash Management and Cash Flow

Cash management is concerned with investing the cash surpluses and financing of cash shortages. Tour operators usually receive full cash payment in advance of the product being enjoyed. Further, operators usually pay suppliers at the end of the season, which is different from general goods that are produced before they can be sold. The management of the cash flow within a company is critical and poor financial management has been the downfall for many companies.

Tour operators' products are usually highly seasonal, affected not only by climate and the destination but also school holidays, festivals and historic travel patterns. This leads to highly seasonal patterns of cash inflows and outflows. Generally, the majority of bookings occur between February and May, while August–October is when they need to make payments to suppliers. As a result, companies have periods when they have large surpluses, while at other times there may only be a small amount of money available to pay suppliers or invest. This seasonality means that tour operators need to manage their funds carefully. In some cases operators may need to borrow from banks to meet their cash requirements over short-term periods.

The long investment cycles from the time it takes to develop the tour product to bringing it to market can be an expensive process involving brochure production, down payments on contracts and marketing. The risk is also increased because the operators need to set their prices at least a year in advance.

Additional Sources of Income

In addition to profit mark-up, tour operators can also raise income from other sources.

Interest

Interest can be earned on customers' monies because they pay a deposit in advance of the full balance of the cost of the holiday, although the current trend for late booking has perhaps reduced the importance of interest on deposits. Full payment of the balance happens in advance of the holiday, but operators tend not to pay the principals until the end of the season, which means that the money is available for short-term investment.

Cancellation and amendment costs

Tour operators usually charge customers if they cancel their holidays. There is no sector-wide charge and each operator will be able to fix their own charges, with some operators charging up to 100% cancellation fees, although there is usually a sliding scale based on the date of cancellation and the date of departure. Operators defend their right for high cancellation charges due to the intangibility of the product and the risks incurred over the whole season. This is a particularly important reason why customers may take out insurance cover through the tour operator, travel agent or independently. A similar situation occurs when customers wish to make amendments to their booking, although it is more usual to have a fixed fee, which varies according to type of package and requirement, e.g. name change or departure date change. Both cancellation and amendment charges must be detailed in the booking conditions.

Commission on car hire or insurance

Operators may earn commission for services sold to customers in the resort, e.g. car hire. Vehicle rental companies often give commission to the resort representative and the tour operator.

Excursions or ancillary products

Selling excursions operated by a local ground handling agent or other agent will also provide a source of income for both the operator and resort representative.

Currency Considerations

For tour operators working internationally, the impact of exchange rates (FOREX) has a substantial impact on their finances. Large tour operators are exposed to substantial risks associated with foreign exchange transactions and this exposure may be far greater than for other industries.

This lack of stability increases the risk for tour operators due to the uncertainty of predicting future exchange rates. If it were possible to predict future exchange rates, pricing holiday packages would be relatively simple! Such exposure to exchange rate movements needs to be managed carefully and monitored, both in terms of the value of payments made in foreign currencies and payments made to suppliers. For example, a UK-based tour operator may:

- Receive payment for the holidays in GBP.
- Pay for accommodation in Euros and other currencies.
- Pay for fuel and policing of aircraft in US dollars.
- Pay staff in local currency.

The impact of a significant rate change can be illustrated by a simple example:

In 2016, £1.00 = €1.1975. For a company purchasing 100 rooms at €30 per night for seven nights, the total cost to the company in GBP would be £17,536.53.

In 2017, £1.00 = €1.116. For a company purchasing 100 rooms at €30 per night for seven nights, the total cost to the company in GBP would be £18,817.20, an additional £1280.67 or £12.81 per room or £1.83 per night.

While this may appear to be a small amount, increases and decreases caused by exchange rate fluctuations can have an enormous impact, particularly for companies selling millions of holidays a year at low profit margins.

Substantial payments are usually made in a hard currency, such as US dollar, euro, yen and British pound. These currencies are internationally acceptable and freely converted and exchanged without restriction. Conversely, soft currencies, such as the Sri Lankan rupee or the Moroccan dirham, are those that are not freely convertible and may have limitations on exchange outside the country of issue. The impact of exchange rate fluctuations means that companies may need to increase the prices of their holidays, but it is unlikely that companies will pass on short-term additional costs to customers because this will have a negative impact on the company's reputation and the long-term result may be losing custom. Furthermore, many tour operators stipulate that there they offer 'no surcharge guarantees', which means that increased costs due to adverse foreign exchange rates cannot be passed on to the customer. Tour operators in the UK that are members of ABTA and European tour operators through the EU Package Travel Directive are required to absorb up to 2% increase in the cost of the holiday. The Directive stipulates that a maximum of 10% can be added, so effectively increases between 2% and 10% may be passed on to the customer. If there are any additional costs above 10%, then the passenger has the right to cancel the holiday and receive a full refund (see Chapter 8, this volume). However, it should be noted that these surcharges are not the same as price rises; tour operators have the right to increase prices that may be imposed on customers after they have paid deposits.

When countries are affected by an increase in exchange rate, this will force up the price of the holiday and as a result operators may look to remove holidays offered in that destination and substitute them with a destination where the exchange rate is more beneficial.

There are a number of ways in which tour operators can attempt to manage the risks of exchange rate fluctuations, and these include methods such as netting and forward currency buying.

Netting

Netting is a management technique used by larger companies to manage performance as an opportunity to yield significant savings. Essentially, netting uses local income in the local currency to make payments to local suppliers. For example, a multinational company such as TUI can develop an American sales subsidiary, and use customer payments in US dollars to pay suppliers in US dollars, thus avoiding exchange rate fluctuations.

Forward currency buying (forward contracts)

Tour operators by their very nature tend to be international and for that reason are subject to these exchange rate fluctuations, but there are a number of options available to help predict and manage such fluctuations. Purchasing currency strategically uses a 'forward contract' or a 'stop loss' order; forward contracts are future purchases of the currency at the exchange rate on the day agreed, but the purchaser does not receive the currency immediately. Such agreements usually last up to two years. This generally involves a payment of approximately 10%, and the balance on receipt of the currency, which should protect operators from adverse currency movements because they can lock into a favourable exchange rate. Forward currency buying is particularly useful for tour operators in order to maintain their prices offered because the brochures, which include prices, are typically produced a year or more in advance.

A stop loss contract specifies the maximum rate at which the currency should be bought or sold. When the agreed exchange rate is achieved, the order for the currency is fulfilled, which effectively guarantees a minimum rate at which the currency will be exchanged. A stop loss contract can be agreed in conjunction with a limit order, which sets a higher target exchange rate. By running both the limit order and the stop loss order together, the exchange rate is guaranteed within a given range, giving the tour operator predictable exchange rates.

These are usually only useful to the large tour operators because substantial amounts of monies are needed to make these beneficial.

Pricing Factors

In addition to the actual cost of producing and distributing the package, there are several other factors that need to be taken into consideration when pricing the offering, including:

- Competition – the prices charged by competitors.
- Demand – products offered by multinational corporations such as TUI will have different prices in different marketplaces. People will pay more if there is high demand for a destination, similarly people will pay less if there is abundance of choice.
- Target market – the willingness of the target market to pay the proposed price.
- Seasonality – supply and demand; low demand in low season and higher demand in high season.

Large operators try to dominate the marketplace by increasing their market share and this may be implemented at the expense of profits by attracting competitors' customers. Smaller companies in general do not have the luxury of being able to reduce prices to increase market share and therefore their products appear more expensive, so to justify the higher prices the products must be unique or specialist. Whether a large or small operator, package prices are nearly always quoted per person based on two people sharing a twin room. Effectively, each person pays for their own flight and transfer plus half the cost of the room. If one person travels alone, then s/he must pay the full cost of the room. Usually, single rooms are more than half the price of a double.

Company Pricing Strategies

Pricing strategies can be developed for a company based on the products offered and the target market and also on the status of the brand in terms of product life cycle and the strategy of the company, for example to gain market share. Each company needs to assess their position in the marketplace and design a pricing strategy appropriate for the market. Pricing strategies are informed by the company's mission statement and objectives. In essence, what does the company want to be and where do they want to position themselves in the marketplace? A company wishing to be one of the biggest operators in the region may choose a low price strategy, whereby their product is sold with minimal profit with the aim of selling high volume. Conversely, a company may wish to remain specialist and concentrate on limited sales but with high profit margins. When devising a pricing strategy, the company needs to reflect the product offering, market share, competition and experience. For example, a company that has a unique product offering with consistent levels of demand in the sector with limited competition would be in a position to charge more for their products. In addition, a company that considers their service levels superior to their competitors can charge premium prices. Conversely, a new company or a company offering a new product may be keen to attract new customers in order to establish the brand and thus may set pricing at a lower rate initially to create demand, as the average customer usually prefers to buy package tours from known branded operators.

Pricing Tactics

Cost plus pricing (marginal pricing)

Perhaps the simplest way of costing a product is to add the costs of the components for each holiday and add on a percentage profit. In the 1990s, First Choice adopted a cost-plus approach to increase market share in specific resorts and achieve an overall price advantage. However, the tour operating sector is now much more complicated and pricing strategies such as these are no longer suitable. Cost plus pricing takes no account of the value of the product perceived by the customer. A low price for a premium product would give the wrong message to the customer. Essentially costs are about production, but prices are about value and this may be considered in three ways.

1. Market based pricing. This is based on what the market will pay and then working backwards. It is an exceptionally delicate and complex approach because it involves estimating prices that the competition will charge.
2. Premium pricing. This is used for niche market products with upmarket images where high prices are expected to be paid, but these must be supported with excellent service.
3. Promotional pricing. This is similar to discount pricing, but rather than offering low prices towards departure dates, promotional pricing is offered to people who purchase holidays in advance and provides an incentive for customers to book early. The benefit of booking early for tour operators is that booking trends and popular destinations become evident, which enables operators to react; for example, if a destination is proving unpopular they may look to introduce promotional activities to stimulate demand. It should be noted that if promotional strategies are employed, it is likely that competitors will copy them and therefore they may lose their effectiveness. If this strategy of promotional pricing does not work, then it may be a waste of resources because the company could have invested in a longer, higher impact marketing strategy.

Fluid pricing

Fluid prices means that agents are supplied with on-screen prices that can change by the hour, depending on how well holidays are selling. This is similar to the stock market, but it allows agents and operators to adjust prices depending on availability and demand. Some tour operators' brochures note that prices may increase or decrease occasionally using the term 'flight supplements', but concerns have been raised about operators using this approach. Fluid pricing makes it difficult for operators to provide prices in brochures and therefore supports their redundancy.

Discount pricing

Sometimes referred to as last-minute/late-booking pricing. This has been a common method used by package holiday operators to fill availability in inventory. It is better to make some sales than to be left with empty transportation seats and accommodation. Discount pricing does come with risks because companies that frequently discount prices to stimulate demand may be perceived by customers as low quality or develop a reputation whereby customers book as late as possible to get the biggest discounts. Last-minute bookings affect the company's ability to forecast sales and price effectively and devalue the brand in the long-term. In order to combat some of the problems of reducing the price of holidays, tour operators may add specific conditions to discounted prices, such as minimum stay or minimum numbers in the booking.

Seasonal pricing

A company may consider a mix of pricing throughout the year to cover high, shoulder and low seasons. This is frequently done to cater for different levels of demand over the year. For example, school holidays and religious holidays tend to see substantial price rises, which compensate for the reduced income during low season.

Competitive pricing

A review of competitors' pricing is important because holiday products are price sensitive, and with the ease of comparing products using the Internet, customers often look towards choosing the lower priced product. Mass market operators within Europe frequently compete using price as the differentiator and if one operator reduces their price and undercuts competitors offering similar products, then they will look towards reducing their prices. As a result, mass market operators frequently publish second and third editions of their brochures throughout the season, reacting to the pricing strategies of competitors.

Options pricing

A company may decide to offer packages with minimal profit, but increase their revenue through sales of optional excursions. For some larger operators, brochures are produced that show the basic holiday cost without including transfers and/or in-flight meals, which allows customers to customize their holidays, but also allows the operator to advertise low prices.

Summary

Any tour operator seeking sustainable success needs a firm grasp of basic accountancy practice and financial management skills. This essential understanding and ability to apply to their business the skills of accountancy and finance are fundamental to all business and are best studied in that context. However, whether small or large, tour operators need also to understand currency markets and fluctuations and manage their cash flows efficiently and effectively. Further, they need to appreciate the complexities involved in pricing package holidays, which as discussed entails far more than simply counting all costs of production and delivery of a good to the point of sale outlet with an added mark-up to achieve the target profit margin. Operators need a clear appreciation of the costs involved, including commissions, and how these might vary with seasonality, which requires informed, accurate sales forecasts. They also need to recognize the range of factors that will influence their package holiday prices, including the potential impact of their competitors' different pricing strategies and tactics. At the same time, they need to appreciate the opportunities that may be available to generate additional revenue streams, which in terms of the generally low profit margins achieved by operators in the mainstream market may well be significant to their overall profitability. Finally, throughout this complex process of pricing their package holidays, tour operators need to manage, as applicable to their operations, variations in the value of currencies in which they work and how most effectively to reduce the impact of unexpected, substantial change.

Discussion Questions

1. Review the booking conditions of several tour operators and compare the costs for the cancellation or amendments made to any bookings. Do you consider these charges to be fair?

2. What measures can a tour operator put in place to manage the risks arising from foreign exchange fluctuations?

3. Why is cash management critical to the success of the tour operator?

4. Why are mass market package holiday customers price sensitive?

5. What incentives can operators introduce to encourage early booking?

6. A tour operator has created a new product for Thailand, designed for the environmentally conscious tourist, and is considering marketing it at a premium price. However, after studying the competition in the package holiday market for the area, they identify that their projected price would be 15% higher than its nearest equivalent. What would you advise them to do?

Key Terms

- **Cash flow:** The sum of money being transferred in and out of the business that affects liquidity.
- **Gross rate:** The price at which the supplier sells the product.
- **Mark-up:** The sum added to the cost price of the package to cover overheads and profit.
- **Net rate:** The price of the package provided for retailers, without commission.
- **Up-selling:** This is a sales technique where a seller, for example travel agent/tour operator, persuades the customer to buy more expensive items, upgrades or other add-ons in an attempt to make a more profitable sale, e.g. car parking, room upgrade, excursions.

INTERNET EXERCISE

Low Cost Holiday, a UK company that relocated to Spain, failed in 2016. Review the news reports from UK newspapers such as *The Guardian* and *The Daily Telegraph* and consider why the holidays were not considered packages and if the Spanish legislation will enable customers to gain refunds.

Questions
- What implications does this have for customers?
- Do you think that all operators need to be bonded?

Recommended Reading

For good standard texts on accountancy and finance, see:

Collis, J. and Holt, A. (2012) *Business Accounting: An Introduction to Financial and Management Accounting*. Palgrave Macmillan, Basingstoke, UK.

Harris, P. and Mongiello, M. (2012) *Accounting and Financial Management: Developments in the International Hospitality Industry*. Routledge, London.

For texts specifically orientated to hospitality and tourism operations, see:

Kotas, P. (2010) *Management Accounting for Hospitality and Tourism*. Cengage Learning, Andover, UK.

Jones, T., Atkinson, H. and Lorenz, A. (2012) *Strategic Managerial Accounting: Hospitality, Tourism and Events Applications*. Goodfellow, Oxford, UK.

References

Cavlek, N. (2006) Travel and tourism intermediaries. In: Dwyer, L. and Forsyth, P. (eds) *International Handbook on the Economics of Tourism*. Edward Elgar, Cheltenham, UK, pp. 155–172.

Dwyer, L. and Forsyth, P. (2006) *International Handbook on the Economics of Tourism*. Edward Elgar, Cheltenham, UK.

Fitch, A. (1987) Tour operators in the UK. A survey of the industry, its market and product diversification. *Travel and Tourism Analyst* March, 29–43.

Harris, P. and Mongiello, M. (2012) *Accounting and Financial Management: Developments in the International Hospitality Industry*. Routledge, London.

Hoeseason, J. and Johns, N. (1998) The numbers game: the role of yield management in the tour operations industry. *Progress in Tourism and Hospitality Research* 4, 197–206.

Kotas, P. (2010) *Management Accounting for Hospitality and Tourism*. Cengage Learning, Andover, UK.

WTTC (2017) Air Passenger Duty. World Travel and Tourism Council. Available at: https://www.wttc.org/research/policy-research/taxes/air-passenger-duty/, accessed 25 January 2017.

8 Tour Operators and Key Travel Regulations

WITH DAVID GRANT

Learning Objectives

After studying this chapter, you should be able to:

- Explain the role of the Package Travel Regulations within Europe.
- Examine the difficulties and challenges in applying package travel regulations to products.
- Provide an overview of legislation pertinent to tour operators in major markets.
- Understand the importance to customers of regulations on the tour operating sector.

Introduction

The aim of this chapter is to present an overview of the law relating to tour operators and the Package Travel Regulations (PTR) with some illustrative case law. It does not examine the wider aspects of the law of contract or the criminal law that also apply to package travel contracts. For that you are invited to read standard travel law texts (see Saggerson, 2010; Grant and Mason, 2012). Our focus here is on the PTR in that, albeit Eurocentric, there is little doubt that these regulations, or similar, have been or are being gradually adopted by other countries. As such, it is argued that the PTR serves to illustrate best practice, whether that is now, as within the EU, or more widely in

terms of operators based in other countries that are seeking to regulate their travel sector. Even when not adopted by other countries, the liability provisions of the PTR will have an impact on suppliers in host countries who must comply with standards imposed on them by EU-based operators who are required by the legislation to accept liability for the defaults of their suppliers. However, as the name suggests, the PTR are concerned solely with the regulation of package holidays and not the liability of hotels, airlines, railways, ferry operators, coach operators and other travel sector businesses who sell single travel products. They do not come within the ambit of the PTR and are not covered here because they fall outside the scope of this chapter.

As with the law generally, legislation and regulation change according to developments in business practice and consumer protection. Not surprisingly therefore, the law relating to tour operators and travel agents is currently in a state of transition. Since 1992, UK tour operators (as in all member states of the EU) selling package holidays have been subject to strict regulation following the implementation of the 1990 Package Travel Directive (PTD1) (Council, 1990) through the 1992 Package Travel Regulations (PTR) (Council, 1992). Now, however, there is a new Directive, the 2015 Package Travel Directive (PTD2) (Council, 2015), which must be adopted into UK law by

July 2018. Yet we do not know precisely what the new regulations will say. In the interim, the travel sector must comply with the 1992 regulations. In the light of this situation, this chapter will discuss the law as it currently stands with respect to the following six aspects of the PTR:

- The scope of the Regulations.
- Pre-departure changes.
- Post-departure changes.
- Liability under Regulation 15 for non-performance and under Regulation 4 for providing misleading information.
- The calculation of damages in the event of a breach of contract by the tour operator.
- How tour operators must protect consumers against their insolvency.

An indication as to what changes tour operators can expect after July 2018 will also be presented. Following on from this, the aim is then to provide insight into current differences between the EU and other countries by way of discussion of major aspects of legislation, principally relating to Asian Pacific countries, which collectively account for an increasingly large proportion of international tourists.

The Scope of the Package Travel Regulations 1992

The purpose of the Regulations is to regulate conventional package holidays, be that a typical 3S holiday, a tour of Rajasthan, a whale watching cruise or other similar arrangements. On this everyone is agreed, but the scope of the definition of a 'package' in Regulation 2 is so wide that it goes far beyond conventional package holidays. There is an amazing variety of travel and holiday arrangements over which unresolved arguments rage regarding their inclusion in the definition of 'package', such as overnight ferry trips to the Continent; business travel; holiday camps and caravan sites; 'tailor-made' packages put together by travel agents; sleeper accommodation on the railways (see para. 17 of the Preamble to the new PTD); holidays provided by **local authority** social services departments for their pensioners; and activity holidays provided by schools or local education authorities. This is perhaps evident in the way the 'package' is defined.

The Regulations define 'package' in the following manner:

2(1) 'Package' means the pre-arranged combination of at least two of the following components when sold or offered for sale at an inclusive price and when the service covers a period of more than twenty-four hours or includes overnight accommodation:

(a) transport;
(b) accommodation;
(c) other tourist services not ancillary to transport or accommodation and accounting for a significant proportion of the package,
and
(i) the submission of separate accounts for different components shall not cause the arrangements to be other than a package;
(ii) the fact that a combination is arranged at the request of the consumer and in accordance with his specific instructions (whether modified or not) shall not of itself cause it to be treated as other than pre-arranged.

Thus, for there to be a package there has to be:

- a pre-arranged combination;
- sold at an inclusive price.

These need to consist of two of the following:

- transport;
- accommodation;
- other tourist services.

At the margins, all these terms cause difficulties. For instance, is a 'fly drive' package caught by the Regulations because it is only two forms of transport? Or what about packages put together by travel agents? Are they 'pre-arranged' combinations? Does the term 'other tourist services' include services for tourists travelling on business? What is meant by 'inclusive price'? Despite the fact that the Regulations are now 25 years old, many fundamental questions like this remain unanswered. However, the vast majority of holidays sold, whether by major tour operators like TUI and Thomas Cook or independents, for example, in the adventure tour market, undoubtedly fall within the Regulations, and some online travel agencies like Expedia have terms and conditions saying that some of their products are sold as packages – although Travel Republic specifically state that they do not. Some of these issues have been addressed by case law – either in the UK courts or in the Court of Justice of the European Union (CJEU). Here we present two key cases by way of exemplification.

Club Tour Viagens e Turismo v Garrido C400/2000 ECJ was a decision on the meaning of 'pre-arranged'. The facts of the case were that the defendant booked a holiday through a travel agency in Portugal. The holiday consisted of accommodation at an all-inclusive resort operated by Club Med in Greece plus flights from Portugal. It was the travel agent who combined the flights (from a different supplier) with the all-inclusive resort. While on holiday the resort became infested with thousands of wasps, which prevented the defendant from enjoying his stay. Despite his complaints, neither the travel agency nor Club Med could provide suitable alternative accommodation. On his return, the defendant refused to pay for the holiday and the travel agent sued him. The domestic court in Portugal referred the case to the European

Court of Justice for a ruling on two issues. The first of these was whether arrangements put together by a travel agent at the request of, and according to the specifications of, a consumer or defined group of consumers fell within the definition of a package. The second was whether the term 'pre-arranged combination' could be interpreted as meaning a package put together at the time when the contract was concluded. In a brief but robust judgment, the European Court of Justice held that both questions should be answered in the affirmative. On the first issue, the Court said that there was nothing in the definition which prevented such arrangements from being a package; and on the second issue, given the answer to the first question, then it necessarily followed that the arrangements were pre-arranged if they consisted of elements chosen by the consumer before the contract was concluded. Note that the travel agent was suing for non-payment, i.e. breach of contract, therefore it was impossible for them to argue that there was no contract.

The case of *ABTA v CAA* [2006] EWCA Civ 1356 revolved around the meaning of 'inclusive price'. The gist of the case can be found in paragraphs 25 and 26 from the judgment delivered by Chadwick LJ:

> *25. The point may be illustrated by examples. Suppose a customer, in London, who wishes to spend a week at a named hotel in, say, Rome. He asks his travel agent what the trip will cost him. The agent ascertains that the cost of the return flight will be £X, the cost of accommodation will be £Y and the cost of the airport transfers will be £Z. Without disclosing the individual cost of each service, the agent offers the customer flights, accommodation and transfers at a price of £(X+Y+Z). The customer accepts without further inquiry. In that case there would be little*

doubt – as it seems to me – that the services were sold as a pre-arranged combination and at an inclusive price.

26. Now suppose that the agent has informed the customer that the cost of flights will be £X, the cost of accommodation will be £Y and the cost of transfers will be £Z; and has explained to the customer that he can purchase any one or more of those services, as he chooses, without any need to purchase the others. He has explained, in effect, that the customer can choose to purchase the other services elsewhere; or to make other arrangements. In that case – as it seems to me – there would be little doubt that the services are not offered for sale as a pre-arranged combination and at an inclusive price.

Although this passage can be criticized, it nevertheless represents the current state of the law – and was relied on by Travel Republic in the case of *CAA v Travel Republic* [2010] EWHC 1151 to establish that they were not selling packages. One later case in which the definition of a package, and in particular the meaning of 'inclusive price', is examined is *Titshall v Qwerty Travel Ltd* [2011] EWCA Civ 1569. Mr Titshall paid £569.16 for a flight and accommodation and 'service fees' for a last minute package holiday in Corfu. The Court of Appeal concluded that this was a package bought for an inclusive price, largely because the service fees could not be broken down and attributed to either the flight or the accommodation and therefore he could not have been buying two separate services at the same time as in the second example given by Chadwick LJ.

Upon Whom is Liability Imposed?

The Regulations impose liability on 'the organizer' and 'the retailer'.

The organizer

2(1) 'Organiser' means a person who, otherwise than occasionally, organises packages and sells or offers them for sale, whether directly or through a retailer.

The test here is how frequently the organizer arranges packages and not, as in other consumer protection legislation, whether the organizer acts in the course of a business. The definition will clearly catch conventional tour operators but, importantly, it will also catch most travel agents in its net on occasion. If tailor-made packages are regarded as 'pre-arranged', then it will be very rare indeed that a travel agent can say that s/he does not 'otherwise than occasionally' put a package together – although the Travel Republic case suggests that evading the Regulations can be achieved. In this context it is important to note that the term 'organizer' cuts across the more conventional terms of principal and agent. That is, to be an organizer it is not necessary to be a principal and, by the same token, an agent is not precluded from being an organizer simply because s/he is an agent; the criterion is whether a person 'organizes' a package, not whether they act as principal.

The chief significance of being labelled an organizer is that the liabilities are much greater that those of a retailer. The organizer is responsible for the performance of the whole package, but the retailer's liabilities are much more narrowly defined. There are also additional criminal offences for organizers to fall foul of, as the following case illustrates.

Hone v Going Places [2001] EWCA Civ 947 is a case where a travel agent fell into the trap of holding themselves out as organizers even though they were only retailers. The facts of the case were that the claimant, who was on a package holiday, was injured during an emergency evacuation of an aeroplane following a bomb scare. Both the tour operator that organized the holiday and the airline that provided the flights were bankrupt and not worth suing, so the claimant sued the travel agent through whom the holiday had been purchased. During the purchase of the holiday the travel agent had not made it clear that they were only acting as an agent for the tour operator; they had given the impression that they were the principals selling the holiday. The Court of Appeal held that they would be treated as 'organizers' because they had held themselves out as such. (Note that although the travel agents could be sued as organizers, they were ultimately not liable because the Court said that there was no failure to take reasonable care of the claimant.)

The retailer

2(1) 'Retailer' means the person who sells or offers for sale the package put together by the organiser.

The definition clearly covers the activities of travel agents. Under the Directive, EU member states had the option of imposing liability on either organizers or retailers or both for failures in the package itself. It is generally believed that the Regulations do not impose such extensive liabilities on retailers, but they do make them subject to the provision of information regime (Regulation 5 and possibly also Regulations 7 and 8) and they incur civil liability under Regulation 4 for providing misleading descriptive matter. However, as discussed above, the Hone case has imposed liability on a travel agent.

As previously stated, a travel agent who puts a package together and sells it in his/her own name falls within the definition of organizer rather than retailer and is, therefore, subject to the more stringent liabilities in the Regulations. Similarly, the agent who packages extra elements with a conventional package is likely to be classified as an organizer rather than a retailer.

In Whose Favour is Liability Imposed?

The Regulations impose civil liability on the organizer and, in some cases, the retailer, in favour of 'consumers'.

2(2) … 'consumer' means the person who takes or agrees to take the package ('the principal contractor') and elsewhere in these Regulations 'consumer' means, as the context requires, the principal contractor, any person on whose behalf the principal contractor agrees to purchase the package ('the other beneficiaries') or any person to whom the principal contractor or any of the other beneficiaries transfers the package ('the transferee').

Traditionally, in English law, only a party to a contract is entitled to take the benefit of it. In other words, there have been doubts as to the extent to which members of a client's family who are named on the booking form but who may not be party to the contract would be entitled to the benefits of the contract, but in the case of *Jackson v Horizon* [1975] 3 All ER 92 the Court of Appeal was prepared to say that the person who makes the holiday contract on behalf of others can sue on their behalf.

However, the definition of 'consumer' in the Regulations, making what amounts to a revolutionary change to a long-established rule of English law (a change that now also applies to other contracts by virtue of the Contracts (Rights of Third Parties) Act 1999) goes some way to eliminating these problems. Furthermore, if a consumer transfers his/her booking to another person, as s/he is sometimes entitled to do now under Regulation 10, the transferee stands in the same position as the original consumer.

Regulation 2(2) identifies three types of consumer:

- the principal contractor;
- the other beneficiaries;
- the transferee.

As a broad proposition it could be said that the legislation was intended to cover three types of person:

- a person who buys the package, but may or may not go on it – the principal contractor;
- a person who goes on the package, but is paid for by another – the other beneficiary;
- a person who acquires a package indirectly from one of the other types of consumer but not directly from the organizer – the transferee.

On this basis anyone who either pays for a package or who goes on a package will get the protection of the Regulations.

Note that under Regulation 10 there are limits to whom the package may be transferred in that the transferee must satisfy '*all the conditions applicable to the package*' – so for instance it would not be permissible to substitute two teenagers for a couple who had booked a seniors' package.

Pre-departure Changes

It is not unknown for tour operators to have to make changes to a package before the consumer departs. This may be for many reasons: political or civil unrest; acts of terrorism; problems caused by extreme weather such as hurricanes or tsunamis; overbooking; insolvency of airlines etc. In these circumstances the consumer's rights are governed by Regulations 12 and 13:

12. In every contract there are implied terms to the effect that –

(a) where the organiser is constrained before the departure to alter significantly an essential term of the contract, such as the price (so far as regulation 11 permits him to do so), he will notify the consumer as quickly as possible in order to enable him to take appropriate decisions and in particular to withdraw from the contract without penalty or to accept a rider to the contract specifying the alterations made and their impact on the price; and
(b) the consumer will inform the organiser or the retailer of his decision as soon as possible.

13(1) The terms set out in paragraphs (2) and (3) below are implied in every contract and apply where the consumer withdraws from the contract pursuant to the term in it implied by virtue of regulation 12(a), or where the organiser, for any reason other than the fault of the consumer, cancels the package before the agreed date of departure.

13(2) The consumer is entitled –

(a) to take a substitute package of equivalent or superior quality if the other party to the contract is able to offer him such a substitute; or
(b) to take a substitute package of lower quality if the other party to the contract is able to offer him one and to recover from the organiser the difference in price between the price of the package purchased and that of the substitute package; or
(c) to have repaid to him as soon as possible all the monies paid by him under the contract.

13(3) The consumer is entitled, if appropriate, to be compensated by the organiser for non-performance of the contract except where –

(a) the package is cancelled because the number of persons who agree to take it is less than the minimum number required and the consumer is informed of the cancellation, in writing, within the period indicated in the description of the package; or

(b) the package is cancelled by reason of unusual and unforeseeable circumstances beyond the control of the party by whom this exception is pleaded, the consequences of which could not have been avoided even if all due care had been exercised.

Thus, under Regulation 12, if a consumer can establish that a tour operator has altered significantly an essential term s/he has the choice of either withdrawing from the contract, or accepting the change with a rider to the price. Presumably, if there is such a major change, then the consumer will withdraw unless the tour operator offers enough by way of compensation. If the consumer does withdraw, or if the operator cancels the holiday for any reason other than the consumer's fault, then the consumer is entitled to the following choices:

- a substitute holiday of equivalent or superior quality, or
- a substitute holiday of inferior quality plus the difference in value, or
- a full refund, and
- compensation, except where the contract was cancelled for **force majeure** or because of lack of minimum numbers.

In *Hook v First Choice Holiday & Flights Ltd* [1998] CLY 1426, the tour operator knew four days before the claimants departed on holiday that their hotel was not available and informed them of this. They were told that the alternative being offered them was in the same resort and of equivalent quality. They were further told that if they chose to cancel they would only receive a 10% refund. The claimants reluctantly agreed to the change. The hotel, although of the same star rating, was of inferior quality. It was decided that the claimants' holiday had not been entirely ruined and they were entitled to a 20% discount on the price for diminution of value (£200) and £250 for distress and disappointment. Of more significance however is that the judge said that the claimants had not been 'properly informed' of their full rights under Regulation 12, including the right to withdraw without penalty, and that in such circumstances tour operators should inform consumers in writing of the options available to them. In this case he felt that there had been 'an element of H being duped into believing he had no right to cancel'.

Post-departure Changes

Some of the problems that cause pre-departure changes may also affect the holiday after the consumer has departed. In that case the consumer's rights are determined by Regulation 14 which provides:

14(1) The terms set out in paragraphs (2) and (3) below are implied in every contract and apply where, after departure, a significant proportion of the services contracted for is not provided or the organiser becomes aware that he will be unable to procure a significant proportion of the services to be provided.

14(2) The organiser will make suitable alternative arrangements, at no extra cost to the consumer, for the continuation of the package and will, where appropriate, compensate the consumer for the difference between the services to be supplied under the contract and those supplied.

14(3) If it is impossible to make arrangements as described in paragraph (2), or these are not accepted by the consumer for good reasons, the organiser will, where appropriate, provide the consumer with equivalent transport back to the place of departure or to another place to which the consumer has agreed and will, where appropriate, compensate the consumer.

Thus, if the consumer can show that:

- a significant proportion of the services are not to be provided, or
- the tour operator becomes aware that they cannot be provided

the tour operator must

- make suitable alternative arrangements for the continuation of the holiday, or
- if it is impossible to make alternative arrangements transport the consumer home again and
- in both cases, compensate the consumer where appropriate.

In *Milner v Carnival plc* [2010] EWCA Civ 389, which is discussed more extensively below, the Milners disembarked a round-the-world cruise in Hawaii and paid for their own passage home to the UK because they were unhappy with their cabin. They claimed this cost under Regulation 14 but the claim was disallowed because the Milners were found not to have had good reasons for rejecting the final cabin offered to them and their disembarkation was treated as consensual rather than a breach of Regulation 14.

Liability under Regulation 15

Until 1992, the position at common law was that tour operators were not liable for the defaults or negligence of their subcontractors (or suppliers as they are often called). This was the issue which was at the heart of the *Wall v Silver Wing Surface Arrangements* (High Court, 1981, Unreported). In that case the plaintiff and her family had booked a package to Tenerife with Enterprise holidays. One night a fire broke out at their hotel. They were unable to exit the hotel via the fire escape because the hotelkeeper had padlocked the gate at the bottom of the escape. The

family then returned to their room and let themselves out of the room via the balcony using a makeshift rope made of sheets. Mrs Wall was injured when the sheets gave way and she fell to the ground.

Although it had been the fault of the hotelkeeper that the fire escape gate had been padlocked, no blame could be attributed to the tour operator in the case. On the contrary, the judge said that the tour operator was a reputable company that had acted properly throughout. It had selected a modern hotel and monitored it for safety and there was nothing more that could reasonably be expected of them.

In practice, this approach meant that because most of a package is made up of elements subcontracted to others – airlines and hotels – much of what went wrong with a package could not be made the legal responsibility of the tour operator. This often left clients either without a remedy or the difficult task of suing a foreign hotel or airline. However, Regulation 15 of the PTR changes that. It provides:

15(1) The other party to the contract is liable to the consumer for the proper performance of the obligations under the contract, irrespective of whether such obligations are to be performed by that other party or by other suppliers of services but this shall not affect any remedy or right of action which that other party may have against those other suppliers of services.

15(2) The other party to the contract is liable to the consumer for any damage caused to him by the failure to perform the contract or the improper performance of the contract unless the failure or the improper performance is due neither to any fault of that other party nor to that of another supplier of services, because –

(a) the failures which occur in the performance of the contract are attributable to the consumer

(b) such failures are attributable to a third party unconnected with the provision of the services contracted for, and are unforeseeable or unavoidable, or
(c) such failures are due to –
(i) unusual and unforeseeable circumstances beyond the control of the party by whom this exception is pleaded, the consequences of which could not have been avoided even if all due care had been exercised; or
(ii) an event which the other party to the contract or the supplier of services, even with all due care, could not foresee or forestall.

The effect of this is that if part of what the tour operator has promised to the client is to be performed by subcontractors, the tour operator is nevertheless held responsible if things go wrong unless they can prove one of four things:

- it was the consumer's own fault;
- it was the fault of a third-party unconnected with the contract;
- it was caused by *force majeure*;
- it was caused by some other event that the tour operator could not predict or avoid.

Most of the most important cases involving personal injury, such as *Evans v Kosmar* [2007] EWCA Civ 1003, *Healy v Cosmosair* [2005] EWHC 1657 (QB), *Japp v Virgin Holidays Ltd* [2013] EWCA Civ 1371 and *Gouldbourn v Balkan Holidays* [2010] EWCA Civ 37, rely on Regulation 15 as the basis of liability.

Liability under Regulation 4

Regulation 4 creates a statutory right to compensation for the consumer that cuts across the traditional boundaries of the common law. It imposes civil liability on both organizers and retailers if they supply misleading information. It states:

4(1). No organiser or retailer shall supply to a consumer any descriptive matter concerning a package, the price of a package or any other conditions applying to the contract which contains any misleading information.

4(2). If an organiser or retailer is in breach of paragraph (1) he shall be liable to compensate the consumer for any loss which the consumer suffers in consequence.

There is liability if the plaintiff can show that a tour operator or travel agent supplied to a consumer a brochure that contained misleading descriptive matter concerning a package or its price and the consumer suffers as a consequence.

The liability is imposed for supplying misleading descriptive matter. The implication here is that it will cover written matter but not oral statements. The word *matter* suggests something tangible. It will obviously cover brochures and other brochure-like leaflets and it would most probably extend to videos of holiday destinations. It probably does not extend to window displays or window cards because the requirement is that the matter be *supplied to* the consumer and it cannot be said that such matter is supplied to the consumer. Press advertisements are potentially different in that it is a moot point whether it can be said that the operator or the retailer has supplied the matter if it comes in a paper or journal supplied by a publisher or newsagent. The other qualification is that liability is only imposed where the consumer, because of the misleading information, suffers as a consequence. For the consumer to show that as a consequence of the descriptive material s/he suffered loss, there will have to be some evidence of cause and effect. S/he must show that s/he relied on the information, otherwise how can it be said that s/he suffered loss as a consequence? A significant point is that the travel agent, as well as the tour operator, could incur liability, thus making them strictly liable for brochure errors they might know nothing about – and with no defence. The only way to combat this liability is to ensure that the agency agreements they have with operators contain indemnity clauses. Whether they do or not may very well be a matter of bargaining power.

The leading case on Regulation 4 is *Mawdsley v Cosmosair Plc* [2002] EWCA Civ 587. The facts of the case were that Mrs Mawdsley and her husband were descending a flight of stairs leading to the restaurant in the hotel they were staying at. They were carrying their baby daughter, Charlotte, in a pushchair between them. In the process Mrs Mawdsley lost her footing, slipped and fell. Mrs Mawdsley claimed that in the brochure advertising the hotel, in reliance on which she and her husband booked the holiday, Cosmos represented that the hotel restaurant could be accessed by a lift when in fact it could not, and that the hotel was suitable for parents with young children when in truth it was not so suitable. The Court of Appeal held that Cosmos were in breach of their duty under Regulation 4 of the PTR in that its brochure contained 'misleading information', and this misleading information caused her fall – she would not have booked the holiday or been descending the stairs if the restaurant had been accessible by lift.

Damages

To compensate the consumer for breach of contract, three heads of damage are recognized:

- damages for difference in value;
- consequential loss; and
- damages for distress and disappointment.

Damages for difference in value: Where the tour operator has provided a holiday which is worth less than the holiday s/he contracted to provide, the holidaymaker is entitled to the difference in value. A straightforward example of this principle is the case of *Mcleod v Hunter* [1987] CLY 1162. In that case the tour operator promised a luxurious villa but what they provided was a cramped apartment. The court assessed the difference in value as £439. This was in addition to damages for distress and disappointment.

Consequential loss: When the breach of contract results in the holidaymaker having to expend further sums in order to rectify the breach, damages for consequential loss can be claimed. Sometimes these damages are referred to as out-of-pocket expenses. In *Harris v Torchgrove* [1985] CLY 944 the court awarded £40 damages for parking expenses because the promised parking at the apartment was not available and a further £300 for the cost of extra meals taken in restaurants because the apartment had no oven and the fridge was 'eccentric'.

Difference in value claims and consequential loss claims cannot be combined to give double compensation. For instance, if a tour operator promises full board but no evening meals are provided, the consumer cannot claim both the difference in value between half board and full board and also the out-of-pocket expenses for purchasing restaurant meals in the evening.

Damages for distress and disappointment: Holiday contracts are almost unique because in appropriate cases the courts will award damages for distress and disappointment caused by a breach of contract. Such damages are not available generally in the law of contract. The rule was established in the case of *Jarvis v Swans Tours* [1973] 1 All ER 71. The plaintiff booked a holiday in the Tyrol at Christmas. He was promised a 'house-party' atmosphere; 'gemutlichkeit'; fondue parties; yodler evenings; afternoon tea and cakes; etc. The hotel was virtually deserted, the skiing was very restricted, almost none of the services were provided and the hotel proprietor spoke no English. The Court of Appeal awarded the plaintiff £125 damages on a holiday that cost £64. Lord Denning said: 'In a proper case damages for mental distress can be recovered in contract … One such case is a contract for a holiday, or any other contract to provide entertainment and enjoyment. If the contracting party breaks his contract, damages can be given for the disappointment, the distress, the upset and frustration caused by the breach.'

The rationale behind the decision is that where the purpose of the contract is to provide peace of mind and enjoyment, then such damages can be claimed, but not for everyday commercial transactions where the provision of pleasure is not the essence of the contract.

Although the Jarvis case forms the basis for claims for distress and disappointment, it must now be read in the light of the Milner case referred to above in relation to Regulation 14. The facts of Milner were these: Mr and Mrs Milner bought a cruise for themselves on the maiden round-the-world cruise of Cunard's Queen Victoria. It was priced at £65,558, but the Milners managed to negotiate a discount and actually paid £59,052. The cruise lasted 102 nights but the Milners disembarked after only 28 nights because their cabin was so noisy – caused by the grinding and banging sounds of the metal plates flexing and vibrating and reverberating in the area of their cabin. Cunard refunded the unused portion of the price (£48,270), but the Milners claimed further compensation for the distress and disappointment they had suffered.

Ward LJ offered the following suggestions for making the assessment of these types of damages (mental distress/disappointment etc.) more consistent:

- The award should be in the nature of a conventional figure, or range of figures. In arriving at this, use should be made of 'comparables'.
- The first comparable was the decisions in large numbers of other cases. These showed modest awards. Ruined foreign weddings got the highest, just over £4000; ruined honeymoons £321 to £1890; other special holidays £264 to £1161; ordinary holidays £83 to £1876.
- The next comparable was the awards suggested by the Judicial Studies Board (JSB) in their Guidelines, for psychiatric injuries and for post-traumatic stress disorder. At the bottom end, modest four-figure sums were considered the benchmark by the JSB.
- Another comparable is discrimination cases in which awards had been made for injury to feelings. These were modest four-figure, or even sometimes three-figure sums.
- Then there are bereavement claims, where even awards to parents for the death of a child did not exceed £10,000.
- Ward LJ also quoted from the House of Lords decision in *Farley v Skinner* [2001] UKHL 49: 'I consider that awards in this area should be restrained and modest. It is important that logical and beneficial developments in this corner of the law should not contribute to the creation of a society bent on litigation.'

Set against these comparables, Ward LJ considered holiday damages. He said: 'Physical inconvenience and discomfort is necessarily ephemeral. Disappointment, distress, annoyance and frustration are likewise the feelings one experiences at the time and which last painfully for some time thereafter. But one is not disabled, the psyche is not injured, and one gets on with life. Every time one thinks back, one relives the horror but the reliving of it is transitory.'

He then considered the award in this case. As to mental distress, he said it was 'wrong to use the price of the holiday as a benchmark for damages'. He awarded £4000 for Mr Milner and £4500 for Mrs Milner, describing these figures as 'exceptional' to cater for the ruination of an exceptional event. Normal awards would be considerably lower.

Mitigation of loss: A victim of a breach of contract cannot simply sit back and collect damages. They must take reasonable steps to mitigate their loss and failure to do so can mean that they will lose their damages. In holiday cases, one of the simplest ways to mitigate your loss is to complain to the tour operator or their representative who may then be able to put things right. Regulation 15(9), in fact, requires tour operators to include in their contracts a term obliging consumers to complain at the earliest opportunity if they have a problem. In *Czyzewski v Intasun* (1990, County Ct. Unreported) the plaintiff complained of an 'offensive' toilet. After several unsuccessful attempts to repair it, the hotel offered him an alternative room but for some reason he declined to take it and remained in his room for the rest of his holiday. The court awarded him only £50 damages based on the limited amount of time he would have had to spend in the room if he had accepted the alternative.

Protection against Insolvency

Expenditure on the average family holiday usually ranks as one of the two or three largest items of expenditure in the family's annual budget. In the vast majority of cases, the money has to be paid in advance to the tour operator. The obvious danger with this is that, if the tour operator becomes insolvent, consumers will lose their money. The problem is exacerbated if the clients happen to be abroad at the time. Prior to 1992, there were various voluntary and statutory schemes in place to protect consumers if this happened. Thus, if a consumer booked an air package holiday they were protected by the Air Travel Organiser's Licence (ATOL) scheme, which required air package tour operators to take out a bond to be paid out to clients in the event of the tour operator's insolvency. ABTA also operated a scheme whereby their members, whether air package operators or not, were also required to have bonds to protect their clients. However, the protection was not universal and it was possible for a client to book a holiday with a non-bonded operator and lose their money. Many coach tour operators fell into this category. Now, as required by the PTD, the PTR require all tour operators to be able to provide evidence of security for the return of pre-payments and for repatriation (Regulation 16). The Regulations provide that this can be done in a number of ways:

- by bonding;
- by insurance;
- by establishing a trust fund.

All air tour operators (but not airlines selling flight-only direct to the public) must have an ATOL. The scheme is administered by the Civil Aviation Authority (CAA), which has created a number of different ways of acquiring a licence. Tour operators can acquire a licence direct from the CAA or indirectly via several different trade association schemes. For instance, the CAA offer a standard licence for large tour operators and a small business ATOL (SBA) for those businesses carrying less than 500 passengers a year. Alternatively, if the tour operator is a member of an accredited body, such as Advantage Travel Centres or Hays Travel, they can trade under the licence of the accredited body – so long as they meet the membership criteria. Tour operators may also acquire a licence by being a member of a franchise such as the Travel Trust Association. ABTA and the CAA have a Joint Administration Scheme by which ABTA members with an annual turnover of less than £1.5 million can obtain a licence. The value of ATOL protection to the customer cannot be overstated in the event of the collapse of a tour operator, as was well illustrated in the summer of 2016 when the Low Cost Travel Group and Anatolian Sky failed. The former was registered in Spain, did not hold an ATOL and had only a small fund to cover liabilities resulting in at best low compensation for customers. In contrast, Anatolian Sky (UK) collapsed due to the marked decline in demand for Turkey, but all their customers' payments were secure because of their ATOL.

The ATOL scheme also covers 'flight-plus' arrangements. This is where an operator, usually a travel agent, puts together separate travel services, but including flights, at separate times but within a 24-hour period. These are not 'packages', but they do attract insolvency protection under the ATOL scheme. For non-air packages, or 'non-licensable business' as it is known, the ATOL scheme does not apply. However, ABTA protects consumers through a scheme that it runs for its members and other tour operators can join schemes run by the Travel Trust Association or Travel Vault, which offer insurance-based or trust accounts.

PTD2 – The Major Changes

When PTD2 is brought into effect by July 2018, there will be significant differences from the current regime. Briefly, they are as follows:

- The definition of 'package' has been radically extended to include, for instance, not only packages as defined already but also much of what is loosely called dynamic packaging; arrangements described as a 'package'; arrangements sold at a total or inclusive price; and 'click through' arrangements.
- 'Fly-Drive' arrangements are now caught by the definition of package.
- There is also a new concept, the Linked Travel Arrangement (or LTA), which resembles the 'flight-plus' concept found in the ATOL Regulations. As with flight-plus, they attract insolvency protection but not the same liability as packages.
- Business travel that is bought via a 'general agreement' is excluded from the legislation.
- The obligation to provide accommodation to travellers where it is impossible to return them to their point of departure because of unavoidable and extraordinary circumstances is limited to three days.
- As far as insolvency protection is concerned, the enforcement of the legislation depends on the tour operator's place of establishment, i.e. tour operators established in Spain are subject to the Spanish rules on insolvency.
- Even if the contract provides for an increase in price because of such events as currency fluctuations, the price cannot be increased by more than 8% and if it is the traveller has the right to cancel the package and terminate the contract without penalty.
- The requirements relating to the provision of information are strengthened.

There is an invitation in the Directive for Member States to make retailers as well as organizers liable for the performance of the package.

Asia Pacific Region and Legislation

The Asia Pacific region is one of the top tourist-generating regions in the world. According to the UNWTO, international tourist arrivals to the Asia Pacific countries increased to 279 million in 2015. In this region the mature destinations are mainly Singapore, Hong Kong, Thailand and Malaysia, which are widely considered to be pioneers in the development of tourism in the region. However, with rising affluence, other countries such as China, Vietnam, Korea and the various ASEAN countries are developing their tourism potential, partly if not totally in recognition of its macro-economic benefits. The Asia and Pacific region is the second largest source of international tourists (24%) after Europe (50%) (UNWTO, 2016, p. 12). The importance of the tourism sector, especially with the growth of inbound and outbound markets, means that there is need for more tour operators offering packaged tours and facilitating travel. In this regard, the need for legislation to control and administer tour operators through licensing as well as to protect consumer interest is of great importance.

In comparison with the EU, many countries and regions outside Europe do not have such comprehensive package travel legislation. For many countries the distinction between travel agent and tour operator is not identified and those regulations that do exist mainly apply to travel agents on the grounds that they create and/or retail packages on behalf of suppliers. This can be well illustrated by an overview of legislation and regulation applicable to travel agents in Asia Pacific countries.

The legislation process in the Asian countries varies in accordance with the stage of travel agent development. Generally, the legislation process is set and administered by the country's respective Ministry of Trade and Tourism, National Tourism Association and Consumer Association. The legislation usually covers the various aspects of tour packages from fee collections, marketing, tour arrangements, breach of contract and booking regulations. Hong Kong, Singapore and China have all established legislative frameworks to set guidelines for tour agents and to protect the interests of their customers (see below). These have been successfully implemented over time and revised where needed so as to be in line with changing trends in tourism. As tourism in the Asia Pacific regions continues to expand, destinations such as Myanmar, Laos, Cambodia and Vietnam are all now looking into new legislation and regulatory procedures for their tour/travel operations sector.

Hong Kong

In Hong Kong, the Travel Agents Ordinance (TAO) (CAP 218) provides the legislation framework for the regulation and control of travel agents and for the operation of the Travel Industry Compensation Fund. Under the TAO, any person operating as a travel agent is required to obtain a licence from the Registrar of Travel Agents and is defined as either outbound travel agent or inbound travel agent. Licensing requires that a travel agent must be a member of the Travel Industry Council of Hong Kong. Consumers on the other hand are also protected under the Travel Industry Compensation Fund and the Package Tour Accidents Contingent Fund.

Singapore

Tourism in Singapore largely developed during the 1950s and it is now a mature destination. Since 1976, travel agents have been guided by the Travel Agents Act, which clearly states all the legal regulations that agents need to comply with, from marketing to key issues such as collection of tour fees and tour cancellation. The Act also established the licensing of travel agents, both inbound and outbound, and is administered by the Singapore Tourism Board (STB), a statutory board under the umbrella of the Ministry of Trade and Industry, which promotes the development of tourism through managing quality, promoting tourism development and marketing. The licence lasts for up to two years and includes listing in the travel agent directory on the STB's corporate website.

The STB also upholds the regulatory environment for travel agents, tour guides (Tourist Guide Regulations) and hotels through a licensing process. In addition, they ensure compliance with the related Acts, policies and regulations and undertake reviews of the pertinent legislation to ensure currency and relevance in the regulatory environment. In order to assess compliance and practice, the STB regularly checks on travel agents to ensure financial stability, thereby assessing that they do not pose a financial risk to the travelling public. The STB also ensures that only licensed tour guides are used to maintain a quality experience for visitors.

The STB states that a travel agent is anyone who:

- 'sells tickets entitling an individual to travel, or otherwise arranges for a person a right of passage on any conveyance (not being a prescribed conveyance);
- sells to, or arranges or makes available for, a person rights of passage to, and hotel or other accommodation at, one or more places (being places within or outside Singapore, or some of which are within and others of which are outside Singapore);

- purchases for resale the right of passage on any conveyance (not being a prescribed conveyance);
- carries out such activity as may be prescribed; or
- holds himself out as, or advertises that he is, willing to carry on any activity referred to in paragraph (a), (b), (c) or (d).

Operators carrying out activities in (a) do not require a licence if they intend to use conveyances owned by them, and operators carrying out activities in (b) do not require a licence if they own both the conveyance and place of accommodation.' (STB, 2016, para 1)

These travel agents are also required to inform outbound customers to consider travel insurance that will insure against the travel agent's insolvency, and the customer's decision must be formally recorded either through acceptance or rejection. The aim of such additional conditions is to remind consumers that they need to safeguard their interests when making travel bookings. If the travel agent does not sell insurance themselves then customers must be referred to the STB's list of insurers. Should a customer decline such insurance, this does not prevent continuing the booking as the purchaser may wish to buy travel insurance later or have alternative policies in place.

Travel agents wishing to handle inbound tourists from China need to sign a Memorandum of Understanding (MOU) with the National Association of Travel Agents Singapore (NATAS). All China-based outbound travel agents are required to work only with agents who have signed a MoU, and therefore, in the case of Singapore, only these Singaporean travel agents will be allowed to apply for China Group Visas from the Immigration and Checkpoints Authority of Singapore (ICA). To protect further the interests of Singaporeans, the Consumer Association of Singapore (CASE) and the National Travel Association of Singapore (NATAS) launched a CASE–NATAS joint accreditation scheme for travel agents. The new scheme is to protect the rights of consumers in a dispute and it covers transparency in their fee policy, accuracy in advertising, refund policy practice and professional business ethics.

China

The travel sector in China is highly regulated and controlled by the Government, which largely dictates how the sector is managed, while tourism in general is closely monitored by China's National Tourism Administration (CNTA). It is important therefore that tour operators, both internal and external, understand China's political landscape. China's travel sector started to develop during the 1970s, a period when the country 'officially opened' in combination with major economic reforms and development. This was particularly notable in 1978 and the start of the Open Door policy enabling outbound travel from China, such that by 1990 residents were allowed to join group tours to Southeast Asian destinations such as Singapore, Malaysia and Thailand (Zhang et al., 2005). All foreign travel was handled by China's International Travel Service (CITS) or China Travel Service (CTS), which restricted the destinations to which they were allowed to travel. Albeit a comparatively late entrant into the tourism market compared with western nations, the tourism sector has grown exponentially since the 1970s. By 2015 China recorded 120 million outbound visitors, supported by 26,650 travel service agents of which 2774 were in outbound tourism and 23,876 in domestic tourism (EU SME Centre, 2015).

Domestic tourism developed from the early 1980s, which is demonstrated by the increase in the number of travel agencies from less than 300 in the mid-1980s to 7725 by the year 2000 (Zhang et al., 2005). This, in part, was facilitated by significant changes in 1985, which allowed collectives and private citizens to operate travel agencies, thereby establishing three categories of agency (CNTA, 2015):

- Category 3: Domestic tourism. Services for Chinese mainland citizens to travel within the territory of mainland China. Category 3 agents work with Category 1 or 2 to process international travel and other administrative matters.
- Category 2: Inbound tourism. Services for foreign tourists and tourists from Hong Kong, Macau and Taiwan to travel within the territory of mainland China; restricted to handling only Chinese passengers or providing ground service arrangements for overseas visitors.
- Category 1: Outbound tourism. Services for Chinese mainland citizens or foreign residents of China to travel overseas or to Hong Kong, Macau and Taiwan and allowed to sell products of all types and conduct sales and marketing overseas (CNTA, 2015).

With the rapid growth in tourism development, the State Council of the People's Republic of China and the CNTA introduced the Travel Agency Regulations (TAR) in 2009, updating the 1996 Management of Travel Agencies Regulations, which aims to protect the interests of tourists, stabilize the market and strengthen the administration of travel agencies within China, thus there is a primary focus on the legislation and licensing process of travel agents. The document defines a travel agency business as involving:

> soliciting for, organizing, and serving tourists and providing other tourism services such as planning for accommodations, food and beverage, sightseeing, leisure entertainment and vacation, tour guide service, and tourism consultation and tourism activities planning services. Travel agencies can also book transportation tickets, reserve hotels, and apply for visas on behalf of tourists; manage the transportation, lodging, food, and conference requirements for all kinds of entities; and provide other tourism services. (Day, 2009, np)

As the definition demonstrates, there is little distinction between travel agents and tour operators, wholesalers and retailers in China.

The Regulations stipulate that travel agents maintain a performance bond by depositing funds at banks designated by CNTA, which can be used in situations where either:

- a travel agency breaches the tourist contract, or
- customers lose their advance payments as a result of bankruptcy or dissolution of the travel agent.

The actual bond cost depends on the type of travel agent and the number of outlets. For example, domestic and inbound agents provide a bond less than that for outbound travel agents. The TAR states that when an agent enters into a contract with a tourist, the contract must include the following: full details of the travel agency, travel details including departure, transit and destination, all included arrangements such as transportation, accommodation and catering provision, included activities such as guided tours, clarification of self-guided activities, tourist payments and payment method, length of time spent at specified retail outlets, and any additional payments that will be necessary. In addition, the contract will also state charges for changing or cancelling the holiday, the dispute resolution mechanism and responsibilities for breach of contract (EU SME Centre, 2015).

The TAR notes that travel agencies often utilize local travel agents (ground handling agents) to provide travel services in destinations and states that the agency must outsource its services to a qualified local agency with the agreement of the tourists, i.e. the tourists must be made aware that the service is subcontracted. It also states that if there is a breach of contract by the ground handling agent (identified as outsourcing agent), the travel agent retailing the trip will be liable, although they note that they may be able to recoup the costs from the ground handling agent. Also, and similar to regulations in the EU, travel agencies in China are required to carry liability insurance. Those that do not have liability insurance are liable to have their operation permit revoked.

China's decision to join the World Trade Organization in 2001 resulted in a number of initiatives and notably led to the lifting of restrictions on foreign investment in travel agencies and allowed for the establishment of wholly foreign-owned travel agents. TUI was one of the first major tour operators to demonstrate early recognition of this and of the potential of the Chinese market. They established the China Travel Company in 2003, which was the first joint venture with an overseas company in tourism.

Recent changes

In 2013 the Chinese government introduced regulations specifically for group travel. The regulations seek to prevent outbound group tour packages to any destination from being sold at unreasonably low prices and to ensure an increased level of transparency. Historically, package holidays had been sold at low, sometimes below-market price, with the travel companies increasing their profits through commissions gained from shops to which the tour groups were taken and from ancillary payments. These regulations are only applicable to group tours and effectively ban zero-based tour fares, i.e. those being sold at a loss; this had the resulting effect of increasing the cost of package holidays. Fundamentally, this new law is meant to protect the legitimate rights and interests of Chinese tourists. It is considered to be a key step forward in regulating and sustaining the tourism market, which is considered as one of the major pillars of economic growth. This increased cost of packages resulted in a decrease in the number of holidays being taken by Chinese passengers, particularly in Australia, Taiwan and other countries within the South East Asia region.

USA and Canada

According to US federal and state law there is no difference between the legal responsibilities of the tour operator and a travel agency (*Travel Weekly*, 2013). Both are considered *sellers* of travel, which also includes telemarketers, travel clubs, Internet websites and informal travel promoters. A travel agent acts as a person authorized to sell products and services of a supplier, in effect as an agent. The travel agent can be liable for any injuries caused to a customer if it can be proved that the agent did not act with due diligence in investigating the safety of the provider/principal. However, if the customer is informed of the identity of the principal, then the agent will not be held individually liable for any breach of contract. According to US law, both travel agents and tour operators are responsible for their own acts or omissions, but not those where

a third party is responsible, unless they stipulate that they voluntarily assume this responsibility. Several US states, including California, Florida, Hawaii, Iowa and Washington, have 'Seller of Travel Laws', which require travel agents to register, regulate the sales of travel agencies and provide financial protection for consumers (Cameron, 2013). Three Canadian Provinces, British Columbia, Ontario and Quebec, also have extensive legislation protecting the interests of consumers.

Summary

Prior to the latter part of the 20th century, customers of tour operators had little redress in the event of an issue arising between the purchase of their package and their return to home. A failing in any element of the product/service, be that on the part of one of the principals, misleading information or the collapse of the tour operator itself, would not necessarily mean the customer could gain due recompense. Indeed, operators invariably considered the delivery of the separate components of the package to be largely the responsibility of the principals concerned. By and large, what redress customers had was based on general law such as consumer protection (comparatively limited at the time) and contract law. The latter, however, was often not particularly helpful given the wide practice of including exclusion clauses in the small print and disclaimers of liability. In effect, in many situations customer protection was only present after the early 1970s to cover for the collapse of the tour operator. Thus, across the EU, until the introduction of the Package Travel Regulations, customers, as elsewhere across the globe, had little substantive protection from poor practices.

This largely changed after 1990 with the introduction of the EU's Package

Travel Directive Regulations, regulations which we now can identify in one form or another in many other countries. These regulations have gone a long way to redress the weaknesses of the past to the benefit of customers. However, it is still very much the case today of *'caveat emptor'* – let the buyer be aware. Indeed, and perhaps even more so today given the growing number of online travel agents (see Chapter 9) and tour operators who can operate satellite offices in countries other than their home country, it is potentially risky to purchase a package through small agents and operators in the absence of clear and professional accreditation and explicitly ATOL or ABTA protection (or similar, dependent on a country's regulations) or awareness of their adoption of the home country's regulations and requirements, which even then might not be adopted to an equivalent level. In practice, it is potentially dangerous for the customer to assume protection, especially as regards the security of pre-payments.

Discussion Questions

1. Why was it necessary to revise the 1992 PTD?
2. Do you think that all countries should adopt a similar set of regulations?
3. Should all tour operators be legally required to identify how their products(s) contribute socio-economic benefits within the destination(s) visited?

Key Terms

- *Force majeure*: Unforeseeable circumstances.
- Local authority: Second tier of government at the local level; often referred to as municipal authority.

Recommended Reading

For a detailed examination of the PTR, see:

DTI (2006) The Package Travel Regulations. Question and Answer Guidance for Organisers and Retailers. Available at: https://www.gov.uk/government/uploads/system/uploads/attachment_data/file/417823/bis-06-1640-package-travel-regulations-question-and-answer-guidance-for-organisers-and-retailers.pdf, accessed 26 May 2017.

For further detail and illustration specifically relating to the PTR, see:

Saggerson, A. (2010) *Package Holiday Law: Cases and Materials*. Tarquin, St Albans, UK.

Tour operators, as with any business, are subject to general law relating to business practices, employment, health and safety and consumer protection, etc., therefore students are recommended to refer to the appropriate sources on legislation/regulations covering business and management specific to their own country. In the case of the UK, the following are particularly helpful:

Grant, D.J. and Mason, S. (2012) *Holiday Law: The Law Relating to Travel and Tourism*, 5th edn. Sweet & Maxwell, London.

References

Cameron, P. (2013) Travel agents: their role and liability. *Vacation Law* 30(3). American Bar Association.

CNTA (2015) Tourism Law of the People's Republic of China (Full Text) China National Tourism Administration. Available at: http://en.cnta.gov.cn/Policies/TourismPolicies/201507/t20150707_721478.shtml, accessed 6 August 2016.

Council (Council of the European Communities) (1990) Package Travel, Package Holidays and Package Tours Council Directive of 13 June 1990 (90/314/EEC).

Council (Council of the European Communities) (1992) Package Travel, Package Holidays and Package Tours Regulations (SI 1992 No. 3288).

Council (Council of the European Communities) (2015) Package Travel and Linked Travel Arrangements. Council Directive 2015/2302.

Day, J. (2009) China Adopts New Travel Agency Regulations and Lifts Restrictions on Foreign Invested Travel Agencies. Jones Day Publications. Available at: http://www.jonesday.com/china_adopts_new_travel_agency_regulations/, accessed 8 August 2016.

EU SME Centre (2015) *The Tourism Market in China. Sector Report*. EU SME Centre, Beijing.

Grant, D.J. and Mason, S. (2012) *Holiday Law: The Law Relating to Travel and Tourism*, 5th edn. Sweet & Maxwell, London.

Saggerson, A. (2010) *Package Holiday Law: Cases and Materials*. Tarquin, St Albans, UK.

STB (2016) Travel Agent Licence. Singapore Tourist Board. Available at: https://www.stb.gov.sg/assistance-and-licensing/licensing/Pages/TRAVEL-AGENT-LICENCE.aspx?, accessed 5 August 2016.

Travel Weekly (2013) Legal briefs. *Travel Weekly*. Available at: http://www.travelweekly.com/Mark-Pestronk/In-US-responsibilities-of-tour-operator-vs-agent-no-different, accessed 5 November 2016.

UNWTO (2016) *UNWTO Tourism Highlights, 2016 edition*. United Nations World Tourism Organization, Madrid.

Zhang, H.Q., Pine, R. and Lam, T. (2005) *Tourism and Hotel Development in China: From Political to Economic Success*. The Howarth Hospitality Press, Binghampton, New York.

9 Distribution (Place)

Learning Objectives

After studying this chapter, you should be able to:

- Identify the channels of distribution and assess factors affecting the choice of channel(s).
- Identify the activities involved in the distribution process.
- Appreciate the role of the travel agent as a channel of distribution.
- Utilize marketing terminology appropriately.

Introduction

The purpose of this chapter is to examine the opportunities for and issues confronting tour operators in relation to the distribution of their products. Thus, our focus herein is on how travel organizers distribute their products to their target market(s). In this context, distribution is how the product can be 'made available to, and be purchased by consumers' (Miller, 2002, p. 95). Unlike traditional goods, holiday products are intangible and therefore distribution is concerned with providing customers with access to the product rather than transporting/delivering goods. The traditional channel of distribution for tour operators is that of the travel agent (see Chapter 6, this volume). Indeed, the establishment of the first signs of a channel of distribution are to be seen in the development of Thomas Cook, which started out as a retail travel agent before developing its tour operations enterprise. As such, it had a ready outlet for the distribution of its own tours through its developing travel agency network. However, as identified in Chapter 3 (this volume), potential customers can access products directly from tour operators and principals. In effect, distribution is the process that links the consumer with the tour operator, the demand with the supplier, providing access to holiday products and enabling their purchase. Significantly in comparison with traditional business operations, the distribution system in tourism is far stronger. Indeed:

> Travel agents and tour operators as well as charter brokers, reservation systems and other travel distribution specialists have a far greater power to influence and to direct demand than their counterparts in other industries do. Since they do, in fact, control demand, they also have increased bargaining power in their relations with suppliers of tourist services and are in a position to influence their pricing, their product policies and their promotional activities. (Buhalis, 2003, p. 179)

The choice of distribution channel(s) is one of the most important decisions a tour operator must make and involves two key considerations. First, where and how potential customers can purchase the product(s). Second, given that customers cannot experience the product before consumption, they rely on information being provided about the product; traditionally, the brochure. Therefore, it is essential that the operator ensures the necessary information is provided for customers to inform their choice and subsequent decision as to which product best suits their requirements. Traditionally, the distribution system of tour operators can be considered as a simple process within which consumers purchase holiday products through travel agents. Over time this chain of distribution has been challenged as the role of the intermediaries has become blurred. Indeed, the distribution landscape has changed substantially over the last 25 years, becoming increasingly complex with the introduction of new players in the market and alternative channels emerging, most noticeably online sales.

Changes in Traditional Distribution

The principle function of travel agents is retailing travel products and services on behalf of the primary suppliers, e.g. tour operator or principal. However, the 1970s witnessed significant changes in the structure of the UK travel agency and tour operator sector, in what became termed by the trade press as the 'March of the Multiples'. Large tour operators expanded rapidly, often through the acquisition of small retail chains, a strategy that continued to the end of the 20th century. Thus, the **multiples** gained greater economies of scale, increased bargaining power with the principals and greater brand awareness leading to increased profits.

The emergence and rapid expansion of the large travel agency organizations saw an unprecedented number of new travel agencies opening, fuelled by the increasing demand for package holidays and travel in general. Non-tourism companies such as WH Smith, the Co-operative Society and the Automobile Association identified opportunities to expand into the travel retail sector, a development continued with the introduction of travel agency

services by some of the major supermarkets today. Other companies in the sector sought to expand; for example, Lunn Poly was bought out by the Thomson Travel Group, which embarked on a rapid expansion campaign, from 60 branches in 1972 to over 600 by 1993, in the process becoming the dominant retailer in the UK. However, since the high days of the 20th century, the traditional travel agency distribution channel has been increasingly challenged by developments in information communication technology, specifically the introduction of computer reservation systems and global distribution systems.

Global distribution systems

The rapid changes in information technology have impacted on all industries, but perhaps none more so than the tourism product. The nature of the tourism product (see characteristics of tourism, Chapter 10, this volume) certainly lends itself to the application of information technology, especially for the supply and exchange of information throughout the production supply chain and distribution, and more so for intra-regional and international travel. The first major evidence of this lies in the development of the electronic distribution systems known as computer reservation systems (CRS) – the forerunners of today's global distribution systems (GDS).

CRS were first developed by airlines in the late 1960s to manage flight schedules, availability, reservations and prices, with the primary objective of selling airline tickets. Prior to this, travel agents would have to phone airlines to request specific flights, while tour operators would manually manage reservations and pricing itineraries. American Airlines was one of the first to introduce a CRS known as Sabre (Semi Automated Business Resource Environment), which was only used internally and travel agents still had to make contact by telephone. Sabre originally had very limited reservation capability, until 1980 when an advanced airline yield management system was introduced (Das, 2009). By the late 1960s the airlines recognized that automating the reservation process for travel agents would make their agents more productive and potentially more loyal to the airlines, as such becoming part of their salesforce. In recognition of this, in 1976 United Airlines offered the Apollo system to travel agents, although this only allowed agents to book on United Airlines. These systems allowed airlines to share their product capacity with retailers and suppliers. The next step was to introduce computer terminals into travel agencies to ensure that their system was used. Subsequently other systems were developed, for example, European airlines invested in creating their own reservation systems, and in 1987 a consortium of Air France and Lufthansa developed Amadeus.

CRS providers have ensured that these distribution systems have developed into a business, becoming a substantial source of income because they charge a small fee per booking and a fee for travel agents for the right to use the system. Ongoing developments in CRS led to GDS, which today can do considerably more than sell only airline tickets and automate procedures and have effectively replaced CRS. These reservation systems, sometimes called automated reservation systems, used by travel agents and tour operators were hugely influential in distributing package holidays to clients. Until the early 1990s, GDS were a closed group limited to the retail travel agency community. Suppliers pay fees to have their products on the system and although lucrative in terms of sales they proved to be expensive due to the cost of the system, transaction fees and commissions. As GDS are distribution software, there was no direct connection with the customer and principals and wholesales looked to find alternative methods of distribution. This situation led to a shift from being passive systems handling only bookings for airlines to include all travel services and becoming a distinct distribution channel.

Three major GDS suppliers have emerged: Amadeus; Sabre; Galileo/Worldspan (after a merger in 2007). Almost every travel agent in the world uses either one or a combination of these three companies to search and book airfares. Tours and activity products are not available through any GDS system. They charge airlines booking fees and require subscriptions from agencies for using the system, which holds no inventories (products) but they can access a supplier's inventory in real-time. Amadeus is the largest GDS but does not have a strong foothold in the USA, whereas Sabre is strong in the USA, but does not have a large presence elsewhere. Travel Port owns both Galileo and Worldspan and used to be the dominant GDS system in Europe, Africa, the Middle East and Eurasia, but is losing its foothold in most markets. Each of these GDS systems has a customer portal for end-users; Sabre has Virtually There, Amadeus has Check My Trip and Travel Port uses View Trip and My Trip (see Chapter 6, this volume). GDS systems enable tour operators to purchase components when putting together packages, particularly packaging tailor-made holidays or buying rooms/seats once allocations are full or additional supply is needed. Some packages may be available through GDS and sold via one of the distribution channels.

Distribution Channels

Today there are alternative distribution channels that can be used by tour operators and wholesalers, which has enabled consumers to interact directly with tour operators. These channels are usually classified as either direct or indirect, as illustrated in Fig. 9.1.

The key question for the tour operator is which channel(s) to use. Channel decisions must be made on information drawn from analysis of the product, the market and the competition. Essentially, it is important to determine which distribution channels are most likely to be effective given the target market(s) (see Chapter 10, this volume). The main options are:

Direct to the consumer:

- telesales/email;
- walk-in;
- call centre;
- online via a booking engine.

Indirect, using an intermediary:

- travel agents;
- online travel agents;

- incentive travel company – these may be professional services that plan, promote and execute their own product or act as an intermediary for operators;
- meeting and convention planners – these may be professional services that plan meetings for corporate clients or act as an intermediary for other suppliers;
- national tourism organization websites, e.g. Japan's National Tourism Organization which hosts packages provided by airlines;
- visitor information centres;
- concierge services.

The benefits of using an intermediary (e.g. a travel agent), although varied, may be primarily considered as they have direct contact with potential customers. They will also reach a wider market that may be difficult for the tour operator otherwise to identify and service.

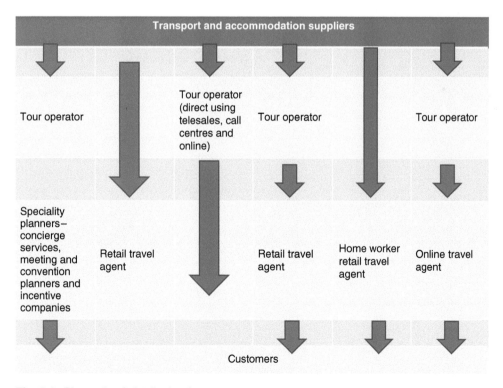

Fig. 9.1. Channels of distribution for tour operators.

Channel choice

The right choice of distribution channel(s) is crucial to the success of any product because it is the link between the supplier of the product offering and the consumer. As Lumsden (1997) indicated, operators need to assess carefully their channel options by considering the following factors:

- Cost: includes consideration of the commission and costs involved in distribution of the marketing material.
- Control: specifically, the degree of control the operator wishes to have in the distribution of their products; for example, selling direct ensures that information given to potential customers is accurate, which may be particularly important for specialist operators.
- Service: the level and quality of service can be controlled if operators sell directly to their customers, whereas they have little control of the service provision when using third-party suppliers such as travel agents.
- Consumer: the target market and their preferences.
- Resource commitment: how much support can they offer to travel agents and other retail intermediaries?
- Competitor activity: how are competitors distributing their products?
- Coverage and access to market segment: can retailers access potential customers more efficiently than the tour operator themselves?
- Image: does the retailer support the image created by the tour operator?

These factors are all particularly pertinent to travel agents.

Travel agents

One of the most efficient ways for tour operators to distribute their product(s) is through travel agents. Basically, a travel agent is a retailer of travel-related products on behalf of suppliers (principals and operators) to customers, who may or may not be the final consumer. Therefore, the agent's role is to act on behalf of principals and consumers – in effect, a 'go-between' – by supplying information on, and opportunities to purchase, travel products, hence the term agent. As such, travel agents act on behalf of the suppliers and can be considered as a broker in that they bring buyer and seller together. They operate on the basis that they will receive commission on sales. Sales primarily comprise prearranged packages on behalf of tour operators; individual components provided by the principals such as airlines or hoteliers; or packages created by bundling components together to create a single holiday product. Agents who do create packages for customers are considered 'travel organizers' under the EU Package Travel Regulations and therefore can be considered as a type of tour operator (see Chapter 8, this volume).

To make such sales, the travel agent needs to provide the necessary product information as opposed to holding and retailing goods, thus they have no stock holdings. Essentially, the agent provides a convenient location for the purchase of holiday products. The key functions of a travel agent include:

- making reservations;
- planning itineraries;
- costing fares and charges;
- providing tickets (or vouchers) for the components of the package;
- communicating with customers, maintaining reservations;
- promoting products using brochures and other marketing collateral; and
- dealing with customer complaints.

A travel agent will only contact the tour operator or principal on the customer's behalf once the customer has decided to purchase the product. Therefore, in comparison with general retail services, they have lower investment costs. Holloway and Humphreys (2012) notes that this has three important implications. First, the start-up costs of operating a travel agency are relatively low because there is no investment in products, thus limiting the financial risk, while revenues are generated through sales commissions. Second, travel agents promote products that are often in competition with other travel agents. Third, because they do not need to sell stock holdings they can be less loyal to the principals involved (unless they are vertically integrated) (see Chapter 3, this volume). Vertically integrated tour operators such as TUI retain high street travel agents so that they can maintain their influence on the way their products are marketed while also promoting their brands. Within the UK, for example, Thomas Cook is the UK's largest travel agency in terms of number of stores with 850, compared with TUI, which has 644, Virgin Holidays 123, Hays Travel 104 and Flight Centre 87 (Mintel, 2014).

Over the past few years it has been suggested that travel agents are in decline, and unlikely to maintain their position in the chain of distribution; this is termed **disintermediation**. For example, in the USA in the mid-1990s there were over 34,000 travel agents, which had reduced to 13,000 by 2013 (CNN, 2013), while in the UK retail travel outlets (ABTA members) declined from 7575 in 2002 to 4435 in 2008 (Mintel, 2016). Both Thomas Cook and TUI have reduced the number of outlets with the aim of increasing their market share of online bookings substantially. Virgin Holidays operate a concession model, which means it has stores inside other shops such as House of Fraser, Debenhams, Tesco and Sainsbury. Furthermore, Virgin Holidays also has recently introduced a 'retail lite' store, which

is designed to cater for customers who have already done their holiday research (potentially including quotes) but want a face-to-face conversation before booking, emphasizing speed and convenience. The fierce competition between agents, the reduction or removal of commission paid by principals and the ever-increasing availability of online distribution is challenging the profitability of the traditional 'bricks and mortar' travel agent. This has led to a deskilling in the sector; once travel agents were seen as consultants with expert product knowledge, but declining revenues have increased the focus on reducing costs, leading to lower salaries and a tendency to recruit staff who are comparatively young and inexperienced.

Overall, the evident trend in the USA and UK is a decline in the use of travel agents, which is symptomatic of the increasing use of the Internet for research and booking. This shift to digital purchasing is substantiated by Mintel (2014) in that 9% of customers booked their holiday package in-store and in-store conversion rates of enquiries to sales were as high as 67%. To compete with online travel agents, some agents have introduced late night openings, Sunday openings, immersive technology, coffee bar style comforts and shops that have become 'destinations' (see Holiday Hypermarkets, which are part of TUI's retail operations). These trends are not replicated in many other countries, wherein agents are still seen as the first choice for purchasing holiday packages. Across the EU, purchasing patterns are very different: Belgian, Danish, Greek and Austrian tourists prefer to book direct with tour operators, the German market still typically arrange their holidays through travel agents, whereas the Spanish are known for also using travel agents for domestic travel products. Within Saudi Arabia, travel agents are used for both leisure and business travel, although their presence has changed from traditional bricks and mortar shops to offering online services. Even so, the majority of customers still paid travel agents directly (Mintel, 2014).

While travel agencies may have declined in mature markets, they are still very much a part of the tour operating sector in young markets such as China. As domestic tourism in China developed notably since the 1980s, the number of agencies increased from less than 300 to 7725 by the year 2000 (Zhang *et al.*, 2005). Subsequent liberalization has resulted in approximately 1400 international travel agencies (those agencies authorized for group and individual travel overseas) (see Chapter 8, this volume).

Types of retail travel agent

Travel agents have historically been classified into three main types: leisure travel agents, business travel agents and home-based travel agents. However, the delineation between these three classifications has become more blurred with leisure travel agents recruiting home-based agents and expanding to include business travel. Furthermore, online travel agents have enabled both business and leisure customers to create and purchase packages.

Leisure travel agent

These travel agents are usually based in the main thoroughfares and/or central business districts in towns and cities. They may also have a presence as an online travel agency. Their primary objective is to achieve the highest level of revenue, e.g. commission, per sale. This sector is highly competitive and generally requires a substantial turnover to generate profits and sustain the business. They may retail products on behalf of tour operators and/or package together different components to create individual packages for clients.

Although the sale of inclusive tours usually accounts for the major proportion of their revenues, they may make additional income from foreign exchange transactions, selling insurance and visa applications in addition to the sale of other travel services such as air flight tickets and so forth. For each of these provisions, the agent will receive a commission. Commissions vary according to the type of product that is sold; typical rates are:

- 10% commission for inclusive tours; however, this may be increased by dealing with preferred suppliers and achieving sales targets. Some agents can achieve 'overrides', which can increase commission by an additional 2.5% when agents achieve a certain level of sales.
- 6% to 8% commission for hotel accommodation, airline and railway.
- 50% for insurance sales.
- 10% for car hire.

However, with increased competition between principals and among travel agents, there has been downward pressure on the levels of commission; for example, many airlines have reduced their commission rates to 2% or less. In some instances, such as British Airways, agents receive 1% commission on their sales, but many airlines in the USA, such as United Airlines, Continental Airlines and North-West Airlines, do not pay any commission (Amadeus, 2007). In the case of the USA, agencies often add a service fee; as The American Society of Travel Agents noted, over 40% of agencies charge a service fee (usually US$25 per booking) for the packages (Amadeus, 2007), which may well be higher for cruise holidays. This approach has not yet been adopted in the UK, so agencies need to find alternative revenue streams, potentially in addition to relying on 'up-selling' and selling ancillary services such as car parking to maintain income in the form of commission.

Types of agencies

There are many different types of travel agency and their titles may well differ, depending on their country and its regulations relating to tour operators and travel agencies; for example, there is little distinction between travel agents and tour operators, wholesalers and retailers in China (see Chapter 8, this volume). In the UK, for example, they are categorized based on their size and links to tour operators.

- Multinationals. Multinational agents have offices worldwide, e.g. the American Automobile Association, American Express. The UK company Thomas Cook is represented in most European countries, North America and the Indian subcontinent, while, for example, the Australian-based company Flight Centre Limited has a UK subsidiary known as The Flight Centre.
- Multiple chains. Most of the travel agents on the high street are part of multiple chains and often vertically integrated with a tour operator, e.g. Going Places, Hays Travel, Trailfinders. These agencies generally operate at a national and/or global level.
- Agents that are part of a vertically integrated chain have been accused of directional selling, i.e. encouraging passengers to book products that are supplied by their integrated operators. Multiples are more likely to operate a racking policy based on selected tour operators, promoting those products that offer greater incentives or are part of the parent company.
- Miniples. These are small travel agency chains, which are usually regionally based and tend to offer a greater range of brochures and may include specialist operators, for example Chan Bros. in Singapore. Regional-based miniples are particularly vulnerable to takeovers by national multiples

such as Hays Travel, a company based in the North of England, which bought out Bath Travel and its 60 branches in the South of England.
- Independent agents, generally a one- or two-outlet operation. They usually cater to specialist niche markets; for example, a well-defined group interested in similar types of activities such as sports or specific destinations, such as CTC Travel, which is based in Singapore and specializes in organizing and operating tours to China. Independent agents, and also some miniples, tend to remain small and focus on having an experienced workforce, quality of customer care and customer retention. They are often located in prime locations in cities and towns and may be operated by a sole proprietor.
- Homeworkers. Homeworkers have been in operation for over 30 years in the USA and are now gradually developing in other countries. Basically, they are anyone seeking to market and sell travel products from a home-based office, usually on behalf of a bonded, accredited travel agency, referred to as 'the host agency'. The host agency will usually support such homeworkers by providing help with administration, finance and marketing, e.g. Hays Travel (UK), which has been supporting homeworkers – known as Travel Counsellors – for over 20 years. Homeworkers design and build packages on behalf of customers and aim to develop a relationship with their clients and a strong client base to encourage repeat customers, which is generally essential to achieve a viable number of sales.

Business travel agents

Business travel is generally considered to be one of the most lucrative sectors of retail travel and is a highly-specialized field requiring prompt, expert service. Although business demand is far less than that for leisure, income from business travellers is often greater due to enhanced product purchase and the comparative lack of seasonality.

Business travel agents, aka corporate travel agents or travel management companies, enable organizations to manage their business travel. Business travel is dominated by multiples such as American Express or Carlson Wagonlit, although many independent travel agents will offer a service tailored to local business needs. Large organizations may be offered 'implants', whereby an agent sets up an office within the organization, e.g. Procter & Gamble, to organize travel for company staff. Most of these agents provide self-booking tools, which allow travellers or those appointed to book travel to do it themselves, although this is usually supported by an advisory service. Even so, face-to-face interactions are far less likely.

Planning packages for business travellers can be demanding because they have high expectations for quality of service and expect efficient itineraries to minimize waiting times and the option to change tickets/destinations as necessary. Flexibility is a major constituent in the higher prices charged for business fares. Business agents may work directly with suppliers to negotiate corporate rates, which requires information on the corporation's travel patterns and expenditure to achieve favourable rates. However, the role of these agents is under threat by business travellers booking their own trips through online travel agencies via smartphone apps and travel platforms, enabling them to make their own arrangements, and the use of peer-to-peer accommodation such as AirBnB, which has grown by 10% in the past two years (Mintel, 2015a).

Online travel agents

Perhaps the greatest concern for travel agents and operators retailing their own pre-packaged holidays is the growth of online travel agencies (OTAs), which has increased the level of competition in the marketplace. Originally, only travel agents could use global distribution systems (GDS). But the development of the Internet has catalysed OTAs, which can access GDSs daily to make reservations for clients. This has enabled customers to search for travel information and to compare prices easily, a development that has been aided by the emergence of metasearch engines (e.g. Kayak, Trivago, Skyscanner) that provide an interface that shows hotel and flight availability and pricing information from multiple sources without the user needing to visit each of these sites separately. These enable customers to compare different brands, products, packages and prices easily. Many OTAs offer this facility.

Although OTAs are available globally, they are still dominated by the North American and Western European market, and have a growing presence in the Middle East; for example, many companies such as Expedia, Agoda and booking.com offer Arabic websites. In contrast, emerging economies are currently still very reliant on traditional retailing. In 2011, the top-four global OTAs were all based in the USA, with Expedia being dominant with major shares in Trivago, hotels.com, hotwire, carrentals.com and Travelocity. Competition though is increasing; for example, from OTAs in Brazil, Russia, India (MakeMyTrip) and China (Ctrip). MakeMyTrip initially focused on US travel to India, but now is a very important player in the Indian market. In China, while the clear majority of international travel packages are still booked through traditional travel retailers, OTAs are rapidly developing, with Ctrip (see Box 9.1) accounting for approximately 50% of the online market (Mintel, 2015b). Although online sales currently account for approximately 10% of the outbound market, it is expected this will grow as more Chinese tourists gain experience of overseas trips and look to travel independently.

The European market was relatively fragmented until Odigeo (eDreams Odigeo) was created in 2011, through the merger of eDreams and Go Voyages and the acquisition of Opodo and its subsidiary Travellink, and is now the largest grouping of OTAs in Europe. Expedia, Orbitz and eDreams have developed affiliation programmes with traditional high-street travel agents. These programmes give OTAs access to a larger customer base while allowing traditional travel agencies the opportunity to maintain their presence in an increasingly competitive market, adopting more of a consultant role providing professional assistance for customers.

The rise of OTAs has led to Lufthansa charging a €16 fee on all bookings made through third-party websites. This was a strategic move to encourage passengers to book direct through the airline's website, although it could be considered a risky move as 70% of airline tickets are booked through third parties. If other companies follow suit, then passengers using price comparison sites will be directed towards the supplier (principal).

Dynamic Packaging

Dynamic packaging is a self-packaging facility, which enables customers to create their own holidays by designing their own package of flights, accommodation, car rental and other products to suit their own needs. These tailor-made packages will be priced based on current availability. As dynamic packages are sold as a single product, the customer does not know the individual cost of each component, meaning that it is not transparent. They will not be aware of the special prices that travel agents can achieve from principals, such as discounted airline tickets and reduced rates for accommodation. In this instance, the consumer may achieve a competitive price for their tailor-made product and the tour operator/travel agent will still maintain their profit margins. Dynamic packaging has been enabled by the growth of computerized software for tour operators. Thus an agent or tour operator can create a package and the software can compare this with traditional package prices, as a dynamically packaged holiday may not be the cheapest option. Conversely, an agent may be able to dynamically package and replicate a tour operator's product at a lower price without having to discount. It should be noted that many people confuse dynamic packaging with customization. Customization, which can also be called dynamic bundling, is when individual components within a prearranged package are changed, for example upgraded.

The benefits of dynamic packaging for customers are that it provides more flexibility in terms of routes and duration of trips, and may offer better value for money. The most likely areas for growth will be in the short-haul market as dynamic packaging can take advantage of low-cost airlines. As a response to the growth of dynamic packaging by travel agents, some large tour operators such as Thomas Cook have introduced dynamic packaging on their websites under the title flexibletrips.com. Utilizing new software, for example Multicon, the software scans for dynamic components and feeds them into this agent's website, allowing greater flexibility and more choice for customers. Online agents offering these packages in the UK need to have an ATOL bond (see Chapter 8, this volume).

As the foregoing discussion suggests, practice in different countries will vary both in terms of agency operations and consumer preferences, which may well be due to variance in historical development and culture.

Travel Agency Selection

Once a tour operator has decided that utilizing travel agencies is the most appropriate means of accessing their target market, they need to decide the degree to which their product should be distributed. Holloway and Humphreys (2012) suggest that this strategy can be intensive, exclusive or selective.

- Intensive – this is where the tour operator maximizes their exposure by utilizing all available channels of distribution and their brochures are available through as many travel agency chains as possible. This is expensive due to the number of brochures needed and the support given to the agency, so this approach is most suitable for mass market holidays.

However, many agencies are owned by tour companies and they will predominantly sell their own products through their own set of agents.

- Exclusive – the operator limits distribution specifically to targeted agents; for example, those specializing in upmarket tailor-made products or specialist retailers. The granting of exclusive rights to one agent to sell products is rare in the tourism sector, although some adventure tour operators allow a small number of specialist travel agents to sell their products, typically holidays that are higher priced.
- Selective – this is where a limited number of agencies are used and can be positioned somewhere between intensive and exclusive. These agents may be identified using specific criteria, such as those who have undergone training by the tour operator and have access to the requisite market segments. For example, an operator may use specific agents that are international to the operator, providing exclusive rights to sell the operator's products in their area/country.

Travel agency branches are usually small outlets and thus have limited shelf space, perhaps allowing for 100–150 brochure spaces (the exception is holiday supermarkets, which can carry considerably more). Brochures are promoted based on links to other levels of the company; for example, Thomas Cook travel agents will promote Thomas Cook holidays, Thomson's, as part of TUI, will promote their products. Agents will also promote those tour operators and principals that offer them higher commissions and thus give their own products and preferred operators premium racking space. Due to the limited space, agents invariably operate different policies on promoting brochures, such as only displaying one copy, or keeping some brochures for 'on request' only. Overall, this situation can prove very difficult for small operators seeking to gain access to the market through agencies. Thus, they need to target travel agents whose customers are in line with their target market segment and who reflect the image of the tour operator – for example, an upmarket independent travel agent such as Gosforth Travel based in an affluent suburb of Newcastle upon Tyne (UK).

Direct distribution

In some cases, tour operators are taking direct control of the distribution by eliminating the need for travel agents. There are a few alternative options to that of travel agents for tour operators to use, which involve selling directly to the customer. This is perhaps the greatest challenge to travel agents. The benefit of direct distribution is most notably the removal of the need to pay commission to travel agents on each sale, hence the interest among operators to sell directly to the public. While initially this may seem an obvious decision for operators, there are costs involved. For example, setting up call centres and sales staff can be expensive and supporting this with national advertising campaigns will also add to the cost. There is also an additional consideration, specifically if operators are selling both directly, and through travel agents. By offering lower prices to book direct, they run the risk of jeopardizing their relationship with the agents, which may have an impact on future sales.

Smaller tour operators frequently sell their own packages direct because they do not have the bargaining power to command good racking positioning in travel agents and sales may be small, thus limiting commission revenues. These operators may choose to distribute their products using a small number of independent travel agents and encourage sales by providing incentives. Within the UK market, small tour operators who are members of AITO have access to agents under the 'Special Agents Scheme', which identifies travel agents willing to handle independent tour operator bookings.

Call centres

By the early 2000s, call centres had become a central element for customer contact and a popular method for selling holidays (Russell, 2008). Inbound call centres (those that receive calls initiated by customers) are very labour intensive and staff costs are estimated to be between 60% and 80% of the overall operating budget (Askin *et al.*, 2007). Many operators have introduced their own telephone-based sales teams, frequently referred to as call centres or the central reservation office, even though they may be located within the company offices.

With increasing operating costs and declining sales, many vertically integrated operators have looked to reduce costs by closing retail premises, but have remained committed to call centres, although online retailing is considered more cost efficient. Direct Holidays, which is owned by the Thomas Cook Group, is a key player in the Irish travel market, with over 750,000 passengers travelling to popular resorts in the Mediterranean such as the Balearics, Greece and North Africa, and further afield to destinations such as Florida and the Dominican Republic. In 2009, in a bid to cut costs, they closed their Dublin premises with the loss of 30 jobs, but retained the 70 back-office and call-centre employees. Centralized call centres have an additional advantage in that they can provide consistent service and the ability to amend prices quickly. However, multi-branded companies may operate several different call centres aligned with each brand, which may dilute the product knowledge of the sales staff.

International outsourcing of call centres has grown considerably because of technology such as Voice Over Internet Protocol (VOIP), which uses the Internet for calls. This has enabled companies such as Thomson to operate a call centre located in India. However, it is noted that the Philippines are predominantly the main location for outsourced call-centre services (BBC, 2012).

Web-based distribution (direct sales)

The impact of the World Wide Web – the Internet – on the distribution of tourism products cannot be underestimated. Travel companies have and continue to exploit the opportunities arising from Internet technology and many operators have set up direct-to-consumer websites. This has resulted in the travel product becoming one of the most commonly sold products on the Internet, although predominantly transportation and accommodation rather than holiday packages.

As a channel of distribution, the Internet is ideally suited to tour operators and travel agents because there are relatively few barriers to setting up an Internet presence. Websites allow companies to make direct contact with potential customers and thereby avoid GDS transaction fees, call centre processing charges and commissions. This also provides excellent opportunities for 'up-selling', i.e. seeking to add on additional services such as airport parking, insurance, accommodation or transport upgrades and car hire. Furthermore, direct contact with the consumer allows operators to engage in customer relationship management to develop the lifetime value of the customer.

Distribution Resources

This section addresses the management issue of distribution of marketing communication material, usually in the form of a brochure. Although technology has enabled operators and agents to utilize information communication technology for the presentation of and consumer access to such material, many people still prefer hard copy material to viewing sources online (Mintel, 2013). Therefore in this section we will consider the process of producing brochures.

Brochure production

Brochures have traditionally been synonymous with booking holidays and are still an important part of the buying process, being an important part of the information search (see Chapter 10, this volume, Fig. 10.3).

The brochure enables potential customers to view and compare different product offerings, including price and key features and indeed may provide inspiration for consideration of new destinations and resorts. They have several positive attributes, such as attracting customer attention when displayed at travel agencies (the pull factor) and being taken away for consideration to enable decisions to be made with other travelling companions. In addition, brochures allow easy comparison between destinations and between different operators. They also provide information about the legal contract between the holidaymaker and the tour operator, specifying the commitment on either side, information on insurance and booking conditions and explaining complaint procedures. As such, they form the basis of the contract between the customer and the tour operator. Criticisms of the brochure include consumers' dislike of the lack of transparency in terms of pricing, with sections often dedicated to supplementary charges such as regional departures, peak season pricing and limited information about the product.

However, they are a significant cost factor, often accounting for the largest share of the marketing budget. While the cost of brochures varies, the average cost is approximately £1–£1.50 per copy for mainstream brochures, although for some specialist operators this may be as high as £5. Mass tour operators can publish between one and five editions of their brochure(s) each year, some of which may be up to 800 pages long, with up to 3 million copies produced due to the need to update prices. Although this is labour-intensive and expensive, brochures cannot be produced within the EU without including prices (Package Travel Directive – see Chapter 8, this volume). The cost of designing each page of the brochure can be between £50 and £100, based on the charges of the design agencies, while distribution costs range from £0.06 for bulk distribution to over £2.00 per brochure for individual postal distribution (*Travel Weekly*, 2007).

It is not surprising therefore to find that tour operators have been seeking to reduce the production and distribution of brochures since the 1990s, a time when, according to Middleton and Clarke (2001), tour operators were producing between 6 and 10 brochures per person booking a holiday in their main summer programmes, adding approximately £20 in costs to each booking. In July 2016, TUI announced that it was going to phase out its Thomson and First Choice brochures by 2020; currently it prints 4.7 million brochures a year with 58 titles for some 5.5 million customers, so it is anticipating substantial cost savings (Dennis, 2016). This may be seen as a move to disintermediate the travel agents because one of the prime motivators for visiting travel agents is to collect brochures that can be taken away.

Brochure contents

It is a legal requirement within the EU that the brochure contents are clear, legible and accurate to enable customers to make a judgement and include:

- price of package;
- destination, itinerary and mode of transport;
- departure dates;
- type of accommodation, additional facilities;
- any meals included;
- standard information on passport, health and visa requirements;
- deadline for payment.

Specialist brochures, such as those prepared for adventure tours, are more likely to contain specific information about the holidays such as difficulty ratings (e.g. for walking and mountain holidays), pictures of attractions, information about the destinations and means of travel. As Page (2009) noted, the brochure can be considered as comprising the following sections.

Front cover

Logo and imagery. The logo needs to represent the company and should be recognizable. This should be supported by any brand imagery that is used by the company. The pictures on the front cover should represent the type of holiday or destination featured, for example brochures that are aimed at families usually include a picture of a family on the front cover.

Introduction

This usually includes information about the company, the uniqueness of their products and the destinations they serve and any specific information that is pertinent to all the products promoted within, e.g. car hire. This section may also include information about the transport used; for example, in the case of air transport, the name of the airline, type and class of aircraft and the operator.

Destination pages

Most of the brochure is given over to information about the destinations and resorts. This will usually include commentary on each of the holidays, such as duration, location, accommodation provider, meals included, activities and facilities included or available, clear indication of price, and any supplements that may be charged.

Information specific to the brochure

This may include regional departures, hotel grading information, upgrade opportunities or surcharges for additional occupants (or single occupancy), health requirements, specific information about meals and other information that may enable customers to make an educated choice, such as same-sex couples restrictions.

Terms and conditions

Full conditions of booking, including cancellation charges and conditions, transferring the booking, pricing errors, insurance, minimum numbers and complaint procedures, are given. Information about insurance may be included, but customers must have the right to choose their own insurance if it covers all the activities.

Visas and general information

It is difficult for tour operators to provide up-to-date information on health matters and vaccinations for destinations. Therefore, they are likely to include useful links to the National Travel Health Network and Centre or recommend visiting a medical practice. Information about visas will be included, such as the need for a visa or Electronic System for Travel Authorization (ESTA), which is the USA visa waiver programme, or other specific requirements.

Back cover

The back cover often includes promotional pictures of other brochures and/or outlets, web address and social media details. In addition it usually lists contact details, membership logos, e.g. ABTA, AITO, **FTO**; travel protection logos, e.g. CAA/ATOL, **IATA**; awards, e.g. British Travel Awards Winner.

Brochures and travel agents

The distribution of brochures is a further expense that tour operators must consider, not only in terms of placement but also the cost involved. Operators must evaluate the effectiveness of each of the retailers they may use and calculate the number of brochures they distribute to each one. This ratio is known as the conversion rate and will determine how many and how often brochures are supplied. For example, high-performing travel agents sell over 100 holidays a year, while low-performing agents may sell as few as five of that operator's products, although this depends on the cost of the holiday (Page, 2009).

There are different ways to deliver brochures. The larger tour operators have a fleet of delivery vehicles, whereas smaller tour operators might choose to use a specialist company that provides this service and acts on behalf of several different operators. The benefits of delivering brochures directly means that their brochure is received alone, encouraging priority racking, whereas using delivery companies means that many operators' brochures are delivered at the same time and less time is spent racking them; some brochures may not be racked at all. Also, to encourage sales, operators may offer additional commissions or prizes to sales agents who achieve defined targets, for example Virgin Holidays offers the chance to win a holiday to Miami with one entry every time they sell a Virgin holiday (*Travel Bulletin*, 2015), while another travel company offers iPads to agents who achieve a specific number of bookings.

The small tour operators encounter difficulties in encouraging travel agents to stock their brochures, given the available display space, which is invariably prioritized for their own company products, operators offering higher commissions or those that are known to sell well. One approach to address this problem adopted by some of these small companies (primarily wholesalers) is to use distribution agencies to promote their brochures directly to travel agents. These distribution agents provide account managers who deal directly with the travel agents to encourage them to promote their products, either by phone or face-to-face visits. More generally, small tour operators need to consider carefully whether a brochure is actually going to be an effective marketing tool.

Direct mail brochures

Some tour operators rely on customers contacting them after seeing advertisements (newspapers, online, social media, radio or television) to request brochures that are then posted to them. This obviously is an additional cost but is likely to have a better conversion rate because the customer has actively sought the brochure.

Producing a brochure

To produce a brochure, operators need to coordinate the information with that available on their website. A brochure can take five months or longer to produce and involve considerable detail and time, as illustrated in Fig. 9.2. Decisions need to be made about the quality of the paper, the colours, the graphics and the style, all of which needs to be attuned to the operator's brand image and be consistent across all marketing communications.

Move to online brochures

There are clear benefits for tour operators to replace the traditional hardcopy brochure with e-brochures, such as a reduction in cost of production, storage and distribution. Originally e-brochures were presented as a PDF format of the hardcopy brochure, but expectations have changed considerably. With the increasing use of 'tablets' and portable devices capable of searching quickly for products, it is increasingly likely that an e-brochure is unnecessary as long as the company's website is easy to navigate and has an in-site search engine.

Summary

In the context of the classic 4Ps of marketing (Product, Price, Place, Promotion), the one which potentially presents the most complexity for today's tour operators is that of place. In operational terms, place translates into distribution; in other words, how does the tour operator reach its target market(s) when it does not have a physical product that a retailer can display for sale, in the process taking ownership of the goods? The tour operator needs to establish a channel through which to communicate their product offerings.

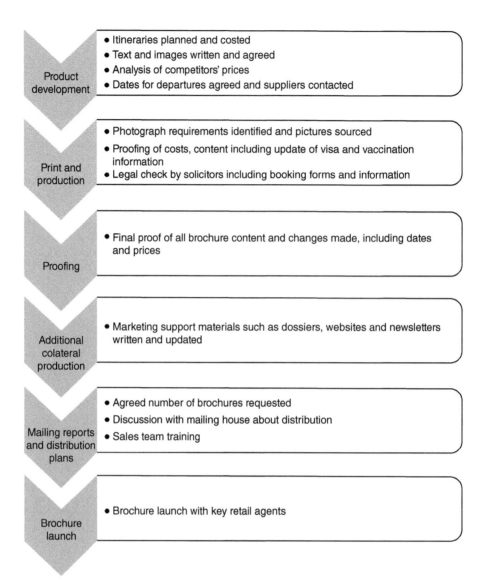

Product development
- Itineraries planned and costed
- Text and images written and agreed
- Analysis of competitors' prices
- Dates for departures agreed and suppliers contacted

Print and production
- Photograph requirements identified and pictures sourced
- Proofing of costs, content including update of visa and vaccination information
- Legal check by solicitors including booking forms and information

Proofing
- Final proof of all brochure content and changes made, including dates and prices

Additional colateral production
- Marketing support materials such as dossiers, websites and newsletters written and updated

Mailing reports and distribution plans
- Agreed number of brochures requested
- Discussion with mailing house about distribution
- Sales team training

Brochure launch
- Brochure launch with key retail agents

Fig. 9.2. Key stages in brochure production.

Traditionally, this was the travel agent, with the operator's products being presented through their brochures, which was logical development on the part of earlier agents who diversified into tour operating. Clearly other entrepreneurs saw opportunities to develop a business in tour operations but then they needed a distribution channel, which was basically ready-made in the developing network of travel agents. In due course, some tour operators sought to merge with or takeover travel agencies (see Chapter 3, this volume), thereby expanding their own operations and being able to prioritize their own holiday packages, giving prominence to their own holiday brochures.

As discussed, developments in information communication technology catalysed opportunities for operators to deal directly with their potential customers, as is manifest through call centres, the Internet and websites. Thus, over the last two decades, the channels of distribution open to tour operators have diversified considerably, bringing into question the role of intermediaries, in particular the travel agent, in these systems.

The adoption of direct channels enabled through the Internet has given rise to questions over the real value of brochures as a marketing tool now that potential customers can garner all the information on possible holiday choices from surfing the Internet. Certainly, visitors to their local travel agent like to browse brochures and take them home to share with other members of the family or friends. But increasingly, such sharing of information can be mutually convenient and simultaneously undertaken within a group using their own smart phones. Brochures are also expensive to produce and distribute and subject to change, which then requires a new issue. Thus tour operators are less likely to produce brochures and increasingly are seeking to use the Internet, particularly their own website, as their channel of first choice.

Discussion Questions

1. What are the benefits of disintermediation for the consumer?
2. What are the implications for the growth of online sales for the traditional travel agent?
3. In the context of responsible tourism, what other benefits arise from tour operators ceasing brochure production?
4. Why is travel and tourism distribution such an important issue and the selection of a distribution strategy so crucial to an organization?
5. Compile a list of considerations that should be made when selecting a distribution strategy for travel/tourism organizations.
6. Consider the impact of IT developments on travel and tourism industry stakeholders.
7. What do you think are the current and future issues in distribution choice in travel and tourism management?

Key Terms

- **Disintermediation** – Disintermediation is the removal of an intermediary from the chain of distribution, for example tour operators selling directly to customers, eliminating the need for a travel agent, or a hotel selling directly to customers, eliminating both the travel agent and tour operator.
- **FTO** – The Federation of Tour Operators was established in 1967 and comprised the major UK tour operators. In 2008 it merged with ABTA.
- **IATA** – The International Air Transport Association is the trade association for 265 airlines (83%). IATA formulates industry policy and standards such as safety and security, and provides accreditation for travel agents to sell tickets on behalf of IATA members.
- **Multiple (as in March of the Multiples)** – The March of the Multiples refers to the rapid increase in travel agents owned by vertically integrated companies, threatening the existence of independent and small travel agency chains.
- **Up-selling** – This is a sales technique where a seller, for example travel agent/tour operator, persuades the customer to buy more expensive items, upgrades or other add-ons in an attempt to make a more profitable sale, e.g. car parking, room upgrade, excursions.

There is much discussion that the future of travel agents is in doubt, with travel industry news articles suggesting they will no longer have a role in the distribution of package holidays (see www.travelweekly.co.uk/articles/40940/mintel-study-casts-doubt-on-future-of-high-street-agents). Other reports suggest that they are still relevant (see www.travelmarketreport.com/articles/Travel-Agents-A-Much-Brighter-Future-Than-You-Might-Think).

Question

- Discuss the future of travel agents and their continued role in the distribution of package holidays and other travel-related services.

MINI CASE STUDY

Virgin Holidays are a long-haul specialist tour operator based in the UK. In 2015, they announced that they would become a direct-sell-only operator, claiming that their reason was they wished to get 'closer to the customer' and control the booking and whole pre-departure experience. They planned to increase sales through their call centre, website and retail shops.

Questions

- How important is the pre-departure experience in the overall holiday?
- How valid are their claims that this is not about cost cutting?

MAJOR CASE STUDY

Sandals launch UK tour operation

Sandals Resorts International is a Jamaica-based, family-owned company operating 15 luxury all-inclusive resorts. They offer romantic and relaxing breaks for couples, family and friends, but do not allow children. The resorts are fully inclusive, meaning that dining in the speciality restaurants is included in the price and no tipping is allowed. The only additional costs are optional tours, spa treatments and some activities, e.g. scuba certification.

Sandals packages were originally sold through Funway Holidays and included in their brochure, but in 2017 Sandals and Beaches Resorts launched a UK tour operation under the name Unique Caribbean Holidays Limited (UCHL). UCHL distribute their packages directly by liaising with key travel agents and publishing a unique brochure advertising only UCHL packages. These agents are supported by Sandals' call centre team, 24-hour helpline, bespoke agent portal and access to a new training programme and industry workshops at the Sandals Luxury Travel Store in London.

Continued

For Sandals, setting up as a tour operator means they will have greater control over the distribution and marketing of their packages. Customers can book direct or through an agency. A new booking engine has been developed with Traveltek that allows travel agents to book online up to two years in advance and manage their bookings with access to a flight and price availability calendar.

Questions

- Why have Sandals decided to expand into tour operations?
- What are the benefits for Sandals?
- Why do you think they have maintained their relationship with Funway Holidays by allowing them to include Sandals packages in their brochures?
- Why are they maintaining their relationship with travel agents in addition to selling direct?

Recommended Reading

For a comprehensive discussion on intermediaries and the challenges facing travel agents and tour operators that still have resonance today, see:

Buhalis, D. and Ujman, D. (2006) Intermediaries: travel agents and tour operators. In: Buhalis, D. and Cosat, C. (eds) *Tourism Business Frontiers – Consumers, Products and Industry*. Elsevier Butterworth-Heinemann, Oxford, UK, pp. 171–180.

For a detailed critique of brochures and their contents, see:

Horner, S. and Swarbrooke, J. (2004) *The Brochures of Tour Operators. Case Study 17 in International Cases in Tourism Management.* Butterworth-Heinemann, Oxford, UK.

For an article examining the skills and experience necessary for luxury travel agents selling wildlife tourism packages on behalf of tour operators, see:

Buckley, R. and Mossaz, A.C. (2016) Decision making by specialist luxury travel agents. *Tourism Management* 55, 133–138.

For a research based paper meriting attention, see:

Harrison, S., Fubger, G. and Hauschka, C. (2014) Insights into web presence, online marketing and the use of social media by tourism operators in Dunedin, New Zealand. *Anatolia* 26, 269–283.

References

Amadeus (2007) Service fees and commission cuts. Available at: http://www. amadeus.com/travelagencies/documents/travelagencies/White%20Paper_ ForWebUse.pdf, accessed 20 June 2016.

Askin, Z., Armony, M. and Mehrotra, V. (2007) The modern call centre: a multidisciplinary perspective on operations management research. *Production and Operations Management* 16, 665–688.

BBC (2012) Call me: tech powers Philippines call centre success. Available at: http:// www.bbc.co.uk/news/business-18061909, accessed 21 March 2016.

Buhalis, D. (2003) *Etourism: Information Technology for Strategic Tourism Management*. Prentice Hall, London.

CNN (2013) The travel agent is dying, but it's not yet dead. Available at: http://edition. cnn.com/2013/10/03/travel/travel-agent-survival/, accessed 25 January 2017.

Das, D.K. (2009) Globalisation and an emerging global middle class. *Economic Affairs* 29, 89–92.

Dennis, J. (2016) TUI brochures to be phased out by 2020. Available at: http://www.travelweekly.co.uk/articles/62336/tui-brochures-to-be-phased-out-by-2020, accessed 12 July 2016.

Holloway, C. and Humphreys, C. (2012) *The Business of Tourism*, 9th edn. Pearson, Harlow, UK.

Lumsden, L. (1997) *Tourism Marketing*. Thomson Business Press, London.

Middleton, V. and Clarke, J. (2001) *Marketing in Travel and Tourism*, 3rd edn. Butterworth-Heinemann, Oxford, UK.

Miller, A. (2002) Tourism distribution. In: Sharpley, R. (ed.) *The Tourism Business: An Introduction*. Business Education Publishers, Sunderland, UK, pp. 95–115.

Mintel (2013) Holiday planning and booking process – November 2014. Available at: http://academic.mintel.com/display/638302/, accessed 25 July 2016.

Mintel (2014) Travel agents – UK– December 2014. Available at: http://academic.mintel.com/display/679727/, accessed 26 January 2016.

Mintel (2015a) Business traveller – UK. Available at: http://academic.mintel.com/display/744282/, accessed 25 June 2016.

Mintel (2015b) China outbound – May 2015. Available at: http://academic.mintel.com/display/718321/, accessed 20 March 2016.

Mintel (2016) Travel agents – UK – December 2016. Available at: http://academic.mintel.com/display/748920/, accessed 24 January 2017.

Page, S.J. (2009) *Tourism Management*, 3rd edn. Butterworth-Heinemann, Oxford, UK.

Russell, B. (2008) Call centres: a decade of research. *International Journal of Management Reviews* 10, 195–219.

Travel Bulletin (2015) Booking incentives. Available at: http://www.travelbulletin.co.uk/archives-magazine/travel-bulletin-16th-october-2015, accessed 15 July 2016.

Travel Weekly (2007) Why e-brochures are better than paper. Available at: http://www.travelweekly.co.uk/articles/23443/why-e-brochures-are-better-than-paper-25-jan-2007, accessed 25 January 2017.

Zhang, H.Q., Pine, R. and Lam, T. (2005) *Tourism and Hotel Development in China: From Political to Economic Success*. The Howarth Hospitality Press, Binghampton, New York.

10 Marketing

Learning Objectives

After studying this chapter, you should be able to:

- Understand the key characteristics and features of the tourism product and evaluate marketing solutions associated with them.
- Appreciate the mechanisms needed to produce a marketing plan.
- Conduct a situation analysis.
- Understand the tourist decision-making process.
- Evaluate the target market and position the packages appropriately.
- Identify key promotional tactics available to tour operators.
- Appreciate the importance of evaluation of campaigns.

Introduction

The purpose of this chapter is to examine the role of marketing for tour operators and their products. The chapter aims to provide an overview of marketing and consider the unique characteristics of tour operator products. In addition, to develop a better understanding of marketing in practice, it is important to appreciate the tourist decision-making process because this shapes the operation of the marketing department and, specifically, the marketing planning cycle.

Marketing is a key activity for any organization, and none more so than for those involved in tour operations. To appreciate the scope, purpose and process of marketing, it would first be helpful to define what the term marketing means. The Chartered Institute of Marketing (CIM) defines marketing as 'the management process responsible for identifying, anticipating and satisfying customer requirements profitably' (CIM, 2016). Thus, marketing is more than just promoting the product and involves the whole organization from product design, distribution, finance and operations through to successful delivery and consumption. This means that a business must first identify potential customers (the market) for whom they are designing the products, anticipate the needs and desires of this market and create a product that satisfies them successfully. Traditionally, marketing activities are examined using a framework comprising the 4Ps – Product, Place (distribution), Price and Promotion. However, recognizing the needs and operations of the service sector, a further 3Ps have been added by Booms and Bitner (1981) namely: People, Process and Physical Evidence. This means that tour operators need to produce the right product, at the right price, promoted effectively and distributed through the right places, while also operating effectively, using appropriate processes and employing the right people in a physical environment that meets the needs of the customer.

Once a tour operator's product is planned and ready for execution at the right price for the right market, part of the role of the marketing department is to promote the product and its benefits to the consumers. The role of the tour operator is to find the most effective way to promote their product(s) to potential consumers and this is inextricably linked to distribution. While promotion is the responsibility of the tour operators it is often customers who provide an effective method of supporting the promotional activities of the tour operator through word-of mouth/ electronic word-of-mouth (WOM/eWOM), such as recommendations, reviews and the use of social media.

Essential Characteristics of Tour Operators, Products

It is generally accepted that goods and services are different, with the main difference being that goods are produced, whereas services are performed. This creates specific challenges from a marketing perspective. 'Goods are tangible objects that exist in both time and space; services consist solely of acts or processes, and exist in time only. Services are rendered, goods are possessed. Services cannot be possessed; they can only be experienced, created or participated in' (Shostack, 1982, p. 52). The most frequently cited service characteristics are intangibility, perishability, inseparability of production and consumption and heterogeneity (see below). There are additional factors that are particularly pertinent to tour operators and the package holiday and these will also be discussed.

Intangibility

Services by their very nature are intangible, meaning that they cannot be tested, touched or seen, unlike products, which have a physical existence. Selling services has been called 'selling the invisible' because services cannot be assessed using physical senses and can only be evaluated after the service has been delivered. As Holloway expressed, a package tour is a 'speculative investment' (2006, p. 8) because the customer does not know exactly what they are purchasing since they cannot examine the service before purchase. The lack of a physical presence means that they may be difficult to sell, although they are easier to distribute as there is nothing to transfer between producer and consumer (Evans, 2015). Thus, the tour operator needs to provide sufficient evidence relating to the holiday product and its quality to ensure that prospective customers are purchasing the product that is most suitable for them. This is especially important given that quality and enjoyment are subjective. The Product Development Manager may visit hotels and restaurants included in tours to evaluate the tangible elements of a package (physical facilities) and enjoy the service, but the experience of the customers may be different.

To reduce such potential dissonance between expectations and reality, operators need to provide physical description and supporting information to potential customers to reduce uncertainty and enable them to make a judgement as to the quality and suitability of the offering. It is therefore crucial that commentaries about what the customer can expect of the package and level(s) of service are accurately conveyed to the customer. Operators do this by providing brochures, details on websites and other supporting information, such as trip dossiers, by which potential consumers can assess the product. This may be reinforced by personal information gathered by the consumer through recommendations by family and friends or reviews found in the media. Therefore, operators aim to create a positive strong brand and organizational image and clear messages in advertising that can reassure customers. Intangibility is one of the reasons why Holloway (2006) considers buying a holiday a risky investment and involves a high degree of trust, especially considering the expenditure involved in purchasing a package. In addition, customers frequently use price to make a judgement about the value and quality of the product, suggesting that low prices infer a lower quality product. Therefore, tour operators need to position their products at a price that the customer feels is worth paying for the experience they wish to have and meets their expectations of both quality and service (see Chapter 6, this volume).

Perishability

Tourism products are perishable; this means that service providers cannot produce and store services for future sales as they could with physical products. For this reason it is imperative that tour operators accurately predict sales capacity. If the quota for any one package is not fulfilled, the remaining allocation cannot be sold at a later date as the departure has already happened. Clearly, such shortfalls in sales have a cost implication and indeed may lead to an overall loss on that holiday departure. A complicating factor is the variance of demand that arises due to seasonality. In the high season, operators may sell all their products, but at off-peak times of year there may be over supply due to lower demand. Supply is difficult to change in the short term, so if the destination proves popular it is hard for the tour operator to increase the supply due to limitations of resources such as accommodation. Thus, tour operators need to factor in the potential for unsold capacity, which will have an impact on the price of the holiday. The most commonly used method to facilitate such forecasting is

yield management, which aims to match supply with demand (see Chapter 7, this volume). Variations in demand and, in particular, oversupply can be tempered using pricing and promotional campaigns to encourage sales, cooperating with other suppliers to share capacity, the utilization of part-time employees, or retailing surplus capacity using specialist websites.

Inseparability

Inseparability refers to the overlap between production and consumption. The production of the service cannot be separated from the delivery/consumption of that service. In effect, the holiday is produced and consumed at the same time, i.e. simultaneous production and consumption. Also, other customers are part of the experience and thus the tourism product is co-produced. This provides a challenge for tour operators because customers may expect differing levels of service or for it to be delivered in a specific way. Therefore they need to ensure that the level of service is comparable with the expectations of the customer. Customers will expect the service to be of an acceptable standard, but because it is consumed at the point of delivery, there is no opportunity to correct mistakes at that time. It must be right the first time. To overcome the challenges of inseparability, operators need to ensure the quality within all stages and components of the package and this can be achieved by training and quality assessments, such as customer feedback and benchmarking (see Chapter 6, this volume). For some tour operators, targeting a specific market segment ensures that customers purchase a holiday suited to their preferences and therefore more likely to be compatible with other guests, e.g. holiday packages for the 'over 50s'.

Variability/heterogeneity

Tour operator products are delivered by people and are therefore subject to variability. In general, every service performance is unique to each customer because it is almost impossible to replicate human behaviour entirely. Staff, from tour guides directly employed by the operator to staff in restaurants included in the package, can vary by the time of day and the day of the week/month/year. This variability is also experienced by the consumers because their service encounters will vary according to their own experience and expectations; for example, two people on the same holiday may have very different ideas about the level and quality of any particular service because their assessment of this is based on their previous experience and expectations. Services, in contrast to physical products which are homogenous, are never identical, evidencing variable degrees of heterogeneity. Therefore another feature of the tourism product is the lack of standardization. To overcome the problems caused by variability, operators and suppliers may attempt to standardize their products and service through staff training (as exemplified by the ubiquitous McDonald's). This may be supported by ensuring customer-focused behaviour, or adopting a more customer-centric approach by customizing the package to the needs of the customer using techniques such as dynamic packaging, add-ons and upgrades (e.g. rooms with balconies, private transfers).

Discretionary

The purchase of a holiday package is discretionary, i.e. people do not need to buy holidays. Therefore, in times of financial hardship, a planned holiday may be one area of expenditure that is sacrificed or lower cost, alternative products are sought; for instance, choosing a short-haul holiday package or holidaying within the home country instead of abroad.

Lack of ownership/composite products

Package holidays are a combination of different, complementary products rather than a single entity. The holiday product covers the complete experience; that is, the transportation element, accommodation, food and beverage services as well as, potentially, travel agents and tour guides. This may be particularly difficult to manage because many of the components may not be owned by the tour operator and be provided by third-party suppliers. This means if there is a failure in any component of the holiday product, it can have a negative impact on the overall experience (see Chapter 6, this volume). Furthermore, as customers buy a service and no product changes hands, there is no physical product to sell. Operators need to convince customers that they are offering a unique product that is superior to that of their competition. This is often achieved through unique selling points that differentiate them from their competitors.

High fixed cost

The package involves high fixed costs, e.g. seats on charter air flights, accommodation paid on commitment, and relatively low variable costs, yet does not guarantee generating a profit. High fixed costs exacerbate the problems of the perishable nature of tour operators' products and the often low profit margins encourage operators to sell surplus holiday packages with minimal profit rather than no sale at all.

Unstable demand/seasonality

Tourism demand is influenced by many factors, including the economic situation, seasonality and global politics. Also, sudden events such as terrorist attacks, geographic catastrophes or fluctuations in currency exchange rates can very quickly influence demand. There are certain times during the year when destinations will see greater demand and this has substantial implication on the provision of services. As a result of demand fluctuations, hotel occupancies may vary from 90/100% to 30% or lower in low season. For this reason, many mass tour operators in northern Europe have attempted to overcome seasonality by introducing new products during the traditional low season, such as winter sun and niche products (e.g. wildlife tours), which may be less affected by seasonality and can enable a more stable cash flow into the company.

Ease of Entry/Exit

In the tour operations/retailing sector it is relatively easy to set up a new enterprise or indeed exit the business compared with many other business sectors, if local conditions and regulations allow. The initial outlay for a tour operator is relatively small because they never need to invest in product as stock, and for travel agents, who only pay the tour operator once the customer has paid for their product, they do not run the risk of having unsold stock. For many small and medium-sized tour operators, their most significant cost is usually that of producing promotional marketing communications such as a website and the brochure. This ease of entry (and exit) has resulted in the tour operation sector being dominated in numerical terms by small and medium-sized enterprises.

Tour operators use their knowledge, the characteristics of their product and the potential solutions to devise a strategy to market and promote their company, as well as to overcome difficulties and the complications involved in retailing intangible products. In order to do this, a company devises a marketing plan. Before we discuss marketing planning, it is important at this stage to develop an understanding of the role and value of the brand for tour operators, which is a key element of marketing.

Branding

A brand is the name given to a product or service from a specific source. The Chartered Institute of Marketing (UK) defines a brand as 'an idea or an image of a product or a service provided by the organisation. Branding is the marketing of this idea or image so that more and more people recognise it and become aware of the brand' (CIM, 2016). As Kotler *et al.* (2014) argue, it exists to distinguish a particular product or service from its competitors. Therefore, a brand is more than just a name and/or a logo; for example, the global TUI logo, which presents the company name as a smile, is considered one of their most valuable assets. The brand is part of the relationship with the customer, a promise made by a particular company about a specific product, a uniqueness, and therefore can be seen as a validation of quality. This is particularly important when purchasing holidays because it is such a speculative investment due to the lack of tangibility. Significantly, a brand can create increased levels of customer loyalty and therefore companies are less vulnerable to competition, which may enable a premium price for the branded product/offering.

Furthermore, branding can reduce competition and substitutability; as Wood opined, 'a brand is a mechanism for achieving competitive advantage for firms, through differentiation. The attributes that differentiate a brand provide the customer satisfaction and benefits to which they are willing to pay' (Wood, 2000, p. 666). A successful brand can act as a barrier and limit the opportunities for competitors in the market or for new entrants. Brand portfolios comprise sets of brands that the company offers and in the case of many large tour operators, each brand is aimed at a specific target market. For example, specific brochures and products with their own individual brand identity, such as Club 18–30 and Manos, are both independent brands within TUI. Tour operators then seek to advertise a company name rather than the individual sub-brands. Overall, the value of a brand over and above its physical assets is described as Brand Equity and is the customers' perception – the feelings that they have about the brand. One of the key strategies for a tour operator is the creation of a brand personality, i.e. human characteristics that are attributed to a brand name.

We can examine brands in more detail by reference to the 'Brand Wheel', which is also known as the Brand Essence model (see Fig. 10.1).

- Brand essence: Strong brands have an easily identified, simple essence, i.e. the fundamental quality of the brand is usually stated in one to three words (an example would be that Disney is 'magical') and is consistently delivered throughout every component of the holiday or visits.
- Personality: Basically, this is what the brand stands for; the words and qualities that describe the brand and that usually have an emotive attachment. Research suggests that customers are increasingly likely to purchase the product from a brand if they share similar personality characteristics or philosophies, which perhaps explains the growth of emphasis on charity work, responsible tourism and sustainability on tour operators' websites.
- Values: These are the core of the brand and what makes customers choose one product or service over another. They can relate to intangibles, such as service quality, or more tangible aspects, such as price, but either way they differentiate one product or company from another.

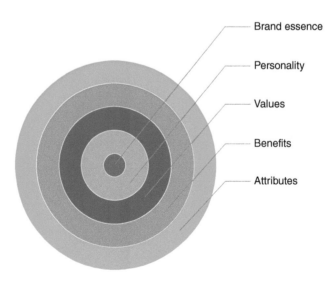

Fig. 10.1. The brand wheel. (From Ward *et al.*, 1999.)

- Benefits: This is why the product/offering would be more beneficial to prospective customers than others. For example, this may be because the company is more experienced than other companies or perhaps they offer unique experiences that cannot be found with other tour operators.
- Attributes: These are the characteristics that define a particular product, for example a family activity tour operator, an operator offering a wide choice of holidays, global reputation or access to unique product offerings.

Marketing Planning

Marketing is often considered in the context of strategic planning on the one hand and tactical (operational) planning on the other. Strategic marketing planning covers a longer timescale and is often embedded in the strategic plan of the company (see Chapter 3, this volume). Operational marketing planning is shorter term, often 12–18 months. In the tour operating sector this short-term planning is more dynamic because of the intense competition within the sector. In summary, the strategic marketing plan outlines exactly what the company is trying to achieve based on the current market situation, life cycle, competition and opportunities. The tactical marketing plan identifies what is required to achieve the strategic goals in the short term. The easiest way to understand the difference between a strategic and a tactical marketing plan is to break it down into two questions.

- What are you trying to achieve? The answer will shape your strategy.
- What do you need to do to achieve that? The answer will shape your tactics.

The marketing planning process therefore starts with developing the overall marketing strategy. The key stages in designing a marketing strategy are encapsulated in the marketing planning cycle (Fig. 10.2). For the purpose of this chapter, we have adopted a simplified cycle.

When devising a marketing plan, the first stage is an assessment of the current situation, i.e. an appreciation of where the company is and where it aims to be in the future. This is often identified through the mission, vision and values of the company.

Mission, vision and values

A marketing plan needs to support the strategic vision of the company, which is identified using mission statements, organizational goals and vision. There are different styles of presenting a mission statement, although the aim is to clarify the purpose of the organization, essentially what it does, and communicate the objectives of the company. The vision of the company can also be presented in several ways; they tend to be future orientated, i.e. what the company aims to achieve, whereas the values provide a set of guiding principles. Many operators provide additional information about their core values on their website; for example, embracing sustainability and responsibility, the philosophy behind the creation of their products and future ambitions. This is exemplified by Haven Holidays.

Situation Analysis

Situation analysis involves examining the company's external operating environment and an internal review examining its own structures, processes, aims and objectives. These reviews will enable the company to decide the direction it should take, based on the organization's capabilities, customers and operating environment.

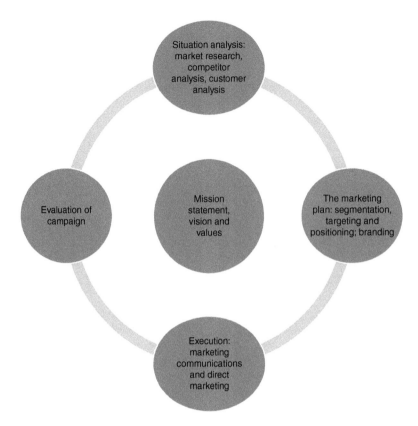

Fig. 10.2. The marketing planning cycle.

Essentially, situation analysis will involve both a SWOT analysis and Porters Five Forces (see Chapter 3, this volume) and may include a '5C' assessment. That is:

- Customer: determining which customers, and their needs, you want to attract by assessing market segments, frequency of purchases, quality of purchases, distribution channels and consumer trends.
- Company: assessing whether the company has the right product(s) to meet the needs of those customers; this can be evaluated using a SWOT analysis.
- Competition: determining who the company will be in competition with to meet the needs of the customers identified. An assessment of products on offer by competitors, alongside their strengths and weaknesses, is valuable in establishing the level of competition.
- Collaborators: identifying other organizations or people that may be able to help the company. This could involve working with national tourism offices, suppliers, airlines or other transport organizations.
- Context (sometimes referred to as climate): determining if there are any limitations that may prevent or limit the opportunities. An analysis of the climate can be achieved by conducting a PESTEL analysis (see Chapter 3, this volume).

Once a company has assessed the operating environment, research may need to be conducted to identify specific information that will enable the operators to identify their market and evaluate the competition.

Market Research

Market research is research that directly focuses on consumers and is essential to inform any marketing activity. It is a central activity and there should be a constant loop or feedback from analysis of market research to inform the management, thereby enabling better informed strategic and tactical marketing decisions to be made. Therefore, tour operators need up to date research relating to the market and their target market(s) through either secondary (previously published information) or primary research. Secondary research sources may be available in the public domain, e.g. data on market trends, tourist flows, visitor numbers, competitors with competing products and services, and general information about market segments (e.g. from market research organizations such as Mintel, Nielsen and Keynote). A disadvantage of such secondary data is that it needs to be used with care. Although it is relatively low cost, marketing managers need to be aware of the suitability of the data in terms of accuracy, reliability, objectivity and currency.

Depending on the quality of available secondary information, the tour operator may need additional data requiring primary research, either through undertaking their own direct research or commissioning a suitable organization to undertake it for them. Primary data collection is often time-consuming and can be expensive, but there are numerous ways in which tour operators can obtain data that may be useful in decision-making. One of the most frequently used data collection methods is that of the questionnaire, whereby customers complete a questionnaire in the final days or on the return journey of their holiday (see Chapter 6, this volume).

Competitor Analysis

A competitor analysis obviously identifies not only current competitors but also should consider potential competitors and this can be achieved in one of two ways.

Competitors can be examined by identifying them from the customer's perspective or from the company's perspective. When examining a competitor from the customer's point of view, the strengths and weaknesses of the company should be identified. This is similar to the SW dimensions of a SWOT analysis (Strengths, Weaknesses, Opportunities and Threats; see Chapter 3, this volume). Questions that will inform such analysis are: why do customers choose their holiday products; what do the competitors do differently or better than us; what makes them successful? Alternatively, examining a competitor from the company's perspective may involve considering that company's size, location, their product(s) and distribution channels.

Customer Analysis and Behaviour

The situation analysis needs to clearly identify consumer trends and potential market development. A fundamental facet of marketing is an understanding of consumer behaviour. This is key to success in tour operations by ensuring that operators plan and develop products that appeal to their target market(s). Second to this is an appreciation of the tourist decision-making process, which enables operators to identify any bias towards specific information sources that can be utilized in the marketing strategy.

The purchase of a holiday package involving a transaction between the retailer or organizer and consumer is only part of a complex process that a potential customer will go through. This process is considered to be characterized by high-risk,

high-involvement and extensive problem-solving behaviour (Clarke, 2005), which in part is illustrated through the numerous decision-making models that seek to explain the process that tourists go through to choose a package. The decision-making process is often considered to comprise five stages (see Swarbrooke and Horner, 2016). In the case of tour operator products, an additional stage can be added because consumers evaluate the product as they are consuming it, as well as in their post-trip evaluation (see Fig. 10.3).

Desire to travel

The first stage of the process is 'need arousal'. In this context, this occurs when a person decides s/he wants to take a holiday. This can be triggered by a host of factors; for example, external stimuli can trigger the desire to travel, such as advertising, promotional campaigns, the media, family and friends, in addition to personal determinants such as socio-economic status, personality, values and social influences.

Information search

Once the desire has been identified, potential customers are motivated to search for solutions to satisfy that need. Information about possible holiday packages is collected, which may involve formal sources such as reviewing advertisements and brochures, talking to intermediaries such as travel agents and searching the Internet, as well as informal sources such as friends, family and colleagues. It is unlikely that potential customers will

Fig. 10.3. The tourist decision-making process. (Adapted from Mathieson and Wall, 1982.)

identify all the potential options, because experience and knowledge will enable them to narrow down the choice to only those that could be considered seriously. These form a 'consideration set' (Wirtz *et al.*, 2012), i.e. those products that can be considered as potential purchases.

Evaluation of the alternatives

Once the consideration set has been identified and key features of the holidays understood, the customer will evaluate the offerings taking into consideration constraints such as time and expenditure, length of trip, personal circumstances and expectations. As the offerings in many destinations will be similar in terms of quality and range of services, then the presentation of the image(s) of the destination (e.g. in brochures or on websites) becomes more important as an influential factor. Previous experience, brand recognition and recall will all impact on the final decision.

Purchase decision

The final stage in the process is the purchase decision, which is made after evaluating all the options identified. This decision will also be influenced by price, convenience, logistics and experience.

Travel preparation and execution

Confirmation of the booking and the travel experience takes place. The tourist will evaluate the experience as it is produced and consumed and, in that sense, is a co-constructor of the experience.

Post-consumption evaluation

Post-consumption evaluation refers to the experiences, feelings and satisfactions that the tourist feels during and after the consumption of a holiday service. It should be noted that evaluation often takes place at the same time as the holiday is consumed and therefore is an ongoing evaluation. The customer will reflect on whether the experience was satisfying or disappointing, and in the case where their expectations are met or exceeded then the customer can be referred to as being satisfied (see Chapter 6, this volume). Alternatively, a customer may begin to experience **cognitive dissonance**, that is, if the consumer has conflicting ideas relating to their experiences and even dissatisfaction in comparison with their expectations, then the experience will be considered to have been disappointing.

Preparation of the Marketing Plan

The next stage of the planning cycle involves the production of the marketing plan. Information derived from the situation, the competitor and customer analysis, and market research will enable a company to produce a strategic plan, i.e. one that supports the company's mission statement, values and vision. The strategic decisions will involve how the company chooses to compete; for example, based on price or quality (see Chapter 3, this volume), identifying sales objectives such as turnover and profit, and marketing objectives such as increasing repeat bookings by a specified percentage. Once these decisions have been made, a marketing plan can then be formulated, which covers a shorter period such as one year, while the strategic plan is based on long-term objectives. The marketing plan is cyclical and dynamic, responding to change, whether in the marketplace, indicated by new data or customer feedback.

In effect, the marketing plan determines in greater detail how a company can achieve its objectives. It usually incorporates the '7Ps', which are recognized collectively as the **marketing mix.**

- Product: the product is usually the first consideration, i.e. to create a product that consumers want (see Chapters 4 and 5, this volume).
- Pricing: a clear pricing strategy is necessary, based on costs, the perceived value of the product and the attractiveness to customers (see Chapter 7, this volume).
- Place/distribution: decisions about the distribution of the holiday product. There are several different platforms available for operators to use to distribute their products (see Chapters 9 and 11, this volume).
- Promotion: the way in which the product is marketed to the consumer needs to be planned. This may involve traditional marketing communications such as newspapers and television, but increasingly will need to include social media (see Chapter 11, this volume)
- People: tour operators rely on people to deliver their product/services. It is important to invest in selecting and developing the right employees in all areas of the organization, e.g. sales staff, tour guides and resort-based staff (see Chapter 6, this volume).
- Process: the way the holiday product operates is critical for customers, so planning the processes such as timescales, transfers, flight times and collection points is critical (see Chapters 4 and 5, this volume).
- Physical evidence/packaging: the quality of the physical evidence is used by customers to assess the value of the product, so it is important that vehicles, hotels, specialist equipment and so forth are in good condition so that customers are confident in the product.

Each of these factors can be manipulated to change the product offering to meet the needs of the market and stimulate demand. They also need to be flexible and incorporate continuous research and reflection.

As noted above, fundamental to the marketing plan is the identification of suitable groups of tourists who will purchase the product. This is called segmenting the market.

Segmentation, Targeting and Positioning

Market segmentation is the process by which organizations divide up the market into subsets of consumers who have similar needs or demand characteristics. The benefit of market segmentation is that the tour operator will have a better idea about the needs and wants of their target market and thus can make more effective use of their budget by selecting appropriate promotional communication tools.

Realistically, tour operators cannot aim to attract all the population, so the market needs to be broken down into groups with whom the operator can try to engage. This is termed 'reach'. This is target marketing, which Kotler and Keller (2012) argued is the way forward for modern marketing strategy. In effect, the operator divides the market into segments, targets one or more of the segments and positions its products – 'market positioning' – and marketing materials so that they will appeal specifically to the needs and wants of the chosen market segment (see Fig. 10.4).

Segmentation

The first stage of target marketing involves identifying the most appropriate customers, i.e. groups with similar needs, and this is usually achieved through market research.

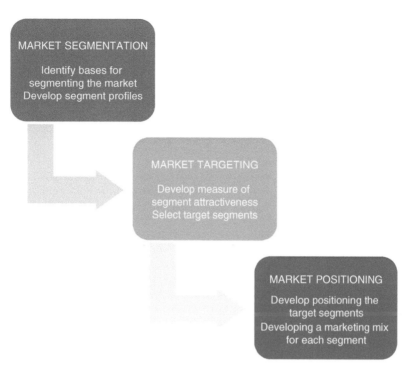

Fig. 10.4. The segmentation, targeting and positioning process. (From Kotler *et al.*, 2014, p. 221.)

To identify market segments, the tour operator should identify who the market is, their requirements, when they want to travel, where they want to find the information and how they can be reached. There are many methods that can be applied to help segment the general market (see Swarbrooke and Horner, 2016), one of which that is specific to tourism is that of Middleton and Clarke (2001), who suggest that the main methods of segmentation are by:

- Purpose of travel, e.g. holiday, leisure break, business trip, visiting friends and relatives.
- Buyer needs, motivations and benefits sought, e.g. relaxation, shopping, education.
- Buyer behaviour/characteristics of the product usage, e.g. families, Halal, grey market, LGBT.
- **Demographic,** economic and geographic profile (see Table 10.1).

- Psychographic profile: groups people on a broad basis of how they live, their priorities, their opinions and their attitudes and interests (see Table 10.2).
- Geodemographic profile (see below).
- Price, e.g. budget/low-cost holidays, luxury.

These segments are not necessarily discreet but overlap and complement each other, thus a tour operator may use two or more methods (and categories within) to identify more accurately a chosen market segment. In addition, it should be borne in mind that the potential means of segmentation may vary, depending on geographic region/country of a source market and changes in societal norms over time.

Another method used in tourism is that of geodemographic segmentation, which is a multivariate classification technique using geographic and demographic details. The most commonly known systems are ACORN and MOSAIC. ACORN

Table 10.1. Illustration of sociodemographic variables.

Variable	Explanation
Age	Segmentation using age-band categories is very common as an indicator of different requirements; these are often given names such as baby boomers (born between 1946 and 1964), tweens (9–12), Generation X and millennials. For example, PGL Holidays offers summer camp activity breaks for 7–17-year-olds, whereas SAGA Holidays targets the over 50s
Life stage	It is often easy for operators to segment their market, linking it to life stage in the family life cycle, for example couples with children and those without. Segments include: young single people, young couples with no children, couples with young children, families with older children, retired couples and retired single people
Gender	Men and women have different holiday choices; for example, women are more likely to choose spa breaks, whereas men may choose golfing holidays
Sexual orientation	Sexual orientation is becoming a key market segment for tour operators. Some tour operators and destinations focus specifically on attracting gay and lesbian audiences, e.g. Mykonos in Greece, which have become a very lucrative market. Also same-sex marriages and civil partnership ceremonies are now packaged by tour operators, e.g. perfectgayhoneymoons.co.uk
Income	This relates to disposable income; for example, a differentiating factor between consumers of 'exclusive tours' or safaris and mass market products, e.g. traditional '3S' holidays or camping. ACORN provides a list of categories from A to F, whereas the UK social class categorization uses a scale of 1 to 8 This method of segmentation emphasizes occupation or social class as a form of segmenting the market
Education levels	Education levels can be used to segment the market under the assumption that higher education levels will mean higher paying jobs, which leads to higher levels of disposable income. Also it is argued they are more likely to be interested in cultural tours, etc.
Ethnicity and cultural background	Services can be segmented according to ethnic group, which is a group of people who have characteristics in common, such as racial background, language or social customs

classifies residential neighbourhoods on the assumption that people living in similar areas will have similar incomes, lifestyles and needs and are likely to share common demographic characteristics. MOSAIC identifies 15 groups and 66 types of consumers (Experian, 2016).

Assessing the segment

A starting point for assessing a market segment by tour operators is the purpose of the customers, travel, e.g. mass market summer holiday, short break, activity-based or family. These segments can be

Table 10.2. Psychographic segmentation.

Lifestyle	Based on tourists' activities, interests and opinions. This approach links product choice to habits and lifestyle, such as Club 18–30 holidays aimed at hedonistic activities, or interests such as bird watching, skiing or spa breaks
Personality	For example, extroverts are more likely to choose busy resorts with various entertainment opportunities, whereas those considered introvert may choose more remote locations
Values	This segmentation method utilizes the VALS framework (values, attitudes and lifestyle). Consumers called Thinkers and Believers are motivated by ideals, whereas Achievers and Strivers are motivated by achievement. Experiencers and Makers are considered risk takers and are motivated by self-expression. Innovatives are at the top of the VALS framework, characterized by high income and high resource individuals who consider independence vitally important and aim to achieve the finer things in life. Survivors are those with the least resources and therefore less likely to purchase new products, but are often considered to be brand loyal

further subdivided to include more specific information, such as a beach holiday with children, beach holidays without children, specific activities such as walking and sailing, or the destination such as short- or long-haul travel.

A key consideration in market segment identification is to ensure that it is large enough to provide a sustainable number of customers and that the segment has longevity. The segment should be assessed in the context of the company objectives. For example, mass market companies aim to have large numbers of sales, whereas smaller companies may aim for higher profit from a smaller client base. Consideration must also be given to the competitors within that market; this is called segment attractiveness (see Porters Five Forces in Chapter 3, this volume).

The identification of the specific market segment(s) is crucial to the tour operator in developing their marketing strategy to target effectively those specific segments.

Targeting

Once the tour operator has identified suitable market segment(s), they need to evaluate their potential in terms of contributing to the company's success and select one or more of those market segments to target. This could involve some re-evaluation of the segment, which may involve identifying segments where they offer advantages over their competition (unique selling points) and/or can provide superior levels of service to ensure that they match the segment(s) to their product offerings.

Positioning

Once a company has identified its target market segment, it must decide on what position to occupy in the market. A product's position is the way the product is perceived by the customer relative to competing products. Positioning involves identifying competitive advantage and communicating this clearly to the target market by creating a detailed and specific marketing mix. There are several different strategies that operators can use.

- Undifferentiated marketing: This is when a company utilizes the same marketing strategy across all their marketing communications. For example,

First Choice uses the same media channels for all their offerings to target the widest possible group of potential customers. This strategy is most effective when the operator's packages are homogenous or customers have the same requirements from a holiday and will be looking for similar experiences, such as First Choice's range of all-inclusive packages, which are not aimed at specific segments but rather focus on the benefits of the holiday being inclusive of all food and entertainment.

- Differentiated marketing. A differentiated marketing strategy involves offering a range of products to different market segments while maintaining a focal brand to differentiate the tour operator from competitors. For example, Voyage Jules Verne present several brochures for both resort and escorted tours while maintaining their brand.
- Concentrated marketing. This strategy, also called niche marketing, is when a company focuses all their resources on one specific market segment. For example, if a vertically integrated tour operator has several different brands, each of those brands may be marketed to very distinct, separate market segments. An example of this would be a ski tour operator marketing their products to those consumers specifically interested in skiing rather than to the general market.

To achieve effective positioning, marketing communications need to focus on the needs of the segment and provide information that identifies the benefits that this group are seeking. Furthermore, because of the large number of products on offer, companies may adopt a strategy of grouping products together or plan their positioning strategy based on their competitors' offerings. Mass market products by operators such as First Choice and TUI often manipulate price rather than promotional campaigns. Smaller tour operators in competition with bigger brands may emphasize their expertise, personal service and additional value to differentiate their product.

Overall, the strategic marketing plan provides the direction of growth for the company and the brand image. The strategic plan will guide and influence the tactical marketing plan, for example the budget that can be spent, and allocate financial resources to each of the promotional methods chosen. The design of the marketing campaign is the implementation of the marketing mix, i.e. communicating the product, the sales price and the distribution channel to the potential customers via a range of promotional activities encompassed by the promotional mix. This is often referred to as the tactical marketing plan.

The Promotional Mix

When devising a tactical marketing plan, companies can utilize several strategies and channels to achieve the aim of the marketing plan, and promote the brand. Promotional campaigns are part of the marketing mix and here we review promotional activities available to tour operators. These activities are encapsulated in the promotional mix (see Fig. 10.5) and are discussed below. Others are examined in more depth in Chapters 4 and 5 (this volume; product development and price) and Chapter 9 (this volume; distribution).

The promotional mix is the coordination of marketing activities which include several different opportunities that enable companies to interact directly with customers or through their channels of distribution. The aim of the promotional mix is to inform, persuade and ultimately encourage the purchase of the holiday

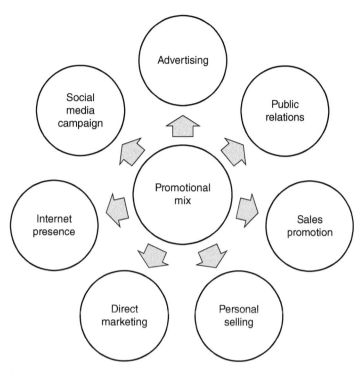

Fig. 10.5. The promotional mix.

products. The tactical marketing plan will stipulate the blend of promotional activities that target the market segment in the most appropriate manner.

Advertising

Advertising involves the design of media plans that aim to deliver the right message to the right people at the right time within budget to generate the right response, i.e. a purchase. A media plan starts with setting the communication objectives, i.e. 'what message do we wish to give potential consumers?' However, this is not as straightforward as one might think due to the number and types of media vehicles available. Furthermore, changing characteristics of the target market means that audience fragmentation is likely and that mass communication methods such as television (TV) and the popular press

may no longer be appropriate or affordable due to budgetary constraints.

To create a media plan, operators need to make decisions about:

- Media selection: the choice of paid media vehicles and channels that can be used to target a specific market and communicate the chosen message. These can include mail, TV and radio, newspaper, magazines brochures, telemarketing and the Internet.
- Media scheduling: the number of occurrences, timing and duration that those messages are exposed to the specific market using the agreed vehicle.

Media selection

Traditional print media such as national and regional newspapers, magazines and trade journals are very effective at delivering messages to large audiences. Advertising in hobby and special interest magazines is a very effective tool for targeting specific audiences. For example, a company offering walking and trekking holidays would look to advertise in magazines focusing on these activities. For tour operators who do not sell directly to the customer, the trade press may be used to promote brand awareness.

Broadcast media takes one of two forms, i.e. TV and radio. The main advantage of these forms of media is that they can reach mass audiences at a relatively low cost per person. Visuals and sound can be used in creative strategies to gain audience attention. TV advertising is normally the most expensive, although prices vary according to the time advertisements are broadcast, with advertising slots during popular television programmes being the most expensive. This is particularly useful for targeting family audiences and thus is used by many mass market operators to advertise their family-friendly products. Radio services often operate on a 24-hour basis allowing consumer segments to be targeted based on the time of day and the type of channel. Outdoor media primarily include advertising boards, transport vehicles (e.g. public buses) and street furniture and can provide effective support when used with other communication, especially in building brand name recognition. It is clear that TV, radio and printed newspapers are losing their centrality within the media landscape as an increasing number of consumers obtain their information through digital sources.

Decisions as to which media to use involve the following factors:

- The reach. This is the number of members of the target audience who were exposed to communications in a specific time period. This is usually expressed as a percentage measurement against the target audience, not the general population. The reach measures how people view the communication, but fails to identify how they react. Coverage is an important consideration because the objective of the marketing campaign may be to create awareness of the brand.

- Frequency. This is the measurement of the number of times on average that a member of the audience is exposed to the media vehicle and is usually measured in opportunities to see (OTS) or opportunities to hear (OTH). Frequency is important because the more times a potential consumer sees or is exposed to the marketing message, the more likely it is to be effective. Marketers will adapt the frequency and scheduling according to the type of products on offer and the market segment. This may include continuous campaigns for nonseasonal products such as city breaks and specialist activities, awareness-raising campaigns where communications are built up over time towards a specific date, such as a particular event, or falling off where advertising campaigns launch and then gradually reduce in activity. Falling campaigns are often used to market mass market products; for example, in the UK traditionally television advertising for summer beach holidays starts in the New Year and gradually declines towards high season.

- Media scheduling. This determines when the messages are transmitted, so it often refers to the pattern of advertising time. Short-term advertising campaigns focus on increasing sales, whereas longer term communications focus on brand-building.

- Purchasing cycle. This is the optimum number of exposures that customers have to the promotional activity. This may vary according to the time of year; for example, in the UK advertisements of traditional summer sun holidays start in January, while European ski tour operators launch their brochures during the summer months.

- Level of involvement. Decisions with higher levels of involvement need less repetitions of the communications because people who are highly involved in the decision process will actively seek additional information, whereas low-involvement decisions need a higher level of frequency to maintain awareness and change attitudes.

Public Relations

Public relations is a communication process that aims to create a favourable image of the company in the target audience, although the audience can be not just customers but also suppliers, investors, journalists and employees. Many tour operators utilize PR companies to represent them in activities such as press relations, product publicity and corporate publicity through writing press releases, E-shots and tailored PR campaigns through social media (e.g. announcing awards, new product launch or charity support). PR also has an important role in offsetting unfavourable publicity and it is extremely useful when dealing with the aftermath of incidents and crises (see Chapter 13, this volume).

Sales Promotion

Sales promotion activities are activities undertaken by tour operators to promote an increase in sales. Sales promotions can be directed either to the customer or to distribution channel members such as travel agents. Tactics used by tour operators for customers include competitions and giveaways, temporary price reductions, free gifts such as free surfing lessons included in the price of the holiday,

or branded items such as passport holders and t-shirts. Promotions are often communicated to customers through specific marketing materials, such as newsletters, emails and flyers. Sales promotions for distribution channel members can include competitions to reward retailers who sell the most packages, temporary increases in commission rates and free gifts.

Personal Selling

Many staff are engaged in personal selling, either directly as part of a vertically integrated travel agent, a telesales agent, or as a travel agent selling products on behalf of the tour operator. Personal selling can increase the likelihood of a purchase and agents can upsell (upgraded accommodation etc.) or switch sell (sell a product of a higher price). B2B (Business to Business), personal selling, i.e. communication between tour operators, retailers, convention, incentive and meeting planners, usually takes place at travel trade events such as the World Travel Market.

Direct Marketing

Direct marketing allows operators to communicate directly with customers rather than through an intermediary such as a travel agent. Copley (2014) describes it as an interactive system that uses one or more communication tools and media to generate a measurable response. The key to direct marketing is to identify the target market and direct promotional material to them, essentially providing in-depth information to customers and prospects that matches the needs of the target group.

Traditionally, direct marketing involved direct mail using mailing lists. The original direct response advertising delivered by mail expanded rapidly in the 1960s/70s as advertising on television increased and potential customers requested brochures that were delivered by post. For several decades, this form of direct marketing was popular, but it has fallen out of favour due to the 'junk mail' image and the relatively high cost for operators in terms of printing and distributing marketing collateral (design and printing, packaging, addressing and postage). However, more recently direct marketing has become increasingly more sophisticated as a direct result of developments in information communication technologies (ICT), particularly the Internet. Basically, the convenience of the Internet and the ability to shop from home have changed the way direct marketing operates.

One of the most common and effective means of reaching the consumer is through email and email addresses are retained by companies to send messages about products and offers. The benefits of contacting customers and prospects directly include the ability to target segments of the operator's own customer database with specific products. Personalized messages are low cost and easy to produce and emails can be sent at specific times of day when customers are perceived to be more likely to be receptive. This medium allows operators to track accurately whether the email has been opened, whether a 'click through' has been actioned and what the result is, thus giving them data which will inform other campaigns.

It should be noted that in many countries the use of personal information is controlled by data protection legislation and although companies may be able to contact their own clients, it is usually illegal for the database of clients to be given/sold to other companies or for other firms to contact clients without their express permission.

Digital Media

The key forms of digital media include the Internet, database technologies, social media, mobile technologies and interactive TV. Digital media have allowed marketers to develop new forms of communication to generate responses from the relevant target audience; these can include email marketing, search engine optimization, pay per click, online advertising, affiliate marketing, text messaging and blogging. One of the benefits of digital media marketing is that the interaction between the customer/potential customer is greater than the traditional one-way forms of communication such as radio and newspapers. Essentially, marketing has moved from a transactional perspective with passive customers to a relationship perspective with engagement in a two-way communication between companies and consumers. As such, digital media allow interactivity between producer and consumer and can disseminate marketing communications through multiple channels.

Internet presence

The Internet is a highly popular and valuable tool for consumers to access travel information, to provide the opportunity to compare prices with ease and potentially obtain faster responses than would be the case with the traditional high street travel agent. In response, travel agents claim that they provide a better service than the Internet and are more adept at creating complex bookings (Cheyne *et al.*, 2006). Tour operators have also been affected in two main ways. On the one hand the Internet offers a direct route for consumers to contact suppliers and principals, thereby omitting travel agents and/or tour operators from the chain of distribution (**disintermediation**). On the other hand, the Internet provides a way of reaching new target audiences outside the areas where they are easily accessible, e.g. international customers. It also allows companies to collect and analyse data to help them make decisions about products, marketing campaigns and competitors. The Internet is particularly useful for small and medium-sized enterprises because it offers a cost-effective communication method, which is particularly useful when targeting niche markets that may be geographically widespread.

Websites

Websites have become important to organizations and increasingly represent the face of the company. Satisfactory experiences in using websites can enhance relationships. However, utilization of websites should not be considered as additional to a marketing strategy, but integral to that strategy, because it will be used to supplement other vehicles, e.g. advertisements that include web addresses. In general, websites are quick to set up, although they are not necessarily cheap to design (particularly if using website designing companies), but they are more cost effective than brochure production. The benefits to tour operators are that they have a local as well as global reach and are available 24/7 and therefore consumers and customers can access information at their leisure. In terms of design, the content of a website needs to include the same substantive messages that will be included in a hardcopy brochure. That is, destinations available, the types of holiday and offer, itineraries and information about the company. In addition, websites have the additional advantage of being able to interact with the customer by encouraging them to sign up for newsletters, send enquiries or request specific information using web chat services.

To develop a deeper appreciation of websites and further understand their design, it is particularly helpful to consider and apply Rayport and Jaworski's (2001) '7Cs' framework (see Table 10.3).

When designing websites, operators may use Content Management Systems (CMS) software applications (collection of programs) that are used to create and manage the digital content. There are many systems available for tour operators to buy off-the-shelf that are targeted at small and medium-sized operators, whereas larger tour operators invariably will design their own purpose-built software. CMS provide operators with the opportunity to update and make changes to the websites with relative ease and may be linked to image banks so that the correct image is viewed on the relevant page.

Search functions are integral to websites, allowing viewers to narrow down product offerings to fit with their own requirements. Such searches will include:

- Date: The ability to search by date range, month of departure, specific dates and flexible dates.
- Country.
- Specific country destination.
- Holiday or brochure code.
- Duration.
- Season.
- Activities involved or specific experiences, e.g. cultural tours, hiking, dog sledding.
- Trip pace, e.g. easy, moderate, strenuous.
- Price range.
- Accommodation style.
- Type of holiday, e.g. self-drive, self-guiding, escorted.

An analysis of website traffic is essential and involves activities such as:

- Online demand: Is your sector growing or declining?
- Visitor numbers: Traffic levels of your Internet footprint. Measurements include the per click campaign.

Table 10.3. The 7Cs framework. (Adapted from Rayport and Jaworski, 2001.)

7Cs	Explanation	Importance for tour operators
Context	Context is the look and feel of the screen and can be classified by aesthetics and functionality. Aesthetics is created by colours, graphics and images, the inclusion of interactive videos and other rich media. Functionality is related to the layout and performance of the website, including tabs, quick access shortcuts, speed, reliability and media accessibility	The division of the site into sections and pages and how new pages relate to other sections, i.e. the linking structure. Thus, navigation tools are important so that customers can access the required information easily, such as internal search engines. For operators with numerous brands, it can be useful to link the brands together and encourage visitors to move between the sites For tour operators working in wide-ranging markets, language options may be considered an investment
Content	Content focuses on what the site offers, the product offering, customer service, information and relevance	The content should include, for example, high-quality photographs and graphics, and well-written in-depth descriptions of destinations. Sites need to be frequently updated How the products are presented and the range on offer are important
Community	Community concerns the interaction between the users and this may include a feeling of involvement or membership of a group	Operators can enable user-to-user communication through a feedback and review section or communication with the company using Instant Messenger
Customization	Customization refers to the site's ability to present different content for each user. Customization can be personalized by the user or tailored by the company	
Communication	Communication is defined as the dialogue between the website and the user. It can be either one-way (broadcast), meaning information is provided for the user, or interactive, which encourages two-way communication between the organization and the user	Broadcast messages can include mass emailing of newsletters, notifications of new products and webcast events Interactive may include customer service through emails or live online communications

Continued

Table 10.3. Continued.

7Cs	Explanation	Importance for tour operators
Connection	Connection refers to formal linkages between sites	Links may be to external organizations, for example links to content from another supplier whereby the user is taken to the supplier's website
Commerce	Commerce is a level of support for transactions such as online purchases, security, order tracking, confirmation and links	Low-level commerce includes the ability to process basic transactions, whereas high-level commerce provides additional support such as customer login and tracking of bookings, additional departure information and destination-specific data

- New sessions: A metric in Google analytics that will identify the number of visitors to your site that are new and those that are returning.
- Direct versus referral: Identifies the point of origin of website visitors.
- Bounce rates: Where visitors enter and leave immediately.
- Conversions: To enquiry, quotation and point of sale.
- Lead to close ratio: The number of people who follow up on a lead and purchase versus the number of people who follow up on the lead but fail to close.

The number of visitors to a website is often referred to as current traffic. A breakdown of this could include the number of unique visitors, i.e. those visitors who are visiting the website for the first time. In addition, it is useful to know the average time spent on the site (stickiness) and the number of pages that are viewed.

Other data that can be collected from websites include the type of device people used to access the pages, the location of those visitors (either domestically or internationally) and probably the most important statistic, the conversion rate to enquiry, i.e. the percentage of people who view the site and then go on to make an enquiry. While the algorithms used by search engines change over time and are fiercely guarded, it is logical to assume that activities on operators' websites may be influential, such as regular updates. In addition, links to and from social media can drive traffic to the website through activities such as shares, retweets and 'likes', and it is more likely that search engines will pick the 'relevance' of the site and it will appear higher up in the search results.

Move to mobile devices

Most websites have been designed for use on personal computers, but this is changing as more customers use mobile devices to search travel information and for bookings. As mobile use increases, tour operators need to adapt their digital strategies, for example ensuring swift and accurate transfer between devices so that searches on one mobile device can be found on another mobile device. This provides an excellent opportunity to strengthen customer relationships by encouraging them to 'register' so they can then log in to their account on different devices – this is particularly important for the millennial generation (Asia Travel Leaders Summit, 2016). By enabling the mobile experience, tour operators can build brands and relationships and provide opportunities for incremental purchases and increase brand loyalty.

Social media

Although there is no universal definition of social media, Chan and Guillet state that it is 'a group of Internet-based applications that exist on the Web 2.0 platform and enable Internet users from all over the world to interact, communicate and share ideas, content, thoughts, experiences, perspectives, information and relationships' (Chan and Guillet, 2011, p. 347). As such, social media is considered to 'build on the ideological and technological foundations of Web 2.0, and that allow the creation and exchange of User Generated Content' (Kaplan and Haenlein, 2010, p. 61). In effect, the rise of social media means that is not sufficient for companies to rely on traditional media for communicating to their actual, or prospective, customers. The availability of information through social media has changed the way that consumers research and plan their holidays. Also, it has had an impact on how we perceive the credibility of that information, essentially eWOM has now become critical to a company's success. Furthermore, social media can be used not only as an online distribution channel but also provides excellent opportunities for relationship building, developing brand loyalty and service recovery.

User-generated content

The rise of Web 2.0 technology has revolutionized how customers research travel products. This includes social networking sites, blogs, wikis, video-sharing sites and hosted services and is characterized by greater user interactivity and collaboration and user-centric social media (Lueng *et al.*, 2015).

Web 2.0 is the development of second-generation Internet-based services that are interactive, context rich and easy to use (O'Reilly, 2007), which has enabled people to collaborate and share information online through social networking sites. These are called User Generated Content (UGC), the 'word-of-mouse', and include blogs, wikis, discussion forums, posts, chats, tweets, podcasting, pins, digital images, video, audio files, and other forms of media that are created by users of an online system or service, often made available via social media websites. This has led to phenomenal growth in social media channels such as Facebook, Twitter, LinkedIn and third-party review sites. International communities are created as people connect through sharing information. According to Salampasis and Matopoulos (2011), travel-related topics are among the most popular issues in this environment – for instance, travel destinations and hotel reviews, excursions, guides, and suggestions for restaurants or attractions.

Many travel companies have recognized that social media now must become a key part of their marketing mix, specifically their marketing communications, as potential tourists look towards social media channels to find information on services and products. Social network sites such as Facebook, Renren and Weibo allow users to construct profiles and share information, write blogs, post pictures and videos and share their ideas. With over 1.7 billion monthly active users, Facebook has become a key platform for many tourism organizations, including tour operators. The power of the image uploaded by the user is often a trigger for other consumers to comment and start thinking about possible holidays. It also provides an excellent platform to promote brands, and many tourism organizations such as airlines and destinations have their own Facebook pages and encourage repeat visits by offering competitions and give-aways. Essentially this has meant that customers have begun to trust comments and feedback left by other consumers on theoretically impartial websites such as Trip Advisor, Trust Pilot and booking.com and are replacing WOM promotion with eWOM as the most trusted sources of information. Review sites such as Trip Advisor can influence purchases because they include quantitative information in the form of statistics and ratings and quali-tative information in the form of customer opinions. Travel bloggers and vloggers have also contributed to travel purchases by influencing potential customers search-ing for inspiration, promoting products or destinations such as Adventurous Kate (adventurouskate.com/blog).

Apps

Tour operators may take advantage of mobile technologies. Mobile technologies have advanced considerably; 25 years ago a mobile phone was used for making phone calls, and now smart phones can be used to access the Internet, use one of a plethora of apps, provide GPS positioning and so forth. Eye for Travel (2013) note that mobile penetration exceeds 100% in most post-industrial countries, with developing countries following a similar pattern. The growth of portable technology such as tablets, smart phones and gaming devices has fuelled media convergence – that is, more opportunities for marketers to engage with customers on different levels using different platforms. Data sug-gest that 85% of travellers take their phone on trips and travellers actively access social media while on holiday, sharing their travel experiences through posts on Facebook, Twitter, Instagram, Snap Chat, each platform attracting different

user groups and content. For example, Instagram, an app that shares only images, is a perfect tool for operators to market their destinations and activities. The app is particularly popular with Generation X, Y and Z and relies on images; operators should add images regularly and link them with hashtags that relate to the organiza-tion to ensure audiences are the type of customers you would like, e.g. #mountain-biking or #sharkdiving. Contiki Tour en-courages their customers to add #contiki to their travel photos they post on Insta-gram. The tour operator then traces these images and reshares them on its Instagram wall. Contiki has managed to build an interactive relationship with clients on Ins-tagram with over 20,000 followers.

The global growth of smart phones has provided opportunities for tour op-erators, and travel agents, to develop their own applications. These apps vary depending on the organization, but offer several advantages for the company and customer. Instead of customers keeping paper-based copies of booking forms, trip, flight and accommodation details, pre-booked tours and activities, they can be stored on the tour operator's app.

However, simply providing storage for details of a holiday is insufficient to meet the expectations of many high-tech users and therefore additional benefits need to be provided. Off-line maps will help customers navigate their resort or destination and further information about the destination or resort can be provided as an off-line travel guide, trip planners and even travel journal opportunities. Some apps allow in-app purchases such as insurance, clothing sales and equipment hire through strategic partnerships with suppliers, and can be a source of revenue through app advertising. Apps can be used to prolong the relationship between the tour operator or travel agent and the customer, because usually the relation-ship between the two parties ends not long after the trip is completed. By providing an app that the customer can access there is an opportunity to prolong the relationship and potentially increase loyalty because customers are exposed to the brand several times a day when they check their phone. An app also provides excellent opportunities to gain feedback from customers and encourage them to engage in other social media to promote the company; for example, by uploading holiday photographs to Instagram or sharing their experiences on Facebook.

The value of apps to tour operators is well illustrated by the following examples. Trafalgar Travel, part of the global Travel Corporation, have introduced 'myTrafalgar', which provides opportunities for customers to access their Travel Director (tour manager) before the trip begins. Significantly, this approach enables the Travel Director to interact with upcoming passengers and learn more about the group and therefore to improve the ability to customize the experience. Crystal Ski Holidays, part of TUI, have developed a phone app, Crystal Ski Explorer, which is designed to help skiers get the most out of their holidays. The app includes Find My Friend, which allows the user to locate friends and/or family on the mountain by creating groups and allows members to call or text them collectively. The app includes recommended resort guides, ski routes and piste maps, as well as enabling the user to track speed, distance and duration. In addition, the app provides updated snow reports to enable customers to identify the best pistes at the correct level for their experience and notifications from the members of the resort teams.

Evaluation

The final stage of the marketing plan is to monitor and evaluate the outcomes of the marketing activities against the objectives set out in the original strategic and tactical marketing plan. Ideally, such evaluation should be continuous because the outcome of such assessment will enable the marketing team to modify their activities or introduce new activities to achieve their goals.

There are several different ways to assess the success of a marketing campaign, with the most obvious being an increase in sales. Comparisons can be made on a week by week basis, monthly or annually. The revenue generated is the simplest and most straightforward way to learn how effective the marketing campaign has been. To identify the success of different promotional activities, companies can track the source of information that has generated a customer enquiry, such as using specific telephone numbers or web addresses related to each unique promotional activity. Monitoring response rates will enable the cost per response to be identified and thus the return on investment (ROI). For example, if spending £1000 returns only £1500 of sales, then it is clear that this strategy is not working and the marketing plan should be re-evaluated and redesigned. Digital marketing allows immediate collection of analytical data, but it is important to choose the right type of metric to monitor, i.e. numeric data, that allows marketers to evaluate their performance. Essentially, these are:

- Traffic generation: overall site traffic, keywords that brought in traffic, cost per click and click through rates.
- Conversion metrics: conversion rate, cost per lead, average cost per view, average time on site, return visitor rate.
- Revenue metrics: ROI, cost to acquire customer (cost of campaign per new paying customer).

Other actions that can be undertaken include reviewing the competitors to identify if the tour operator's marketing campaign has affected them; for example, if they start to mimic the operator's marketing techniques and campaign, then it is evident that the competition feels under threat. Feedback from customers (see Chapter 6, this volume) about the campaign is also very useful and will enable the operator to customize future marketing campaigns.

Overall, the evaluation of the campaign enables companies to use the information to inform decisions for the next campaign, building on areas that were successful and either removing or adapting those aspects which achieved less successful results.

Summary

Overall, the chapter has provided an outline of the key principles and practices involved in marketing tour operators' products. In the process, the key challenges that tour operators face when marketing intangible products have been identified. Further, while each tour operator will evaluate their own circumstances, and produce a company-specific marketing plan, key decisions to be addressed before embarking on a promotional campaign are identified and discussed.

The efficient and effective marketing of the tour operator's products is a core activity of the management and key to the ongoing development of a successful enterprise. In terms of their products, it is also one that presents a number of additional challenges when compared with traditional retail goods. This is because of the essential characteristics of services inherent in the products of tour operators and also, as discussed, those particular traits associated with the sector's operating environment. In combination, these bring a degree of complexity to the fundamental task of marketing planning.

The development of the marketing plan covers the whole process of the establishment of the enterprise, based as it is on the development of package holidays, through to its continued success and development. In many ways, therefore, the marketing planning process follows similar stages as that of strategic planning and is both informed by, and informs, the strategic direction of the operator (see Chapter 3, this volume). Central to this is a good understanding of the competition and demand and where the operation's products fit in this context, which is well demonstrated in the successful establishment of a widely recognized brand.

Based on such strong foundations, the marketing plan can be developed, aided by adopting the 7Ps of the marketing mix, each of which play key parts in achieving the maxim of 'the right product, in the right place, at the right price'. This leads to identification and targeting of the right market and in turn informs the tour operator's promotional planning mix, how they will reach the target market(s) and the distributional channels to be used. The marketing activity of tour operators is crucial to their success, but no amount of expenditure on marketing will overcome an unsuitable product that is targeting the wrong market segment. Since the rise and development of ICT, this has become more complex as traditional channels such as travel agents, TV and the general press are being usurped by social media in its increasingly myriad forms and applications that demand the attention of tour operators. The chapter has acknowledged the importance of the Internet and social media as a way of targeting increasingly sophisticated consumers and identified opportunities for tour operators to embrace new communication platforms and further promote their unique selling points.

Once the marketing plan has been satisfactorily completed and implemented, it must be recognized that this is not the end of the process. The implementation needs to be monitored and outcomes evaluated very much as an ongoing process. The information gained from this can be reviewed and fed back into the planning process, creating a continuous cycle of planning action – reaction – revision and adjustment accordingly, thereby enabling action as appropriate to address any failings or emergent opportunities. This process should also inform strategic planning and be informed by ongoing environment scanning. Through such processes, the tour operator is far better positioned to withstand external threats, manage opportunities and sustain success in this very competitive marketplace.

Discussion Questions

1. How do the characteristics of the tourism product affect the marketing of package holidays?
2. What is the relationship between tour operators and marketing?
3. Examine the factors that affect a consumer's decision to purchase a specific holiday. What are the implications for the marketing department?
4. What tools can a marketer use to launch a new product for a tour operator?
5. Examine a selection of brochures available and discuss the market segment targeted and how the company has positioned themselves in the marketplace.
6. Based on researching the websites of a variety of tour operators, seek to identify to what extent they may or may not be using 'green' or 'responsible tourism' ideas in their company profiles and/or promotional material. Can you identify any differences between the types of tour operator examined?

Key Terms

- **Cognitive dissonance:** Cognitive dissonance happens when there is conflict between attitudes, beliefs and behaviour.
- **Demographic:** A particular sector of the population based on statistics relating to people and society, e.g. sex, age, births.
- **Marketing mix:** The marketing mix is also called the 4Ps and the 7Ps. The 4Ps are price, place, product and promotion. The 7Ps also include physical evidence, people and process.

INTERNET EXERCISE

Review the TUI brandbook:
www.tui-travelcenter.ro/uploaded_docs/TUI_brandbook.pdf

Questions

- How important is it for TUI to have one logo across many of their brands?
- Why do you think that TUI have not rebranded all their brands?
- Use Rayport and Jaworski's (2001) 7Cs framework to review one of the websites for a TUI brand, e.g. World Challenge, Crystal Ski, Hayes and Jarvis.
- Utilizing the brand wheel, create a wheel for one of the brands.

In 1998 the German operator C&N took over the UK travel company Thomas Cook and decided to launch the Thomas Cook name in Germany. In 1999/2000, a decision was taken to amalgamate many of the Thomas Cook sub-brands into one overarching brand 'JMC' (as in John Mason Cook, founder of Thomas Cook), thus launching JMC Airlines and JMC Holidays. This would replace longstanding, well-known Thomas Cook brands such as Sunworld, Sunset, Flying Colours, Inspiration and Caledonian Airways. The launch cost £10 million and was criticized for lack of brand awareness, with commentators citing the lack of brand personality, brand values and positioning strategy. Within three years, the Company reverted to the original Thomas Cook for all but its family holiday packages and reintroduced the budget brand Sunset Holidays.

Questions

- What are the risks involved in redesigning or deleting brands?
- Why was the launch of JMC unsuccessful?

Club Méditerranée

Club Méditerranée (Club Med) is a French company specializing in all-inclusive holidays in over 100 'vacation villages', which it owns and operates in over 40 countries, and a forerunner of the Sandals, Dreams and Beaches brands of the 2000s. The company, founded in the 1950s, was the first operator to offer all-inclusive packages. The product was synonymous with private club getaways and exotic locations for European jetsetters, providing active holidays for families. The appeal of the all-inclusive was that everything was paid for and thus there was little need for extra spending money. In addition to the original summer holidays, winter villages were introduced which provided skiing and winter sports tuition. Originally the main market target was singles and couples; later it became more attractive for families. Club Med offerings included lodging, food, use of facilities, sports activities, games and shows.

Club Med introduced a new informal working environment, which involved Club Med staff being called 'GOs' (*gentils organisateurs* – gracious/nice organizers) and clients 'GMs' (*gentils membres* – gracious/nice guests/members). The company culture became more relaxed as the GOs and GMs now integrated at mealtimes, during activities and at the evening shows, with both being regarded as equals and therefore no tipping was allowed. As a French company, the staff spoke French and French customers were dominant.

By 2000, the original concept became outdated and new suppliers were creating intense competition and customers were demanding more sophisticated products. Club Med accepted that it needed to refresh its image. The company conducted a brand analysis where it identified that it had high levels of brand recognition but its position in the market seemed unclear. It was perceived as being expensive and therefore loyalty was hard to achieve and new custom harder to gain.

Continued

As part of the repositioning in the market place, Club Med decided to:

- renovate their vacation villages;
- increase the marketing budget and specifically increase their online presence;
- restructure their pricing levels;
- reduce promotions that were confusing the brand reputation;
- add additional product offerings such as new activities, e.g. climbing walls, circus arts and rollerblading;
- upgrade shows and entertainment;
- reorganize the structure of the company by moving the headquarters from New York to Florida.

Although the launch of the new positioning strategy coincided with the September 11 attack on the Twin Towers in New York, these changes enabled Club Med to reposition themselves. They started to see improvements in visitor numbers and an increase in operating profit. The rebranding of Club Med focused on building relationships and responding to opportunities to changes in the environment. By 2015 the Company operated 65 villages in Europe, Africa, the Caribbean, South America, the Middle East and Asia. Club Med also decided to construct 40 villas for private purchase. The owners would have free access to use the amenities and participate in activities in the village and to rent out their villas when they were not occupied.

Questions

- Club Med offer a single product which is an all-inclusive holiday and aim to attract a global market. Do you consider that a global approach to marketing and customer segment is achievable for Club Med?
- Club Med are introducing new products such as private villas. How do you think these fit into their product development and marketing strategy?

Recommended Reading

For a comprehensive text that provides an excellent introduction to marketing, relevant theory and application in the various sectors of the travel and tourism industry, see:

Holloway, J.C. (2004) *Marketing for Tourism*. Pearson Education, Harlow, UK.

For an examination of the barriers to introducing specialist activities to a new market, see:

Jin, X. and Sparks, B. (2017) Barriers to offering special interests tour products to the Chinese outbound group market. *Tourism Management* 59, 205–215.

Online bookings have seen year-on-year growth, a trend that is likely to continue. For an overview about how tour operators can generate and sustain traffic to their websites, see:

Joergensen, J.L. and Blythe, J. (2003) A guide to a more effective world wide web presence. *Journal of Marketing Communications* 9, 45–58.

The following paper examines the extent to which Danish tour operators use the internet as a tool for marketing their products and in particular generating and sustaining traffic to their home pages:

Senders, A., Govers, R. and Neuts, B. (2013) Social media affecting tour operators' customer loyalty. *Journal of Travel & Tourism Marketing* 30, 41–57.

For a very informative text on the themes of demand for tourism and within that context consumer behaviour and types of tourists, which is well illustrated through a comprehensive collection of case studies, see:

Swarbrooke, J. and Horner, S. (2016) *Consumer Behaviour in Tourism*, 3rd edn. Butterworth-Heinemann, Oxford, UK.

References

Asia Travel Leaders Summit (2016) Yoursingapore. com. Available at: http://www.yoursingapore. com/content/dam/MICE/Global/bulletin- board/travel-rave-reports/Capturing-the- Asian-Millennial-Traveller.pdf, accessed 4 September 2016.

Booms, B.H. and Bitner, M.J. (1981) Marketing strategies and organisation structures for service firms. In: Donnelly, J.H. and George, W.R. (eds) *Marketing of Services*. American Marketing Association, Chicago, Illinois, pp. 47–51.

Chan, H.L. and Guillet, B.D. (2011) Investigation of social media marketing: how does the hotel industry in Hong Kong perform in marketing on social media websites? *Journal of Travel and Tourism Marketing* 28, 345–368.

Cheyne, J., Downes, M. and Legg, S. (2006) Travel agent vs internet: what influences travel consumer choices? *Journal of Vacation Marketing* 12, 41–57.

CIM (2016) The Chartered Institute of Marketing. Available at: http://www.cim.co.uk/ more/getin2marketing/what-is-marketing, accessed 18 June 2016.

Clarke, J. (2005) Marketing management for tourism. In: Pender, L. and Sharpley, R. (eds) *The Management of Tourism*. Sage, London, pp. 102–118.

Copley, P. (2014) *Marketing Communications Management: Analysis Planning Implementation*, 2nd edn. Sage, London.

Evans, N. (2015) *Strategic Management for Tourism, Hospitality and Events*, 2nd edn. Routledge, Abingdon, UK.

Experian (2016) MOSAIC – the Cross-Channel Segmentation. Available at: http://www. experian.co.uk/marketing-services/know- ledge/infographics/infographic-new- mosaic.html, accessed 24 June 2016).

Eye for Travel (2013) *Social Media and Mobile in Travel Distribution Report: Online Strategies, Consumer and Industry Trends, 2013*. Eye for Travel, London.

Haven Holidays (2006) About us. Available at: https://www.haven.com/support/about-us. aspx, accessed 29 October 2016.

Holloway, J.C. (2006) *The Business of Tourism*, 7th edn. Prentice-Hall, Harlow, UK.

Kaplan, A.M. and Haenlein, M. (2010) Users of the world, unite! The challenges and opportunities of social media. *Business Horizons* 53, 59–68.

Kotler, P. and Keller, K.L. (2012) *Marketing Management*, 14th edn. Pearson Education, Harlow, UK.

Kotler, P., Bowen, J. and Makens, J. (2014) *Marketing for Hospitality and Tourism*. Pearson Education, Harlow, UK.

Lueng, X.Y., Bai, B. and Stahura, K.A. (2015) The marketing effectiveness of social media in the hotel industry: a comparison of Facebook and Twitter. *Journal of Hospitality and Tourism Research* 39, 147–169.

Mathieson, A. and Wall, G. (1982) *Tourism: economic, physical and social impacts*. Longman, Harlow, UK.

Middleton, V. and Clarke, J. (2001) *Marketing in Travel and Tourism*, 3rd edn. Butterworth-Heinemann, Oxford, UK.

O'Reilly, T. (2007) What is Web 2.0: design patterns and business models for the next generation of software. *International Journal of Digital Economics* 65, 17–37.

Rayport, J. and Jaworski, B. (2001) *Introduction to Ecommerce*. McGraw-Hill, New York.

Salampasis, M. and Matopoulos, A. (2011) *Proceedings of the International Conference on Information and Communication Technologies for Sustainable Agri-production and Environment.* Hellenic Association for Information and Communication Technologies in Agriculture, Food and Environment, Skiathos, Greece.

Shostack, G.L. (1982) How to design a service. *European Journal of Marketing* 16, 49–63.

Swarbrooke, J. and Horner, S. (2016) *Consumer Behaviour in Tourism*, 3rd edn. Routledge, Abingdon, UK.

Ward, S., Light, L. and Goldstine, J. (1999) What High-Tech Managers Need to Know about Brands. *Harvard Business Review* 77(4), 85–96.

Wirtz, J., Chew, P. and Lovelock, C. (2012) *Essentials of Services Marketing*, 2nd edn. Pearson Education South Asia, Singapore.

Wood, L. (2000) Brands and brand equity: definition and management. *Management Decision* 38, 662–669.

11 Human Resources and Managing the Workforce

Learning Objectives

After studying this chapter, you should be able to:

- Understand the contribution effective people management activities can make to overall business success.
- Explain the critical links between workforce planning, recruitment and selection, learning and development, performance management and employee reward.
- Identify the methods for recruiting a workforce with the skills and experience aligned to the needs of the business.
- Outline the approach towards managing individual employee performance and learning.
- Assess the range of benefits that a tour operator can offer to motivate and retain a skilled workforce.

Introduction

Human resource management can be described as 'getting the right number of right people into the right place at the right time' (Douglas, 2002, p. 291). This definition emphasizes the importance of recruiting the appropriate number of staff with suitable skills and positioning them within the company in order for them to make a positive and effective contribution. A wide variety of issues have to be integrated into the planning process to guarantee optimal staff deployment,

e.g. not only current staffing requirements but also future ones, short-term peak loads (for example, school holidays), staff availabilities, holidays, sickness absences, budget allowances, skills, employment law-related restrictions, as well as salary and contractual terms. Furthermore, through training and performance management, the individuals may be able to take advantage of opportunities, such as promotion, as the organization develops. Evans (2015) suggests that because of the labour-intensive nature of the tourism sector, the human factor is often key to differentiating competing operators and a critical factor to sustained success. Indeed, many employees in tour operations will be in direct contact with the customers and the quality of their service will not only influence sales but also the level of customer satisfaction (see Chapter 6, this volume). Therefore, recruiting employees who are talented and knowledgeable is critical, as are the interpersonal skills and the ability to adapt to change.

For many tour operators, cost saving is paramount to their survival. Therefore, it is imperative that they recruit (and retain) the best people in the first instance, whether they are from within their own country or local to the resort or destination. In the latter case, a tour operator may gain potential cost savings as the remuneration package for staff drawn from within the destination may be comparatively lower than for expatriate employees. However, it is important to check on employment law obligations in the country in question before reaching this conclusion.

Tour operations is generally viewed as an attractive sector in which to work, despite the oft-cited negative aspects of working in tourism, which relate primarily to the hospitality sector (see Morris, 2003). Not only are the general working conditions viewed as comparatively better but there are the perceived benefits such as the opportunities to travel, discounted rates for accommodation and travel, and the interactive nature of the roles. Even so, the sector does experience relatively high workforce turnover, notably regarding resort representatives, tour managers and sales teams, which is predominantly attributable to the variations arising from seasonality. It is especially for these reasons that best practice in Human Resources Management (previously known as Personnel Management) is very important. Undertaken and delivered effectively, with the accent on employee development and engagement, this can go a long way to addressing high staff turnover.

This chapter introduces the core people management activity that needs to be undertaken in a tourism organization to ensure that the workforce can effectively support the successful achievement of the business strategy. The way in which people are managed, motivated and deployed, and the availability of skills and knowledge, should all link to and inform the business strategy. Hence, here we explore the role of human resource management from a strategic perspective, which leads on to the broad principles and objectives of workforce planning and how this links to other aspects of HR management policy and actions. This helps ensure that the various aspects of people management work together to develop the performance and behaviours necessary to be successful in achieving the objectives of the business. Workforce planning is therefore seen as a key element of the business's strategic planning, i.e. the strategic plan informs workforce planning and thus the attention then turns to recruitment and subsequently the core elements of managing employee performance and related benefits.

As previous chapters have identified, tour operators vary considerably in both size and scope, from micro enterprises to global companies with brands and sub-brands, and present diverse employment opportunities, as illustrated by the range and scope of career opportunities in this dynamic sector. Even so, the organizational structure of these tour operators will vary according to their size and remit, with larger organizations having clear departments with fixed roles and smaller organizations having roles that encompass several different activities. Therefore, although each tour operator will have their own requirements and processes, the fundamentals of planning and managing the workforce are the same; the difference will lie in their scale and complexity. There are five broad areas encompassed by Human Resources Management: recruitment and retention, employee engagement, learning and development, pay and reward and performance management.

The overall focus here, as noted, is on workforce planning and thus establishing the company's workforce requirements, subsequent recruitment, performance and reward. These fundamental aspects of human resource management are subject to myriad legal and regulatory requirements, which are applicable to all employers within the EU (see Nickson, 2013). By and large, similar regulatory requirements will be found in most post-industrial nations, but will differ in many other countries of the world. Tour operators should therefore ensure they establish employee legislation and regulations pertaining to their country of residence. Any business needs to be aware of and compliant with these requirements, which are accessible in a variety of ways, such as trade organizations, municipal authorities, employment law websites and the websites of the appropriate government department. However, it is to be noted that new regulations and practices relating to employment are regularly introduced or amended and thus tour operators should seek to keep abreast of changes in legislation and employment-related practices through suitable journals and the professional press, establishing their own relevant policy framework.

Strategic Human Resource Management

Strategic Human Resource Management (HRM), although considered complex in some quarters, is arguably essential to the success of a business's strategic management and planning. This is well illustrated by how it is defined by the Chartered Institute of Personnel and Development (CIPD): 'The undertaking of all those activities affecting the behaviour of individuals in their efforts to formulate and implement the strategic needs of business' and 'the pattern of planned human resource deployments and activities intended to enable the organisation to achieve its goals' (CIPD, 2016a, para. 4). On such a basis, company HRM strategies need to be incorporated to support the strategic plans of the tour operator.

In practice, strategic HRM is an approach towards managing an organization's people resources in a way that supports long-term business goals and outcomes within a strategic – joined up – framework, as illustrated in Fig. 11.1.

This approach focuses on longer-term people issues, matching resources to future needs, and joins activity relating to organizational structure, quality, culture

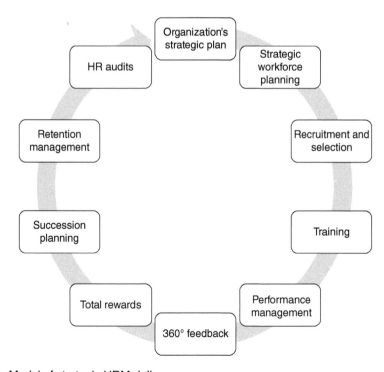

Fig. 11.1. Model of strategic HRM delivery.

and behaviours. Within the UK, the CIPD and other organizations have been investigating the impact of people management practices on business performance. Much emphasis has been placed on the importance of 'fit', in other words, human resource interventions should align with other HR practices and with organizational strategies for maximum impact (CIPD, 2016a). In practice, it is critical that the organization's approach towards workforce planning, recruitment and selection, learning and development, performance management and reward all link with each other, and promote and endorse the types of activity and behaviours that lead to a culture that the organization seeks to deliver through its workforce.

A key area of HRM strategy is workforce planning, which helps organizations meet their future skills needs and support their long-term business goals. Workforce planning involves putting business strategy into action. Therefore, it is an iterative process – feeding information to senior management on the capability and capacity of the workforce to deliver, and acting on forecasted needs for skills and capabilities to take the tour operator forward. On this important aspect tour operators may be failing, because the sector is highly competitive and many companies focus on the day-to-day running of their operation rather than the future needs of the business. However, recently there has been a renewed interest in workforce planning, largely driven by the realization that in a fast-changing economy some degree of planning is vital to ensure the organization is developing sufficient capacity to adapt to new trends and take advantage of emerging opportunities.

Although there is no single HRM strategy that will deliver success in all cases, organizations need to define their own unique strategy based on their specific context, culture and objectives. This is where HR professionals are instrumental in applying their expertise in helping managers understand organizational circumstances and interpret HR interventions that will make the most of, and retain, the talent within the organization, thereby reducing defection to other tour operators.

What is Workforce Planning?

The original concept of workforce planning fell out of favour in the early 1980s because it was considered to be unable to adapt to fast-paced changes in the external environment (Gilmore, 2013), such as being unable to predict or allow for downturns in economic growth. Simply looking at workforce numbers was too narrow an approach. However, workforce planning is now considered a high priority by many organizations, recognizing the need for skills development and adaptability rather than stability. More recent interpretations of workforce planning place a greater priority on forward planning informed by the organization's future ambitions. As such, it is increasingly being recognized as an essential feature of HRM. Considered in its widest sense, it is about making the best use of the human resources available to the organization while also planning for workforce requirements for the future. Therefore, in effect, it is a process designed to ensure the right number of people, with the right skills, are employed at the right time to deliver an organization's short- and long-term objectives. The CIPD (2016b) suggests it can embrace a diverse and extensive range of activities, such as:

- skills gap analysis;
- succession planning;
- labour demand and supply forecasting;
- recruitment and retention planning;

- **talent management**; and
- future scenario planning.

However, what is essential is that any activity in this regard must be linked to the business direction of the tour operator.

In an increasingly competitive marketplace, tour operators are faced with the need to improve efficiency and profit, which in turn means maximizing the return on resources whether these be financial or human resources. Consequently, they need a quality workforce that is responsive and adaptable. Due to the nature of tour operations, which is usually highly seasonal, many employees are employed on a part-time or temporary basis, resulting in high labour turnover, which can be problematic. Operators need to consider this when planning for the workforce.

Workforce planning can be approached in two ways: operationally and strategically. The operational dimension aims to ensure that resources are allocated to projects correctly, or sufficient staff are available to fulfil day-to-day customer needs or demand for products and services. Examples of this might include the need to ensure call centres are appropriately resourced or that sufficient people are recruited to fulfil a predicted demand for certain products or services on a seasonal basis. The strategic dimension supports the company's strategic goals by forecasting future needs, succession planning and replacing/ensuring key skills in the workforce are replaced as employees leave the organization. Arguably, it is better to address these two approaches together, i.e. from the outset, and therefore plan to ensure that the best talent is in the right roles, at the right time. Further, such planning needs to be undertaken in the context of the longer-term scenario plan and with a better understanding about what type of workforce is likely to be needed in the future based on the operator's strategic objectives.

To take this one step further, this means linking workforce planning to talent planning (or succession planning) and feeding the results into the operator's business plans, which are then implemented locally by line managers. Whatever its precise form, workforce planning should be linked to strategic business goals and viewed as an important part of the tour operator's strategic business planning process. A tour operator that is making major changes in its product distribution strategy from travel agents based in urban areas to online sales, also recognizing the trend for self-packaging because the traditional roles of sales agents and the associated skills will be required less, will be seeking staff with specific skills sets such as in web page design, as well as IT specialists and data analysts. These modern approaches to workforce planning are often informed by management information and analysis systems such as PESTEL (see Chapter 3, this volume).

What does workforce planning involve?

Workforce planning is a core HR process and presents an important opportunity to support the organization's strategic planning to achieve business objectives. In a volatile, fast-changing economy, this can help to enable sustainable performance by providing the basis for better decision-making about the future needs of the business in terms of its people resources. Basically, it involves generating and analysing information to inform future demand for people and skills and then translating that into a set of actions that will develop and build on the existing workforce to meet future business need. Good-quality information is vital for good workforce planning and this information must flow both from within the organization and from external sources. Essentially it is about operationalizing the business strategy into a set of actions to ensure a workforce is established that can deliver the organization's strategic goals and objectives. This process must be organization-wide and requires effective communication across all the management functions. Therefore, it is important to involve stakeholders from all parts of the organization and that they can understand the data and what it means for both short- and long-term resourcing needs.

According to the CIPD (2016b), the process of workforce planning should not be overly complicated and involves the following stages:

- Determine business strategy, people strategy and associated operational action plans.
- Analyse the available data – input information from data collection exercise, input resourcing information from HR and business managers.
- Agree objectives of the plan – review labour supply data (internal and external) and review workforce capability to deliver the plan.
- Determine actions and implement plan – agree assessment of the status quo, scenario plan, projected workforce requirements, identify actions to close gaps, implement and monitor the plan.

Implementation of workforce planning

Implementing workforce planning basically starts with the company's business plan and therefore it is essential to make sure that HR management is involved in the business planning process. In this the CIPD (2016b) notes that the following points should be considered:

- The plan needs to be future-focused to enable the organization to deliver the business strategy while at the same time remaining flexible enough to deal with constant change.
- It is a dynamic process and therefore should be subject to constant feedback and review to ensure it remains relevant in a rapidly changing environment.
- It is not just about numbers, it is also about skills, employee potential and how these are deployed and organized. As such it links into development, career planning, talent planning, organization design, among the other HR practices.
- The process encompasses the whole organization and requires buy-in at all levels to be effective. It should seek to enable co-operation between managers and minimize any competition between departments for people resources.
- It brings together the operational and the strategic planning processes. There is a need to be able to think strategically while acting practically to ensure that the technique is carried out as effectively as possible.
- No single formula exists that will give a 'correct' workforce plan. However, with a wealth of data available, the art is about bringing this together and interpreting it in a meaningful way.

Once the requirements for the workforce are assessed for both the short and the long term, securing the right talent is achieved by using effective recruitment and selection techniques. For operators, many of their staff deal with customers and it is essential to recruit people who have the skills and ability, or the potential to develop them, to represent the company in a professional manner and support the image of the organization.

Recruitment

The UK's CIPD publishes a Code of Practice on recruitment and selection (CIPD, 2017b) which aims to promote high standards of professional practice. The code contains advice on a range of aspects, including achieving equality and promoting diversity in the process while complying with current employment legislation. Here we consider the operational actions required to be undertaken when recruiting and selecting workforce members, which is considered in six key stages.

1. Identifying the business need and analysing the job

Before recruiting to a new or existing position, it is important to invest time in collating information about the job and considering whether in the prevailing economic situation and organizational context the role is required or is required in a different format. Many organizations use natural turnover in the workforce to consider savings opportunities, either through not replacing a staff member who leaves or redesigning the nature of the role more fitting to the projected needs of the organization. This should be the first consideration by any manager looking to plan and manage a recruitment and selection process. In aiding such a process, it is obviously important that each employee who leaves voluntarily should be given an exit interview to reveal why s/he is leaving, so that appropriate action can be taken if a resignation is due to some failing or other on the part of the company. The main causes of turnover are wide-ranging and can be attributed to pay and reward, managerial relationships, lack of training opportunities, boredom, frustration, discrimination, harassment, victimization or an accumulation of petty irritants.

If the business assessment is that a role does need to be filled, then an analysis of the work involved is required. This means reviewing not only the content, such as the tasks making up the job, but also the purpose of the position, the outputs and how the role fits into the operator's structure. This analysis should form the basis of a job description and person specification. These are key documents in the recruitment and selection process and pivotal to the way candidates will be judged and selected. Designing appropriate job descriptions and person specifications ensure that candidates are judged on a similar basis and will help the organization to comply with ever-increasing employment law in this area.

Many tour operators are reliant on seasonal staff recruited at specific times of year; for example, operators offering mainly summer seasons will recruit in the preceding autumn, whereas ski tour operators will recruit during the summer in preparation for their winter season. Operators also need to identify specific requirements that may be necessary; for example, the ability to speak other languages, experience of having lived and worked in specific destinations and previous experience.

Job description

The job analysis leads to the manager writing a job description. The job description explains the scope, purpose, duties and responsibilities of the job to candidates (Boella and Goss-Turner, 2005) and helps in the recruitment process by providing a clear guide to all involved about the requirements of the job. It can also be used to communicate expectations about performance, and how they will be measured, to potential employees and thus help managers ensure effective performance in the job. Current thinking suggests that job descriptions should focus on the work someone needs to achieve rather than the skills and experience (CIPD, 2017b), as this is more likely to result in selecting someone with the right abilities. Therefore, there is also a move away from very detailed job descriptions, which can be seen as creating inflexibility in roles.

Person specification

When the information has been collated for the job description, it will be possible to determine the knowledge and skills required to perform the job successfully. A person specification states the necessary and desirable criteria for the role. Increasingly, such specifications are based on a set of competencies identified as necessary for the performance of the job, such as knowledge (what people need to know to be able to do the job), skills (technical or management skills necessary to complete the role) and competencies (attitudes and behaviours that underpin how people do the job). For example, recruiting for a website designer for a tour operator will require applicants to have specific IT knowledge and experience. Traditional tools for developing a person specification include Rodger's Seven Point Plan, which provides a range of headings against which individual candidates can be measured (see Torrington and Hill, 2004). It can be used when preparing the person specification by identifying requirements under each heading as either essential or desirable:

- Physical make-up, e.g. speaking voice.
- Attainment, e.g. academic and other achievements.
- General intelligence, e.g. intellectual capacity.
- Special aptitudes, e.g. foreign languages, IT skills.

- Interests, e.g. practical, physically active, artistic or social.
- Disposition, e.g. preference for working in a team, dependability.
- Circumstances, e.g. where they live, travel abroad, ability to work unsocial hours.

While Rodger's framework provides a list of attributes, care should be taken not to make some attributes essential when they may only be desirable.

A competency framework may be substituted for the job or person specification, but these should include an indication of roles and responsibilities. In addition, many person specifications will also indicate how during the recruitment and selection process each of the required areas of knowledge, experience and/or competencies will be assessed in the process. Furthermore, in the UK it may be necessary for applicants to have undergone a Disclosure and Barring Service (DBS) check.

2. Attracting talent

There are many ways to generate interest from potential candidates with the key aim of creating a strong pool of candidates from which to select individuals. Many organizations go to some lengths to create a strong organizational brand to ensure in the longer term they attract the best talent in the market place. For example, TUI operates an Intentional Graduate Leadership Programme to recruit their future leaders, which has two intakes each year. As outlined below, there are a number of approaches which can be taken.

Internal methods

It is important not to forget the talent pool that already exists within the business when recruiting. Providing opportunities for development and career progression through promotion or transfer increases employee commitment and retention, and supports succession planning. For example, tour managers/leaders who have spent considerable time working in overseas destinations may prove ideal candidates for office-based roles such as Product Manager or roles dealing with customer relations and the customer experience.

Employee referral schemes

Some organizations operate an employee referral scheme. These schemes usually offer an incentive to existing employees to assist in the recruitment of friends or contacts, but employers should not rely on such schemes at the expense of attracting a diverse workforce. Such schemes should be in addition to other methods.

External methods

There are many options for generating interest from individuals outside the business and a growing expectation from candidates of being able to search and apply for jobs online and via mobile devices. Increasingly, the most popular methods for seeking candidates include directly (e.g. a tour operator advertises on their company website, offering roles as they become available), specialist recruitment agencies, commercial job boards and professional networking sites such as LinkedIn, and most importantly, the travel press. Some organizations also use social media to identify candidates, but employers need to exercise caution and ensure guidance is taken if they establish this approach as part of their policy framework, to ensure equality and privacy requirements are not breached.

If an employer uses online or other media for advertising roles, advertisements should be clear and indicate the:

- requirements of the job;
- necessary and desirable criteria for job applicants (to limit the number of inappropriate applications received);
- organization's activities;
- job location;
- reward package;
- job tenure (for example, contract length);
- details of how to apply and the deadline;
- DBS requirements.

Other ways to attract applications include building links with local colleges/universities, working with the local jobcentre and holding open days.

External recruitment services

Some organizations use external providers to assist with their recruitment. Recruitment agencies or recruitment consultants offer employers a range of services, including attracting candidates, managing candidate responses, screening and shortlisting, (or) running assessment centres on the employer's behalf and on occasions assisting on the interview days. It is important that the recruitment agencies have a good understanding of the organization and its requirements. Those employers and agencies committed to collaborative partnerships are more likely to achieve positive results.

3. Assessing the candidates

There are two main formats in which applications are likely to be received: curriculum vitae (CV) and/or an application form. It is possible that these could be submitted either on paper or electronically (increasingly common). All applications should be treated confidentially and circulated only to those individuals involved in the recruitment process. It is good practice that all applications, whether solicited or not, are acknowledged, although this is often time-consuming and expensive and many organizations only reply to applicants who have been shortlisted. Prompt acknowledgement is good practice and presents a positive image of the organization. The development of a 'sorry you have been unsuccessful for the role you applied for' card/email often speeds up this process.

The recruitment process is not just about employers identifying suitable employees for the future, it is also about candidates finding out more about the business and considering whether the organization is one they would like to work for. The experience of applicants (both successful and unsuccessful) at each stage of the recruitment process will affect their perception of the organization both as potential employee and potential customer.

Application forms

Application forms provide a standardized format comprising the same questions, which must be answered by the applicants and allows for information to be presented in a consistent way. This makes it easier to collect information in a systematic way and assess objectively the candidate's suitability for the job. The job application form is a legally defensible listing and thus requires factual responses and includes the potential employee's signature, verifying that the statements are true. Application form design and language is important – a poorly designed application form can mean applications from good candidates are overlooked, or that potential candidates are put off applying. Devoting lots of space to current

employment could disadvantage a candidate who is not currently working. Also, any form of discrimination should be avoided; if not, it may fall foul of a country's laws (e.g. the UK's Equality Act 2010). It may also be a legal requirement to offer application forms in different formats, such as braille or large print, or to help a prospective employee who is blind to complete the form. Also noteworthy is that personal questions relating to sex, marital status, children and age need to be considered very carefully and with legal advice.

CVs

The use of CVs allows candidates the opportunity to promote themselves in their own way, unrestricted by the confines of application forms. However, CVs make it possible for candidates to include additional, potentially irrelevant material, which may make it harder for the tour operator recruiter to assess in a consistent way.

4. Selecting candidates

Selecting candidates involves two main processes: shortlisting and assessing applicants in order to decide who should be offered a job. Selection decisions should be made after using a range of tools appropriate to the time, level of role and resources available. Care should be taken to use techniques that are relevant to the job and the business objectives of the tour operator. They should be validated and constantly reviewed to ensure their fairness and reliability and that they are not discriminatory in any way.

A range of different methods can be used to assess candidates. Some are more reliable than others in terms of predicting performance in the job, while some are easier and cheaper to administer than others. Whatever method is used, recruiters should tell candidates in advance what to expect from the selection process, including how long it will take and the type of assessment they will undergo and when they will be notified of the decision. Employers should also check whether the applicant has any need for adjustments because of a disability.

Selection interviewing

After reviewing the applications, the operator should shortlist suitable candidates. The next stage is usually to ask the candidate to attend an interview in person (or, according to the circumstances, by video or skype link). Interviews are very widely used in the selection process, as demonstrated by successive CIPD surveys of recruitment practices. Such interviews invariably involve five key areas:

- **First impression**: This takes account of everything that is heard or noted in the first few minutes of the interview: speech, manner, dress, personal attitude towards the interview.
- **Qualifications and expectations**: General, further and technical education, and signs that at every stage the interviewee has lived up to the expectations one would expect from their background.
- **Intelligence and ability**: Observations on their understanding of the questions asked; use of standard ability tests.
- **Motivation**: Achievement of goals in every phase of life: school, sport, pastimes, work; with special regard to initiative, ambition and determination.
- **Adjustment**: Ability to cope with pressure or unexpected situations; indications of ability to take responsibility if necessary/required.

Interviewing is generally considered to be the least effective method because it often bears no resemblance to what the candidate is likely to do once employed and many managers are not properly trained in interview techniques (Boella and Goss-Turner, 2005). The global nature of tour operators means that it may be necessary to conduct phone interviews or video interviews using webcams or smart phones. Many UK-based tour operators use video interviews for resort representative posts and ask the candidates to prepare a 20-minute video presentation answering a selection of questions and demonstrating their skills.

As well as being relatively simple to set up, interviews provide both parties with an opportunity to meet face to face (or virtually via video link), exchange information and gain a sense of whether they would like working together.

For the employer, the interview is an opportunity to:

- assess a candidate's experience, ability to perform in the role and suitability for the team;
- discuss details such as start dates and terms and conditions;
- explain the employee value proposition, including training provision and employee benefits; and
- give the candidate a positive impression of the organization as a good employer.

For the candidate, the interview is an opportunity to:

- understand the job and its responsibilities in more detail;
- sell themselves in terms of potential, skills and benefits they will bring to the organization;
- ask questions about the organization; and
- decide whether they would like to take the job if offered it.

Assessment centres

Assessment centres vary in structure from employer to employer, and the role involved. They are used by many employers to test those skills that are not easily accessible from the traditional interview. For many customer-facing roles, an assessment centre test may last the whole day and will only be attended by applicants who have passed an initial screening process based on information provided in their CV and/or application form. Essentially, candidates are expected to complete different tasks as part of the selection process and the tasks set should relate closely to the person specification and reflect the reality of the job. They must be administered in a systematic way, with candidates being given the same tasks to complete in the same time, so that they have equal opportunity to demonstrate their abilities. Depending on the nature of the job, the tasks might include individual or group work, written and/or oral, and tasks prepared in advance as well as those performed on the day.

For resort-based jobs, the ability to sell the tour operator's products and services (e.g. excursions, car hire) is crucial for the success of the operator and the employee, so it is likely that candidates will be expected to present to the interview/assessment panel. Some operators may expect applicants to prepare a presentation on a predefined topic (e.g. favourite holiday destination) or to demonstrate their sales skills (often involving an everyday item such as a pen or cup).

Group tasks may be included to identify applicants with good time management skills and the ability to prioritize, other tasks may include analytical work, individual problem-solving, group discussions, group problem-solving, simulations of business activities, personal role-play and functional role-play. Group exercises should be as realistic as possible based on a detailed brief with clear goals and have

a time limit. Typically, they require candidates to undertake a defined activity, share information and reach decisions within a limited time period to assess their ability to perform under pressure and to aid evaluation of leadership skills. For example, when recruiting for holiday representatives, operators often ask applicants to present a Welcome Meeting to the others because this would be a task that they would do in the resort and therefore potentially demonstrate confidence in public speaking and remembering detailed information. Other tasks may include basic mathematics, e.g. to work out sales prices, commissions and currency conversion calculations. They might encourage co-operation and/or competition to test for creativity or the ability to build on the ideas of others in a productive manner.

Psychometric testing

Many large tour operators recruiting for their graduate training schemes use psychometric testing as a way of filtering applicants at an early stage. Online testing is growing in popularity, especially if there are many applicants. These tests are standardized and objective and employers often value the results because they provide a fair way of comparing candidates' strengths regardless of their background. Used correctly, psychometric tests allow employers to assess systematically individual differences (for example, in ability, aptitude, attainment, intelligence, personality).

Most tests are designed and developed by occupational psychologists and are accompanied by detailed manuals providing the data to establish the reliability of the test and how test scores might be judged so that employers can compare their test candidates against the scores of similar people. Administering tests and analysing the results is a skilled task, and the services of a qualified tester should be secured by the recruiting manager should they wish to use such tools. The use of psychometric testing before interviewing candidates can allow employers to inquire into an area that may be a cause for concern.

Evaluating the candidate

After each interview, the candidate should be evaluated based on their answers to the interview questions and activities. Evaluation may be based on whether the candidate's response met, exceeded or failed to meet the criteria for the question. Once the interview is completed, a comparison of candidates' responses based on scores achieved for pre-defined criteria will help evaluate objectively and provide a sound basis to compare candidates with each other. It should be noted that applicants can request a copy of their evaluation forms, so comments made by the interviewer need to be fair and objective.

Making the appointment

Most employers will have a policy on pre-employment checks, usually by taking up references provided by the candidate. But, and particularly significant to tour operators, prior to making an offer of employment, employers have the responsibility for checking that applicants have the right to work in the location(s) required by the company. The offer does involve a legal relationship between the employer and employee, which is based on a contract of employment. As with other contracts, there must be:

- The offer, which may be made orally, in writing or by implication.
- The acceptance, which may be made orally, in writing or by implication.
- The consideration, which will be, on the one hand the remuneration and other benefits offered and on the other hand the performance of the job.

As with other contracts, any agreement based on misrepresentation is voidable. It is therefore all the more important that the offer is presented in tandem with an employment contract detailing the terms and conditions of employment. In the UK, for instance, employees have a legal right to have written terms and conditions within 13 weeks. The composition of a general contract of employment is presented in Box 11.1.

This statement may be issued to the employee before 13 weeks of service has been completed. It does not have to be signed by either the employer or employee, but it is good practice to sign the copies, and retain them for the employment records.

5. References

A recruitment policy should state clearly what kind of references will be necessary (for example, from former employers), when in the recruitment process they will be taken up and how these will be used, and these rules should be applied consistently. Candidates should always be informed of the procedure for taking up references and usually references are sought after the applicant has been given a provisional offer. Some organizations may refuse to provide references based on concerns over legal ramifications and will provide only summary details about length of employment and position held. If a reference is not provided for a candidate, this should not be held against the candidate because it may simply be company policy; in this instance, the candidate may be requested to provide alternative sources of references.

6. Induction

No matter how carefully the recruitment and selection procedures have been

Box 11.1. General terms and conditions of an employment contract

- The name of the employer.
- The place of work or where the work is required or permitted at various places; an indication of this would be the address of the place of work.
- The date on which employment/continuous employment commenced.
- Where employment is not expected to be permanent, the period for which it is expected to continue or, if it is for a fixed term when it is to end.
- The scale and method of remuneration and the intervals at which it will be paid.
- Length of any probationary period.
- Any collective agreements that directly affect the terms and conditions of employment, including, where the employer is not a party, the persons by whom they were made.
- Any terms and conditions relating to hours of work, including normal working hours and contractual overtime.
- Any entitlement to holidays, including public holidays, and holiday pay, including entitlement to accrued holiday pay on termination of employment, to be precisely calculated.
- Terms relating to sickness, notification of sickness and pay for sickness.
- Pension arrangements, including a statement as to whether or not a contracting-out certificate is in force.
- The length of notice which an employee is entitled to receive and the amount they must give if they wish to terminate their employment.
- Any pay in lieu of notice clause.
- The title of the job that the person is employed to do.
- Disciplinary rules, or an indication of where the person can go to find out about the rules.
- The name of the person to whom a grievance should be taken, and the steps or stages of the appeals procedure.
- Any restrictive covenant clauses, non-solicitation or non-competitive clauses.

carried out, the new employee will need assistance if they are to become fully effective in their role. The administrative detail must be handled effectively to ensure that the employee understands the terms and conditions on which they are employed, the day-to-day expectations of their line manager and the company, and any technical skills training that they will be expected to undertake in the early months. In many organizations this forms the probationary period.

It is important that initial induction activity is well planned because this will help the new employee to integrate more effectively into the organization. Induction will usually involve introductory sessions about the organization, their products and job-specific information such as computer programs, policies and procedures, while also being a mechanism for identifying longer term training and development needs for the individual. It will also include relevant health and safety procedures, although new employees may be required to complete online training for this.

For staff who will be working abroad, e.g. holiday rep, the induction process may involve intensive training within the organization's home country. For example, Thomas Cook provides a seven-day intensive training session in the UK and, if successfully completed, the potential holiday rep will be sent to work with the team in the resort destinations. These training sessions are usually administered by in-house training teams who specialize in developing selling skills, customer service skills and incident management procedures.

Training and Development

While the induction introduces the organization, the culture and job specific requirements, training continues throughout the employees' employment with the organization. Training is vitally important to an organization to ensure that they have the right skills and the right people in place at the right time.

According to Douglas (2002), training provides many benefits to an organization, such as:

- providing employees with specific skills;
- improving productivity and performance;
- reducing waste;
- reducing accidents;
- reducing labour turnover; and
- individual advancement.

Training is directed towards a change in knowledge, skill or attitudes, or a combination of these factors. Some training may be essential for employees to perform their role (e.g. complaint handling, equipment usage), whereas other training programmes will aim to develop their skills (e.g. appraisal techniques). If training is to be carried out in an efficient manner, then it is important to be systematic and this is best approached using a training cycle, as illustrated in Fig. 11.2.

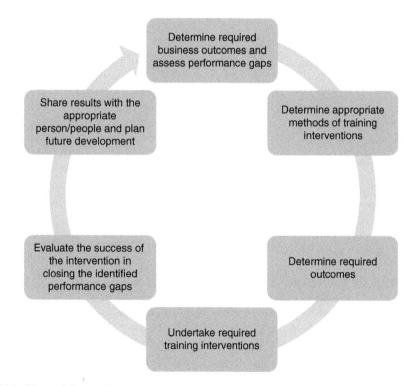

Fig. 11.2. The training cycle.

- Identifying training needs. In order to identify an individual's training needs, it is important to conduct a training needs analysis (TNA). Once opportunities for training have been identified, then the training can be planned. This may be developing skills, improving productivity, performance and the customer experience to reduce actions or be a result of changes in legislation.
- Set objective and choice of method. The training should have clear objectives and this will inform the organizers about which method of delivery is most suitable, e.g. on the job or off the job training, online sessions.
- Plan the training. This includes the specific events and activities that will be used.
- Evaluate. Once the training has taken place, then the success should be evaluated, from the perspectives of a participant and the organization, and ultimately whether it has led to the changes identified as necessary in the TNA.
- Feedback.

Training should be considered an investment for an organization. Unfortunately, when companies experience financial difficulty, this is often one of the first areas where companies make cuts. Therefore, it is essential that companies identify the most important areas for staff development which will enable the organization to achieve its strategic objectives.

Managing Employee Performance and Learning

Performance management should be a holistic process that ensures that employee performance contributes directly to the achievement of the business objectives. Armstrong and Baron define performance management as 'a natural process which contributes to the effective management of individuals and teams in order to achieve high levels of organisational performance' and stress that it 'is a strategy that relates to every activity of the organisation, set in the context of its human resource policies, organisational culture, style and communication systems' (Armstrong and Baron, 2005, p. 2). Thus effective performance management is considered to bring together many of the elements of best people management practice and relies on both formal and informal processes. Not surprisingly, the processes involved will vary depending on the scale of a tour operator, the business climate and culture within which it operates. In an international setting where employees are drawn from many different cultures and nationalities, this process will be influenced by what is appropriate and acceptable from an employee, employer and trade union perspective (where relevant).

In practice, some common tools of managing employee performance include an annual performance appraisal meeting, the setting of objectives and performance standards, identification of learning and development needs, establishing learning and development plans, the use of 360° feedback mechanisms, and maybe performance-related pay.

Performance appraisal

Performance appraisal is a process where individuals and those responsible for their performance (line managers) discuss the employee's performance and development, alongside the support that they might need in their role. It is used to assess recent performance and focus on future objectives, e.g. learning and development needs. While this is an important part of performance management, as outlined above, it is one of a range of tools that can be used to manage performance. Typically, performance appraisal takes the form of an annual meeting between the line manager and employee. Key elements of an effective appraisal meeting would include:

- employee's achievements being recognized and reinforced;
- scope for reflection and analysis between employer and employee;
- performance and behaviour being analysed;
- open exchange of views on performance;
- discussion on future objectives;
- future capability and individual development needs discussed; and
- agreement on an individual action plan for the following year.

While the majority of large organizations continue to use performance appraisal meetings in their performance management framework, there is a growing body of debate that has highlighted perceived deficiencies in traditional appraisal approaches, giving rise to alternative approaches being introduced by organizations such as Google, Netflix and Deloittes (CIPD, 2017a). Specifically, these criticisms include:

- The frequency of an annual appraisal does not match the speed of change in business priorities which require immediate feedback.
- A lack of added value related to the time invested in the process, e.g. completion of associated appraisal paperwork.
- Focus on past performance with too little attention paid to future performance, improvement and/or learning needs.
- Feedback often coming from a single source (the line manager), which may not account for the experience of peers, customers and the individual themselves.

Alternatives include one-to-one coaching, year-round communication and bottom-up evaluations. In considering the needs of an organization in the tourism sector, these newer approaches are worthy of note given the fast-moving fluid nature of the tourism business. For example, the demand for holidays and travel can be affected by a range of factors, from weather conditions, to the current strength/weakness of the main currency used and political unrest, and as such it continues to be a dynamic, fast-moving business. Given the necessary speed of engaging the workforce as new priorities emerge, tour operators need performance management processes with a high degree of flexibility.

360° feedback

360° feedback is an alternative to complement line-manager appraisal. This is a form of performance appraisal based on a collection of performance data from several sources, typically including people who report to the individual, peers, team colleagues, internal and external customers, in addition to the line manager. Feedback from this diverse range of sources can help identify areas for improvement and manage employee expectations, enabling them to see how their role fits into the whole organization. The employee is usually asked to provide names of one or two peers s/he would like to be involved in her/his 360° feedback process as well as those approached by the manager.

Learning and development

Performance appraisal reviews may be regarded as learning events, during which individuals can be encouraged to think about how and in which ways they want to develop. This can enable managers to write a personal development plan (PDP) setting out the actions they propose to take to meet their development needs. In turn, these should be linked to organizational goals to ensure they are appropriate and relevant and add value for the organization.

Objectives and performance standards

Many organizations set performance objectives for individuals, departments and the business overall, which may be directly work-related or personal. Work-related objectives refer to results such as sales targets, standards or timelines, which can be expressed as targets to be met (such as sales levels) or as tasks to be completed by specified dates (for example, in product development or marketing). Personal objectives take the form of developmental objectives, such as increased level of accuracy in proofreading website documents, and these should relate to the overall purpose of the job, department and the business. They need to be agreed with the individuals or teams concerned, that is they need to be SMART: Specific, Measurable, Achievable/Aligned, Relevant and Time Bound.

Alongside objectives are performance standards, which are used when it is not possible to set time- or volume-based targets, or when there is a continuing objective that does not change significantly from one review period to the next and is a standing feature of the job. These are usually encapsulated in quantitative terms; for example, time management or communication.

Pay

The relationship between pay and performance is a widely debated aspect of performance management (see Armstrong,

2012; Brown and Reilly, 2013). Recently, many employers have adopted an increasingly individualistic approach towards employee reward, transferring more of the risk (and potentially reward) and cost of the provision to their employees. For example, there has been a move from collective bargaining, across-the-board pay rises and service-related increments towards performance-related pay and incentives. Linking levels of pay to individual, team and organizational performance, e.g. performance-related pay (PRP) or payment by results (PBR), is a traditional and commonly used approach within many tour operators, e.g. sales bonuses for individuals and teams.

Proponents such as Belfield *et al.* (2007) argue that PRP:

- is the most tangible and effective way to incentivize people in their work;
- better links the pay budget to the employer's finance;
- delivers a clear message that performance is important;
- can reward employees without promotion; and
- is the fairest way to reward performance.

Recent evidence has challenged these claims, arguing that while PRP can increase performance, it may also have a negative effect on a wider range of factors, including:

- an increased focus on measurable and/or immediate performance targets, potentially undermining the organization's purpose and mission;
- inhibited teamwork because of its competitive nature;
- reduced intrinsic motivation, as focus shifts towards pay as the primary incentive;
- an increased sense of unfairness in an organization; and
- erosion of trust and inability to have open conversations about performance.

Employee Reward/Benefits

Employee reward or benefits is a much wider area than solely monetary reward. This section seeks to describe in more detail the range of reward packages that tour operators may offer to attract and retain the best talent in the market. Both strategic and total reward approaches have the potential to be very powerful management tools and change catalysts. The reward package can be very powerful in helping employers align their reward approach with HR and organization strategies, in addition to employee needs, with the aim of improving organizational performance. It can also have wide-reaching implications for the culture within the organization as it can focus in part on employee empowerment.

Employee benefits are no longer regarded just as a retention tool. In fact, research indicates that there are many factors in an organization's employment proposition and what makes them attractive depends on the individual employee's circumstances (such as family, caring responsibilities) (Lupton *et al.*, 2015). This has led to the concept of 'total reward', where the company adopts a bundle of mutually supporting financial and non-financial rewards (such as flexi-time, gym membership, health insurance) that aim to align the needs of the business and the employees. As such, the employee benefits package is increasingly seen as a strategic tool to assist recruitment and retention.

Total reward and benefits

The concept of total reward encompasses all aspects of work that are valued by employees, including elements such as learning and development opportunities and/or an attractive working environment, in addition to the wider pay and benefits package. Total reward packages may include:

- flexible benefits;
- access to professional and career development;
- a challenging role;
- freedom and autonomy;
- opportunity for personal growth;
- recognition of achievements;
- preferred office space or equipment;
- capacity to raise matters of concern;
- involvement in decisions that affect the way work is done;
- flexible working hours;
- opportunities for home working;
- administrative support.

In addition, more forward-thinking companies may also offer:

- opportunities to undertake charitable work;
- opportunities to work-shadow different post holders.

These are the less obvious benefits that can be considered alongside the more traditional elements of a pay and benefits package, such as annual paid leave, pension provision, healthcare and risk benefits (e.g. death in service).

Holidays and time off

Employers are required by law, in many countries, to offer a minimum level of paid annual holiday leave. There are also statutory entitlements to other types of time off work, including time off for dependents (unpaid), maternity, paternity, adoption and parental leave. As with holiday leave, employers often provide more generous entitlements than required legally.

Pensions

One of the more expensive parts of the employee benefits package for the employer is workplace pensions. The provisions for this will very much vary according to a country's regulations and indeed individual business practice. For example, since 2012 the UK Government has decreed that employers must offer a workplace pension to eligible employees. This is being phased in according to the size of the employer's business. Eventually all employers will automatically have to offer to enrol staff into a pension scheme and make contributions to the pension if the employee:

- is aged between 22 and State Pension age;
- earns at least £10,000 per year; and
- works in the UK

However, employers do not have to contribute if employees earn less than a certain amount unless the employee requests to be enrolled. If an employee requests that they be enrolled the employer must comply, even if the employee does not comply with the basic eligibility clauses.

Healthcare and risk benefits

These benefits may be provided to ensure both the welfare and productivity of employees. Common types of benefits include:

- occupational sick pay;
- private medical insurance;
- life assurance;
- permanent health insurance;
- critical illness insurance;
- employee assistance plans; and
- dental insurance.

Career Opportunities

To work within the tour operations sector requires a combination of knowledge and skills. Therefore, education and training are important factors in both gaining a suitable position as well as undertaking the duties of that position, but experience and effort are also very important.

Many employers, and not just tour operators, are increasingly seeking employees capable of multi-skilling. In other words, they are seeking employees with the ability to carry out different functions and tasks. In parallel with knowledge and specific task skills are what are called transferable skills. These are the skills that we may all have to varying levels. They include numeracy, good communication skills, personality, co-operation and flexibility. Also, and particularly important within tour operations, are interpersonal skills; particularly the ability to interrelate and deal with customers, sometimes in difficult situations while also being polite in the process is not to be undervalued. Similarly, the ability to get on with colleagues and to be able to work successfully in groups and teams. Employers are also always on the lookout for motivation, while further strengths include foreign language skills. In combination, these are fundamental for anyone seeking to develop a career in tour operations.

Rather than attempt to illustrate all careers available, it is more informative to identify the activities possible within the broad departmental titles. The way tour operators are structured varies according to size and operational capacity, but generally the medium/large enterprises will have similar departments/sections.

Director/CEO

The director (or titled equivalent) will coordinate the activities of the company from a strategic point of view. The departmental heads will report to the Director.

Accounting

The accounting department, which is usually headed by a company accountant, has responsibility for recording all financial transactions, e.g. salaries and expenditure within their home country and foreign currency payments to suppliers/principals. In addition, they will provide monitoring of the financial position of the organization by controlling cash flow, payments, deposits etc. and providing insights in all kinds of business-critical areas, from working out cash flow to providing real-time financial information. The accounting department will need to make payments for all components of the package holidays (see Chapters 5 and 7, this volume), including:

- flights, accommodation, transfers and excursions;
- salaries, both within the organization and to any overseas representatives;
- office costs: rent, rates, heat, etc.;
- IT and communication: computers, telephones, access to computer reservation systems/global distribution systems, brochure production, website design;
- travel agents and commissions;
- cost of recruitment and training, etc.

In addition, the accounting department will be responsible for:

- customer deposits;
- payments to suppliers;
- insurance payments;
- financial promotion contributions from national tourist organizations; and
- revenue from ancillary sales.

Product department

The product department is responsible for the development of the tour operator's products and the planning of the itineraries. This will involve the initial design of new products and the review of existing products in their portfolio. This department may also be required to:

- manage current products;
- research new products;
- contract accommodation, which particularly requires negotiation skills (there may be a specific department for contracting, particularly if it needs to be completed in a number of destinations);
- accommodation inspections for health and safety requirements; and
- producing brochure copy.

For many tour operators, it may be necessary to have a dedicated air travel section (possibly within the product department). This section organizes the purchasing of flights for passengers from the generating country and, as appropriate, flights within the destination, e.g. domestic flights in China.

Operations department

As with many companies, the titles and roles within the operations department will vary, with larger companies having separate sections for product development, operations, contracting, etc. The operations department may involve many administrative functions, including:

- confirming travel arrangements, creating and despatching customer documentation;
- general office services; and
- contracting/accommodation negotiations.

Sales and reservations

By and large, the sales of the major tour operators (i.e. with the exception of small and micro-enterprises) are made either by travel agents, online or by a dedicated department. Direct sales by tour operators reduce the need to pay commission to agents, although it is likely that there will be some form of reward for staff achieving/surpassing sales targets.

Sales teams deal directly with customers and need to be knowledgeable about the product on offer to be able to advise customers about the holidays and their suitability. Larger tour operators may have a separate department for handling group bookings and/or specialist itineraries.

Reservations administration

This department has a varied remit, including processing and checking bookings, ensuring that documentation and invoices are sent out and providing manifests (passenger lists), rooming lists and transfer lists to ground handling agents and service providers, including resort reps and accommodation suppliers.

Marketing and PR

The marketing and PR department is responsible for producing marketing collateral such as brochure design, website design, copy writing and all promotional activity. Specialist teams may be employed by large tour operators to focus on data analysis, such as web analysts, to maximize search engine optimization, etc.

Human resources

As discussed above, the HR department is responsible for ensuring that the workforce can effectively support the successful achievement of the business strategy. This is achieved by planning for the workforce in terms of projected needs by recruiting, training, deploying and retaining suitable members of staff.

Customer services

The customer service department may be part of the operations department in smaller tour operators, but larger tour operators will have a dedicated team that liaises with customers. The department can be considered to comprise:

- Pre-departure customer service: handles queries made by customers prior to departure, changes to bookings such as name changes and additional pre-booking of activities and excursions.
- Post-departure customer service: deals with customers who contact the operator on return from their holiday. This team may deal with post-holiday enquiries, including complaints which they will be expected to respond to, investigate and resolve in accordance with company protocol, procedures and travel industry guidelines.
- Guest experience: from looking after customers in resorts to solving problems and delivering 'moment(s) of truth'.

Overseas positions

There are many different roles available overseas, all of which are dependent on the size and the activities of the company. These roles may be undertaken by employees of the tour operator or they may be provided by ground handling agents.

The terminology varies from company to company, so in this section we have used the most common titles. Many overseas positions are seen as the face of the company and represent the company in the destinations.

Resort representatives

Large tour operators often employ resort representatives in the larger destinations, either employing staff from their own country or from within the destination region. Some countries impose restrictions on employing non-locals and therefore it may be necessary to hire local staff. There are several different roles, such as resort representative, senior representative and head representative, whereas other companies may use terms such as resort manager. The role can vary in terms of responsibility and the function, with some reps being expected to look after customers in a number of hotels, which they will visit on a regular basis. In the case of ski tour operators, their resort representatives are usually expected to provide an après ski entertainment programme.

Due to the competitive nature of tour operators, some high-volume destinations have reduced the number of reps and instead of being based in hotels they are based in a local office in the centre of the resort (contact centres) and customers are expected to contact the office. Although this may be seen as a cost-cutting measure, it is more likely due to the fact that customers are more experienced in travel and are less likely to need the guidance of a rep. The role will involve handling general enquiries about the destination, dealing with problems, organizing hotel-based activities and selling excursions, for which they will usually receive a commission once sales targets have been met. Some tour operators offer welcome meetings or parties for their customers (providing an ideal opportunity to promote excursions) and it is the responsibility of reps to arrange these.

Adult representatives

Adult representatives are reps who look after young adults on what are often termed 18–30 holidays, where the emphasis is on partying and clubbing, and the role involves organizing events and activities for this group of people.

Children's representatives/children's entertainers

Children's representatives are responsible for providing activities for large groups of children over a wide age range. This may involve organizing games and competitions, overseeing meals and providing activities. Tour operators generally expect these reps to have a formal qualification in childcare or nursery nursing and experience of working with large groups of children, and they must have a successful DBS check (UK).

Transfer representatives

These representatives deal solely with the movement of customers from the airport to the hotels (and vice versa). These are roles offered by the very large tour operators.

Animateurs

These are overseas staff employed specifically as entertainment staff for the shows put on by the tour operators. Staff are usually recruited through acting/entertainment journals such as the UK's *The Stage*.

Tour managers/tour leaders/ couriers/escorts

Tour managers accompany their tours throughout the holiday and have a multifaceted role. They have to ensure that tours run according to the itinerary and therefore they may have to make alternative arrangements in case of unforeseen circumstances, such as bad weather, strikes or accidents. They will be required to perform group check-ins at airports and accommodation, provide information to passengers about the destination through welcome meetings and throughout the trip, and make sure all travel arrangements run according to plan. The exact role depends on the type of tour, e.g. adventure tour managers may be expected to drive overland vehicles, arrange and cook meals when camping, lead mountaineering trips, etc.

Many coach companies refer to their tour managers as couriers and like adventure holiday tour managers/leaders they accompany the passengers providing commentary and support throughout the trip. Escorts accompany tourists throughout the tour and they may perform the role of the tour leader.

Cruise managers

For operators who include river or sea cruises in their itineraries, a cruise manager often accompanies the passengers and provides a similar role as that of a tour manager. Some operators also supply a cruise director if dealing with large numbers of passengers. Roles will involve the coordination of schedules, dealing with operational issues and guest relations.

Activity specialists

Activity specialists are recruited for their experience and qualifications in specific activities, although some larger operators may offer their own training. These roles have varying levels of seniority, with new recruits and trainees rising to management roles that will involve appropriate training, risk assessments and so forth. Examples of specialist roles include:

- ski and winter sports instructors;
- sailing/dinghy instructors;
- multi-activity instructors, e.g. swimming, orienteering, horse-riding, football, tennis, windsurfing, archery;
- deckhands and stewards for yachts; and
- camp site organizers.

Chalet staff

UK ski tour operators often use local chalets instead of hotels in ski resorts and this is a unique element of this form of package. Chalets range in capacity from four to over 20 beds and can be booked by small groups, couples or individuals. The guests are looked after by chalet staff, who cook and serve breakfast, packed lunches and an evening meal, with some operators offering afternoon tea. The informality and sharing of facilities is a key to the popularity of chalet-based ski holidays and the chalet staff are a critical factor in this success. This hosted accommodation has been replicated in other forms such as gulet (sailing boat) holidays and club-style hotels.

Guides

A guide's role is dependent on the nature of their employment. In many countries, guides need to have achieved specialist qualifications to receive certification. In some countries, such as India, guides are categorized depending on their specialism: monument guides, museum guides, wildlife guides and city guides.

Summary

Businesses in the service sector invariably start from a small enterprise employing few people. The tour operating sector is no exception to this and indeed an enterprise could start up with as few as two people. For example, an inbound destination management company based on arranging tours for overseas clients might comprise initially just two people – the entrepreneur and an administrator. Similarly, an enterprising tourism graduate based in Chengdu

(China) might identify the potential for small group, guided tours of Nepal. The initial staff would comprise the entrepreneur, a part-time administrative assistant and a known family friend based in Nepal to assist in making local arrangements (equivalent to a ground handling agent – see Chapter 5, this volume). Clearly, the two staff members of this embryonic enterprise have been selected on the basis of being known and considered to hold the requisite knowledge and skills for their tasks and longer term potential. As the enterprise develops, so the entrepreneur becomes less and less 'hands on' and consideration needs to be given to the next stage in development and the staff requirements. While still a micro-enterprise, the entrepreneur logically automatically includes the potential need for more staff as the business develops and may recruit through direct approaches to suitable personnel. However, as both operations and the workforce expand, this becomes increasingly unlikely and often unwise in terms of complying with employment legislation.

The enterprise becomes departmentalized and within that developing structure an HRM department arises and with it defined policies and procedures for managing the workforce and for recruitment, selection and personal development. This all needs to be attuned to the needs of the business, not only in regard to current and short-term operations, but also informed by the overall strategic plan for the business. Hence the need for strategic workforce planning based on ensuring the operator has the right staff in place to meet their longer term strategic objectives.

Discussion Questions

1. Seek out three or four examples of job descriptions and application forms and compare them. What do you consider to be good points about each one? Why do you think they have included the questions featured on the application form?
2. Discuss the costs and benefits of using resort representatives and how the role may change in the future.
3. Discuss the benefits of performance-related pay.
4. Present an argument in support of the view that tour operators should only recruit employees from within the destinations they visit and similarly, only engage as required the services of locally based, small enterprises.

Key Term

- **Talent management:** An organization's commitment to recruit, retain and develop the most talented prospective employees available in the job market.

INTERNET EXERCISE

Try to obtain at least one example of a contract of employment from a company with which you are familiar. Compare the contents of that contract with the general terms and conditions of an employment contract.

Identify a selection of tour operators offering differing products and review their recruitment/job section. What skills and qualifications are they looking for?

Adventure tour managers

Adventure tour managers are employed for their travel experience and their knowledge of destinations. Their roles involve running tours often with little contact with the UK due to the remote locations. Many tours are run back-to-back, which involves repeating the same two-week itinerary several times. Many managers are self-employed and may work continuously throughout the year or pick and choose when they want to work. Some adventure tour operators are no longer using generating-region-based staff, but employing local staff to manage the tours.

Questions

- What are the benefits of using local staff?
- What difficulties could you envisage when trying to manage local staff in remote regions?

MAJOR CASE STUDY

Workaseason.com

Workaseason is the recruitment department for three specialist ski companies, Inghams, Esprit Ski and Ski Total, plus Santa's Lapland, Inghams Lakes and Mountains and Esprit Sun. These operators form the largest specialist independent tour operator in the UK and are part of Hotelplan Ltd.

Workaseason recruits staff for many different positions, including resort reps, chefs, bar staff, childcare and chalet staff.

Chalet staff, also termed hosts, are employed to look after the guests in the chalet. This involves catering, cleaning and general customer service. As the food is included, and critical to the enjoyment of the holiday, Workaseason offers training programmes to teach potential chalet staff basic food hygiene and how to cook and plan meals, and provides recipe books. By successfully completing the programme, candidates are offered chalet host roles.

Staff are recruited using an online application form or via the recruitment portal online. The application form is supported by a CV which should detail the candidate's previous experience. Applicants are then contacted to attend interviews either at the head office or other locations throughout the season.

Questions

- What are the benefits of asking candidates to apply online?
- What are the advantages of offering training programmes for chalet staff?
- What personal skills do you think chalet staff need?

Recommended Reading

For an overview of human resource management and a comprehensive introduction to key concepts and a range of examples, see:

Nickson, D. (2013) *Human Resource Management for Hospitality, Tourism and Events*. Routledge, Abingdon, UK.

For a comprehensive overview of employment law pertinent to the UK, suitable for tourism students, using case examples to illustrate the topics, see:

Nairns, J. (2011) *Employment Law for Business Studies*, 3rd edn. Pearson Education, Harlow, UK.

References

Armstrong, M. (2012) *Armstrong's Handbook of Reward Management Practice: Improving Performance through Reward.* Kogan Page, London.

Armstrong, M. and Baron, A. (2005) *Performance Management: Performance Management in Action*. Chartered Institute of Personnel and Development, London.

Belfield, R., Benhamou, S. and Marsden, D. (2007) Incentive pay systems and the management of human resources in France and Great Britain. Centre for Economic Performance. Available at: http://eprints.lse.ac.uk/3628/1/Incentive_pay_systems_and_the_management_of_human_resources%28CEP%29.pdf, accessed 20 January 2017.

Boella, M. and Goss-Turner, S. (2005) *Human Resource Management in the Hospitality Industry.* An Introductory Guide. Elsevier, Oxford, UK.

Brown, D. and Reilly, P. (2013) Reward and engagement: the new realities. *Compensation and Benefits Review* 45, 145–157.

CIPD (2016a) Strategic human resource management. Available at: http://www.cipd.co.uk/hr-resources/factsheets/strategic-human-resource-management.aspx, accessed 9 August 2016.

CIPD (2016b) Workforce planning. Available at: https://www.cipd.co.uk/knowledge/strategy/organisational-development/workforce-planning-factsheet#8039, accessed 22 January 2017.

CIPD (2017a) Performance appraisal. Understanding the basics of performance appraisals and how to ensure the process adds value to the organisation. Available at: https://www.cipd.co.uk/knowledge/fundamentals/people/performance/appraisals-factsheet, accessed 22 January 2017.

CIPD (2017b) Recruitment: an introduction. Available at: https://www.cipd.co.uk/knowledge/fundamentals/people/recruitment/factsheet, accessed 22 January 2017.

Douglas, H. (2002) Human resource management. In: Sharpley, R. (ed.) *The Tourism Business: An Introduction.* Business Education Publishers, Sunderland, UK, pp. 291–312.

Evans, N. (2015) *Strategic Management for Tourism, Hospitality and Events*, 2nd edn. Routledge, Abingdon, UK.

Gilmore, S. (2013) Recruiting and selecting staff in organisations. In: Gilmore, E. and Williams, S. (eds) Human Resource Management. Oxford University Press, Oxford, UK, pp. 89–110.

Lupton, B., Rowe, A. and Whittle, R. (2015) Show me the money: the behavioural science of reward. Available at: https://www.cipd.co.uk/knowledge/culture/behaviour/reward-report, accessed 12 December 2016.

Morris, J.A. (2003) Emotional labour in the hospitality and tourism industry. In: Kusluvan, S. (ed.) *Managing Employee Attitudes and Behaviours in the Tourism and Hospitality Industry*. Nova Science Publishers, New York, pp. 223–245.

Nickson, D. (2013) *Human Resource Management for Hospitality, Tourism and Events*. Routledge, Abingdon, UK.

Torrington, D. and Hill, L. (2004) *Personnel Management: HRM in Action*. Prentice-Hall, Harlow, UK.

12 Crisis Management

Learning Objectives

After studying this chapter, you should be able to:

- Define and explain the term crisis.
- Understand the diversity of causes of crises.
- Understand the role and production of risk assessments.
- Examine the production of management plans for tour operators to manage crises.

Introduction

In the last decade, international tourism appears to have experienced an increasing number of crises arising from environmental, political or economic factors that have impacted on tourism in general, at a destination level and on tour operators. Furthermore, international tourist flows are highly susceptible and responsive to external factors beyond their control. Indeed, it might be argued that no other sector in the world can suffer more from a **crisis** than tourism. As an economic sector of global reach, tourist flows rely on perceptions of destination safety, security and a positive reputation, all of which can be quickly undermined in the wake of an **incident**, of a crisis, which, to quote Coombs may be 'unpredictable but not unexpected' (2014, p. 3). As such, tour operators should plan and be prepared for crises.

It is the purpose of this chapter to consider the causes of crises and the impact on tour operators and the application of suitable processes for the management of those impacts. The first stage is to establish what is meant by a crisis and in this context, related terms of catastrophe and **disaster**, before exploring situations recognized as a crisis for tour operators and to consider their responses. Initially we will address major incidents that can be termed crises and subsequently examine the management of minor small-scale incidents which brings into focus **risk** assessment.

Definitions

A crisis can be defined as 'an occurrence of an unexpected event which introduces uncertainty about the future and it involves a threat to the status quo' (Holloway and Humphreys, 2012, p. 690). Therefore a crisis could be something that impacts on a business sector or an organization and could threaten the future of both. It might then be an incident which could be specific to that sector or quite possibly to the organization or enterprise. As such, a crisis can range from an event of global concern such as a natural disaster or terrorist incident to an unexpected downturn in cash flow for a tour operator that is already financially over-extended. Potentially confusing the matter, the term disaster is often used instead of crisis. To clarify, we can draw on

Faulkner (2001), who makes a clear distinction between a crisis and a disaster by examining the root cause, i.e. internal or external to the organization. Thus a crisis is that situation 'where the root cause of an event is, to some extent, self-inflicted through problems such as inept management structures and practices or a failure to adapt to change', whereas a disaster is 'where an enterprise is confronted with sudden unpredictable catastrophic changes over which it has little control' (Faulkner, 2001, p. 136). The apparently interchangeable way in which these terms are used suggests little consensus as to whether a crisis is the event or the subsequent reaction to an event, whether it is internal or external to the organization and the level of its severity. For the purpose of this chapter, we have retained the term crisis for both internal and external events.

The examination of crises and the associated impacts on tourism has grown substantially in recent years, although predominantly focusing on destination reactions to crises rather than within the context of operational management. Several models of crisis management have been devised. Moore and Seymour (2005) analysed the speed at which a crisis develops, describing those that happen very quickly as the Cobra, 'a fast attack and paralysing bite', 'a disaster that hits suddenly and takes the company completely by surprise and leaves it in a crisis situation', whereas the Python is 'the slow burning crisis, gradually curling itself around an unresponsive or paralysed company' (2005, p. 34). In the case of tour operators, the Cobra could be an incident that is unexpected (e.g. transport accident, extreme weather conditions), albeit this should have been planned for. A Python incident would be the lack of response to slow changes such as ongoing negative currency exchange rates or declining demand. Ritchie (2009) suggests that crises can be divided into three categories.

- Immediate crisis: This is where there is little or no warning in advance of the situation. For tour operators, this means that the crisis is unforeseeable and therefore there is an inability to prepare or plan for such an event, similar to the Cobra.
- Emerging crises: This assumes that the crises are slower in developing and that signals are given to the organization enabling them to limit the impending crises, similar to the Python.
- Sustained crises: In this case, crises may last for many weeks, months or years and have developed over a long period of time.

Internal Crisis

Adopting Faulkner's stance, the root cause of an internal crisis from a business perspective is in part at least self-inflicted. For a tour operator, this could be the result of management failure, be that poor management planning, inappropriate strategy, cash-flow problems or staffing issues. The source and scale of the crisis will determine the significance of the consequences to the tour operator. For example, small-scale incidents such as understaffing due to sickness will involve short-term disruption; conversely, large-scale incidents such as an environmental disaster will result in longer term disruption and have a greater impact on the operator and the destination(s) involved. As Meyers (1986) identified, crises can arise through a variety of causes: public perception, sudden market shifts, product failures, top management succession, finances, industrial relations, hostile takeovers, adverse international events and regulation/deregulation. These may be exacerbated by media coverage.

Internal factors can be assessed and controlled through best practice in business planning and management.

External Crisis

Faulkner also brings into focus the use of the term 'catastrophe', which while considered similar to a crisis refers more to the outcome. As Glaesser (2003) proposed, a catastrophe is an unpredictable, negative event with clearly unavoidable outcomes, which might be the cause of a crisis for an organization. However, external factors, by definition, cannot be controlled by individual companies and therefore there is a greater degree of uncertainty. Even so, tour operators need to respond appropriately, whether that means a quick intervention or longer term resolution. For example, a tourist resort hit by a terrorist atrocity requires the tour operator to bring back their customers safely and promptly. In the short term, demand will drop dramatically with no opportunities to off-load ongoing bookings, thus the operator will need in place a management strategy to address those bookings and have in place alternative opportunities. In the event of a forecast recession, longer term strategies will be needed such as cost-cutting or product withdrawal. Irrespective of the cause, it is largely possible to plan for such crises arising. In practice, this amounts to 'What if' **scenario planning**.

Sources of external crises

Recognition of the catalyst of an external crisis (see Table 12.1) leads to attempts to define them and analysis of the cause and consequences, which then facilitates examination of management reactions and any preventive measures.

Table 12.1. Examples of external crises. (Adapted from PATA, 2003, p. 2.)

Natural	Man-made
Avalanche	Terrorism
Earthquake	
Fire	Transport crash or disaster
Flood	Industrial or political action
Hurricane	Crime kidnapping/ murder/hostage
Mudslide	Mechanical/systems failure
Medical epidemic	Riots
Violent storm	Civil unrest

Scale of Crises

When considering the impact of a crisis it is important to review the scale of the event, which will affect the recovery (Holloway and Humphreys, 2012). This can be assessed in conjunction with the likelihood of such an event occurring as well as in partnership with persons who may have experienced such an event and include personnel who would be directly involved.

Low

Singular localized event, e.g. hurricane: recovery period relatively short. Hurricanes and cyclones are known weather features in many tourist destinations, particularly in China, Japan, Mexico, the USA and the Caribbean. These types of events can be planned for, particularly as they usually occur at similar times annually.

Medium

A multiple impact event, e.g. pandemics: recovery period increased. Large-scale events that happen over substantial geographic areas occur infrequently, but the impact can be over a greater area.

High

Global event, e.g. financial shocks or global terrorist atrocity: recovery period significant. For example, the terrorist attacks in New York on 11 September 2001 were not aimed at tourists or tourism, but initiated a global tourism crisis as consumers started to perceive that cross-Atlantic travel was dangerous.

Lee and Harrald state that 'natural disasters can disrupt the supply and distribution change for even the best prepared businesses.... Service businesses are increasingly vulnerable to electrical, communication and other critical infrastructure failures' (1999, p. 184). This further serves to highlight the risky nature of tour operations, as well illustrated by destinations that have suffered from major incidents (see Table 12.2).

Each of the destinations involved witnessed an immediate decline in visitor numbers and a subsequent impact on

Table 12.2. Major incidents and destinations.

Incident	Example
Aircraft crash or hijack	September 11, 2001: World Trade Centre – major impact on demand for travel in and out of the USA; 8 March 2014 loss of Malaysia Airlines flight causing immediate impact on demand for their airline; 2016 Egypt Airline flight crash due to terrorism: major drop in demand for both carrier and Egypt as a tourist destination
Terrorist activity or bomb alerts in hotel/destination/ transport provider	1997: 62 people, mainly tourists, were killed near Luxor 2002: 202 people killed and 209 injured in a bomb attack in Bali; hotel occupancy reduced from 69% to 19% (Ritchie, 2009) 2005: 80 people killed in an attack in the Egyptian resort of Sharm el-Sheikh – reason for the attack was partly to destabilize an economy so dependent on tourism 2015: 38 people killed in Tunisia
Building fire or collapse	2017: Couple fell 40 feet when their balcony collapsed in the Dominican Republic
Coach, car, train, boat-related incident	2004: 12 people killed when a bus overturned in Jordan 2017: Bus crash in New Zealand, no fatalities
Civil unrest or riot, strikes, political or industrial action	2015 Riots in Baltimore; reduced tourist numbers to USA 2017: Political unrest in The Gambia; longstanding issues in Yemen
Natural disasters, such as avalanches, earthquakes, floods, hurricanes, volcanic eruptions	2004: Tsunami in Indian Ocean led to the deaths of over 200,000 people in 14 countries 2010: Volcanic eruption of Eyjafjallajökull, Iceland. The floating ash cloud threatened the safety of aircraft and so flights into the USA and Europe were cancelled. The concern was that it was impossible to predict how long the volcano would continue to spew ash and how long the ash would take to disperse and allow flights to recommence
Medical epidemics such as Norovirus, SARS, bird flu	2003: SARS epidemic in Asia. The health and well-being of tourists is of great concern for many travellers and tour operators. Health disasters such as infectious diseases and disease outbreaks can have an immediate impact on tourist demand for a destination. Norovirus on cruise ships
Accident resulting in injury or death	Accidents on ski slopes, scuba diving, mountaineering, etc.

operators offering products to these destinations. Turkey, which welcomed some 37m visitors in 2014 (BBC, 2016), is estimated to have experienced an overall decline in visitor numbers of 40% in 2016 due to terror attacks and political incidents, with an expected decline of 95% from the Russian market as a result of a ban on operators selling package deals to Turkey.

Risk Assessment

For tourists, the tour operator is seen as being an expert in the destinations in which they operate and they are reliant on the operator to provide a safe experience. When operators are offering activities as part of the package, it is best practice to assess the risks not only to protect the company's reputation, but also from a legal perspective. It is generally accepted that tour operators have a degree of responsibility for the health and safety of their customers. Today, such responsibility is often enshrined in law and this is especially true for customers within the EU (e.g. Package Travel Directive (PTD), EU Fire Safety Recommendations and Corporate Manslaughter/Corporate

Killing legislation) and increasingly so in other countries across the globe (see Chapter 8, this volume). Furthermore, in some destinations (e.g. Iceland) tourist boards provide safety guidelines for operators and professional organizations such as ABTA provide codes of conduct to advise operators on best practice. While such provisions are guidelines, to ignore them may be considered a breach of trust and thereby support a litigious customer in the event of an accident. It is therefore best practice on the part of a tour operator to undertake a risk assessment for any activity they may offer.

Risk assessment is a management plan concerned with establishing and evaluating possible risks of negative events and identifying interventions and precautions to reduce or remediate the impact, and the subsequent impact on the tour operator. There are many models of risk assessment, but essentially they all follow a similar process (see Fig. 12.1). Risk assessments enable operators to plan and improve safety, and substantially reduce liabilities. Within the EU, tour operators are responsible for carrying out checks on all components of their packages, such as transport and accommodation, and frequently work

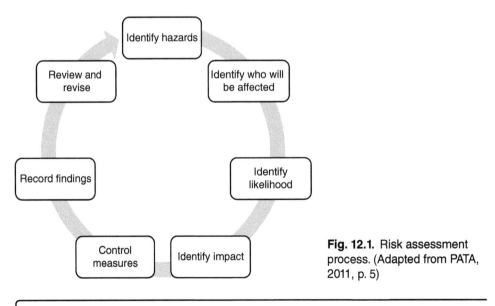

Fig. 12.1. Risk assessment process. (Adapted from PATA, 2011, p. 5)

in conjunction with ground handling agents to evaluate provision.

- Identification of hazard: A hazard is something that has the potential to cause harm or injury. For tour operators, these hazards could include thefts and accidents and they should identify what is reasonably foreseeable, although it is logical to concentrate on significant risks with those that are specific to an event.
- Identify who could be affected: Identification of who could be harmed, whether it is the entire group or individuals.
- Identify likelihood: Likelihood is the probability of the hazard causing injury to a person/persons. There are many ways to categorize likelihood when assessing the risk, which are usually evaluated as unlikely, possible or likely (see Fig. 12.2).
- Identify impact: This stage concerns evaluating the impact that such an

incident would have on the individual(s); these may be cuts or more serious issues such as broken bones.

- Control measures: These are measures that can be put in place to reduce the likelihood of any incidents and maintain the safety of the tourist (see Table 12.3). The first level of control is that of group management and supervision, which may be the role of the tour leader/manager or resort rep. The second level of control concerns the information that should be given to the tourists in advance, which usually comprises a checklist or briefing. The final level is ensuring that all participants have the correct equipment for any activity they may be undertaking.
- Record findings: A written record of the assessment is important and may be necessary to demonstrate to insurance companies when purchasing liability insurance.

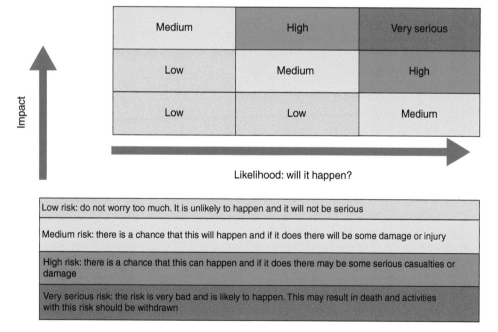

Fig. 12.2. Risk matrix.

Table 12.3. Control measures.

Participant: tour manager ratio	Code of conduct	Appropriate footwear
Distribution of group leaders	Pre-tour briefing	Appropriate clothing
Group member needs	Daily briefings	Specialist equipment, e.g. lifejackets, riding helmets, ski helmets
Make-up of group	Activity-specific briefings	
Qualified instructors		

- Review and revise: It is good practice to review tours and packages once complete and revise any documentation or decisions as necessary.

Once the risk assessments have taken place, they are recorded in a Standard Operating Procedure (SOP) document, which provides guidance for the daily operation of activities and identifies procedures derived from the risk assessment. Essentially, tour operators must reduce the risk of any injury to passengers. For high risk or very serious risk, a tour operator would most likely remove the activity or reduce the risk by identifying specific strategies. For example, an operator offering a boat trip in the Halong Bay (Vietnam), which is an area that suffers from strong winds that may destabilize the boat, would have an SOP that states that the trip should only take place once any storm has passed. Alternatively, operators may choose to replace dangerous activities with alternatives that offer a similar experience. The SOP would also state pre-activity assessments that must take place (equipment, staffing qualifications, roles and responsibilities), activity guidelines (client briefings, emergency action procedures), accommodation requirements and assessments (fire exits, emergency lighting, balcony) and guidelines for emergency situations.

A risk assessment is therefore an examination of what in the trip could cause potential harm to a member of the party, usually termed a hazard. If you consider for a moment a standard package holiday there are many potential hazards in the constituent parts, as the following examples serve to illustrate.

Accident

Within the UK, the most common incidents involve tripping, swimming pools, falls and issues with electrics. The PTD states that adequate safety measures should be in place to ensure the protection of guests and visitors from reasonably foreseeable risks. As the tour operator could be held responsible for accidents that happen either in the accommodation, on transport or during excursions, it is important that risk assessments have been conducted to minimize the chance of accidents.

In the UK, operators offering activity-based itineraries may be certified by a British Standard, in particular the BS 8848:2014 – Safer Adventures: Managing the Risks of Adventure Travel. This set of standards aims to minimize risks of adventure travel, in particular operators offering adventure holidays, volunteering projects, charity challenges, expeditions and field research or educational visits. British Standards are not compulsory, but it is illegal to claim that the company complies with the standards when it does not.

Accommodation

The majority of accidents happen within the accommodation and therefore accommodation needs to be assessed carefully, especially as regards safety, so the presence of fire doors, evacuation procedures and firefighting equipment should all be clearly marked and available. Fire doors and fire exits should be closed but unlocked and access ways must be clear. Although provision may vary depending on the locality of the accommodation, it is reasonable to expect in major resorts that hotels will have emergency lighting and a fire alarm system including sprinklers. Hotel windows should be lockable and may have safety devices fitted to prevent fully opening on higher level floors. The height and designs of balconies may vary from country to country and very few hotels are legally obliged to install 'toughened' or safety glass in their windows, doors and panes.

Albeit not an accident as such, the catering within accommodation is also a potential liability for the operator. The expectation is that if customers suffer from any form of illness, especially food poisoning, they should contact their representatives or the accommodation management, who should record the complaint in writing and provide the customer with a copy.

Swimming pools

There are several risks associated with swimming pools, in particular the quality of the water. Signage must be provided for the depth of water, the opening hours, if the pool is supervised or not and emergency action information. The area around the pool must be nonslip and free from cracks, broken tiles and glass.

Gas water heaters

Gas water heaters can be a cause of carbon monoxide poisoning. After high-profile incidents resulting in the death of occupants, gas water heaters are not advised to be used in rooms.

Activities

For many tour operators, the activities included in the package are one of the main attractions for customers, but it is essential that these activities are safe. Specific risk assessments need to be conducted for each activity, such as dogsledding, animal riding, hot air balloon trips, snorkelling and so forth. Risks can be reduced by ensuring that clear information is provided to all passengers. When assessing the likelihood of the hazard and the severity of the outcome, operators may decide to no longer offer the activity or to insist that additional equipment is provided. For example, white water rafting should only be conducted when every passenger has a helmet and a lifejacket and a full briefing about safety procedures should be delivered before starting the activity.

However well prepared a tour operator is, there is always the potential for more serious incidents to occur. Although the tour operator needs to prepare for 'most likely' scenarios (e.g. small accidents, customer problems and changes of itinerary) using a risk assessment, they also need to prepare for 'worst-case scenarios' (e.g. threat of terrorist activity or a fatal incident involving passengers or staff). The preparation of a **crisis management plan** is the attempt by organizations and stakeholders to manage or prevent crises from occurring (Pearson and Clair, 1998), whether resulting from internal or external events.

Crisis Management Plan

The following section illustrates the creation of a crisis management plan (CMP) and examines the procedures that need to be put in place to deal with a major incident that involves serious injury or fatality of passengers. Many tour operators purchase crisis management insurance policies to cover the cost of their response to a crisis, whether they are legally responsible or not.

Many of the models used to analyse disasters and crises (see Glaesser, 2003) have various shortcomings; in particular, they are based on business crisis management theory without considering the perishability and intangibility of the tourism offering. Few authors evidently have been able to adapt crisis management models to the tourism sector and those that do tend to fail to appreciate the lack of predictability that tourism crises demonstrate. The assumption with many models is that crises will develop following a linear trajectory as, for example, demonstrated by Coombs (1995). To be effective, crisis management responses need to be viewed as a strategic response to ensure an organization's survival (Pforr and Hosie, 2009). Derek Moore, the chair of AITO, emphasizes the need to have a plan in place (TTG, 2014), stating that it is not a matter of if a crisis happens but when. In recognition of this, tour operators have introduced CMP, frequently called incident response plans, which are prepared in advance to guide teams to handle incidents that happen. These plans can save lives and the company's reputation by minimizing negative publicity and preventing unnecessary distress (ABTA, n.d.). In support of such pre-emptive planning, professional organizations in the sector such as ABTA and the Council of Australian Tour Operators (CATO) provide guidance with supporting documentation, while the members' website noticeboards provide for the sharing of experiences and an array of contacts. As a matter of course, it is necessary to review the strategies implemented and update plans on a regular basis and reflect on operational procedures after an incident.

When developing a CMP, the operator will need to ensure it is suitable for the size of their company and the type of operations and as such generic plans are of limited application. That said, a CMP would usually comprise event forecasting, execution and evaluation strategies and are generally based on the 'four Rs' of crisis management: reduction, readiness, response and recovery.

Reduction

This element of the plan involves the initial identification of potential risks and crises and also the strengths and weaknesses of the organization and/or destination should an incident arise, the significance of which will vary according to the prevailing circumstances. The understanding of these elements is the first step to reducing the impact of potential crises. Therefore the production of the CMP should involve an assessment and evaluation of the business and the core activities so that the company can evaluate the risks. ABTA (n.d.) suggests that consideration be given to the following:

- Management. Identification of who will be responsible for the management of any crisis or emergency. This may involve deputies if key members of staff are not available.
- Finance. Is there provision for an emergency budget and who is the signatory for the account?
- Human resources. Identification of lead staff who will deal with each of the teams and whether they have received appropriate training.
- Communications. Is a member of staff contactable 24 hours a day and how does the system work, e.g. rota system? Identification of a spokesperson on

behalf of the tour operator who will manage the media or identification of a suitable organization to act on behalf of the company.

- Logistics. Are contact details for all relevant personnel available, including details of overseas staff?

The preparation of the plan will depend on the size of the company, the locations of customers and the likelihood of an incident(s). Establishing an incident response team is critical so that everyone knows exactly their responsibilities.

Readiness

The second step involves the development of a plan of responses and tactics. To be most effective, this plan must be regularly reviewed to identify if changes are needed and/or if additional resources are required. This may be because of changes within the company, information from destination management companies (supply chain) or environmental scanning. The CMP should include the identification of key teams and their members and map out a clear reporting structure and areas of responsibility for all staff involved in the incident (see Fig. 12.3). Obviously, the extent of detail will vary according to the scale of the tour operator's operations; a small operator may not have teams as such but a designated person for each area.

Response

This step occurs if a crisis takes place and involves the operational response of an organization or destination. This response is based on damage limitation as well as a communications strategy that focuses on reassurance. Strong leadership is needed within an organization if a CMP is to be put into action effectively.

Thus, a crisis management team is often formed as part of the plan to ensure effective implementation.

Once an operator is notified of an incident, it is critical that the CMP is implemented immediately. In the 21st century, with hyper connectivity through social media, communication is very fast and companies have very little time to react. For example, the tour operator may be informed of an incident through their suppliers, but at the same time tourists may be calling, emailing or tweeting to family and friends.

The initial assessment must involve a decision as to the severity of the incident and thus the protocols to be instigated. The tour operator Chameleon Worldwide that operated under a number of brands such as Wildlife Worldwide and Walks Worldwide assesses severity using a traffic light system yellow, amber and red, and each level can trigger a different operational response. Contact details for advisers and professionals such as the insurance contact, sector contacts, legal advisers, trauma counsellors and PR specialists need to be available immediately. Major emergencies are rarely handled in-house and a tour operator will usually contract outside agencies for assistance.

The crisis coordinator, usually the managing director, will assume control from a central base and make major decisions. According to the company structure/size, s/he will be assisted by the four teams: the incident location team, the public relations team, the customer information team and the company information team.

The incident location team

The incident location team (ILT) of the tour operator are the staff on site, i.e. they are situated where the incident has occurred. This team would usually be led by

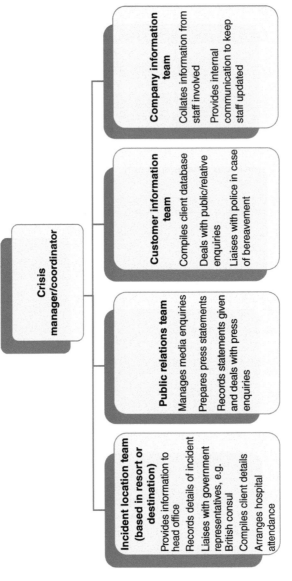

Fig. 12.3. Key teams of a critical management plan. (Adapted from ABTA, 2015.)

the most senior person in the locality, although it is likely that a representative from head office will travel to the location immediately. The ILT put into practice the prepared emergency procedures, which will usually involve contacting the police, medical authorities and key representatives of the customers' home countries, e.g. British Consul. They are responsible for compiling a list of all customers involved in the incident, their physical condition and where they are currently located, e.g. in hospital. Details of the incident must be recorded, including how and why it happened as far as can be ascertained, for example a description of the incident, weather conditions and any information that may be considered relevant. When passengers have been hospitalized, the incident team will arrange for visitors and ensure the comfort of the passengers where possible, recording all details of interactions. An assessment will need to be made as to whether the holiday can continue or whether it should be terminated, in which case repatriation of the remaining passengers needs to be arranged.

The public relations team

The public relations team will be based in the tour operator's office and may include their own PR staff or representation by a PR consultancy as per the emergency plan. It is important that nobody other than the allocated member of staff speaks to the press, in particular the ILT must not make any statement without approval from the PR team. When a major emergency occurs, the PR team should issue a press statement clearly giving the latest details of the incident and an undertaking to provide further accurate information when it is available. Regular updates should be provided and emergency hotline numbers announced to deal with immediate queries. How the tour operator handles

the media, and the way in which information is communicated, is critical to the final outcome of the crisis on the company and how the public judge the company (see Ucelli, 2002). The news value of the crisis depends on several variables such as the number of people affected, human interest, novelty and the relevance of the incident to the public. Therefore, it is imperative that the operator has the support of the PR agency to handle the press during a difficult situation, which also enables the operator to focus entirely on the crisis itself. Ideally, it is best to appoint a company to work with before any incidents arise, to develop a relationship and understanding of the activities of the operator. The PR agency will represent the company, with a spokesperson ensuring that a single message is reported to the press rather than a collection of mixed messages, which may be incorrect and could damage their reputation.

Reputation management is critical. The tour operator must be seen to be concerned and caring about the situation. On the proviso that the destination is safe, a senior member of management should be sent to the crisis location and ensure the accuracy of information disseminated to the press.

The customer information team

The customer information team usually has the lowest profile but is vitally important. The list of passengers is passed on to this team and they ensure that all information, including next of kin and details of the travel agents who made the booking, is available. If death occurred, then next of kin must be informed through official police sources before they learn of this from the media. If passengers have booked through travel agents, then the travel agent should be notified immediately of the incident, as they will have passenger details including next of kin. Names of any fatally injured passengers will not be released until next of kin have been notified and agree.

The company information team

The company information team collects and provides information for employees of the company, such as liaising with travel agents and providing information detailing the incident and actions being taken, and this information is circulated internally.

Recovery

After an incident or crisis, an indication of how effective the CMP has been is the speed with which normal operations resume and the pre-crisis level of business is reached.

The Reality of an Incident

In the event of an emergency that affects a company, such as a coach/bus crash, it is important to assess the situation and make decisions quickly and effectively. Procedures must follow those expected at the destination, for example notification to the police and officials. For an overview of how a political crisis could be managed, in this instance in the case of Thailand (see Kanlayanasukho, 2015), see Table 12.4.

Accidents that involves injuries or potential threats to passengers can involve emergency repatriation. If the situation is notable, then special arrangements

Table 12.4. Crisis: an operational response. (Adapted from Kanlayanasukho, 2015, p. 125.)

Stage and operator procedure	Customers at destination	Customers scheduled to travel	Accommodation suppliers	Transport suppliers
One				
Compile update of political crisis situation	Locate all customers	Prepare statement	Contact hotels where customers are staying	Contact airlines that customers are scheduled with
Two				
Evaluate crisis situation by levels of severity	Communicate with customers about the situation	Update crisis situation by phone or email	Maintain contact with hotel regarding guests' safety	Monitor airline press releases, cancellation policies and seat availability
Three				
Provide response to stakeholders	Suggest evacuation if necessary	Inform advance purchase customers of cancellation or delay	Communicate tour operators' decisions about customers to hotel management	Evacuation needed, accommodate customers to different airlines to leave the affected area
Four				
After evacuation, maintain strong contact with customers	Evacuate and continue to inform customers about the situation	Maintain contact with customers who postponed their travels	Contact hotels to negotiate cancellations of upcoming bookings	Keep contact with customers until after they have left the affected area

may need to be made. For example, if there is a fatality, then the relevant consulate needs to be notified and either arrangements made for local burial (according to religious beliefs) or repatriation. Injured passengers may need hospital care or specialist transport for their return home.

Summary

Tourism, given its worldwide presence, may often find itself affected by a disaster situation due to unpredictable external events of one form or another. In many such an instance, tour operators will be involved and it will be how they manage their own operations which largely influences the extent to which the consequences of the disaster become a crisis for them. But, as discussed, it is necessary to also recognize that a crisis for an operator can also occur due to some fault with its own management and operational planning, as well as due to an unexpected occurrence, which leads to sustained consequences such as a major drop in demand for its products. Evidently, the tour operating environment holds a range of risks for which, as illustrated in Table 12.2, operators should be prepared. The first step to be taken is therefore to undertake a risk assessment(s). This is not just a matter of an operator adopting best practice but in many countries, notably so within the EU, the health and safety of customers is part of the PTD as well as consumer protection regulations. Thus, operators should assess potential hazards that could be present throughout the entirety of their operations. Once so prepared, it is possible then to formulate crisis management plans. These are not just a question of addressing possible customer accidents but also 'what if' scenarios, such as a terrorist incident. In all such cases, CMPs can be drawn up (and regularly reviewed).

For tour operators, it is not a matter of 'if' but rather 'when' a crisis will arise. Therefore, it is essential to be prepared in order to avoid an 'event' turning into a crisis for the tour operator.

Discussion Questions

1. Why has terrorist activity become a major concern for tour operators?
2. Why are tourists targets for terrorists?
3. Why is it important for tour operators to prepare crisis management plans?
4. What type of crises do you think tour operators may face in the next decade?
5. What role should tour operators play in tourist destinations that have been affected by an environmental crisis?
6. Why is it good practice to introduce standard operating procedures for dealing with resort-based incidents?
7. What role does the media play in heightening concerns about issues in resorts?
8. Tsunamis and snow avalanches have been the cause of catastrophes involving substantial loss of life. Tour operators may be partly considered at fault, albeit indirectly, through their promotion of accommodation close to the sea and the development of ski resorts. Do you consider they should accept some degree of responsibility for the consequences of such catastrophes and therefore address such responsibility in the context of crisis management planning? What might be the implications for the operator of adopting such action?

Key Terms

- **Crisis:** An unexpected problem seriously disrupting the functioning of an organization or sector nation.
- **Crisis management plan:** Management document developed by the tour operator that outlines the steps for

handling the unplanned event. Involves preplanning, reacting to the crisis and recovery.

- **Disaster:** Unpredictable catastrophic change that can normally only be responded to after the event.
- **Incident:** Situation which may lead to a crisis if not contained.

- **Risk:** The level of probability of an undesirable event or incident occurring.
- **Scenario planning:** Involves hypothetical scenarios and discussion of possible decisions. Planning responses for different situations; but it is often difficult to foresee the full implications of crises.

INTERNET EXERCISE

Review the British Standard 8848, which can be found at www.bsigroup.com/Local-Files/en-GB/consumer-guides/resources/BSI-Consumer-Brochure-Adventurous-Activities-UK-EN.pdf

---

MINI CASE STUDY

Norovirus

A not infrequent crisis that is readily picked up by the media is that of an outbreak of infectious diseases on a cruise ship. The most common source is the norovirus, which is a highly contagious, very common and uncomfortable stomach virus resulting in severe vomiting, abdominal cramps, nausea and diarrhoea. It is often termed stomach flu. An outbreak is considered if over 3% of the population is infected. Such outbreaks can arise in different situations, though generally where there are large numbers of people in a small area.

The US Centre for Disease Control and Prevention (CDC) monitors cruise ship outbreaks and requires cruise lines to immediately report when more than 2% of passengers report symptoms to the Medical Officer. On cruise ships, the most usual source of a norovirus outbreak is contaminated food or water. The virus can spread through physical contact with sick people or handling objects that have been contaminated, for example sharing food, caring for sick relatives, or poor hygiene such as not washing hands. Numerous studies have suggested that hand sanitizer does not kill the norovirus, so it is imperative that good hygiene standards are implemented and maintained.

Question

- Why has the US government made it mandatory for cruise ships to report incidents of gastrointestinal symptoms to the Centre for Disease Control and Prevention?

Tunisian terrorism

Tunisia has always been seen as a laid-back destination for package holidays, with a post-revolution economy dependent on foreign tourists and beach resorts, particularly favoured by Northern European tourists, providing an alternative to the Mediterranean resorts. In 2014, tourism accounted for 7.4% of GDP, with a total contribution overall of 15.2%, and 230,500 jobs directly (6.8% of total employment) (WTTC, 2015). It attracted over 6 million visitors annually, of which 500,000 were from the UK (UNWTO, 2015). The country is not without problems and has high unemployment rates and social unrest.

In 2015, Tunisia had two separate terrorist attacks. On 18 March, two Tunisian gunmen attacked the Parliament building and then went to the nearby Bardo National Museum, where they took many hostages, killed 21 and injured at least 44 tourists. The tourists were from Japan, Italy, Colombia, Spain, Australia, Russia, South Africa, Poland and France. They were on package holidays or land excursions from cruise ships. Then, on 26 June, a lone gunman shot and killed at least 38 people on a beach at Sousse, 30 of whom were UK citizens. The resort of Sousse relies heavily on package tourism, probably more than any other Tunisian resort.

ABTA estimated that over 20,000 British holidaymakers were in Tunisia at that time, but this did not include those tourists who travelled independently, i.e. not as part of a package. According to the BBC, thousands of customers booked emergency flights out of the country, with over 3500 leaving within the week. Tour operators such as TUI UK (which owns Thomson and First Choice) immediately started the repatriation of their 6400 holidaymakers and cancelled all further flights to Tunisia (initially until 4 July).

Many tour operators had the legal right to enforce their booking conditions, which state that passengers could lose bookings if they do not take their flights, because according to Foreign and Commonwealth Office advice Tunisia was a safe destination. The UK's Foreign Office updated its travel advice, noting that further terrorist attacks in Tunisia, including in tourist resorts, were possible. Thomas Cook offered customers about to travel to Tunisia the opportunity to amend their flights free of charge until 31 July. Thomson offered its customers the opportunity to change bookings until 24 July. EasyJet provided additional flights for customers to return home and stated that passengers due to travel within the next 14 days could change their booking or obtain a voucher equal to the value of the unused flights.

The long-term implications of such actions affect many stakeholders. Tunisia was already recovering from the Arab Spring of 2011, which saw a dramatic decrease in tourism. According to the UNWTO, tourism in Tunisia in 2015 decreased by 3% in contrast to the 2% estimated increase for the African continent as a whole. For local businesses, the disappearance of the tourists has had an enormous impact on their livelihoods because over half a million people depend (directly and indirectly) on tourism for their income. The impact of such terrorism affects not only the Tunisian economy but also the companies facilitating package holidays to these destinations. On 29 June travel agencies such as TUI predicted the unrest in Egypt and Tunisia would cost the company over £20 million, and airlines such as IAG and EasyJet saw their share prices fall.

Continued

Questions

- According to the booking conditions provided on webpages or in brochures, what is the legal position of the customers wishing to cancel their holiday immediately following the terrorist incidents?
- Prepare an outline for a crisis management plan dealing with a major emergency such as the Tunisian terror attacks.
- What options do independent tourists have for repatriation?
- Bali has also suffered from terrorist attacks (2002 and 2005). Utilizing data from the WTTC, examine how long it took for tourist numbers to recover to pre-2002 figures.

Recommended Reading

The following two texts provide opportunities to examine the range and scope of crisis management in greater depth as well as an interesting array of case studies and examples. They merit attention when considering the discussion and review questions.

Evans, N. and Elphick, S. (2005) Models of crisis management: an evaluation of their value for strategic planning in the international travel industry. *International Journal of Tourism Research* 7, 135–150.

Stanbury, J., Pryer, M. and Roberts, A. (2005) Heroes and villains – tour operator and media response to crisis: an exploration of press handling strategies by UK adventure tour operators. *Current Issues in Tourism* 8, 394–423.

Further to the above, readers are referred to:

PATA (2011) *Bounce Back: Tourism Risk, Crisis and Recovery Management Guide.* Pacific and Asia Tourism Association, Woolloomooloo, Australia.

References

ABTA (n.d.) Dealing with a crisis or emergency situation. Available at: https://c0e31a7ad 92e875f8eaa-5facf23e658215b1771a91c2 df41e9fe.ssl.cf3.rackcdn.com/publications/ HR_CEP_A5_Brochure_FINAL.pdf, accessed 17 December 2015.

BBC (2016) Turkey tourism: an industry in crisis. Available at: http://www.bbc.co.uk/news/world-europe-36549880, accessed 26 October 2016.

Coombs, W. (1995) The development of guidelines for the selection of the 'appropriate' crisis response strategies. *Management Communication Quarterly* 4, 447–476.

Coombs, W. (2014) *Ongoing Crisis Communication: Planning, Managing and Responding*, 4th edn. Sage, London.

Faulkner, B. (2001) Towards a framework for tourism disaster management. *Tourism Management* 22, 135–147.

Glaesser, D. (2003) *Crisis Management in the Tourism Industry.* Butterworth-Heinemann, Oxford, UK.

Holloway, C. and Humphreys, C. (2012) *The Business of Tourism*, 9th edn. Pearson, Harlow, UK.

Kanlayanasukho, V. (2015) An analysis of the tourism industry's management responses to political crisis in Thailand. In: Ritchie, B.W. and Campiranon, K. (eds) *Tourism Crisis and Disaster Management in the Asia-Pacific.* CAB International, Wallingford, UK, pp. 116–131.

Lee, Y.F. and Harrald, J.R. (1999) Critical issue for business area impact analysis in business crisis management: analytical capability. *Disaster Prevention and Management* 8, 184–189.

Meyers, G. (1986) *When it Hits the Fan: Managing the Nine Crises of Business*. Mentor, New York.

Moore, S. and Seymour, M. (2005) *Global Technology and Corporate Crises: Strategies Planning and Communication in the Information Age*. Routledge, London.

PATA (2003) *Crisis. It Won't Happen to Us. Expect the Unexpected. Be Prepared*. Pacific Asia Travel Association, Bangkok.

Pearson, C.M. and Clair, J.A. (1998) Reframing crisis management. *The Academy of Management Review* 23, 59–76.

Pforr, C. and Hosie, P. (2009) *Crisis Management in the Tourism Industry: Beating the Odds?* 1st edn. Ashgate, Farnham, UK.

Ritchie, B. (2009) *Crisis and Disaster Management of Tourism*. Channel View Publications, Bristol, UK.

TTG (2014) Derek Moore: crisis management planning – like painting the garden fence? Available at: https://www.ttgmedia.com/news/news/derek-moore-crisis-management-planning--like-painting-the-garden-fence-244, accessed 27 December 2015.

Ucelli, L. (2002) The CEO's 'how to' guide to crisis communications. *Strategy & Leadership* 30, 21–24.

UNWTO (2015) *Tourism Highlights, 2015 edn*. United Nations World Tourism Organization, Madrid.

WTTC (2015) *Travel & Tourism Economic Impact 2015 Tunisia*. World Travel and Tourism Council, London.

13 Challenges and Issues: A Look Ahead

This, the concluding chapter, aims to bring into focus the challenges and issues that the tour operating sector may face over the coming years. The intention is not to try and foretell the future, for who knows? For example, who forecast the phenomenal rise of the package holiday or the decline of the coach market in the 1970s or the resurgence of the cruise market in the 2000s? More widely, who foresaw the rapid development of email and the internet? Over the last decade, electronic media have and continue to have substantial impacts on work practices, business operations and social networks. By and large, most forecasting within the context of tourism has been extrapolations based on the trends and issues of the time. Thus the attention here is first on 'where are we now?', before moving on to consider opportunities and challenges across a range of areas facing tour operators in the coming years and issues drawn from the wider environment that potentially will impact on their operations.

Where Are We Now?

The international mass market for package holidays to popular destinations will continue. The main constraints on demand – time, disposable income, transportation and opportunity – will not change. As such constraints ease in developing economies, then there will be continuing global expansion of tourism. How such demand is manifest will be more influenced by leisure, e.g. interests and hobbies, than a brief escape from work, which traditionally was considered a major influencing factor in the industrialized economies of the world. This is also a reflection of changing work practices (e.g. less physically demanding, increased flexibility, freelancing) as well as an outcome of improvements in home environments, which is also driving up standards in accommodation provision – the latter an influence on the emergence of AirBnB.

Demographics

As an economy grows, general conditions improve, birth rates tend to decline and prosperity increases, leading to a growing proportion of older people, who are often healthier, fitter and more affluent compared with their forebears. Ageing populations are a major factor of all post-industrial populations and will become so in comparatively emergent economies of the world, for example South America or Asia. Significantly this 'grey' market is far more flexible as to where and particularly when to go on holiday. Many older people consider safety/risk-free holidays as essential in their choice of package.

But what about today's younger generation, preoccupied as they are with social media, more tuned in to ICT than the active outdoors? Are they going to follow in the tourist footsteps of their parents and grandparents? Indicators suggest that this is less likely in the future, given societal changes; what is different is the influence of information and social media, relaying what their peers are doing. It is likely that they will want more and want it quicker (and easier to organize), but will not necessarily want higher quality or higher prices, preferring low-cost carriers (LCCs) and more fun-based, 'do as we like' style holidays. In contrast, older customers will be seeking added value in creating bespoke packages, informed by knowledge of the destination(s) and surrounding region.

Opportunities will certainly develop for small enterprises and new entrants to niche markets. There is a growing range of special-interest-based holidays, such as wine tours, food tours, geographic tours (e.g. Antarctic), visiting renowned gardens of the world, art and heritage, and an increasing popularity of guided tours hosted by 'celebrity experts'. Also packages can be based on specific personal factors, e.g. gender, 'pink' (gay), 'purple' (less able tourists) or single persons.

Tour operations

Tour operations in many countries, notably so across Europe, have reached maturity, evidencing a history of greater competition with tour operators integrating, concentrating, forming alliances and investing in mass distribution techniques. They will be challenged by competition from operators developing in major new generating regions, e.g. China, India. As demand and opportunity for tourism expands, so too will the potential for indigenous tour operators. As these companies grow, they will mirror the same strategies as their European/American counterparts, with supply becoming increasingly dominated by a small number of transnational companies following similar expansion strategies as have happened in Europe, leading to mergers and takeovers of operators in other countries to further their expansion and a possible shift in power.

Further increasing competition and innovation will be the expansion of major transnational role players, with ownership increasingly concentrated in the hands of a relatively small elite. As yet, this is not replicated in developing markets such as Korea and India, where distribution is more fragmented and suppliers remain independent. That is, tour operators act as wholesalers and travel agents are retailers (or prepare tailor-made packages). In those countries we will witness a similar pattern of development and growth as seen in Europe and America, but this will be in a far quicker time frame.

As regards innovation within tour operations, it is difficult to see how any innovation will influence the mainstream market. Certainly there will be some development in managerial and operational practices, but arguably little else. Without product changes, and that has not happened to date, the package holiday as we know it now is basically the same as 50 years ago.

Destinations

Access to tourist destinations growing in popularity will become easier as the destinations' transport infrastructure develops. Tour operators will be able to exploit the rise in demand and offer packages at lower prices. Demand for emerging and new destinations in comparatively less affluent regions of the world will similarly increase. This is especially so as established tourist resorts become perceived to be too popular, which will encourage the comparatively more affluent tourists to go elsewhere, to less 'spoilt' destinations and environments. But, the world is finite. This is rather like a waterfall with a ladder of rock pools – the water cascades down gradually filling the first pool, then overflowing into the next one, and so on. Today, just as previously, adventure tours based on low-key, small groups visiting little known areas could well be considered one of the first pools and as the superstructure and infrastructure develop, tourist capacity increases. Thus, those low-demand, low-impact tours in hitherto largely unknown or limited destinations begin to expand and quite rapidly so, irrespective of the potential barriers to touristic development; tour operators invariably find ways to overcome them, including using helicopters to fly in tourists! Destinations with iconic climbs, e.g. the Himalayas, Toubkal or Kilimanjaro, have become so popular that they are being despoiled. Other outstanding physical attractions are suffering from the volume of tourists, e.g. the Grand Canyon, Machu Picchu, the Pyramids and Great Wall of China. Ultimately, ways of restricting access will be introduced, which ironically will make such renowned places all the more attractive. We may see access to particularly fragile environments being limited to only pre-arranged tours by accredited, specialist tour operators.

The question is: where next? Cruise operators continue to seek new routes and places to visit as the popular destinations in season become clogged with ships and their passengers. They have certainly reached places hitherto unseen by the average tourist, be that along the Alaskan coast or the shores of Antarctica. Suitably designed ships can now go further; for example, One Oceans' ice-strengthened cruise ship is promoting 'Pathways to Franklin' through the fabled North-West passage. But the strength of the competition is such that this sector may have reached its peak in terms of traditional markets. There is a strong Chinese market, but will the international tourists of developing economies be similarly interested?

Competition between destinations will increase, which will encourage new developments and attractions. The comparatively developing economies of the world will build Exhibition and Conference centres to attract business, as globalization continues apace, and stadia, with the aim of targeting international sporting events. Further development, particularly of the infrastructure, coupled with rising demand could attract interest in creating mega-attractions like Disneyworld. But destinations are not limitless and through technological advancements we can expect new innovations, perhaps under the sea or in polar regions. Unique propositions are needed as consumers demand ever more unusual innovations, such as created attractions based on action movie films or computer games offering virtual worlds wherein tourists can enact fantasies.

However, the most distant destination is that of space, which may not be that far in the future (Lappas, 2007). There has been some activity already in advance of flights into space for the exceedingly wealthy consumer; the logical next stage on the drawing board, building on the expertise involved in the space station, will be creating a visitor stay section attached to a space station or even a space hotel.

Competition

Key to tour operators' success is either offering something that cannot be replicated by self-booking or where a defined group is necessary. Operators with specialist knowledge of destinations will come to the fore and, given such knowledge and expertise, be better positioned to create well-targeted 'unique' products, to diversify with a focus more on quality and difference.

Long-haul packages will increase, encouraged by further developments in aircraft technology that will lead to lighter, quieter and more fuel-efficient planes that can fly longer distances without the need to refuel and so reduce flying times. Increasing competition between airlines, as well as airline companies seeking opportunities to expand and/or diversify their operations (e.g. LCCs operating across Europe), will seek to develop opportunities in the tour operating sector – a move that will be reflected in other countries as their LCCs develop.

Turbulent times

In the short term, tour operators are facing more turbulent times. The 2010s witnessed a state of political flux across the European Union (EU) with the UK's decision to exit the EU, ongoing wide dissatisfaction among the peoples of the EU with the EU's governance and also in the USA with the election of Donald Trump. Meanwhile, countries in North Africa and the Middle East continue to be politically unstable. In combination, this contributes to the unsettled state of the financial markets and particularly the value of major currencies. This leads to relatively short-term shifts in demand away from those countries where the value of the tourist's own currency has declined. Conversely, this makes the home country more attractive to foreign tourists. Certainly, some tour operators gain, but others, particularly those heavily committed to a foreign country, may well find their financial security significantly challenged. However, this is basically reflecting what has gone on for decades.

Terrorism is arguably the biggest ongoing problem facing tour operators and the effects appear to be longer lasting and less readily managed than many other extraneous factors. An outcome of this is that destination choices may be increasingly dictated by safety concerns and more stable countries may become more attractive destinations.

Transportation

Diversity between carriers, or within their own brands, will increase as they seek to maintain and expand their market share. Potentially a dichotomy may develop between quality and comfort on the one hand and 'cheap and cheerful' on the other, the latter particularly for short haul/short trips. In general terms, it can be expected that the options in terms of speed and/or quality and comfort will increase with tour operators, especially those offering dynamic packaged bundles or who are involved in upmarket operations, offering ease and comfort as an integral element. In this area tour operators in the long-haul category may place the emphasis on the transport element rather than just as the means of transfer from home to destination (and return) as part of the holiday experience. Similarly, coach tour operators will seek ongoing improvements in interior design, facilities and comfort of their coaches and better quality accommodation to promote thematic tours.

Travel by train will gain new interest, either in its own right or by virtue of being an alternative to cruises or all-inclusive packages. Thus, the current list of Great Rail Journeys will expand. An example demonstrating that the railway is still very much a part of travel for tourists and the importance of direct government action is the aim of opening up Tibet to more visitors (between 2009 and 2017, tourism demand tripled, to more than 21 million visitors). This has been facilitated by improving the speed of obtaining visitor permits and the development of the Sichuan–Tibet railway, which certainly holds the potential to become a 'great rail journey' attraction to complement the existing Qinghai–Tibet line. Also the high speed train from Singapore through Malaysia will probably include Thailand, thus opening up another route. This may reduce the reliance on LCCs for short-haul trips, so they may seek to develop routes to medium-haul destinations.

ICT

Developments in ICT will generate easier, quicker and more accessible (cheaper) communication systems and devices with more options and more detail. This will lead potentially to new channels of distribution that are more effective than current channels, further encouraging disintermediation on the part of tour operators. Further, such applications will facilitate better communication between operators and their principals, as well as aid the development of tour packages and their subsequent monitoring and evaluation. But it will also facilitate the growth of online travel agents or travel organizers throughout the globe. This century has seen their expansion in number and increasing concentration in the hands of a few; for example, in the USA Expedia and Priceline now own a number of other major sites and have retained their titles, thus appearing as different and separate companies. For those companies to expand further they will need to seek companies in other countries, most likely starting with Europe. Equally, the major players in the markets in China and India will be seeking to acquire such operators in other countries. Also, major role players in ICT hitherto with little involvement in tourism operations will seek to establish a presence, e.g. Google, Amazon.

The rise of online agents may well come with a cost to consumers and with that there is a potential loss to the customer in terms of protection, whether that be about financial expenditure or health and safety. To some extent, the forthcoming changes to the EU's Package Travel Regulations will partly address the lack of regulation relating to online agents who present opportunities for customers to book travel and some other element, e.g. accommodation and car hire, but which is currently not within the regulations in Europe. In the absence of similar regulations in other countries, that may be of little value.

There will be developments in the online-sharing economy, such as AirBnB and Homeaway, known as 'peer-to-peer'. This bypasses everyone and potentially therefore regulations that tour operators are expected to abide by and, to varying degrees, to which their principals have to adhere. This presents further challenges to tour operators. Will this become more regulated? Certainly, more tourists will arrange their own holidays, but at the same time overall demand for holidays will increase, thereby partly compensating for that shift in the marketplace.

Consumer Concerns and Protection

There is evidently growing consciousness among tourists of their security when arranging holidays with regards to their choice(s) of destination. This is largely due to the speedy and extensive coverage of terrorist incidents by the world's press and social media. It includes personal safety from risk, such as terrorism, and financial protection in the event of something untoward happening that affects their holiday, e.g. the airline company or their tour operator going bankrupt. This is well illustrated by the terrorist attack on the resort of Port El Kantaoni, Sousse (Tunisia) in 2016, which led to a dramatic fall off in demand for the region. The actions of the main tour operator, TUI, demonstrated the true value to customers of ABTA and

ATOL customer protection regulations. Furthermore, under EU regulations tour operators are required to take appropriate measures in the interests of the safety/security of their customers, including their principals, e.g. fire precautions in hotels. These measures, coupled with the attention expected of tour operators to the quality of provision by their principals, will counteract demand for holiday packages from less regulated suppliers. However, this only applies within the EU. Are other countries likely to adopt similar measures? Is it likely there will be a shift to globalization of consumer protection? Tourists will learn to check that online companies offering package holidays provide similar levels of consumer protection, which is evidently not the current situation.

Issues

The rise of the agenda for sustainable development and that unsustainable patterns of consumption are to be discouraged raises serious questions over tourism. First, tourism is a particularly conspicuous form of unsustainable consumption. Could tourists become the pariahs of conspicuous consumption? Unlikely, especially given the economics of consumption and a free market economy, which point towards the ongoing promotion of tourism. Second, transportation contributes to climate change through emissions released from fuel consumption causing atmospheric pollution, major culprits being air travel and sea travel, the latter predominantly from sulphur emissions. Although airline technology developments will reduce the negatives (fuel, noise), such gains will be counteracted by increased demand.

There is concern over emissions and pollution from cruise ships, although there are regulations in place, both general and specific to particular destinations. However, the standards of adoption of the best environmental management practices vary greatly (see www.foe.org/cruise-report-card). This could lead to tighter regulation and monitoring of their effective application, which has implications on costs and therefore customer prices in what is already a highly competitive tour operating market. The car, the mainstay of domestic tourism, is equally problematic, even if electric, which just transfers the emissions to the source of the electricity production process. Fossil fuels will continue to be the major source of energy for transportation. There are alternatives, such as biofuel, but with little potential to meet demand. Furthermore, all too often the opportunity costs of the production processes involved are not taken into account. Oil will continue to be the predominant fuel supply, even allowing for market fluctuations in the price. World stocks of oil, as yet, are not considered finite in the sense that the forecast is that there is sufficient for the next 20 years – a time frame that is long enough for forward planning business strategists.

Is it likely we will see some form of regulation on travel? Unlikely. First, it would be difficult to apply, given the diverse reasons for travel. Second, given the issues that have long vexed worldwide agreements on establishing climate change protocols, such an initiative is logically a non-starter in the absence of substantive change in attitudes throughout the globe. A possibility for the distant future is a personal carbon allowance. Such an initiative would undoubtedly generate a market for allowance trading, thereby enabling over-consumers of carbon to increase their usage; for example, residents of the USA, which has the highest level of personal consumerism, could buy the allowance credited to comparatively poor people in the USA or potentially in other countries.

We can expect the rights of indigenous peoples supporting tour operations in whatever field will gain further support. This will raise the costs, but operators will be able to adjust their prices accordingly and potentially promote their positive actions as evidence of their social responsibility. For example, this has already been demonstrated by some operators in response to concerns over animal welfare, e.g. removal of elephant rides from many tour operators' brochures and better regulation of tours involving whale watching.

What of cities that in the high season are swamped with tourists? Will some form of local taxation be introduced? More local authorities may seek the introduction of a local tourist tax, perhaps under the umbrella of maintaining the environment, but tour operators invariably complain.

There is no doubt that tour operators are key role players in tourism destination development. However, in terms of the environmental agenda, the response of the tour operators to date has been limited (as is the case in all other categories of tourism activity). Most major players in the market are taking some action, but this is arguably little more than window dressing. In comparison, small and micro-tour operators are doing far more by way of supporting the local economy and environment in the destinations they visit. This may be argued to be more a function of their size and that they are very dependent on the quality of the environment and local support for their tour operators and/or the owners themselves are environmentally conscious and proactive. Will operators come under pressure to adopt more proactive environmental actions? This is unlikely in the absence of a substantial political shift among the international organizations with an interest in tourism.

Could green consumerism drive such change? Again unlikely, particularly as 'green consumers' tend to be less green in their environmental behaviour when it comes to holiday choices! It is highly unlikely that tour operators will change their *modus operandii* substantially. Ultimately, perhaps the most significant question to consider here is: are tour operators responsible for the impacts of their customers?

What may well affect their operations more are two aspects attributed to climate change. First, the projected rise in sea levels is a substantial threat to low-lying islands such as the Maldives. This could lead to a major decline in tourism demand for such places, resulting in tour operators seeking similar opportunities elsewhere. The effect on the Arctic and Antarctic regions could facilitate cruise liners to make further inroads to hitherto unspoilt environments. Second, predicted fresh water shortages could bring into sharp focus the comparatively very high levels of water usage by tourists in areas that may already have limited supplies, leading to restrictions which will affect demand.

How these challenges and issues affect tour operations will vary in scale and depth, depending on their exposure and responses to the opportunities and threats that arise. However, throughout the history of tour operators, there is one very evident factor, which is that successful operators appear to have an innate ability to metamorphose according to the needs of the time.

Reference

Lappas, V. (2007) Space tourism. In: Buhalis, D. and Costa, C. (eds) *Tourism Business Frontiers: Consumers, Products and Industry*. Elsevier Butterworth-Heinemann, Oxford, UK, pp. 157–168.

Index

Note: Page numbers in **bold** type refer to **figures**
Page numbers in *italic* type refer to *tables*

accidents 252
accommodation 66–67, 73–75, 98, 136,
    174–175, 189–190, 250–253
  local 67
  upmarket 99
accounting department 238–239
ACORN 199
activity specialists 242
actors 25
ad hoc booking 98
ad hoc chartering 76
ad hoc contracting 75
adult representatives 241
adventure holidays 45, 63
adventure tourism 17, 28, 87–98
adventure tours
  basic costing 95, 97
  designing factors 91, 92–94
  guides 91
  itinerary 95, 96
advertising 203–205
Africa 5, 14, 26
  North 267
Air France 168
Air Passenger Duty (UK) 132
air tax 132
Air Transport Licensing Board (CAA) 15
Air Transport Organizers Licence
  (ATOL) 15, 22, 137–138, 157–158,
  164, 176, 269
air travel 3–4
Air Travel Reserve Fund (UK) 15
Air Travel Trust 137
airlines, commercial 3
Airtours 53
All Leisure Group 43
all-inclusive coach luxury tour 101, *101*
all-inclusive packages 14, 23, 34, 62, 72, 99,
  202, 267
allocation (allotment) 74–75, 98
  on arrival 81

alternative tourism 26–27
amendment costs 138–139
American Airlines 167
American Express 12
American Society of Travel Agents, The 172
ancillary products 78, 139
ancillary services 67
animateurs 241
annual leave, paid 237
Ansoff's Matrix 48–50, **49**, *55*
Antarctica 5
application forms 228–230
apps 211–212
Asia 5, 25, 32, 62, 89
Asia Pacific Region 159–163
assessment centres 230
Association of British Travel Agents
  (ABTA) 15, 29, 33, 157–158, 164,
  250, 254, 268
Association of Independent Tour Operators
  (AITO) 15–17, 177, 254
Association of Southeast Asian Nations
  (ASEAN) 159
Audley Travel 20
augmented product 67
Australia 4, 28
  CATO 254
  Intrepid 44, 90, 119

backward vertical integration 53–54
Balanced Score Card (BSC) 121–123, **123**
Balearic Islands 26, 29, 40
  Sustainable Tourism Tax 40
Barcelona (Spain) 29
basic factors (customer satisfaction) 109
beach holidays 43, 63, 201
Beijing (China) 4
Belize 5
Benidorm (Spain) 26
bespoke holiday packages 16

Biewei (55) 17
Black Tomato 14
booking
    ad hoc 98
    conditions 178–180
    self- 174, 266
Boston Consulting Group Matrix (BCG
    Matrix) 64–65, **64**
Botswana 21
brand
    building 210
    equity 192
    portfolios 192
brand wheel (brand essence model) 192, **192**
branding 191–193
Brazil 5
breach of contract 157
British Airways 52, 172
broadcast media 204
brochure production 78–79, 178–179
    direct mail 181
    key stages 181, **182**
    mainstream 179
    online 181
    specialist 179
Brundtland Report (1987) 27–31
budget coach tour 102
build it yourself holiday packages 16
business
    assessment 225
    crisis management theory 254
    market, oligopolistic 86, 105
    objectives 60
    strategy 220, 224
    travel agents 173–174

call centres 177–178, 223
    international outsourcing 178
campaigns, promotional 202
camping 101
Canada 49, 163
    Vancouver 4
cancellation charges 138–139
candidates
    evaluation 231
    selection 228–231
capacity 66, 72
    management 135–137
car hire 78
carbon monoxide poisoning 253
career opportunities 238–242

Caribbean 3–5, 14, 19, 26
Carnival Cruise Lines 19, 52
cash
    flow 138, 143–144, 239, 247
    management 138
cash cow 64
chain of distribution (disintermediation) 38,
    50–52, **51**, 206
chalets 242
Chameleon World-wide 255
charges 132
charter flights 3, 67, 75–77
Chartered Institute of Marketing (CIM, UK)
    187, 191
Chartered Institute of Personnel and
    Development (CIPD, UK)
    221–225, 229
chartering 76
    time series 76–77
    whole season 76–77
children's representatives 241
China 5–6, 30, 90–91, 159–163, 172–173,
    239, 268
    Beijing 4
    TAR 161–162
China International Travel Service
    (CITS) 161
China National Tourism Administration
    (CNTA) 161–162
China Travel Company 17, 162
China Travel Service (CTS) 161
city break packages 49
Civil Aviation Authority (CAA) 157–158
civil liability 150, 154
Clarkston 55
climate change 29–30, 40, 269–270
Club Med 18, 148
Co-operative Travel, The 52–53
coach holidays 65
coach operators 99
coach tours 18, 99–104
    all-inclusive luxury 101, *101*
    budget 102
    escorted 102
    9-day costing 102, *103*
    specialist 102
cognitive dissonance 197
commercial airlines 3
commission 134, 171–172, 176–177
    sales agent 134
commitment contract 74
company information team 258

comparables 156
compensation 121, 156
competition 266–267
competitive pricing 143
competitor analysis 195–196
complaints
    customer 120–121
    monitoring 113
computer reservation systems (CRS) 40, 56,
    167–168
concentrated marketing 202
consideration set 197
Consumer Association of Singapore
    (CASE) 160–161
consumerism 269
    green 270
consumers 73, 89, 150, 153–157, 188–190,
    266–269
    demand 61
    expectations 115
    green 270
    potential 188
    protection 16
consumption 166, 188–189, 197, 269
Content Management System (CMS) 207
contract
    breach of 157
    commitment 74
    employment 232
contracting 72–78
    ad hoc 75
    commitment 74
control measures 251, 252
convenience 14–15
Corfu 149
cost base analysis for tour packages 67, 68–71
costing
    adventure tour 95, 97
    model, basic tailor-made tour 99, 100
    9-day coach tour 102, 103
costs
    amendment 138–139
    breakdown 131–132, **131**
    distribution 134–135
    fixed 131–135, 190
    operating 131–135
    operational 132
    plus pricing 142
    tour 95–98
    variable 132
Council of Australian Tour Operators
    (CATO, Australia) 254

Court of Appeal 149–150, 155–156
Court of Justice of the European Union
    (CJEU) 148
Court Line 15
Cox & Kings 12
credibility 210
crisis 247–249, *248*
    management 246–263
        insurance policies 254
        theory 254
    operational response 258, *258*
crisis management plan (CMP) 8, 253–259
    key teams 255, **256**
critical incident technique 113
cruises
    managers 242
    market 14
    ships 2, 5, 19, 28, 43, 50, 269–270
cruising 19, 63
Crystal Ski Holidays 52, 212
Cuba 3
Cunard Cruises 52
currency 66, 130, 139–140, 160, 191,
    235, 267
    forward buying 140–141
    local 139–140
curriculum vitae (CV) 227–230
customer lifetime value (CLV) 119, 125
Customer Loyalty Ladder 118, **118**, 124
customer relationship management
    (CRM) 119–120, **119**, 124–125
customer-based research 112, *113*
customer-centric culture 117
customers
    analysis 196–197
    behaviour 196–197
    centric 110
    complaints 120–121
    expectations 117
    feedback 63
    information team 257–258
    interviews 112
    loyalty 108, 117–118, 122–124
        schemes 119, 124–125
    perceptions 110
    potential 169
    preferences 61
    protection 15–16
    satisfaction 63, 108–111, 117, 121–125
    service 108–129, 240
        questionnaire 114
customization 175

damages 155–157
data
    collection
        qualitative 112–114
        quantitative 114–117
    sales 63
decision-making process 196, **196**
Deloitte 235
democratization 2
destination marketing organizations (DMOs) 4
destinations 62, 66, 81
    development 27
    popular 90
    short-haul 14
developing economies 21, 264–266
developing markets 43, 52
diagonal integration 54
dichotomy 267
differentiated marketing 202
digital marketing 212
digital media 206
direct distribution 177
direct mail brochures 181
direct marketing 205–206
    personalized messages 206
directional selling 53
disaster 247
Disclosure and Barring Service (DBS)
        check 226–227, 241
discount pricing 142–143
discrimination 228
disposable income 2–3
distress and disappointment 155–156
distribution 166–186
    channels 166–175
        for tour operators 169, **169**
    costs 134–135
    level one (direct) 51
    level two 51
    system 166
    traditional 167–168
diversification 11, 14–18, 48–52, 54
diversity 17, 30, 267
dogs 64–65
domestic tourism 3–6, 22, 31, 161, 269
domestic tours 22, 87
Dominican Republic 27
Dubai 17, 27

e word-of-mouth (eWOM) 109, 118–121,
        124–125, 188, 210–211
Eastern Europe 5, 77

Easyjet 52
eco-bubble 14
economic development 30
economic growth 11, 26, 222
ego-tripping 14
electronic media 264
emergency plan 257
employees
    benefits 237–238
    development 220
    referral schemes 227
    rewards 237–238
    satisfaction 122
employment contract 232
empty leg 133
entrepreneurs 19–20, 29, 104, 182, 243
environmental management 29–31
environmental scanning 41
escorted coach tours 102
escorted packages 111
escorted tours 18
established resorts 13
Europe 2–7, 11–22, 47, 76–77, 99, 102,
        159, 265
    Eastern 5, 77
    Package Travel Regulations (PTR) 54,
        137, 146–149, 153–157, 163,
        170, 268
    Western 16
European market 175
European Union (EU) 4, 54, 146–147, 179,
        220, 250, 267–269
    CJEU 148
    member states 149, 158
    Package Travel Directive (PTD) 16, 120,
        140, 146, 157, 164, 259
exchange rates 40, 130, 139–140, 191, 247
excitement factors 109
excursions 139
    optional 95
expectations 117
Expedia 148, 174, 268
experience, guest 240
external crisis 248, *248*
external sales data 63

Facebook 210–212
familiarization trip 79
Family Adventure Company (UK) 90
Far East 8
Federation of Tour Operators (FTO)
        15, 183

feedback
    customer 63
    360° 234–235
finalizing sales 79–80
financial considerations 130
financial planning 130–145
financial risk 74, 171
financial stability 160
findings recorded 251
First Choice 18, 45, 52, 121, 142, 179, 202
fixed costs 131–135, 190
flexibility 174
flights 75–78
    charter 3, 67, 75–77
    long-haul 76
    night 77
    scheduled 3, 76–78, 102
Florida (USA) 5
fluid pricing 142
fly-drive tours 19
focus groups 113
forecasting 135–137
forward vertical integration 54
fossil fuels 269
4Ps marketing 181, 187
France 2–3, 62
    Paris 3

gas water heaters 253
geodemographic segmentation 199
Germanwings 77
Germany 49
global distribution systems (GDS) 40, 56, 167–168, 174, 178
global positioning system (GPS) 211
globalization 6, 9, 25, 266, 269
Google 235
Great Rail Journeys 267
Greece 62
    Club Med 18, 148
green consumerism 270
ground handling agents (GHAs) 87–90, 95, 98
Grupo Piñero 53
guest experience 240
guided tours 18
guides 242
    adventure tour 91
Gulf War (1991) 20

Haven Holidays 193–194
hazard identification 251

Headwater Holidays 52
heterogeneity 188–190
high season 135
high-energy tours 101
holiday pay 2, 12
home-based travel agents 172–173
Hong Kong 6, 159
    Travel Agents Ordinance (TAO) 159
    Travel Industry Council 159
Horizon Holidays 13
horizontal integration 45, 50–53, 104
hoteliers 73
human resources (HR) 223–224, 237, 240, 254
human resources management (HRM) 219–245
hyper-communication 80
hyper-competition 108
hyper-connectivity 255

Ibiza 26
Immigration and Checkpoints Authority of Singapore (ICA) 160
Importance Performance Analysis (IPA) 114–115, **115**, 125
inbound tour operators 22–24
inbound tourism 161
incident location team (ILT) 255–257
incidents
    logs 113
    major 249, *249*, 259
    reality 258–259
    small scale 246
Inclusive Tour by Excursion (ITX) fare 78
inclusive tour planning stages 60, 62
income, disposable 2–3
independent holidays 13
independent tour 19
independent travel agents 54, 111, 173
India 5, 21, 30, 52, 87, 242, 265, 268
inductions 231–233
industrialization 1–2
information, misleading 155
information communication technologies (ICT) 206, 213, 264, 268
inseparability 188–189
insolvency 157–158
Instagram 211–212
intangibility 188–189
Intasun's Club (18–30) 18
Intentional Graduate Leadership Programme (TUI) 226

interactions 110–111
interest 138
internal crisis 247–248
International Air Transport Association
    (IATA) 183
International Airlines Group (IAG) 52
international banking crisis (2008) 21
International Council of Cruise Lines (ICCL) 28
International Federation of Tour Operators
    (IFTO) 29
international holidays 13
International Leisure Group (ILG) 15–16,
    55, 133–135
international outsourcing 178
International Standards Organization
    (ISO) 29–31
international tourism 6, 13, 246
international travel 6, 25
International Union of Official Tour
    Operators (IUOTO) 15, 27
International Union of Overseas Tour
    Operators (now UNWTO) 6
internationalization 6
Internet 45, 171, 183, 203, 206–207,
    210–213
interview selection 229
Intrepid 44, 90, 119
Italy 2
    Venice 28
itineraries 59, 82, 91–95, 99
    adventure tour 95, 96
    development 59–60
    new 59
    planning 59, 67, 91
    static 59
    tailor-made 75, 98–99
    well-established 90

Japan 6
job description 225–226
Judicial Studies Board (JSB) 156
junk mail 206

Kathmandu 21
Kenya 5
Korea 52, 159, 265

land-based transport 78
learning and development 219, 235–236

Leisure International 20
leisure travel agents 172
liability 149–155
    civil 150, 154
liberalization 172
line-manager appraisal 235
Linked Travel Arrangement (LTA) 158
LinkedIn 210, 227
load factor 132
local accommodation 67
local currency 139–140
local economy 207
long-haul flights 76
loss mitigation 157
low season 143
low-cost carriers (LCCs) 77–78, 265–268
loyalty
    customer 108, 117–118, 119, 122–124,
        124–125
    maintenance 118–119
luxury market 102
    all-inclusive coach tour 101, *101*

macro environment 39, 42, 55
macro niches 88
major incidents and destinations 249,
    249, 259
Malaysia 5, 159
Maldives 5
management strategy 38, 248
Marco Polo 47–48
mark-up 131, 138, 143–144
market-based pricing 142
marketing 187–218, 240
    campaign 213
    concentrated 202
    differentiated 202
    digital 212
    direct 205–206
    4Ps 181, 187
    materials 72
    mix 198, 201–202, 214
    niche 202
    plan 79–80, 187, 191–193, 197–198,
        202–203, 213
    planning cycle 187, 193, **194**, 197
    positioning 198
    7Ps 198, 213
    short-term plan 193
    strategy 196, 201
    undifferentiated 201–202

markets
  developing 43, 52
  development 48–49
  European 175
  growth 64–65
  luxury 101, *101*, 102
  mature 43
  oligopolistic business 86, 105
  penetration 48–49
  research 195
  segments 61–63, 73, 199, 202–204, 213
  share 64–65, 141
  of tour operators 22, *23*
Marriott International 52
mass market 13, 74, 264
  model 16
  operators 18, 22, 66, 78
  products 62, 80, 132, 202
mass tourism 6–7, 16, 27, 88
media 203–205
  broadcast 204
  digital 206
  electronic 264
  print 203
  social 120–121, 188, 209–212, 255, 265
Mediterranean 4–6, 22, 26, 33
Mediterranean Sea 14–15, 20
Memorandum of Understanding (MOU) 160
mental distress 157
Mexico 14, 18, 26
micro environment 39–42
micro niches 88
middle class 3, 17
Middle East 267
miniples 173
mitigation of loss 157
mobile devices 209–210
moments of truth 111–112, 124–125
Morocco 90
MOSAIC 199–200
multi-destination tours 91
multinational travel agents 173
mystery shopper 113
MyTravel plc 53

National Association of Travel Agents
    Singapore (NATAS) 160–161
national tourist organizations (NTOs) 4
natural disaster 246, 249
Nepal 26, 243
Netflix 235

netting 140
new contemporary tourism 89
next of kin 257
niche
  marketing 202
  micro 88
  tourism 87–89, **89**, 104
night flights 77
nineteenth century 2, 5, 11–12
non-governmental organizations (NGOs) 30
non-tourism companies 167
North Africa 267
North America 5, 11–14, 20, 25, 76

off-peak 189
off-season 136
oligopolistic business market 86, 105
online brochures 181
online reviews 114
online testing 230
online training 232
online travel agents (OTAs) 40, 171,
    174–175
open jaw tickets 78, 82
operating costs 131–132
  air tax 132
  fixed 131–135, 190
  variable 132
operational marketing plan 193
operational response, to crisis 258, *258*
operations department 239
opportunities to hear (OTH) 204
opportunities to see (OTS) 204
optional excursions 95
options pricing 143
Organization for Economic and Cultural
    Development (OECD) 24
Orient Express 3
outbound tour operators 22
outbound tourism 161
outsourcing, international 178
overbooking 75
overcapacity 72
overseas positions 240–242

P&O Cruise 52
package holidays 2–8, 11–37, 44, 81, 111,
    130, 264, 269
  planning timeframe 60, *61*
  revolution 13

package tourism 11
Package Travel Directive (PTD, EU) 16, 120, 140, 146, 157, 164, 259
Package Travel Regulations (PTR, Europe) 54, 137, 146–149, 153–157, 163, 170, 268
packages
    all-inclusive 14, 23, 34, 62, 72, 99, 202, 267
    bespoke 16
    build it yourself holiday 16
    city break 49
    cost base analysis 67, *68–71*
    escorted 111
    sun, sand and sea (3S) 4–6, 14–16, 22, 44, 60, 86, 124, 147
    tailor-made 19, 104, 149, 175
packaging, dynamic 175–176
paid annual holiday leave 237
Paris (France) 3
payment by results (PBR) 236
peak season 179
peak times 135
pensions 237–238
performance
    appraisal 234–235
        reviews 235
    factors 109
    management 219, 234–236
    objectives 236
performance-related pay (PRP) 234–236
perishability 188–189
person specification 226
personal computers 209
personal development plan (PDP) 236
personal selling 205
personality 192
personalized messages 206
PESTEL 38–42, *41*, 48, 55, 195, 223
PGL Travel Ltd 17
political instability 62
popular destinations 90
popularized resorts 13
Porter's Five Forces 42–46, **43**, 55, 195
Porter's Generic Strategies 46–50, **46**, 55
Portugal 148
positioning 201–202
post-consumption evaluation 197
post-departure changes 152–153
post-departure customer service 240
post-industrial countries 13, 40, 86
post-industrial nations 220
post-tour management 81

potential customers 169
pre-arranged combination 148–149
pre-departure changes 151–152
pre-departure customer service 240
pre-employment checks 231
premium pricing 142
press advertisements 154
price
    competition 42
    elasticity 44, 56
Priceline 268
pricing
    competitive 143
    discount 142–143
    fluid 142
    holiday packages 130–145
    marginal 142
    market-based 142
    options 143
    premium 142
    promotional 142
    seasonal 143
    strategy 72, 142–143
print media 203
product
    department 239
    development 48–49, 59–85
    launch 80–81
    planning 66–72
    review 81
    strategy 63
Product Development Manager 188
Product Life Cycle (PLC) 64–65, **66**, 141
productivity 117, 121
profit margins 72, 130–132, 141–143, 190
profitability 59, 95, 102, 110, 121–123, 144, 171
promotional campaigns 202
promotional mix 202–203, **203**
promotional pricing 142
promotional tactics 187
protection, customer 15–16
psychographic segmentation 199, *201*
psychometric testing 230–231
public relations (PR) 205, 240
    team 257

qualitative data collection 112–114
quality, service 108–112, 117
quantitative data collection 114–117
question marks 65

rail travel 2–3
    Great Rail Journeys 267
    Orient Express 3
recession 52
recruitment 219, 225–233
    agencies 227
    policy 231
references 231
regulations, travel 146–165
related diversification 54
Renren 210
reports, tour 113
reputation management 257
research
    customer-based 112, *113*
    market 195
reservations
    department, and sales 239–240
    systems 80
        computer (CRS) 40, 56, 167–168
resort-based jobs 230
resorts
    established 13
    popularized 13
    representatives 240–241
    tourist 6–7
responsible tourism 28–30
retail travel 12
retailers 50–51, 149, 154, 173, 180, 265
return on investment (ROI) 212
revenue management 136
reviews, online 114
reward
    employee 237–238
    packages 237
risk, financial 74, 171
risk assessment 246, 250–253
    process 250, **250**
    risk matrix 251, **251**
Rodger's Severn Point Plan 226
Russia 5–7
    Ministry of Transport 77

Sabre 167–168
SAGA Holidays 23, 54
sales
    agent commission 134
    data 63
    finalizing 79–80
    promotion 205
    and reservations department 239–240

seat-only 76
staff training 79–80
team 240
satisfaction
    customer 63, 108–111, 117, 121–125
    employee 122
    tourist 111
Saudi Arabia 171
Scandinavian Air Systems (SAS) 111
scheduled flights 3, 76–78, 102
seasonal pricing 143
seasonality 60, 134–138, 141–143, 174,
    189–191
seat-only sales 76
segmentation 198–201
    targeting and positioning process
        198, **199**
self-booking 174, 266
selling
    direct 53
    prices 134
series charter 76, **76**
service
    ancillary 67
    customer 108–129, 240
    encounter management 110–111
    quality 108–112, 117
    recovery 108, 120–121, 125
Service Profit Chain (SPC) 121–122, **122**
service-based sector 108
SERVQUAL 115–116, *116*, 125
7Cs framework 207, *208–209*
7Ps marketing 198, 213
Shearings 102
short-haul destinations 14
short-term marketing plan 193
Singapore 159–161
    CASE 160–161
    ICA 160
    NATAS 160–161
Singapore Tourism Board (STB) 160
ski tour operators 67
small or medium-sized enterprises (SME) 47,
    59, 74, 86–107, 119, 191, 207
small operators 66, 72
small scale incidents 246
smart phones 211
Snap Chat 211
social media 120–121, 188, 209–212, 227,
    255, 265
social networking sites 210
social networks 264

social responsibility 270
sociodemographic variables 199, *200*
Solo Holidays 23
Spain 3–4, 26, 29, 33, 62, 158
    Barcelona 29
    Benidorm 26
Special Agents Scheme 177
Special Group Inclusive Tour (SGTI) fare 78
special-interest holidays 14
special-interest tourism 86–88
specialist brochures 179
specialist coach tours 102
specialist tour operators 22
Sri Lanka 78
staff
    chalet 242
    training 80
        sales 79–80
Standard Operating Procedure (SOP) 252
standardization 47, 53, 190
stars 65
state pension 238
static holidays 18
static itinerary 59
Strategic Human Resource Management
    (HRM) 221–222, **221**
sun, sand and sea packages (3S) 4–6, 14–16,
    22, 44, 60, 86, 124, 147
Sunwing Travel 53
sustainability 192–193
sustainable competitive advantage 109
sustainable development 27–30
sustainable tourism 29–31
Sustainable Tourism Tax, Balearic Islands 40
swimming pool 253
Switzerland 12
SWOT 42, 55, 195–196

tailor-made holidays 47
tailor-made itineraries 75, 98–99
tailor-made packages 19, 104, 149, 175
Taiwan 5
talent management 243
tangible product 67
terrorism 15, 20, 39, 151, 267
terrorist attacks 39, 64, 246
testing
    online 230
    psychometric 230–231
Thailand 5–7, 21, 26, 40, 159
theme parks 17

Thomas Cook 3, 20, 47–49, 52–53, 148,
    171–173, 232
Thomson 47, 121, 179
Thomson Travel Buddy scheme 121
Thomsonfly 75
360° feedback 234–235
tickets, open jaw 78, 82
time series chartering 76–77
total quality management (TQM) 110
tour managers 113–114, 241–242
tourism 1–7, 24–30, 110–111, 166–167,
    187–192, 219–220, 246–247,
    269–270
    adventure 17, 28, 87–98
    alternative 26–27
    domestic 3–6, 22, 31, 161, 269
    inbound 161
    international 6, 13, 246
    mass 6–7, 16, 27, 88
    new contemporary 89
    niche 87–89, **89**, 104
    outbound 161
    package 11
    responsible 28–30
    special-interest 86–88
    sustainable 29–31
    worldwide 6
tourist–employee encounter 111
tourisurbanization 30
tours 18–19, 53
    coach 18, 99–104
    domestic 87
    escorted 18
    fly-drive 19
    guided 18
    high-energy 101
    independent 19
    multi-destination 91
    see also adventure tours
training
    cycle 233, **233**
    and development 233–234
    initiatives 123
    online 232
    staff 79–80
training needs analysis (TNA) 234
transferable skills 238
transfers 67, 78
    representatives 241
transport 62, 67, 91
    flights 75–78
    land-based 78

travel agency 38, 44, 79
    chain 52
Travel Agency Regulations (TAR, China) 161–162
travel agents 12, 51, 79, 159–161, 170–172,
       180–183, 190–191, 223
    business 173–174
    home-based 172–173
    independent 54, 111, 173
    leisure 172
    multinational 173
    OTAs 40, 171, 174–175
    traditional 175
Travel Agents Ordinance
       (TAO, Hong Kong) 159
Travel Corporation, The 102
Travel Foundation 29
Travel Industry Compensation Fund 159
Travel Industry Council (Hong Kong) 159
Travel Republic 148–149
Travel Trust Association 158
Travel Weekly 79, 113
Trip Advisor 118–120, 211
Trump, D. 267
TUI (Touristik Union International) 20–25,
       52–54, 75, 120, 140–141, 176–179,
       202, 268
    Intentional Graduate Leadership
        Programme 226
Tunisia 62
Turkey 26, 62–64, 158, 250
twentieth century 2, 11–12, 16, 99, 163, 167
twenty-first century 20, 255
Twitter 210–211

under capacity 72
United Airlines 168, 172
United Kingdom (UK) 1–5, 11–17, 98–99,
       137–140, 146–148, 171–173,
       176–177, 232
    adventure tour supply chain 89, 90
    Air Passenger Duty 132
    Air Travel Reserve Fund 15
    All Leisure Group 43
    ATOL 15, 22, 137–138, 157–158, 164,
       176, 269
    Beiwei (55) 17
    Chartered Institute of Marketing
       (CIM) 187, 191
    Chartered Institute of Personnel and
       Development (CIPD)
       221–225, 229

    Clarkston 55
    Family Adventure Company 90
    Shearings 102
    Thomas Cook 3, 20, 47–49, 52–53,
       148, 171–173, 232
    Wendy Wu 44
United Nations World Tourism Organization
       (UNWTO) 24, 159
United States of America (USA) 12–14, 25,
       49, 78, 163, 171–174, 268–269
    American Airlines 167
    American Express 12
    American Society of Travel Agents,
       The 172
    Carnival Cruise Lines 19, 52
    Florida 5
    PGL Travel Ltd 17
up-selling 117, 134, 144, 172, 183
upmarket accommodation 99
User Generated Content (UGC) 210
utilization 75–78, 134, 189, 207

value-added services 109
Vancouver (Canada) 4
Venice (Italy) 28
vertical integration 50–54, 78, 104, 171
    backward 53–54
    forward 54
Vietnam 159
Virgin Holidays 181
Virgin plc 54
Voice Over Internet Protocol (VOIP) 178

war 39
web-based distribution 178
webinars 79, 82
websites 207–209
Weibo 210
well-established itineraries 90
Wendy Wu 44
Western Europe 16
Western world 16
What If scenario planning 248
wholesalers 50–51, 59, 173, 265
word-of-mouth (WOM) 109, 118–121,
       124–125, 188, 211
workforce
    management 219–245
    planning 219–224
    requirements 222

working class 3
workplace pensions 237
World Tourism Organization of the United
    Nations (UNWTO) 6
World Trade Organization (WTO) 162
World Travel Market 73, 82, 205
World Travel and Tourism Council 29

World War I (1914–1918) 102
World War II (1939–1945) 12, 102
world wide web (www) 178
worldwide tourism 6

yield management 136–137